# A SERIES OF LETTERS

FROM

# LONDON.

# A SERIES OF LETTERS

FROM

# LONDON

WRITTEN

## DURING THE YEARS 1856, '57, '58, '59, AND '60.

BY

GEORGE MIFFLIN DALLAS,

THEN MINISTER OF THE UNITED STATES AT THE BRITISH COURT.

---

"Point de fiel permet beaucoup de franchise."—GUIZOT, *Mém.*

---

EDITED BY HIS DAUGHTER JULIA.

TWO VOLUMES IN ONE.

PHILADELPHIA:
J. B. LIPPINCOTT & CO.
1869.

# PREFACE.

---

THERE were many incidents connected with the post of American Minister in London, from 1856 to 1861, which may be usefully, and perhaps not disagreeably, recalled from the oblivion into which they must otherwise hasten. To do this, no departure from the reticence lastingly exacted by diplomatic function is necessary. A book, in which the scenes and conversations of Paris at the outbreak of the Revolution of 1848 are portrayed by a British diplomat and peer, was doubtfully received, because this reserve was in a measure relaxed. The example should be followed with watchful self-restraint.

As a general rule, *Despatches* addressed by a public agent to his government, on the business of that government, pass out of his control and merge into the mass of executive archives, to be thenceforward reached under a responsible authorization only. Exceptions nevertheless will occur to every mind:—as when mooted topics, ceasing to agitate, have subsided into History; or when they involve no question of State policy and are purely personal.

The series of letters addressed to Mr. William L. Marcy and Mr. Lewis Cass—although those gentlemen were Secretaries of State, in succession—partook, however, neither in design nor fact, of official character. They were essentially private letters:—uniformly so termed, regarded, and treated. Very probably, an exaggerated estimate of their merit as such, has been caused by the complimentary language with which their continuance was constantly urged.

The purpose of these volumes will be seen with more distinctness than it can be described. Their bearings are various. As constituting, in the aggregate, a running commentary upon events during five years, they take the undisguised aspect of a familiar journal. While the personal opinions of the author upon every subject springing into notice are perhaps decidedly perceptible, yet nothing savoring of dissertation, treatise, or argument, political or social, was indulged, save in one or two instances. Although touching, occasionally and obscurely, on matters behind the screen of diplomacy, the letters to the Secretaries of State were wholly apart from the official correspondence of the envoy, maintained in at least three hundred and thirty *numbered* despatches. They were meant to be by-the-by:—to convey friendly and informal hints: to help the conclusions of public functionaries by widening the sphere of facts and observations: and to relieve dry and onerous labors with short and sketchy allusions. How far this design succeeded, it is impossible to judge better than by the encouragement to persevere often and warmly expressed.

There is one light in which this publication particularly recommends itself to the writer:—that is, as an authentic report to his fellow-citizens (altogether divested of the multitudinous communications on file in the Department of State) indicating, with sufficient distinctness, his whole course of action, sentiment, and thought, from week to week, and year after year, while filling the United States mission to the British Court.

G. M. D.

# LIST OF LETTERS, VOL. I.

# LIST OF LETTERS, VOL. II.

# LETTERS FROM LONDON.

---

## No. 1.—TO MR. MARCY.

NEW YORK, February 29, 1856.

MY DEAR SIR,—Your letter of the 26th was received about the same time that I suppose you got mine.

I ought to have made this acknowledgment at once, but it was lost sight of in the distractions of departure. We quit here on board the Atlantic, punctually at 12 to-morrow.

I must confess that when reading the correspondence at the department, I was slightly surprised to notice with what little account the conversational suggestion as to an arbitration had been regarded. No doubt it was so made as to leave no impression that it was meant as a serious proposal; our minister would otherwise have formally submitted it for decision. Lord Clarendon was bound to give it directness and distinctness, or to abstain afterwards from saying that the offer had been made at all.

I cannot say whether it would be wholly safe to refer the construction of the Treaty to any "State or Power" in Europe; but if it be a case for reference, and it can be esteemed so only because of the moral weight of an offer of that sort, then I think we should be safer in relying upon the judgment and independence of an *individual* of recognized political ability, experience, and integrity. There are such men even in these modern times. Recollecting his Life of Washington, his Portrait at the Patent Office, and his general estimate of our government, I should feel no apprehension that his British attachments would blind the sagacity or warp the honesty of Mr. Guizot. I put him as an instance only; there are others.

My numbered despatches will of course be always official; and as to other communications, I shall leave them to be classed as public or private, as your good discretion may determine.

I am very truly and respectfully yrs.

G. M. DALLAS.

---

## No. 2.—TO MR. MARCY.

LONDON, March 28, 1856.

MY DEAR SIR,—The arrival here of the America, after a detention of several days beyond her proper time, and the sight of boundless fields of ice, through which, by filling and backing, she made her way with difficulty, have thrown a pall over the last hopes for the Pacific. This unfortunate ship excited so much interest that I ventured to write a private note to Lord Palmerston about her. The admirals of the Admiralty had all given her up, and discountenanced the idea of sending a government steamer in search; and being told that nothing would avail unless the Premier could be induced to act, I, very impudently, invoked his co-operation in a purpose of general humanity, and sent my billet by an American merchant, to explain the plan of exploration. My messenger returned perfectly enchanted with the prompt and decisive manner in which my note had been received and acted upon. Lord P. wrote notes to the admirals, and an order immediately issued to the commanders of *two* steamers, Tartarus and Despatch, to proceed in search forthwith, and according to the programme matured. So much for a first step in diplomatic audacity.

Our travelling military commissioners, Messrs. Delafield, Mordecai, and McClellan, took pot-luck with me yesterday, in the house to which I have just removed my family and the legation. They are not talkative men; but I thought I could discern that they are going home full freighted with a large mass of useful information.

If ever you issue another decree for reform in the diplomatic service, pray devise some mode by which a minister may be relieved from the deluge and distraction of visitors. If the department would assume the responsibility, and not quarrel with the consequences, he would be able to do twice the usual amount of business by closing his doors three days in the week.

I am drawn to my last ten minutes before the Bag is closed.

Truly and respectfully yrs.

---

## No. 3.—TO MR. MARCY.

LONDON, March 30, 1856.

MY DEAR SIR,—The *Times* of this morning announces that orders have been issued to the officers at the outposts and the Tower to hold themselves in readiness for firing salutes on receiving to-day from the department news of peace being made: and one of the correspondents says that Lord Clarendon will probably be in his seat in the House of Lords on next Tuesday, and may then communicate the incidents of the conferences at Paris.

I received yesterday your "confidential and unofficial" letter of the 14th instant. The very day before it reached me I had a visit from Sir Henry Bulwer, who, I could not help thinking, came to discharge himself of certain reflections on the treaty, of which he was one of two fathers. He very soon entered upon that subject, first, however, with a preface that he was in no manner connected with the government, and that our conversation was, of course, "as between gentlemen." He had read Mr. Clayton's speech, and really there was very little difference between their impressions. I told him that whatever might be the views of others, the fathers of the bantling were bound to unite in defending it against mutilation, if not destruction, by opposite constructions. He remarked how difficult it was, in framing such an instrument, to choose language which would admit of a single construction only; that Mr. Clayton and he had conceived themselves particularly safe in employing the words of Mr. Abbot Lawrence in his communication to Lord Palmerston, accepted and affirmed by Lord Palmerston's answer. He went on to say that so far as respected the Bay Islands, the question appeared to him primarily to be, whether at the time of ratifying the treaty, they were dependencies of the Belize; and as to that, he observed, with what appeared to me some significance, their subsequent formal colonization rather indicated the sense of the British government that they were not. The protectorate was really recognized by the treaty, and only restricted in its possible modes of exercise; fortification and dominion were excluded. I interrupted him by asking *how* then was the protectorate to be exercised? He paused an instant; thought there were modes of exercising it not prohibited by the treaty; but added that he did not wish to argue the matter, as argument was too apt to make those engaged in it obstinate in their respective views. The Protectorate was a point of honor. Yes, said I, a most attenuated point: you reduced it to a semblance or a shadow, a thing under which, without violating the clear terms, intention, and scope of the treaty, you could do nothing effective, and then you tell us that you hold to it as a *point of honor!* But it is quite as possible to disembarrass yourselves of this fanciful point of honor as of anything else. A trustee must act with honor as long as he holds the trust; but he can with perfect honor withdraw from and transfer the trust to another; and how cheaply and under how many guarantees this could be done with the Mosquito savages!

Sir Henry recurred to the Belize, and seemed to regard the matters of which we complained in that quarter as topics between England and the adjacent States, Mexico or Guatemala, rather than with us. Such an idea, I said, seemed to me to render the treaty with the United States, so far as the Belize was concerned, quite nugatory; it left England at liberty to extend her progress as far as she liked, without authorizing an interference of any sort by the United States.

This conversation, which I consider private, was protracted for some time. I have endeavored to sketch it faithfully, as you may deem it of moment to know the general theories of Sir Henry Bulwer respecting the conflict over his own treaty. He left me under very agreeable impressions of his intelligence, and more than half inclined to think that he rather leans to our interpretation than to the adverse one. You are much better acquainted, probably, with Sir Henry than I am, and can appreciate what he says more correctly. His reputation here is that of a man of ability, but prone to indirection.

Our officers were repulsed by Marshal Vaillant in Paris in a manner alike singular and rude. If it had not been ascertained by them to be the effect of personal eccentricity and *brusquerie*, we might draw from it a warning. They wanted to visit certain military establishments. "No! you can't be permitted; we don't like you enough." They wanted some drawings, which they specified: "No! we have a quarrel with you; we are going to fight you; good-by, till we meet to exchange cannon-balls:" and so they were dismissed. We must not be caught napping, though I can as yet discern no proof of a belligerent plan.

Very truly and respectfully yrs.

---

## No. 4.—TO MR. MARCY.

London, April 4, 1856.

My dear Sir,—In a letter received from the bankers, after giving me a memorandum of the credit opened in my favor by the government on account of salary, they go on to say, "we beg to add that we have received no advice respecting the allowance for contingent expenses." This, I presume, is the result of a casual oversight; but as it precludes my checking on them for contingent expenses, and will embarrass the despatch agent and the messenger of the legation, pray have it put right as early as possible.

By a letter from the Foreign Office of April 1, I was apprised that the Queen, who returned to town the day before, would grant me an audience at Buckingham Palace, on Friday, the 4th, at 1 o'clock, to deliver my credentials. Her Majesty has been entertaining for the last two weeks, at Windsor, the King of the Belgians.

Yesterday, in the House of Commons, Mr. Cobden asked Lord Palmerston whether he had yet fulfilled the promise of producing the correspondence between this country and ours. The reply was that the correspondence was still in the Foreign Office, which had recently been severely pressed, but that he expected to lay it on the table in two or three days. Our own pamphlets, transmitted by you, have been in some demand, and have enlightened not a few.

Every day gives birth to some fresh conjecture as to the terms of the Treaty of Peace. Lord Clarendon is either extremely cautious, or dissatisfied with what he has been obliged to sign;—he will neither come home, as was anticipated, and explain a little in the House of Lords, nor will he open his mouth at a dinner in Paris to support Walewski's praise of the Treaty, although that praise was pronounced with unusual solemnity. The Conservatives, and opposition generally, are ready to pounce upon the instrument as soon as it appears.

* * * I have just returned from Buckingham Palace, having delivered to the Queen my credential. Her Majesty asked about the health of the President, about my former visits to this country, and so on. She is not handsome, but her expression of face and her manner are engaging, and very soon put her visitors at ease. I was also presented to Prince Albert, who stood by the Queen on her left. While in the Picture Gallery, I made the acquaintance of Lord Lansdowne, Sir George Grey, Earl of Harrowby, Count Coloredo (the Austrian Minister, recalled to be sent to Rome), Mr. Vernon Smith, of the Cabinet, and many others, who, I am happy to tell you, were in no wise repelled from the American Minister by his plain suit of black, but, on the contrary, made his time, while waiting her Majesty's readiness, pass very pleasantly. My coat, which I am bold to say was as well made and of as good cloth as any in the Palace (except perhaps Prince Albert's!), came from the shop of a tailor in Philadelphia, Sixth above Arch, of the name of Kelly! The truth appears to be that our common sense is gradually getting the better of traditional fooleries, in honest reality, greatly improving social intercourse. Sir ——, a son of the minister we had in the United States, and who seems quite attached to our country, confessed, though himself an assistant of Sir Edward Cust, the Master of Ceremonies, that these idle points of court etiquette were gradually wearing out.

I have neither had matter nor time for a formal despatch, and must beg you to be content with this unceremonious letter.

Very truly and respectfully yrs.

## No. 5.—TO MR. MARCY.

LONDON, April 7, 1856.

MY DEAR SIR,—My effort is to let you have something from me, be it ever so small and indifferent, by every regular steamer. I would have prepared a formal despatch to-day, though there is nothing to tell that will not keep for a few days; but that, suddenly, the Queen has laid her commands upon me, and I must eat my dinner at the Palace.

And pray, Mr. Secretary, what is your minister to do or say if he be placed at the royal table alongside of Soulouque's representative, whose fine ebony our friend, Mr. Mason, has estimated at $1000?

Political parties here are squaring off for a regular set-to, on two subjects, the Treaty of Peace and the Relations with America. On the former, the public dissatisfaction is growing every day; shoulders are shrugged, and a sense of disappointment and humiliation expressed in all quarters, to such an extent, indeed, that I doubt whether an illumination can be safely ventured. On the second topic, Mr. Gladstone has broken ground in the House of Commons with considerable animation;—so much so as to cause Lord Palmerston to lose his temper, a thing he very rarely does, and to occasion quite a general surprise. He would seem, though not yet very decidedly, to be resolved on standing by Mr. Crampton, and to regard his omission to communicate to you for two months the letter of Lord Clarendon, offering to arbitrate the Central American difficulties, as of no importance, because the offer had been repeatedly made to Mr. Buchanan, and communicated by him to you long before. A vague impression prevails that upon these two questions united, the ministry will go by the board, and that Mr. Gladstone, certainly the only fully competent man presenting himself, will, in the new combination, take the place now filled by Lord Palmerston.

I wish our well-wishers here, who are becoming loud and more numerous hourly, could be spared, for a time at least, the shock they will certainly receive on the President's declining to arbitrate. There is a moral weight in an offer of that sort which nothing but a perfect knowledge and correct appreciation of the matter in controversy can entirely repel, and it is absolutely amazing how few among our best friends understand the subject even superficially! For my own part, I am against arbitration, as involving something that savors of concession, and I am convinced that if we calmly but firmly, and especially with quiet and steady preparation for the worst, hold on to the obviously just construction we have given the treaty, this government will give way, indirectly, perhaps, by proposing to nullify the treaty and begin again, or directly by removing in some such fashion as Mr. Squier's project, all possible motive to persevere in their misinterpretation. We have distinctly and ably, in the face of the world, taken our position on both the matters in difference; it is entirely too late to change that position, or even to seem to hesitate about it. Lord Palmerston must be looked coolly in the eye, so that he may gather from our composure as well as from our words, the conviction that he can expect no substantial change in us. Still, a short postponement of the President's final determination on the question of umpirage, would give to many in both houses of Parliament, now that the ball is opened, an opportunity to inform themselves accurately, and so to avoid being shocked by the refusal when it comes.

I was somewhat struck by a remark which was made to me by a gentleman, rather high in office, at a soirée on Saturday last. In the course of conversation I had ventured to say that what surprised me was, that a man so personally good-tempered and courteous as the Premier, could use such words and evince such bitter feelings as he sometimes did towards the United States. "Perhaps," was observed, "it may not be his fault." "How so?" I immediately asked; "and whose fault can it be?" "Well," was the reply, "I think it all originates with Clarendon!" This may be an effusion of personal grudge against the Earl, worthy of very little reliance; and yet we sometimes get a peep behind the curtain by casual remarks of this sort.

Mr. C., just returned from Paris, tells me that Mr. Buchanan proceeds home by the Arago on the 9th instant, —the vessel which takes this note.

I cannot forbear repeating to you my anxiety that you

should not permit any importunity to persuade you to remove our consul at Leeds. He is, as a public officer, first-rate.

Majors Delafield and Mordecai, and Captain McClellan, have not yet obtained the visiting permits for the several military offices which Lord Palmerston promised me a week ago. I hope he has not been thwarted by the respective Boards, and that the papers will be forthcoming soon.

There is to be a grand naval review off Portsmouth, the chart and programme of which will accompany this letter. It was prepared and presented to me by Captain John Washington, of the Hydrographical Office. At this moment the exhibition is fixed for the 17th of April—a day which I cannot give to it—but Captain Washington tells me that the naval officers wish it postponed for a week, and that the Queen may probably so command;—and if so, I will endeavor to be a witness. Captain Benham, of our Coast Survey, may, as an engineer, deem it important that he also should be present.

The scientific gentleman whom I have just mentioned, Captain Washington, has told me of the discovery of a process by which the place at which a submarine cable, sunk in the sea for telegraphic purposes, breaks, can be immediately ascertained. At the point either of beginning or ending, the spot is determined in a very novel but certain manner, by time, or intensity in the action of the fluid. He regards it as of immense importance, in encouraging the laying of submarine cables, but he could give me no more definite or accurate account of it. It may possibly not be wholly new to the Superintendent of our Coast Survey.

You must not hesitate to let me know if you think I waste your time.

Very truly and respectfully yrs.

---

## No. 6.—TO MR. MARCY.

LONDON, April 18, 1856.

MY DEAR SIR,—My despatch has gone by the steamship on Wednesday last, but I think it probable that this epistle, by the Persia on to-morrow, will reach you quite as soon, if not a little earlier.

I regret that Major Delafield and his colleagues could not give another week to the pursuit of their researches, as I have latterly received from the Foreign Office notes which might have facilitated their progress.

If the statements made to me by very many of our leading friends in the House of Commons can be relied upon, a most determined and formidable assault on the ministry, in respect to our relations, may be looked for. As far as I have yet acted, my desire has been to strengthen the position of our parliamentary advocates by removing all pretence of a hostile feeling on our part, and putting the hostility of the ministry on the grounds of some "*inexorable state policy*," in reference to their commercial encroachments by the colony of the Bay Islands, or some "*foregone conclusion*" as to the enlistment question, quite inaccessible to reason or manly conciliation. Such you will see to have been my intimations at the Lord Mayor's dinner to me of yesterday.* I send you an exact copy of

---

* The table-address at the Mansion House referred to in the foregoing letter, was the following:

My Lord, Ladies, and Gentlemen,—The very kind and complimentary language with which his lordship prefaced the last toast, and the cordial manner in which it has been received by this distinguished assemblage, are entitled to, and I hope you will accept, the return of my gratitude. I am, in truth, however, almost bankrupt in thanks; for since landing in the dominions of your illustrious Queen, as the representative of the government and people of the United States, I have met nothing but a series of flattering welcomes and hospitalities. Although perfectly conscious that these manifestations are not in the remotest degree addressed to an individual so utterly unentitled to them as myself, but that they are profusely lavished as a generous tribute to a nation as whose messenger I come; still, on its behalf, and with the sensibility which I know it would unanimously feel, I must beg you, my lord, ladies, and gentlemen, to receive this expression of profound acknowledgment.

There are some topics on which it would be ill-timed, if not unwise, more enterprising than safe, to touch on this occasion, and in this presence; indeed, my arrival is so recent that the subjects which would be most acceptable to you are as yet unknown to me. I dare say, however, that I can venture, without much hazard (in the provincialism natural to Western tongue), to *guess* that the spirit and purpose of a new-comer are matters of at least partial curiosity. Well, my lord, I am neither authorized to feel, nor do I feel any desire other than that of giving all my energies and efforts unreservedly, to the restoration of the most harmonious sentiments and friendly relations between America and England. Animated by such a spirit, and aiming at such a purpose, if I fail,

my remarks, for I took care to premeditate carefully, and rely more upon my memory than upon the extemporaneous afflatus of the occasion. Allow me to analyze briefly. You will note that—

1. I ignore all the balderdash about mother country, kindred, and so forth. One of to-day's papers, referring to a short speech made by me at the most republican of the London clubs, on the evening of the 16th inst., puts nonsense of this kind very falsely into my mouth. The truth is that such terms as "mother," "daughter," "cousins," etc., are their own familiar ones, and if you refer to England and America, their version makes it a reference to mother and daughter. I have resolutely, and from principle, eschewed any phrase of the sort.

2. My reception has been such as to exact the strong acknowledgments made; and this was not only due, but in harmony with my purpose.

3. I designedly forebore expanding on the points of difference, but asserted that if, with the conciliatory spirit and purpose I avowed, the government made my mission fail, it would be because they had found out that the Clayton-Bulwer treaty checked their commercial ambition at a most interesting point, or because Mr. Crampton and the consuls (who are said to be ready to vindicate their course by publishing their instructions) were to be sustained at all hazards. This was said in terms not as here stated, but to the intelligent perfectly clear.

4. I introduced a congratulation on the Peace, because I thought it would quietly and respectfully imply a perfect and cool contempt for the idea that our government could in the slightest degree be affected in their pursuit of right by the powerful attitude in which that Peace left England.

---

as fail I may, it will be because of some overruling and inexorable policy of state, or some foregone conclusion not to be undone by manly and honorable conciliation.

Allow me, my lord, in conclusion, to offer my congratulations to your lordship, and to all the guests who surround you, on the great event consummated since my arrival—the restoration of peace to Europe. War, though undoubtedly accompanied by moral benefits or alleviations, is still, and at best, an evil; and the vast industrial power of the empire, however for a time gallantly enlisted and ably directed, will find more genial and fruitful employment in those channels of agricultural, commercial, manufacturing, and mechanical exertion, which have so eminently distinguished her people in their march of improvement.

Renewed acknowledgments, etc.

The support given to my remarks was very decided. Lord Stanley (who, as the son of Lord Derby, was called upon to respond to a toast complimentary to the House of Peers) did not hesitate to say that that body would echo my sentiments, and that the man in England who would venture to assail the institutions and government of the United States would be regarded as a dangerous public enemy. Mr. Cardwell (responding for the House of Commons), while all the members present stood up as expressive of their adhesion to his views, went so far as to say that he "could almost pledge the Commons of England to sustain the American Minister in the assertion of his country's international rights against any ministry whatever." An eminent and eloquent clergyman put in the same sentiment from the Church; and Mr. Roebuck, sitting by me at the time, said that I could now see that Lords, Commons, and Church agreed with the great body of the British people, and would never submit to quarrel with America on the pretexts got up: he added, with emphasis, we fear no power on earth, and I am incapable of hypocrisy—my only wish is that you should know the truth.

Lord Lyndhurst, whose great age has in no respect impaired his powers of mind, is said to be preparing to take the field for us in the Lords. A trifling, but to me most agreeable incident, gave countenance to this idea, at the recent Levee, which I attended as *chaperon* to three of our countrymen. I was passing, in the line of diplomats, to the throne-room, when I felt myself caught by the arm, and heard the exclamation: "Welcome, my countryman, welcome to England!" I turned, saw a very venerable man in court costume; did not know him, for I had never seen him before, but thanked him cordially, and hurriedly passed on. After performing my duty in presenting my *protégés*, I waited close by the Queen to see who the old gentleman might be; ascertained that he was Lord Lyndhurst, and then, going up to him, renewed my thanks for his welcome, which he very cordially received.

I forward to you in the Bag to-day an interesting communication from Mr. Mason, received yesterday. I have, as he requested, carefully read it; and should the emergency to which he refers arise, or be seen approaching, I shall not fail to advise him promptly. Although my impressions are as yet like his own, there is no knowing what a whim may bring forth, and I think it might be prudent to instruct the Commodore either to affect, for a month or two to come, some business with the ships of his squadron in such of the Mediterranean ports as would prevent any abrupt attack, or gradually to disperse them on the lookout. I will write to Mr. Mason this suggestion, and perhaps he will see the expediency of applying it at once, and until some time has elapsed after the grand review at Portsmouth on the 23d inst.

By-the-by, the frequency with which I have been advised and almost solicited, by the officers of the government, to attend this naval review, has rather confirmed my disinclination. It will be a grand and ostentatious display of British naval power, at which, as an American, citizen or minister, I shall be reluctant to play the part of a wondering spectator. I was told that * * * * had said he would rather have Mr. Dallas attend than all the others of the diplomatic body; as indicative of something like this peculiar desire, I send you the copy of a short note this moment received from the Foreign Office, and I add a copy of my reply. I do not intend, unless *commanded* by a direct *invitation* from the Queen (which I have feared might come), to swell the exulting crowd at that demonstration, but shall, of course, abstain gracefully.

Very truly and respectfully yrs.

---

## No. 7.—TO MR. MARCY.

London, April 20, 1856.

My dear Sir,—Lord Aberdeen was kind enough to pay me a visit this morning; and the result of a long conversation with him is my conviction that, in the course of two or three days, I shall receive, to be forwarded to you, the reply of Lord Clarendon to your letter of the 28th of December last, requesting, at its close, the recall of Mr. Crampton, and the removal of Messrs. Rowcroft, Barclay, and Matthew.

This reply will be calm and moderate in tone, but definitive in declining to do what you have asked. It will found its reasoning upon fresh statements and evidence furnished by Mr. Crampton, and affect to be unable, without doing injustice, to determine the question of veracity on points of fact. Of course, neither Lord Aberdeen, nor any one else out of the Foreign Office, has exact knowledge of what the facts are upon which Mr. Crampton has raised, or rather bolstered up, the issue for the relief of the ministry. It is conceived that, unless by some harsh and unexpected course of action on the part of our government, a reaction in sentiment shall be suddenly provoked, Lord Palmerston will be unable to sustain himself. No one will be surprised if Mr. Crampton be dismissed ultimately; but it may be (as was said to me) that a plausible case of contradictory proof may be the burthen of Lord C.'s reply, and that many will expect it to be met before the final blow is struck. Lord Aberdeen is a calm and judicious man. His political position here you perfectly well understand. He would undoubtedly desire to preserve good relations between the two countries, and is by no means satisfied that a similar disposition on the part of the ministry would not, especially at their commencement, have avoided existing difficulties. But he is a loyal, high-minded statesman, and is obviously not prepared to prejudge the new testimony sent forward, and of which he can have no accurate knowledge until it shall be laid upon the table of the House of Commons, as repeatedly promised by Lord Palmerston.

Since reading the *Globe* of the 18th instant, I have been in very little doubt as to the "foregone conclusion" in respect to the matter of foreign enlistments, upon which this government had settled. That newspaper, in my opinion a reliable representative of cabinet policy, when commenting upon my address at the Lord Mayor's dinner, and after many compliments to it and my sentiments, with an expression of a desire to keep the best relations with us, yet closed its article with a strong "trust" that notwithstanding all this, "no considerations, even those arising from the prospect of war and its calamities, will ever lead the British nation to *deflect* one inch from the path of uprightness and honor."

Considering, then, that the British ministry refuse your demand, I take it for granted that you will send Mr. Crampton his passports, and that, as soon as your having done so is officially known here, I shall receive mine. It will, in all probability, be in your power before that to apprise me at what time you intend acting, and what course the President would wish me to take on being tendered "my ticket of leave." Certainly I will comply with his and your instructions as far as I can; but my inclination is, as I think my true representative duty and policy are, to quit England instantly, and to remain for a limited period either in Paris, or Brussels, or Geneva, until I receive your final directions. Of course, I cannot do this without incurring serious and most inconvenient loss:—but this is a consideration by which you cannot be "deflected one inch from the path of uprightness and honor;" and it is only mentioned as a reason for my adding that I presume my receiving my passports and going on the Continent do not cancel my commission as minister, or suspend my credit with the Barings for salary, until I am recalled by the President. My functions, although not exercised in diplomatic intercourse with the government here, are at the discretion of the President only.

* * * I have just received your private letter of the 7th inst., in which you say that, having heard Mr. Crampton had sent to his government an elaborate defence of his course, you "inferred that the discussion is to be further protracted. This inference squares with what Lord Aberdeen seemed to consider as highly expedient: and, indeed, as the matter of foreign enlistment has taken the foreground of our differences, and has been managed by you with so much force and labor, I should regret your omitting anything by which your powerful argument of the 28th December can be fortified, so as to repel the new assault. I would cheerfully take the labor upon myself, in order to relieve you; but your familiarity with the subject will probably make it easy, and the additional evidence in your hands has not been sent here. Besides, a reasonable delay on our side, for a substantial reason, after the long delay on theirs, merely on the ground of Lord Clarendon's absence, can only enure to our benefit, by letting the parliamentary scene of action be fully developed. It may be that a change of ministry on the Peace question would save trouble all round.

This peace is very generally regarded as one forced upon the government, and in truth a botchery and a sham. Rumor will have it that Louis Napoleon has been too lavish in personal as well as national expenditure, and that he *insisted* upon closing a war whose next campaign (not necessary to preserve the military prestige of France) might drive himself and his public chest into bankruptcy. One of the already apparent effects of the peace is the universal bitterness against England on the Continent, and the general chorus in praise of France.

The ministry are trying to make capital out of the Italian question. But nothing will give brightness to the illumination which has been resolved upon; and to maintain the tranquillity of which, in this discontented and mortified metropolis, Horse Guards and Life Guards are deemed necessary. Riot is anticipated; but the affair is too lifeless to kindle excitement; it will pass off as a mockery.

Some attention is given here to our fermentation preparatory to the coming Presidential election, and I am frequently asked as to its probable result. Of course, I can give them nothing better than conjecture; and they regard it as "quite odd" that, notwithstanding the character of the new House of Representatives, and the election of a *Black* as Speaker, I should be confident of a democratic success. They do not seem to speculate upon deriving any advantage from our defeat; indeed, they rather despise the doctrine of "America for the Americans;" and what they consider the total disappearance of the Whig party, their old allies, leaves them very suspicious of the new factions. I think, too, our steady adherence to republican doctrines, accompanied by the constantly augmenting prosperity and power of the country, are visibly undermining their former prejudices, and letting in upon their thoughts, their manners, and even their conversation, a great deal more democracy than they themselves are conscious of. I see this in every rank of society, and perhaps more among the nobles and titled than in other classes.

As soon as Lord Clarendon returns to the Foreign Office, Herran says he will open upon him the recession of the Bay Islands to Honduras, upon Mr. Squier's plan. I will bear in mind the views of your No. 7. The Earl is reported to me as decidedly favorable to the scheme; and it is possible that he may catch at it as the only mode of disentangling this government from the absurd misconstruction he gave to the treaty of 1850.

Very truly and respectfully yrs.

## No. 8.—TO MR. MARCY.

LONDON, April 25, 1856.

MY DEAR SIR,—Last evening Lord Palmerston laid upon the table of the House of Commons the papers relating to our differences. Of what the packet consists I have not yet ascertained. It can hardly contain the reply to your letter of 28th December, because up to this hour that reply has not been sent to this legation. In the Lords, Lord Clarendon promised the papers early next week.

I wrote by the Hermann, which steamed from Southampton last Wednesday, a rather lengthy letter to you on the subject of the expected reply. I was anxious that you should get my views as early as possible, founded, as they are, on information perfectly reliable. I presume you will get that letter either before or about the same time with this, and will not, therefore, repeat its contents further than to say that your request for the recall of Mr. Crampton will be declined *upon the basis of fresh statements and proof furnished by Mr. Crampton*, and in a tone vastly improved from the former envenomed one.

All London is laughing at the ridiculous mishaps which occurred owing to the mismanagement of the arrangements for the great Naval Review of the day before yesterday. Both Houses of Parliament discussed them for an hour last night, and a morning journal contains a long article, full of fun, but considering the whole affair as somewhat a failure, and as a sort of representation of the mismanagement of Balaklava. The Peers and Commons, pompously invited to be near the Queen, were left in the lurch. Lord Palmerston was twice, in the tumultuous mélée, turned out of rail-cars by the conductors. Lords of Council and high Church dignitaries, and Chief Justice Campbell underwent all sorts of annoyances and delays. What became of the Diplomatic body nobody can tell. A huge steamer ran down a gun-boat. The manœuvring was indistinct and uninteresting, and finally nothing seems left to comfort the originators of this magnificent turn-out, but the certain facts that the number of vessels of war was 240, and their aggregate armament

3002 guns! I am not sorry that I abstained from being "there to see."

Lord Clarendon reached London on the evening of Monday, the 21st instant. I received the usual official notification on the afternoon of the 22d, and on the following morning requested an interview. Late last night I got his reply, assigning 4 o'clock this afternoon as the hour, and the Foreign Office as the *locus in quo.* I am therefore afraid that I cannot send you by this opportunity my first impressions of her Majesty's principal Secretary of State for Foreign Affairs. Indeed, as I have nothing to discuss with him, I shall be lucky if I can get him to say anything worthy of crossing the Atlantic.

The ministry have lately been several times in the minority in the House of Commons; and some of the newspaper sentinels carefully point to each case as a significant sign of what is coming. But I cannot yet perceive any really heavy weights tacked to the heels of the administration, but the Peace and the American question. These are certainly pressing them down more and more every hour; but the Premier is a man of great adroitness in extremities, and may yet, by sudden movement, twist round upon his tight rope, and dance off, with Parliament blinded and in tow, and in another direction. Pray observe how, in the distribution of the immense land and naval forces on hand, he is sending a larger force to Canada than they have ever yet had there; other troops to Bermuda; a most extraordinary supply of many millions of ball-cartridges, etc., etc. We have in cotton, to be sure, pretty good bail for the peaceful behavior of this country, as a general thing; but there are epochs and circumstances in which I should not think that bail sufficient. I have a strong mistrust of France; but that is Mr. Mason's province, not mine.

Allow me to intimate that in these critical times there may be some doubt as to the entire security of the arrangements made by the department with the Cunard steamers, reposing more confidence in them than in the Collins line, by instructing the despatch agent that it is unnecessary to have a special bearer of despatches when the Bag is sent by a Cunarder. No expense is incurred by these bearers of despatches; and our travelling countrymen are always proud to take charge of and faithfully protect what is meant for you. I don't question the integrity of the Cunard officers, but the public impression may be the other way; and all on board steamships are not officers.

You will have read in the newspapers the Treaty of Peace. The entire document breathes a spirit of tenderness for Russia and indifference to England. Public opinion here has become so pronounced about it, that the formal illumination preparing by government is universally sneered at, and even in the House of Commons has been laughed at and ridiculed.

I have just received a communication from Mr. Mason, dated Paris, the 24th instant. He tells me that he has embraced my idea about our Mediterranean squadron (which I think I sent to you in my letter of the 18th April), and has written to that effect to Commodore Breese.

I sometimes wish, for your sake, that I wrote a larger and bolder hand. I am conscious that eyes of a respectable period of life ought not to be severely taxed; but my habit is inveterate, and I am forced to this tiny chirography, if I write at all.

I have got nothing requiring the solemnity of a despatch.

Very truly and respectfully yrs.

P. S.—I have opened this to add that I have had my interview with Lord C.; that I said I had come, first to pay my personal respects, and second to enquire within what reasonable time I might expect, for transmission to you, the reply to your letter of the 28th December last. He was, of course, exceedingly pleased to form my acquaintance, and said he would send *me* a note, perhaps on Monday next, certainly before the next steamer left. This led me to suppose that there is something coming separate from the reply.

We talked over the negotiations at Paris. He is certainly not satisfied, but remarked that he had had no wish to humiliate Russia by the terms of the treaty. More at another time.

## No. 9.—TO MR. J. Y. MASON.

LONDON, May 2, 1856.

MY DEAR SIR,—It will be agreeable to you, no doubt, to know that your despatch to Governor Marcy, respecting the course things took about privateering, was received here just in time to enable me, after hastily reading it, to seal and put it in the Bag for the steamer Asia to-morrow.

Governor Marcy, who long ago took into his own management the correspondence on the Enlistment question, still retains it. We shall probably know nothing on that subject, beyond what we at present know, for six weeks to come; and then I do not, under the existing circumstances, expect a definitive stage to be reached. Possibly the controversy may drag its slow length along until Congress rises. If our State Department continue firm, Baron Brunow (to whom I send my cordial and most respectful remembrances) will, I feel assured, be proved a better prophet than either Count Walewski or Lord Cowley. I refer, of course, to the contents of your letter.

Your exceedingly kind invitation to Paris has given us all much pleasure. The ladies would enjoy nothing better; and the opportunity of one of "the sights"—the sight of yourself and family—would be sure to compensate them for the annoyances of travelling. But this distracting legation requires incessant watchfulness, especially now that the opening spring induces such shoals of our countrymen to come abroad; and as to a compulsory visit, if it occur at all, it will hardly occur until the middle of summer.

Sincerely yrs.

---

## No. 10.—TO ADMIRAL BEECHEY.

24 PORTLAND PLACE, April 3, 1856.

Mr. Dallas, the American Minister, has the honor to acknowledge the receipt of Admiral Beechey's note of to-day, apprising him that the Council of the Royal Geographical Society had awarded to Dr. Kane, of the United States, the Gold Medal of the Society, for the distinguished conduct and discoveries of that gentleman in the Arctic regions, and for the great zeal and energy displayed, under circumstances of great privation and suffering, in the search for Sir John Franklin.

Mr. Dallas hears of this tribute, alike generous and just, to the services of his countryman, in the cause of science and humanity, with much sensibility and pride. He will attend at the Anniversary meeting, on the 26th instant, agreeably to the invitation of the Council, and in receiving the medal will undertake its safe transmission to Dr. Kane.*

---

* When Admiral Beechey, in the presence of the Royal Geographical Society, handed this Gold Medal to the American Minister, it was acknowledged by the following short address:

Mr. President,—On behalf of my fellow-citizen, Dr. Elisha K. Kane, I receive, with equal pride and pleasure, this testimonial, awarded by your learned body to his ability and services in that branch of human knowledge to which you are specially devoted.

His country also, even now engaged in expressing her high sense of his deserts, will be gratified to learn that her judgment, which might possibly be ascribed to partiality, has been thus sanctioned.

Young as he yet is, and fairly entitled to count upon many years of zealous intellectual activity, he can never achieve a prouder recognition, considered in all its aspects, than this Medal of the Royal Geographical Society of London.

Dr. Kane, as is personally known to me, entered upon his career of Arctic exploration under the influence of sentiments which were strengthened rather than shaken by its depicted terrors. In the medical department of the Navy of the United States, on a remote station, his government scarcely intimated a disposition to join in the search for Sir John Franklin before he hurried forward to volunteer an enlistment for that noble purpose. There was a voice upon the breeze that had caught his ear. An ardent fondness for scientific studies impelled him to a fresh field of research. A daring and irrepressible spirit of enterprise co-operated with much experience and peculiar attainments. He went—he went twice; and, though he vainly offered his own life to rescue another's, he brought back with him observations, verifications, discoveries, and delineations worthy to be accepted by the masters of Geographical science. If, as I believe was the case, he penetrated to, and actually beheld, the ice-encircled yet open Sea, whose existence had been predicated of the periodical northern flight of aquatic birds, of certain currents, and of other *indicia*, he may justly feel that the practical solution of an interesting problem has earned the honor of your approbation.

I do not wish, Mr. President, to eulogize my countryman. You are far more competent than myself to appreciate the exact value of what he has effected. Your Council have affixed to his record this, their Great Seal, and, at your invitation, and with alacrity, I assume the grateful task of transmitting it safely to his hands.

## No. 11.—TO MR. MARCY.

London, May 6, 1856.

My dear Sir,—After the despatch sent you by the steamer of Saturday, the 3d instant, I have not enough on hand for another of that formal character by to-morrow's. Perhaps Lord C.'s reply to yours of the 28th December, will be enough for some time to come. I was surprised at finding it printed in the *Times* and *Post* on the very morning the steamer sailed. You will probably have received it in that shape.

This reply is more than commonly conciliatory in tone, and its concluding paragraphs are thought to evince a sincere desire to avoid a breach. Although it imports a refusal to recall, it avoids saying so expressly; and it may be construed as withholding a definitive answer until you have had an opportunity to consider the denials of the four honorable gentlemen, with the budget of loose and wanton affidavits. Of all the acts to which this government has resorted in defence of their officials, I cannot help regarding the procuring and publishing such a mass of gossiping slander as the most disgraceful. To be sure the letter of Strobel to Mr. Crampton, demanding £100, and threatening to turn State's evidence if he be not sent the means to quit the country, is very, very bad, and he must cease to be relied upon, whatever may have been his former character. That letter, however, like those of Mr. Crampton and others, adduced on the trial of Hertz, is substantive proof in itself; it is incapable of being explained away. Not so the absurd tittle-tattle and hearsay, often three degrees removed, invoked from ignorant and prejudiced men to destroy the statements of Hertz and others. This is all garbage with which Lord Clarendon and Mr. Crampton should have disdained to foul their pens. Still, it will have its intended effect upon the minds of superficial examiners, and I need not say that these count as a thousand to one against the reflecting and analyzing. Hence the expediency of commenting upon it, and, if within your power, of dispelling it by some strong testimony, such as that to which you have referred in one of your private letters. Even if you decide to send Mr. C. his passports, I would accompany that final measure with reasons, incorporating a complete refutation of these pretences of a Quarter-sessions character, why you regard further correspondence or argument as unnecessary and uncalled for.

There are gentlemen here who take another view of Lord Clarendon's reply. They represent it as an effort to persuade you to let him off upon the basis of a generous adherence to public agents misled by zeal in the service of their country; upon the ground that they were not lawyers, and did not exactly apprehend the legal character of the steps they were taking; upon the unwillingness to rest a quarrel on evidence derived from sources partially tainted and equivocal; and, more than all, upon what they regard as an appeal to your magnanimity, not to persevere after reiterated expressions of regret, and upon receiving renewed and cordial assurances of good will and friendship. If I could take this view I would certainly and frankly urge you to act upon it, as it must, I think, be admitted, that your doing so could only be ascribed to a forbearance in favor of peace. But I cannot so construe the sweeping and merciless and foul attack to which Lord C. has lent his high station and higher name against the motives, the officers, and the proceedings of the American government. Our judges are all under executive or party control; our district attorneys and marshals are all subservient and venal; our citizens, if witnesses, all corrupt and perjured; and our juries, grand and petit, unworthy of confidence! Such is the impression which this extraordinary paper, if not repelled conclusively, must have upon the general mind of Europe. I do not, I cannot, believe that Lord C. had carefully considered the miserable tissue of wanton scandal he was sending you, or the extent to which it necessarily carried him. There it is, however, and you are forced to deal with it exactly as he has shaped it, and as the world will understand it. Had it been read to the assembled representatives of the seven Great Powers, in the Congress at Paris, it would have been hailed with smiles as an exposure precursive of the downfall of republicanism, and might have formed a protocol, or at least an annex to a protocol, like the menace against the free press of Belgium. I wonder whether it may not in fact have had the *imprimatur* of a majority of this great league of rulers against the rights and liberties of the ruled? Orloff is the only one—no, his colleague, Brunow, is another—from whom I should expect resistance to its adoption. You must excuse this latitude of remark. I am generally cool, but now and then heated by trifles; and I know your temperament too well to fear that any sudden extravagance of mine can possibly mislead you.

I am just now struck with the idea that, if you inclined to postpone giving the final blow on the enlistment question, your object might be best attained by simply asking Lord C. if it was intended by her Majesty's government to superadd to the many unpleasant features of the correspondence, the adoption, as true, of the various imputations grossly made in the affidavits which accompanied his reply, against the integrity and honor of the judicial and executive officers of the United States? I think such a brief interrogatory would let him understand your sense of the proceeding, and would oblige him to do one of two things, either to say Yes, in which case you would have a unanimous feeling at home, or to say No, and that would take from the affidavits all title to any respect whatever, and leave you free to act upon the general tone of his reply. If we are to quarrel, let us do it with the entire approbation of the American people, and then consequences need not be apprehended.

I returned Baron Brunow's visit to-day, and had a long conversation with him as private friends. I knew him intimately when in St. Petersburg in 1838. He is here only for a short time, to announce the death of Nicholas! I reproached him for having, at the Conference in Paris, entered into the English project of abolishing privateers, although his country had so little interest in the matter, and he perfectly knew that it was aimed exclusively at the great defensive weapon of the United States against British disposition to go to war with us. I observed to him, see what the result is of having sympathized with Russia for two years!—we have a fierce contest about enlistments in violation of our neutrality laws, and at the very first occasion Russia throws her weight into the scale of our adversary, and enables her to claim to be backed by all Christendom! He made many efforts at excuse, but said, finally, "What could we do?" "I'll tell you what you could and what you ought to have done," said I. "You might have admitted the general plausibility of the idea, and expressed a readiness to co-operate in abolishing privateering, provided, in advance of any combined declaration on the subject, the assent of *all maritime* nations be obtained. You should have abstained from an unwillingness to exercise a species of moral coercion over Powers not represented in your Conference. In that way, without naming the United States, you would not have lent yourself to putting them in the wrong." The baron was quite overthrown by the suggestion, and treated it as unanswerable. I think it very likely that Mr. Stoeckl will be instructed to make all sorts of explanation. In the course of the talk, which was quite protracted, I asked him his opinion about our points of difference with this government. "Don't be worried," he replied, "they will be settled. They may not recall Crampton; but if he be dismissed, they will make light of it, or their indignation will be mildly expressed and of very short duration. No ministry would last a month, in the present condition of England, that should quarrel with the United States. As to a war with you, they dare not attempt it." He thinks Count Kreptovitch, a son-in-law of Nesselrode, will be sent to this Court as ambassador from the Czar.

I have just got your two private letters of the 20th and 25th April, and cordially thank you for them. You are somewhat more costive than I am, and therefore every word is of greater value.

Very truly and respectfully yrs.

---

## No. 12.—TO JUDGE JOEL JONES.

LONDON, May 9, 1856.

MY DEAR SIR,—I find private correspondence to be a luxury very difficult to enjoy at this post. The perpetual stream of visitors from the United States, the exactions of Court ceremonials, the endless series of entertainments and hospitalities, combine, with the necessities of business and the despatches to Governor Marcy twice a week, to run me fairly out of all time. I have no objection to the hardest work, but I would really delight in an hour or two occasionally for private and personal intercourse with such absent friends as you. That I should have been able to write you but one letter since I came here is a conclusive proof of my slavery. At this moment the mail for the Liverpool steamer of to-morrow morning is making up, and I scribble under whip and spur.

I cut the enclosed paragraph from one of the London newspapers. It is probably coined in the mint of an adversary who had his own purposes in view. As far as it refers to me, it is without the shadow of foundation. On its topic, I have no correspondent to whom I could or would write but yourself. The Committee of which you are the leading member have that matter in their own hands, and I do not intend in the remotest manner to interfere with it.

You perceive that out of the conferences at Paris, and especially out of the alliance of France and England, has emerged a more formidable league of sovereign powers against peoples than has yet been witnessed by modern times. The end is not perceptible at first glance; but I am much mistaken if the principle of rapid decay be not seated in the very heart of that league, and if its rotten fragments be not shaken to the earth by popular convulsions, and that at no distant day.

Of course I cannot write about my prospects as minister to any one *extra mœnia* of the State Department. Let me, however, intimate my opinion that I have gone far in accomplishing one of two things—putting our country in the right, if we are obliged to quarrel, or leading men's minds to a purpose and tone of conciliation. Governor Marcy has now the world before him, and with Providence as his guide he cannot fail to achieve a great result.

Always truly and faithfully yrs.

---

## No. 13.—TO MR. MARCY.

LONDON, May 13, 1856.

MY DEAR SIR,—We have quite a difference of opinion, in private circles and in the newspapers, whether it be safer to illuminate for the Peace or not to illuminate. The night assigned is the 29th instant. Many say the mob will attack the non-illuminated; but others allege the Peace to be so unpopular that he who ventures on glorification will be in danger. The diplomats, who care only for the safety of their windows, are puzzled how to act. One of my colleagues, residing opposite me, is so much of a courtier that he is bent upon a great blaze; while another, who adjoins me, looks rather glum and doubtful, and talks of *les lampions* with distrustful shakes of the head. I must own that my inclination is to keep dark, and leave tomfoolery to the rest of the world; but then, peace is *per se* a good, may certainly be innocently rejoiced over without becoming a party to it, and the smashing of panes of glass by a crowd around one's house, if to be done at all, is to be preferred as against the spirit of the police, rather than with their quasi connivance. If you were accessible by the telegraphic wire, I should, as I suppose all the European representatives have done with their courts, ask for instructions, and abide the consequences. That small obstacle, the Atlantic Ocean, shields you from the necessity of deciding the important point.

Now, although this treatment of the crisis be jest, the very doubt as to the course safest to be taken speaks strongly the character of the treaty as respects England. It has passed the ordeal of Parliament, though with some hard hits. The abandonment of Schamyl and his Caucasians to their fate, the forbearance toward Nicholaief, the abolition of privateering, the surrender of established legal rights of belligerents, the shameless truckling to the indecent attack upon the freedom of the Belgian press, and, after all, the little security obtained against Russian ambition,—although they were not pressed as matters to justify opposition to the address of the Queen, were, nevertheless, put in, *protestando*, as items in reserve for future attacks upon the ministry.

Lord Palmerston, just at this moment, seems to be in as victorious an attitude as any British premier has ever held. He has baffled the combination on the surrender of Kars, has boldly carried the peace through, has vindicated the protocols, even when defying Walewski's effort "to gag a free press," and has dexterously managed to postpone our American differences to a distant day. In the mean time, he sides with Sardinia on the Italian question, and stands by Turkey in a separate convention secretly made between her, Austria, France, and England, much to the offence of Russia. His majorities are large, and his party is full of exultation. Still, there is that thorn of America in his side—*hœret lethalis*—and if it do not bring him to the ground, it will be because you may come to his relief, or he may suddenly, by the indications in France, discover the expediency of greater conciliation in his relations with us. All men of opinions worth anything agree in saying—I should not be surprised to hear it from his own lips—that a conflict with the United States is the only thing he could not stand for six months, or even half that time. His power is immense, but that is a rock on which, if he touch, he founders.

I have carefully watched, from day to day, the official distribution of the recent armada off Portsmouth, and must confess that I have not been able to detect any such disposition of the force as would warrant anxiety. If there be any hostile preparation going on, it is most successfully veiled. Lord Elgin has a motion *in petto* respecting the troops recently sent to Canada; but his object, as I gather from himself, is not so much to complain of what has been done, as to make an occasion to warn against going further, so as to arouse our susceptibilities and jealousies. I feel confident that the result of the experiment tried a year ago, of ordering a squadron abruptly to the West, was not such as will encourage its repetition. The ministry, if set upon quarrelling with us, and I am yet to perceive any decidedly amicable disposition, will not go to work in that way, but will coolly strive to put us in the wrong, and make us at least appear to be aggressive enough to rouse the loyalty and passions of their people. Lord Elgin's motion will come up soon after the holidays, say about the 20th instant.

The special instruction to ask for an answer to your despatch of the 28th December came *too late.* I had mooted the matter with Lord C. as soon as he reached the Foreign Office from Paris, and his reply will, upon a fair calculation, be in your hands the day after tomorrow. I hope you may rest, after its perusal, for a week, and give my letter of last Saturday a chance of conveying a hint or two of some importance.

I have nothing worthy to be worked up into a formal despatch. I send you, however, a parliamentary document of some interest—"Correspondence respecting the late negotiation with Japan"—recently laid upon the tables of the two Houses. It shows a neat and exact imitation of the example set by Commodore Perry.

You introduced to me citizen * * * * of California, and of course he was cordially welcomed. With a generous ambition, he sought the eye of royalty, and I presented him at the Levee. By some mistaken movement of her arm, the Queen led him to kneel and kiss her hand! If you remember him you will smile. Our democrats make pretty good courtiers, for they are generally men practically of the world.

Politics at home look to be in a fine state of fermentation; the democracy, sanguine as usual, preparing to go it blind. Rest assured that the adversary's fragments, which appear now to be so disjointed and broken, will at the eleventh hour fly together and form a powerful whole. It is so obviously their only chance that I cannot presume them silly enough to overlook it. And if we do not, at Cincinnati, shun the loadstone rock, which seems, at this distance, to be attracting all kinds of floating craft, and to be drawing out the bolts and rivets of our party, we shall sink. And at what period of constitutional history are we incurring this risk! If the administration are forced to back down on the great Kansas question, and they will assuredly be so if gentlemen like Mr. ———, and Mr. ———, and Mr. ——— are to attain their purpose, we shall have a restoration of the ruinous Monroe doctrine, "*the era of good feeling*," sapping and subverting every honest and solid principle of the democratic creed. It really "behooves you, then, to apply your finest art," "*ne quid detrimenti capiat respublica!*"

I hope you will not fail to write me precisely the wishes of yourself and the President in regard to my course of action, should you dismiss Mr. Crampton, and I be dismissed in return. Although public considerations must not bend for a moment, or to the breadth of a hair, to considerations of personal convenience, yet, when they can be perfectly harmonized, attention may justly be paid to both.

Very truly and respectfully yrs.

## No. 14.—TO MR. MARCY.

LONDON, May 16, 1856.

MY DEAR SIR,—A great contest, big with the ultimate disruption of Church and State, has been going on here for some time, and has, to the surprise of almost everybody, brought Lord Palmerston plump on his knees before the Archbishop of Canterbury. About three weeks ago, Sir Benjamin Hall, First Commissioner of Works, Parks, Palaces, and Public Buildings, after obtaining the sanction of the Premier, ordered some fine military bands to play for an hour or more in the parks on the afternoons of Sunday. The music attracted immense crowds. In Regent's Park, close by me, the number assembled, counted officially at the gates, fell little short of 100,000 men, women, and children, on a single occasion. The Sabbatarians, scandalized and alarmed, rushed to the rescue. All the newspapers took sides—some in favor of amusing the toil-worn populace in so harmless a way, others decrying it as the prolific source of demoralization and turbulence. At last the pillars of the Church are shaken into action. The Archbishop writes to Lord Palmerston. Lord P. sulks, reiterates his liberal opinion and advice on the matter, and formally abates the music. A slight apprehension is entertained that the disappointed, on Sunday next, the day after to-morrow, will show their spunk and vexation by some outbreaks. No fear of that at the present epoch. John Bull is as effectually nozzled, and foot-tied, under the auspices of police, Horse Guards, and Life Guards, as his majestic representation, the Lion, in the Zoological Gardens, is caged in iron.

Further reflection upon Lord Clarendon's reply to your letter of the 28th December last has settled down into a very general opinion that the President will dismiss Mr. Crampton as soon as you receive it. This impression is strengthened by the intercepted correspondence of the Foreign Office with the Costa Ricans—a correspondence, to be sure, which we have very little to do with, but which shows Lord C.'s meddlesome and inimical spirit and policy to be rather worse than had been supposed in relation to Central America. Had the President recognized the existing government in Nicaragua I would have been disposed to ask his lordship whether these intercepted letters were genuine, and what he meant by lending arms against an independent State on the Isthmus. Such a question would hardly need a reply, and yet his lordship would be put to his trumps in making a civil and honest answer. As it is, however, I suppose we can't find fault with his helping a friendly power to resist a filibuster. I am not sure that you have not been too scrupulous and cautious in your policy as to Walker. At all events, I hope that these meddling manifestations from this quarter may be made the avowed platform of a decisive movement on our part. We should displace this entering wedge by a quick and well-aimed stroke.

By the time you get this you will be in the midst of the agitation of the Cincinnati Convention—from which I wish ourselves a safe deliverance.

Very truly and respectfully yrs.

---

## No. 15.—TO MR. J. P. H.

London, May 16, 1856.

My dear H.,—Did I not know your friendship, as well as your constant engagements, I should take it for granted that you had finally given me up as one of the lost. Are you always too busy to write letters?

We have got into a quiet, comfortable house in Portland Place, and we are gradually introducing ourselves to the mysteries of London housekeeping. The system is simple enough, as it devolves the whole trouble upon servants, allowed to expend what they think necessary, and expected to account at the expiration of every week. Simple, certainly; but as to economy, quite another thing.

I am kept hard at work in the legation in a variety of ways; but never having contracted a distaste for labor, I get along tolerably well. Phil is indefatigable and always at hand.

Politics are anything but satisfactory. I found on my arrival a fixed anti-American set in the ministerial and social classes, and entered upon a determination to break that down, first, by frankness and conciliation, if they would answer, if not, then, second, by open defiance. Our countrymen here tell me that my success has been complete:—but let us wait a little longer before too confident a conclusion. To go to war with us is an extravagance which I am certain would upset any ministry in less than six months, if not on the instant; but I doubt much their disposition to forego their great luxury of treating us with insult and contumely. Their hospitality and kindness to me and my family have certainly been unmeasured; but the region of national relations and policy is widely separated from that of mere personal intercourse. Should Mr. Crampton be dismissed by Gov. Marcy I think we may look out for a series of retaliatory and recriminating acts between the two countries, which must lead, at no distant day, to the final trial of strength. When we are driven to that, we must throw the scabbard away, and tie the hilt to the hand.

The ladies up stairs are all well, and not yet tired, as I am heartily, of the gaieties of the great London season. I wish you would bring two or three of your circle over, and give them a chance while I am here (not long, mark that!) to see the Court of Queen Victoria, as splendid now as it ever has been or ever will be. All this magnificence of ceremonial and pretension is fast being undermined, even among the proudest peers, by our republican principles accompanied by our wonderful prosperity; and before any one of your children reaches fifty, it will have vanished, like the hues of a rainbow, forever. Let them see it before it fades away.

Many affectionate remembrances to yours.

Ever truly and faithfully.

---

## No. 16.—TO MR. J. Y. MASON.

LONDON, May 24, 1856.

MY DEAR SIR,—I have had the enclosed letter by me for some time, undetermined what direction to give it, and now it occurs to me that I may enclose it to you, and beg you to address it for me to wherever the Commodore may be. I have put on an extra envelope and leave it unsealed, so that you can perceive its subject is a purely private enquiry, having no connection with public topics.

The matter on which we have heretofore exchanged views is not yet sufficiently developed to be decided upon finally one way or the other. I have been unable, though always on the watch since the great review of Portsmouth, to perceive any such naval distribution as would warrant anxiety. As, however, I have reason to expect, in the course of the coming three weeks, something definite from Washington in reference to the Earl of Clarendon's last communication on the recruitment question (a communication, by-the-by, of a tone so remarkably calm and conciliatory that it would have had a strong effect towards entire adjustment had not its writer, heedlessly, and without some disclaimer of official adoption, connected with it a series of wantonly vituperative affidavits), and therefore think it safest to let things remain as they are for a month longer.

Always sincerely yrs.

---

## No. 17.—TO JUDGE KANE.

LONDON, May 27, 1856.

MY DEAR JUDGE,—It gave me peculiar pleasure to attend the Royal Geographical Society yesterday. Their Gold Medal, a very beautiful piece of art by-the-by, which I received on behalf of the Doctor, was accompanied by a handsome notice from the President, Admiral Beechey. My short reply I have written out for the especial benefit of my valued friend, Mrs. Kane, and take the liberty to enclose it. As no important business closes in London without a dinner, and a series of table-speeches, the Doctor was toasted, and, as the guardian of his fame for the nonce, I addressed about 200 philosophers and explorers with a review of his whole life. He was cheered from beginning to end. The medal is transmitted in a small screwed box to the Department of State by my despatch bag. Let me hear of its safe arrival.

I suppose all this should take the appearance of stately form, but I am bound to fulfil other engagements, and really must throw myself upon the indulgence of yourself and the Doctor. Mr. Marcy waits for me.

My warm regards to all the family.

Ever truly yrs.

---

## No. 18.—TO THE BISHOP OF OXFORD.

24 Portland Place, May 28, 1856.

My dear Lord,—No one has yet, to my knowledge, arrived from the United States to whom I could venture to refer you as a person fully and accurately informed on the topic of the note I have had the honor to receive from your Grace to-day. Nor can I hope to meet one so early as by Friday next.

The comparatively private mode of inflicting capital punishment has not been long practised, and has probably not attracted the general and careful attention to which it is entitled. Opinions as to its effects on the people, contrasted with the effects of the old public executions, may not be uniform; but I am disposed to think that experience is fast dispelling the jealousies and doubts which were felt when the change was introduced. Of course this remark refers exclusively to my own country, and it is not made with the confidence which a thorough knowledge of facts and a close investigation might inspire.

If I am fortunate enough to meet a fellow-countryman on whom, in regard to this enquiry, perfect reliance can be placed, I will hasten to apprise you; or, if it be likely that your movement may be protracted so long as to enable me to write home, and receive back the views of one or two gentlemen whom I have in my eye, I will undertake to do so with great pleasure.

With sincere respect, I am, truly yrs.

## No. 19.—TO MR. J. Y. MASON.

(*Private.*) LEGATION OF THE UNITED STATES.
LONDON, May 31, 1856.

SIR,—Incidents affecting the relations between this country and the United States are crowding so rapidly upon us that too much vigilance and precaution cannot be exercised to ward off or to mitigate the consequences of an explosion which may possibly happen at any moment.

You will therefore excuse me for suggesting the expediency of warning the Commander of our Mediterranean Squadron to be, at this juncture, extremely careful not to put himself in a situation open to surprise, and to keep himself and his force ready for any sudden emergency. The clouds which now threaten may blow over; but as experience has not taught us to rely upon the plausible professions of British statesmen, unconfirmed by ascertained facts, I am anxious to put every one on guard. The detection of the correspondence with Costa Rica, the intermeddling of Capt. Tarleton with our steamer, the Orizaba, the reception by the government of the new minister, Padre Vigil, from Nicaragua, and the overwhelming denial given by Mr. Clayton to one of Mr. Crampton's boldest assertions, combined with the daily expectation of hearing that this latter gentleman has been dismissed, maintain the public pulse at fever heat, which may precipitate secret action.

I am, most respectfully, very truly yrs.

---

## No. 20.—TO MR. E. G. SQUIER.

(*Private.*) LONDON, June 1, 1856.

DEAR SIR,—Your letter of the 28th May, '56, did not reach me until the 30th, after I had seen Mr. Brown, and requested him to convey to you my sentiments.

I thank you for the clear and full statement you have given me of your position and views.

It has, no doubt, occurred to you that our government cannot, especially at this juncture, participate in any negotiation having for its object a new disposition of islands over which they can pretend to claim no right of sovereignty whatever. The group, headed by Ruatan, is really part of Honduras, but is occupied and colonized by Great Britain. The question is, therefore, to be adjusted by those two governments exclusively. If the latter can be persuaded by Señor Herran to do what is just and restore the islands unconditionally to Honduras, such a course will be cordially approved by the United States—first, as a measure of right; second, as a measure favorable to the independence of their own commerce and intercourse; and third, as a measure removing practically one of the leading causes of difficulty with this country.

If, however, the restitution cannot be effected, except upon terms or stipulations which would divest it of substantial and permanent character, leaving the islands subject in the remotest degree to English influence or law, and ready to relapse at a more prosperous moment into their present colonial dependence, the United States could not fail to regard it with disfavor—first, as a source of future quarrel between Honduras and Great Britain; second, as on the part of the latter only a plausible evasion of an exciting issue; and third, as legalizing, without substantially disarming, the actual usurpation.

I do not think that the government at Washington would find anything in the *three conditions* you have enumerated at all questionable; but there is something in your suggestion about admitting the inhabitants to the enjoyment of special municipal rights which savors of keeping up the distinction between the English citizens and the other citizens of Honduras, and so facilitating the future relapse to which I have adverted. To this the President would probably seriously object. Perhaps you have stated it somewhat vaguely; and, indeed, until the "special municipal rights" are distinctly enumerated, I do not wish to hazard a positive opinion.

The moment is perhaps unfavorable to action. The two nations are much excited by the recent events, and are watching each other with extreme jealousy. It is not merely impossible for me to leave London for an hour, but I should fear that my meeting Messrs. Herran and

Alvarado just now anywhere would excite suspicions and impede their progress. In a short time the cloud will either disappear or burst.

I am very respectfully yrs.

---

## No. 21.—TO MR. D.

LONDON, June 6, 1856.

MY DEAR SIR,—A watchful solicitude induces me to send you the enclosed slip from one of the newspapers.

My best regards wait on you and yours. If the *Times* and the *Post* are reliable organs, I shall probably quit England soon, *never* to return; an undiscriminating retaliation amounts to an original insult, and will require many years to be forgotten. It will not surprise me if I should turn out to be the last minister from the United States to the British Court, and that will certainly be fame if it be not honor.

Always faithfully yrs.

---

## No. 22.—TO MR. MARCY.

LONDON, June 6, 1856.

MY DEAR SIR,—I have nothing worthy of a formal despatch by the steamer of to-morrow.

The report of Captain Tarleton on the affair of the Orizaba has not yet been received. I shall wait a day or two longer, and if I do not get from the F. O. by that time the copy I expect, the case of Captain Tinklepaugh will be spread out in writing, as it was in conversation, and definite replies be asked to definite interrogatories.

Lord Palmerston said last evening in the House of Commons that this government had received *indirect* information of Mr. Crampton's having been dismissed. This information, if your letter of the 23d May be, as it of course must be, accurate, cannot be well founded. No later intelligence than that of the Atlantic, which reached here on the 4th inst., after leaving New York on the 24th May, has been received. The recognition of Vigil is fast passing into the same category of permanent, but incurable, and therefore to be tolerated, causes of reproach to our government and people as the annexation of Texas, the displacement of the poor Indians, or the constitutional recognition of Slavery. There is no use in crying over spilt milk; the thing is done, cannot be undone, can in fact do no harm, and may as well be forgotten, except so far as it serves the purpose of an occasional fling at the mobocracy of America.

If mischief grow at all out of Vigil's reception, rest assured it will be quickened by compost from France. The rumored Spanish movement against Mexico—a movement which should put General Gadsden and our Home Squadron on the alert—involves an ulterior purpose of Louis Napoleon's:—either to send a scion of his imperial house to the hall of the Montezumas, or to extirpate Walker, or so to involve Spain and Mexico in war as to furnish to the former a plausible excuse for transferring Cuba to England. I am inclined to adopt the last hypothesis. Lord Palmerston, having served the purpose of Louis Napoleon for some months back, is requiring a reciprocation, and Spain is the cat's-paw which the Emperor puts in to stir the fire.

My uncertain position is of course not without its inconveniences, and I am now and then tempted to exclude myself altogether from the world, until the world lets me know definitely whether I am to be decapitated or let go without day. The measure of dismissing me, as *in pari delicto* with that honorable gentleman, Mr. Crampton, savors of an undiscriminating vindictiveness which strongly marks an original insult. Indeed, I am disposed to think that the dignity of our country will make it necessary so to regard that measure, if it be resorted to, and that, without the amplest apology, we ought never to permit an American minister, or diplomatic agent of any sort, even a consul, to shew himself in her Majesty's dominions. My longing for historical fame would certainly be satiated if it were to turn out that I am to be the last of our ministers at this Court. As it could not be ascribed to any fault of mine, and would unerringly indicate the moment at which the doctrine of *delenda est Carthago* began its practical operation, I should be borne down to future ages identified with the commencement of a great period. *Ultimas Romanorum* is better than merely Consul or even Imperator.

The dread of a war with the United States is very general; and the two great interests, manufacturing and mercantile, are beginning to bestir themselves to prevent it if they can. I do not rely so much upon the parliamentary movements of the opposition as upon violent agitation in these interests. The ministerial majority is too great and too mercenary to be in any danger of defeat, until terrified by the clamor of the constituencies. *That* can scarcely be brought to bear upon them until after Lord Palmerston has tried their mettle, and forced them, as he has already once done since I have been here, to stick to him and brave the storm. My conviction, however, is firmer than ever, that if he advances any farther on the road to a quarrel with us, he will suddenly close his administration.

Pray pardon me if I request you to let the President know that I give my adhesion to his reception of Vigil, as indeed I believe I did in one of my former letters.

Always very truly yrs.

---

## No. 23.—TO COL. PEREZEL.

LONDON, June 7, 1856.

DEAR SIR,—Your letter of the 4th inst., requesting a passport from this legation for your wife, on a visit to Hungary, and one for yourself enabling you to accompany her to France, has been received. The circumstances of your case are such as awaken my warmest sympathy, and I sincerely wish it was in my power to send the documents you so urgently desire. But I am without discretion, and under explicit instructions from my government on the subject. You are not a citizen of the United States, and I am expressly prohibited granting a passport to any but a citizen. The declaration of your intention to become a citizen would avail you much while remaining in the United States, but abroad its efficacy is not recognized. I entertain no manner of doubt as to your character and merits, and would cheerfully rely upon your assurances of discretion and care;—but I cannot break through a rule positively prescribed.

Enclosed I return to you the introductory note of Mr. Sedgwick, and the certificate of Mr. Henry Ward Beecher.

I am very respectfully yrs.

---

## No. 24.—TO MR. MARCY.

LONDON, June 10, 1856.

MY DEAR SIR,—Fortified by the mail of the Asia, I feel strong hopes of bringing to a close the bickerings of the two countries. The sentiment condemnatory of Mr. Crampton augments in force every day, and is almost as general in this as in our own country. The programme of your course has been, in conversation, anticipated by me, and every reflecting mind accepted it as a desirable termination to the affair. I do not think the ministry will make further stand and hazard a war, in defence of a person now proved so unworthy. If they do, Parliament will drive them from their places.

Should this government, contrary to my *present* expectations, retaliate the dismissal of Mr. Crampton by mine, it is probable that I shall immediately quit London with my family, and fix myself within a promptly accessible distance from our legation at Paris, in rural and private quarters. You have made no disposition to relieve me from the necessary expense of this movement, and, if it has to be made, I shall be driven to borrowing for the first time in my life: a consequence of *no outfit.* My time is up.

Very truly and respectfully yrs.

---

## No. 25.—TO LORD ABERDEEN.

LONDON, June 11, 1856.

MY DEAR LORD ABERDEEN,—Agreeably to my promise I now have to inform you that Mr. Crampton was sent his passports by the President, and the exequaturs of the three consuls were recalled; but the reasons for doing this are set forth in a despatch addressed to me, which I propose to read in the course of the day to Lord Clarendon. The despatch is in terms and tone of a most conciliatory character; accepts frankly and conclusively the assurances of Lord Clarendon's last letter, so far as her Majesty's government is concerned; but expresses an unchanged conviction as to the personal misconduct of Mr. Crampton and his coadjutors, who have, by disregarding the instructions sent them, and by continuing, even up to January last, to act in violation of our laws, and by misrepresenting the conduct of our public functionaries to the government here, embroiled the two countries, and made themselves objectionable residents in the United States. The despatch is accompanied by a mass of fresh evidence, chiefly from the very witnesses whose affidavits were appended to Lord Clarendon's communication of the 30th of April.

My only purpose is to describe the features of the despatch I have received, not to make a single comment. Should there, in your lordship's opinion, be no indelicacy in my doing so, it will afford me pleasure to submit the paper to your own perusal.

With the most cordial respect,
I remain very sincerely yrs.

---

## No. 26.—TO SIR H. BULWER.

LONDON, June 15, 1856.

MY DEAR SIR HENRY,—Your note from Brighton was really very agreeable to me as proof of regard, but in no respect was it at all necessary as explanatory of the circumstance to which it refers. My amiable countryman, Mr. Peabody, omitted to look at the thing on both sides; and while he was anxious that the toast should come from the person most acceptable to me, he forgot that it could not but be personally embarrassing to you. It would be a wretched sort of life, this of ours, if such a long-continued and kindly intercourse as yours and Mr. Crampton could be coolly sacrificed to a table compliment to another. Even my comparatively slight acquaintance with him suggests to me that I shall undergo, when meeting him, an unpleasant struggle between official decorum and individual feeling.

Pray be assured that I appreciate and sincerely applaud what you did. I place a much higher value upon the note you have written me than upon any specimen of formal eloquence (though aware of your power) with which you could possibly have addressed Mr. Peabody's guests.

I am, very truly and respectfully yrs.

---

## No. 27.—TO MR. MARCY.

London, June 17, 1856.

My dear Sir,—The Hermann leaves Southampton to-morrow, but she has so little repute that I shall do no more than write this short note by her.

Everything since I communicated your two last despatches to Lord Clarendon has worked to a charm. The public excitement augmented every hour. The opposition in Parliament took an attitude not to be mistaken, and on Friday last, headed by Lord John Russell, opened their battery. Yesterday Lord John put his questions to the Premier in a handsome and impressive speech, and Lord Palmerston announced formally the determination of the cabinet, "not to terminate their present amicable relations with Mr. Dallas." The breakers are avoided; the legation is in deep water again; the Crampton squall has passed over, rather clearing the sky than otherwise; and there is bright promise of a goodly day to-morrow. No time shall be lost to improve the returning swell of kindly feeling. It is not impossible that prompt negotiation may put an end to all controversy about the treaty. If not, and we resort to arbitration, let me know your preferences and be prepared.

The war, as between the parliamentary parties, will continue; and Lord Derby has threatened a fierce overhauling of the ministerial conduct in the recruitment business. But this last feat of Lord Palmerston secures his position.

Our countrymen here are in great exultation, and lavish upon "Old Marcy" eulogies which my jealousy forbids me to repeat.

Very truly and respectfully yrs.

---

## No. 28.—TO MR. MARCY.

LONDON, June 24, 1856.

MY DEAR SIR,—I have as yet nothing from the Foreign Office for a despatch. The replies to your letters on Central America and recruitment seem to require great care and elaboration. Much effort and skill are certainly necessary to steer through the straits in which the ministry find themselves. The Opposition are resolved to hold them to their responsibility, and nothing but the highest exercise of the imperturbable temper, adroitness, and ability of Lord Palmerston can save them. In my opinion, however, he will prove himself equal to the task. What may be the tone and purport of the forthcoming answers it is impossible to conjecture; but they cannot incur the extreme hazard of continuing, on either question, the war of words which has already so nearly ruined them; such a course will inflame their adversaries and produce a reaction of panic. If they are calm and moderate, no matter how strongly tinctured with self-esteem, they will pass current, dispel the existing mortification, and disarm many who only insist upon no further provocation to the United States. A vote in either House in such a case would probably be in favor of government.

I constantly hear your two despatches praised, and cannot help thinking that they are producing on the general public an impression of our having been right, and the ministry wrong from the beginning. Even the newspapers, the *Times* and the *Post*, are slowly but obviously retreating from the positions they have heretofore so audaciously maintained. My colleagues of the diplomatic corps, who unanimously foretold my dismissal, chuckle over what they regard as the discomfiture of Palmerston, and give me, *en passant*, an extra smile and squeeze of the hand. I could entertain and perhaps surprise you with particulars of a similar spirit in other quarters; but there are spheres as to which pen and ink are indiscreet agents of communication.

Messrs. Herran and Alvarado are now here. The former asked this morning by note an interview with Lord Clarendon. They both, with Mr. Squier, called on me yesterday. We conversed freely, but agreed that, before going formally into business, it would be prudent on all sides to await the answers preparing to your despatches, as some clew to the most politic and promising mode of proceeding might be derived from them, and we should, at all events, better understand the dispositions of the British government. These answers, you must recollect, will be put, in print, on the tables of the two Houses of Parliament, as soon as they reach the American Legation. I suppose they will come to me, as Mr. Crampton's passports came to him, after the steamer of to-morrow has sailed.

I enclose, as worthy a moment's conference with Mr. Dobbin, two notes, one from Mr. Hawthorne to me, and the other from Mr. James Rae to Mr. Hawthorne. The quadrant of Paul Jones ought certainly to be among other Revolutionary relics in the Navy Department, and it would give me pleasure to secure it. Should you gentlemen agree with me, let me be duly authorized to purchase, at a reasonable price, on proof of its identity, and give orders how to pay.

The Italian question, you will have noticed, is fast ripening to the dropping point. One of two things must take place, and that speedily, or a popular rise will occur:—either Austria must be allowed to *repress* with her iron squadrons, or vast reforms must be inaugurated under the auspices of Sardinia directly, and of France and England indirectly. Manin eclipses, at least for the time, Mazzini (who, by-the-by, meditates retirement in America) in boldness and prudence; and the liberal Whig Cabinet of St. James are intensely on the *qui vive*. History, a half century hence, may possibly attribute the recent forbearance of Lord Palmerston, under an indignity from the United States, to his forecasting preparations in favor of Italian unity.

Our nomination for the next Presidential term is rather favorably commented upon here. It is supposed to be auspicious of external tranquillity. But when I express the opinion that its success is certain, they treat me with an incredulous smile, being assured by their wise correspondents and their equally wise newspapers that Mr. Fillmore's election by the House is far more likely. *Nous verrons.*

Our countrymen are prodigious travellers. Every steamer comes loaded with them, on their way first to this legation for passports, and then "*partout en Europe.*" Some have families of eight(!) children with them; others are spending their "honeymoon;" and wandering bachelors sharp-set for Paris, the Pope, the Pyramids, St. Petersburg, or Persia, are countless. What a sinecure of a place has the American Minister in London!

Always truly and respectfully yrs.

---

## No. 29.—TO MR. M. M.

LONDON, June 26, 1856.

MY DEAR SIR,—The "contretemps" experienced by me at the Levee yesterday is inaccurately stated in the *Times* of to-day, and I can't think that *you* would knowingly sanction a misrepresentation as to myself. I will briefly tell you the facts without a comment.

I took with me to the Palace three American gentlemen. One of these is an eminent professor of civil and military engineering in our Military Academy at West Point, and has the assimilated rank of major in the army. He wore his official costume:—a blue dress coat, with buttons of the engineer corps, blue pantaloons, white vest, black stock, and the common hat.

It was objected, in a manner exceedingly kind and courteous, that he wore a black cravat, had no chapeau, and no sword, and could not thus pass the Queen. I tried once, twice, or thrice to surmount the difficulty by adverting to the *official* character of his dress; but the rule was express, and there was no discretion to relax it. Pained at the position in which my estimable countryman was placed, among strangers, and in a place to which he was entirely unaccustomed, I unhesitatingly offered to go home with him, and in this suggestion his companions joined. We retired. It was impossible to do less, and we did no more.

Truly and respectfully yrs.

---

### No. 30.—TO SIR EDWARD CUST.

24 Portland Place, June 26, 1856.

My dear Sir Edward Cust,—It has occurred to me that you, as the gentleman best knowing the incidents immediately preceding the opening of the Levee on Wednesday last, the sudden discovery of the insufficiency of a particular costume, and the consequent retirement from the Palace, must be the proper person to whom to address this short note on that subject.

Allow me then to say to you frankly and unreservedly that the idea that what then took place can possibly be attributed to a want of respect to her Majesty, either in my countryman, Professor Mahan, or in myself, occasions surprise as well as sincere pain. No sovereign has more just and more universally recognized claims to affectionate attachment and veneration than your Queen; and I might hope that avowals of sentiment, in public and in private, strengthened by an unaffected gratitude for the generous distinction and kindness with which I have been honored, ever since my arrival, as the diplomatic representative of the United States at her Majesty's Court, would render it impossible, even with those who do not personally know me, that I should be suspected, and on an occasion, too, so casual and light, of failing in the respect so eminently due. I disclaim it, Sir Edward, with emphasis, on my own part, as wholly foreign to my nature, and equally foreign to the government and people of the United States; and I disclaim it as unjust to Professor Mahan, and irreconcilable with the high and honorable character he has long maintained in the service of his country.

I remain, Sir Edward, always, etc.

## No. 31.—TO MR. MARCY.

LONDON, July 3, 1856.

MY DEAR SIR,—I sent you a despatch by the Fulton, which left Southampton yesterday. Nothing worthy of a fresh one since.

The effort to make of the affair at the Levee something of importance has entirely failed. I have not recognized it as worthy to interfere with the public interests and business under my care. It is dying out as another of the gross exaggerations of the *Times*, springing from hostility to the United States. The pretence that it originated in an intentional disrespect to the Queen was promptly exploded. As to the merits of the Master of Ceremonies' decision against the admissibility of Professor Mahan's costume, I am disposed to think Sir Edward Cust, though very polite and courteous, acted erroneously, and I suspect he has been told so by those to whose opinions he would be more deferential than to mine. It was a quasi military official dress, so stated to be by me. The Professor was not an attaché, and was therefore not bound, by what Sir Edward kept harping on as an agreement between himself and Mr. Buchanan, to add anything to his full dress uniform. The dress of the members of the legation is controlled by the understanding—not so the dress of others, citizens or officers. I have already presented many, on whose persons not a symptom of the diplomatic equipment could be traced beyond the chapeau and sword, and no objection hinted. Even on this very occasion Sir Edward was willing to pass as unexceptionable the militia dress of an adjutant-general of New Jersey, which, though certainly showy (especially with the blue ribbon and gold eagle of the Cincinnati hanging at a button-hole), and highly respectable, can scarcely claim to be on a footing with the *national* costume prescribed by the President for officers in the national service, ranking by assimilation as majors. I find many distinguished connoisseurs of the rules of etiquette entertain the opinion that Sir Edward was confused in his notions and made a blunder.* It is perhaps from the prevalence of this sentiment that it has been thought expedient to invent two utterly unfounded subterfuges—first, that Lord Clarendon, upon being told what had happened, sent in haste to stop my going away, and to say that her Majesty would receive the Professor; and, second, that her Majesty herself had done so. We left the Palace tranquilly, after shaking hands with Sir Edward Cust, and without the slightest intimation that the decree of exclusion had been rescinded.

This really frivolous matter has worried me personally more than I would be willing to admit; but I have been extremely guarded and forbearing to prevent its having any influence whatever upon the discussions now proceeding as to Central America. The French newspapers hailed its first appearance in the *Times* with delight, and seemed to gloat on a fresh opportunity of fanning discord between England and the United States. They fired up incontinently at the effort to advance another step in the usurpations of democracy! We may yet have a Congress of sovereigns to teach dress and manners, whose protocols will be accompanied by photographic illustrations of the only tolerable "shorts," "tights," "vests," "cravats," "rapiers," and head-gear!

---

* "COUNCIL HALL, SHEFFIELD, July 7, 1856.

"SIR,—I have to acknowledge, on behalf of the Sheffield Foreign Affairs Committee, the receipt of your very courteous note of the 24th ult.

"The Committee, in reference to the recent circumstance at the Queen's Levee, further instruct me to say that if your countryman, as is now represented by a portion of the Press, holds a recognized military rank in America, and wore his official costume on the occasion in question, they are of opinion that Sir Edward Cust made an error of judgment in not admitting him, without reference to the components of that dress. The Committee conclude this from their knowledge that Turkish, Persian, and other officials have the right of entrance in their peculiar national dresses. They believe that the regulations on which Sir Edward Cust relied refer only to cases of private individuals, that is, persons not holding office nor rank, which it is now stated your countryman did.

"The Committee also believe that the misrepresentation which the *Times* in the first instance made of the circumstances was designed with a view to still further complicate the differences between our country and yours.

"I have the honor to remain, sir, yr. obed. serv.,

"WM. CYPLES, S. S.

"The HON. G. M. DALLAS,

"American Minister, etc."

Since my interview with Lord Clarendon on Monday last, I have twice conferred with Mr. Herran, who has been received by Lord C., and whose course of action as to the Bay Islands is alike intelligent and frank. He carefully advises with me at every step, and he assures me that he confidently expects to get the islands back. That point worked through, we ought really not to quarrel.

I send you the whole American debate in the House of Commons, as reported in the *Times*. You will recognize the ability of Mr. Gladstone's speech. Lord Palmerston, by dropping Crampton, found it easy to float. I believe I told you that if assailed by the Opposition upon the bygone recruitment business, he would triumph. The majority was enormous.

Always truly and respectfully yrs.

---

## No. 32.—TO MR. MARCY.

LONDON, July 4, 1856.

MY DEAR SIR,—In the House of Commons last evening, and in answer to a question put by Mr. Baillie, Lord Palmerston is reported by the newspapers of this morning to have said that—

"Mr. Dallas had received full powers to discuss the Central American question with government." (*Advertiser.*)

"Mr. Dallas had full powers to discuss with her Majesty's government all the questions which have arisen with respect to the affairs of Central America, and that he has powers which Mr. Buchanan had not; as I understood from Mr. Buchanan that he had no instructions upon these questions." (*Post.*)

"The government understood that Mr. Dallas had full powers to discuss with them the questions connected with the affairs of Central America, and therefore he had powers which Mr. Buchanan had not." (*Times.*)

It is difficult to see precisely what is meant by the language imputed to Lord Palmerston. The shades of difference between Mr. Buchanan's powers and mine, if any exist, are slight. I have laid before the British government, on the 11th June, your despatch of the 24th of May, the last paragraph of which contains all the powers you have given me on the special subject of Central America, independent of my letter of credence. Certainly these powers are, as Lord P. describes them, *full powers to discuss*, but how, as such, they differ from those of Mr. Buchanan, I cannot perceive, except it be as to the details and conditions of arbitration, and even as to those I don't know that, had the proposal of arbitration been regularly made and entertained, Mr. Buchanan's *powers to discuss* would not have been precisely as broad as my own. Perhaps it is on this hinge that Lord Palmerston's distinction turns. The matter will, of course, engage Lord Clarendon and myself at our next meeting; for I cannot, with the frankness I am resolved to pursue, permit any misconception to continue as to the existing extent of my powers.

Suspicion seems, more or less, inseparable from the diplomatic "rôle;" and it has struck me that possibly the heavy ministerial majority of the 2d instant has encouraged them to take a bolder stand; to recall their readiness to reopen the Central American discussion; and to put *that* on the ground that they understood my powers to be more full than Mr. Buchanan's, and find they are pretty much the same. Such a course would undoubtedly be utterly inconsistent with past professions and explanations, and though I have suspected it as a possibility, I do not believe it will occur.

Our quondam minister from Nicaragua arrived here last Sunday. I am told that he is loud in animadversions upon the conduct of our government, and that he proposes to demand an audience of Lord Clarendon. He will probably try his hand at mischief; and as there is certainly no particularly favorable sentiment felt here at this moment for the actual state of things in Nicaragua, he may, to some extent, succeed.

Always very truly and respectfully yrs.

---

## No. 33.—TO MR. MARCY.

LONDON, July 8, 1856.

MY DEAR SIR,—Your despatches from 16 to 20, both inclusive, were received in one batch this morning, and will be formally acknowledged hereafter. I have not now time to do more than will suffice to keep you, by means of a hasty note, up to the times.

The discussions on Central America continue, and in an unchanged humor to try our best to effect an arrangement. I think I see land.

My powers were frankly considered. They rest exclusively upon the concluding paragraph of your No. 13. Unless, however, they are greatly enlarged, and instructions made full, I foresee much delay and embarrassment.

Complaints are coming in upon me on the score of the inconveniences which spring out of a want of international regulation about seamen who desert from merchant vessels. I find that the active and repeated efforts of Mr. Buchanan during last year, to get a consular convention, embracing this matter, failed, though aided by Lord Clarendon. It may be that the recent incidents have opened their eyes to the absolute necessity of some provisions on the subject. If I propose to you to send me authority to act, it will only be after having ascertained that the prospect of doing something is better now than it was last year.

Parliament is restive under the heat. They are pushing on to an early prorogation. If nothing starts up, I think they will adjourn by the 20th instant.

I got also to-day your "unofficial" of the 16th June I have not had a richer treat for a long time. It is the first symptom you have thrown out, in our correspondence, of a relaxation in that costiveness which I once charged upon you. By-the-by, solve me this diplomatic etiquette of epithets! Some of your letters are marked "*private*," that I undertand perfectly; some "*strictly private*,"—what's the difference? Again, some are headed "*unofficial*;" does that imply more than merely personal or private? Some "*confidential*," that means—does it not?—" on public official business, but not for public use." Others are doubtless shades of difference; but it may be well to say what my own understanding is, as between myself individually and my records representatively. If you mark "*private*," the word "*strictly*" is supererogatory, and your missive goes quietly into my pocket; so also as to "*unofficial*," except that its contents are not esteemed to be under the injunction of secrecy; but if you merely say "*confidential*," then it goes into the archives as a secret paper of the legation.

I want to be agreeable at the close of a dull epistle, and must therefore tell you that everybody here, without an exception, regards your despatches Nos. 13 and 14 as first rate specimens of diplomatic ability and skill. General Scott and Lord Clarendon are in the same category of vanquished. My cordial respects all round.

Always truly yrs.

---

## No. 34.—TO MR. MARCY.

LONDON, July 11, 1856.

MY DEAR SIR,—You must not be appalled by the length of to-day's despatch. I promise not to repeat it often, especially at a season when you are probably (notwithstanding the comfortable coal fire before which I am writing) perspiring under a sun of 100° Fahrenheit, at Washington.

Everything here is tranquil. Even the tea-pot tempest of the *Black-tie* and *Gamboge* vest has subsided to the common level. Parliament is packing up, and will soon be *noncomeatibus in swampo*, that is if pheasants and grouse are tenants of marshes. Nothing remains to keep one awake but the drowsy hum of the Italian question; and even that Lord John Russell proposes to put at rest. In a little while all London will have fallen asleep in the green lap of rural retirement, and nobody, no! nobody, be left to keep watch and ward for international safety and peace but Lord Clarendon and me. Genii of Central America, hover over and protect us! for we mean well.

We have just had the Guards, returned from the Crimea, some four thousand lads of 19, in bright red coats and huge fur caps, pass through the highways and file in procession before the Queen. One could not help thinking, as they moved onward, "hardly heavy enough for effective fight!"

No talk yet, not a whisper, as to sending a successor to Crampton. Many I know would like the place, notwithstanding their awe of the American Secretary. There's Lord Howden—*no me gusto!* Lord Elgin—capital! The Duke of Newcastle and his fine daughter—excellent! Sir Edward B. Lytton—agreed! Mr. Charles Pelham Villiers, Lord Clarendon's brother—admirable! Sir William G. Ousely, with his American antecedents *et uxor*—quite acceptable! Give them time to recover from the galvanic shock of the Cramptonian smasher, and when they once resolve to let by-gones be by-gones, I shall be mistaken if your diplomatic corps will not be adorned and strengthened by an Englishman of higher rank, greater ability, better temper, and more winning manners, than any our terrible but resistless democracy has yet welcomed.

The steady stream of American travellers through this city and onward to every point of the Continent, and then winding backwards, is a sort of moral Mississippi or Amazon. There is really a miraculous character about it. One would imagine that our migratory people, having reached their Ultima Thule on the golden coast of the Pacific, were resolved to turn their faces once more to the rising sun, and trample over Europe to Tartary and Japan. Only think for a moment of the rushing rapids that pour into the American Legation, on the arrival of every steamer, for Passports! Passports! Where to? Everywhere.

The ministerial white-bait dinner is fixed for the 19th inst., and therefore prorogation may be looked for by the 25th. Lord John's motion on Italian affairs is for Monday next, the 14th.

Always faithfully yrs.

---

## No. 35.—TO MR. JOHN EVANS.

London, July 14, 1856.

Sir,—Your letter of the 12th instant has been received. Without knowing you, I cannot assume the responsibility of advising you on your project of emigrating to the United States. It might be that although you possess the means, and the personal qualities, which would give promise of success in a new and rising country, yet your fixed tastes and habits would make you miserable there. Your safest course is to cross the Atlantic during this summer, pass by the cities, and speed directly to St. Louis, in Missouri, or Chicago, in Illinois; stay ten days or more, look about, and consult the men of business whom you will find as plentiful as blackberries, see what pursuit would suit you best, how you can most safely and profitably invest your £3000 (which is an ample fund to start with out there), and then determine for yourself whether to remain or return. At your age, with your health, after 20 years of active life in Liverpool, and with the money at your command, if you scrupulously keep off the snags and sawyers of politics for five years, I should deem it quite an exception to the ordinary and natural current of things, if you were not rich, influential, and respected by the time you are fifty.

Respectfully yrs.

---

## No. 36.—TO MR. MARCY.

London, July 15, 1856.

My dear Sir,—I have no reason for writing except the desire for letting you have something, however unimportant, by every good opportunity.

Murray, the publisher of the *Quarterly Review*, sent me the June number yesterday. It contains an animated article on Central America, which vindicates the Mosquito Protectorate, and then surrenders it to some arrangement like what I sent you, but moving the Indians off in a body to Canada; it vindicates the English title to Ruatan, rather as a West India Island than a dependency of the Belize, and then surrenders it to Honduras; and it is willing to stop the Belize settlement at the Sarstoon, provided that be a final adjustment. You will see by this article, though it is crowded with haughty pretension and dogmatic assertion, that public opinion here is fast coming to the point of amicable arrangement at any sacrifice. The writer, at the close, mounts the jaded steed of the Recruitment question, and caracols for Crampton at a furious rate.

Some of the newspapers are anxious about Parliament adjourning before the definitive settlement of the differences with us. They don't like leaving unchecked in the hands of Lord Palmerston the power to make war, and they ask why so much naval force has been sent to the West Indies. We have got the ministerial assurances, both public and private, on this last point, and we can get nothing more. As to hurrying a convention with Lord Clarendon, that is impossible; for I have as yet no power to propose or reject anything. Without guide, except as I am able to distil your views from despatches to Mr. Buchanan, I can only listen and suggest. Our friends in Parliament take it for granted that I am armed at all points, and seem every day to enquire how the matter gets on, under the delusive expectation that I will hint the signature of a complete arrangement! Lord Clarendon and I must, I suppose, while away full another month before we can go seriously to work; nor do I think there is any harm in our doing so; on the contrary, it gives me time to see how Mr. Herran gets on with the Bay Islands, for their devolution is a *sine qua non*, and time also to receive any instruction you may think proper to send about Mr. Alvarado. It is not improbable that they may persuade themselves to believe that Col. Fremont will be elected in November next; and if they adopt that notion, they would like to take the chance of the new administration's adopting their interpretation of the treaty.

I attended the House of Commons last evening to hear the debate on the Italian question. Lord John Russell introduced it reasonably well. Lord Palmerston talked much, but left the matter without a ray of light. Disraeli went the whole figure of conservatism, and dread of revolution. On the whole, the discussion was flat, unmeaning, and unproductive. There is a singular stagnation in the political atmosphere of Europe at the very moment when ours is all in motion.

I hear, now and then, from our friend at Madrid, Augustus C. Dodge. He last wrote me for a hint as to what course it would be best for Commodore Breese, who was at Cadiz, to take. I could only answer that I could perceive now no cause for alarm or misgiving.

Always truly and respectfully yrs.

## No. 37.—TO MR. WILLIAM BROWN.

24 PORTLAND PLACE, July 16, 1856.

MY DEAR SIR,—The rumor, which you tell me prevailed in the House of Commons last evening, that "all our differences are settled," is, I hope, connected with that description of events which are said to cast their shadows before. It is, however, no better founded now than it might have been three weeks ago.

We are all deeply sensible of the kindness of yourself and Mrs. Brown in proposing to us a visit to Richmond Hill, and have many thanks to give. Until, however, I am able to see land on the business so important and interesting to our two countries, which brought me here, I do not think I shall find an excuse to my anxiety, for leaving London a single day.

I hope to see you before you go.

Always truly yrs.

---

## No. 38.—TO MR. MARCY.

LONDON, July 18, 1856.

MY DEAR SIR,—The accounts from Spain are full of excitement. They are given in the newspapers in homœopathic doses. Whether this be precautionary design, or the natural shape of telegraphic news, is not easily determinable. It is said that the insurrection in Madrid has been completely suppressed—*dubitatur*. At any rate, it is buoyant in Saragossa and in Barcelona. There is a drawback in this movement; for I am told that they who have proclaimed a republic have also pledged themselves, if successful, to emancipate the slaves in Cuba.

The gentlemen who represent Honduras here are not as discreet as perhaps they should be. They go into the newspapers and explain their objects. Lord Clarendon will be apt, I should fear, to take offence at this exchange of the Foreign Office for the Press. I have intimated my opinion both to Mr. Squier and Mr. Herran. It is an imprudent invocation of hostile views.

It is whispered that Louis Napoleon has retreated into the country, owing to his suffering from the attacks of some severe and serious disease.

Very truly and respectfully yrs.

---

## No. 39.—TO MR. MARCY.

LONDON, July 22, 1856.

MY DEAR SIR,—Notwithstanding your letter to him of the 28th May, 1856, assuring him that the prosecution against him should be discontinued, and that orders to that effect had been issued to the United States Attorney at Cincinnati, Mr. Rowcroft writes to Lord Clarendon within a week past that he cannot quit Cincinnati, as he is still under recognizance to answer, and that the District Attorney says he has repeatedly written to Washington upon the subject, but can get no reply. Pray enquire about this, and have what is right done, letting me know where the mistake lies.

I have just got back from the Foreign Office in time to write this, but without anything sufficiently important for a despatch. His lordship had not had leisure to finish *his* sketch of a plan for ending the protectorate; it was begun, however, and he promised to send it in the course of the week. He complains of being dreadfully fagged by the expiring throes of the present session of Parliament. He can't get to bed before five in the morning.

Spain, you see, is in a ferment. Italy will next spring upwards. Louis Napoleon thinks the opportunity come to play his great uncle's game with Ferdinand and to find a throne for the Prince, whose nose the Empress has so unkindly disjointed. He has offered to assist Queen Isabella, which means to devour the kingdom, and extinguish the hazard of a republicanism too near at hand. Nothing yet heard of Espartero.

Very truly and respectfully yrs.

## No. 40.—TO MR. MARCY.

LONDON, July 25, 1856.

MY DEAR SIR,—You will perceive by the newspapers that, two days ago, a question was addressed to Lord Palmerston, in the House of Commons, by Mr. Milner Gibson, as to whether her Majesty's government had determined to send a minister to Washington. Mr. Gibson is a friend, and a watchful one to boot. The reply of the Premier was to the effect that the cabinet had come to no decision, and that it was by no means unusual that delays should take place in appointing diplomatic representatives. There was neither word nor look to intimate an indisposition to fill the mission; in fact, the answer produced the impression that no decision had been come to, because it was difficult to select the person, rather than from any other motive. Be that as it may, I have ascertained, from a source entirely unquestionable, that there are gentlemen in Washington, "distinguished for ability and position," who amuse themselves by writing letters to their friends here, intended for exhibition to the ministry, and inculcating in the interest of the American Party, that the manner in which Mr. Crampton's dismissal was treated by this government has worked advantageously for the democracy, and they strive hard to have something done which may rekindle the panic, as to the danger of war, among our mercantile classes. I asked for no names, because I was frankly told in advance that they could not be given. But I characterized the letter-writers, in strong terms, as mischievous partisan intermeddlers, who, for the sake of carrying their Presidential candidate, were willing to hazard the peace and interests of their country. I do not feel entirely at liberty to go into details. They would surprise you. But you are entitled to know, and I violate no principle of delicacy in letting you know, the incontestable fact I have stated. If a minister to Washington be withheld, though I do not think one will be withheld beyond a reasonable time, it will be owing, in my opinion, to the effect produced by these secret and treacherous letter-writers. It is amazing, if not almost incredible, that any "distinguished" American citizen should not revolt from such a proceeding. How far, too, it has a tendency to dissuade from the contemplated adjustment of the Central American differences, or at all events to protract the negotiation, it would be hard to say. I hope those with whom that business must be transacted are too sagacious and honorable to permit themselves to be misled by the wretched zealots of abolitionism, now playing a game of despair in our canvass; and yet England has so long and so obstinately deemed our democratic party her natural and unalterable enemy, that the force of habit may exert its power.

The *coup d'état* of Louis Napoleon has got its parallel—no, not quite its parallel, but its servile imitation—in the conduct of O'Donnell at Madrid. The citizens are butchered by wholesale, and the legislature coolly Cromwellized. France may find a pretext for occupying the Spanish capital as she occupies Rome. Wherever a popular commotion occurs she may like to occupy. According to all sound modern doctrine, occupation, whether for one or seven years, is perfectly consistent with non-intervention. There is something singularly accommodating in that word "occupy,"—is there not? The Premier begins to "*scent the tainted gale.*" (See slip.)

The prorogation is put off till the middle of next week. To-night, according to a strange and recently established practice, Mr. Disraeli will review the session, and elaborately set forth the mismanagement, omissions, and commissions of the ministry, during the five legislative months. He represents, for the occasion, the Opposition; Lord Palmerston will reply. A regular set-to by champions.

As yet we have had sight of summer only in fruits and flowers. Two or three days of warm sun, no more.

Always truly yrs.

---

## No. 41.—TO JUDGE JOEL JONES.

LONDON, July 25, 1856.

MY DEAR JUDGE,—Warm weather is of slow progress here. I have yet had no cause to thin the clothing put on during the extreme cold of January last in Philadelphia. And yet the newspapers represent *you* as frying under 96° of Fahrenheit!

From this distant stand-point, our politics appear excessively angry, confused, and critical. The Americans have taken up Fremont upon the principle and in imitation of our nomination in '52. Will it run the same wild and victorious career? If Providence still favors the Union, reserving it even in despite of our numerous extravangances and follies, we may succeed. I can see no reliance but in Providence. We have tried our best, or worst, to exasperate Providence; let us hope still that the real and unaltered excellence of our Constitution may keep her on our side. A great pother is made in these old fogy regions about the series of violences which accompany the fermentation of our great canvass. One governor declares martial law; another administers it, with a kick, in the State capitol; one member of Congress shoots down a table servant; and another selects higher game for his bludgeon in the Senate chamber; civil war has its licensed playground in Kansas; and droves of foreign fighters are rushing to Nicaragua; belligerents throng to hiss and shout at every public gathering; and rows and riots are—everywhere! Such is the picture drawn by an European artist. Its features come to you in detached doses, and are therefore not so striking; crossing the water, they cluster into an intolerable bouquet.

I have to thank you for your agreeable letters. They tell me all the political incidents and the social occurrences, of which I should otherwise remain unconscious. I wish this stagnant part of the world furnished me something to send you in return. By-the-by, Spain has just opened the revolutionary movement. O'Donnell, mimicking the *coup d'état* of Louis Napoleon, has drenched Madrid with the blood of its citizens, and dispersed the Cortes. Many think that the train was fired from Plombières, the mysterious summer retreat of the French Emperor. Certainly, he has promptly shown his sympathies on behalf of unconstitutional government. Lord Palmerston, yesterday, in the House of Commons, had the audacity, while seeming to vindicate, to give him a cool warning. I send you this remarkable intimation to England's great ally. All the Parisian journals will exclaim "Morbleu! Par exemple!"

Parliament has but few days longer to live. The session must have its "*oraison funèbre.*" They have a singular practice of permitting the leader of the Opposition in the House of Commons, just before the session closes, to review the ministerial conduct, and to concentrate in a single philippic all the grounds of accusation and complaint. Mr. Disraeli has given notice that he intends doing that matter to-night.

Always faithfully yrs.

---

## No. 42.—TO MR. MARCY.

LONDON, July 29, 1856.

MY DEAR SIR,—Your private letter of the 13th instant reached me yesterday, and was heartily welcome.

My despatches during this month will have shown you that I have been actively "*feeling the ground in relation to Central American questions.*" I cannot say that I have reached bottom yet, although the *Morning Advertiser* of Saturday last formally announced that all matters were settled. I suspect the editor of that paper was anxious to pour out an *amende honorable* by extravagant eulogy of myself, and found no excuse for doing so except by inventing a consummation which he knew would attract attention and be universally acceptable. It is possible that he may know more of British Cabinet secrets than I do; and that a suggestion I once made to Lord C., as to the manner in which the Gordian knot of our difficulties might be cut, has been adopted, to wit,—that the Queen should take the responsibility and initiative in restoring the Bay Islands to Honduras. I threw the notion out, certainly not dreaming that it would stick; but the *Advertiser* predicts it positively. We shall know at the prorogation today.

Lord C. has sent me, two or three days ago, my *pro-forma* scheme of getting out of the Protectorate, modified and changed according to his views. I would send you this paper, but he accompanied it with a note, requesting me to consider it *private*, as he had not even been yet able to show it to his colleagues. It contains some things, too, the real bearing of which I apprehend he has not sufficiently weighed, and which I hope and believe he will readily forego. Your despatch, No. 13, had he remembered its contents, would certainly satisfy him that *I* could do nothing in the nature of recognizing the Mosquitoes as an independent sovereignty or nation; and that I had it as little within my competency to overlook the ultimate eminent domain of Nicaragua, or to complicate the foreign policy of the United States in a joint protectorate. These are matters as to which, to be sure, I will carefully fulfil any instructions you may transmit; but, without instructions, they do not meet my judgment or approval. I am preparing a reformed sketch; adopting what I can, retaining what he has adopted of my former view, and showing what I conceive, as at present advised, to be impossible. My opinion is that we shall ultimately adjust a plan by which the British obligation of honor may in no respect be violated in the abandonment of the protectorate; unless, indeed, your promised instructions, which I anxiously look for, open a new field of discussion, and give my labors a different direction.

So much has been said in periodicals, in weekly and daily newspapers, evincing the acceptableness of the proposed restitution of Ruatan to Honduras, that I can scarcely doubt, after the conversations that I and Mr. Herran have separately had with Lord Clarendon, that it is a point which will be conceded to the spirit of peace. I would therefore suggest whether, if that be done, especially if done handsomely, it would be becoming in us to take our position *inter apices juris* about the Guatemalian title to the land between the Siburn and Sarstoon? The truth is, that if trade across the Isthmus once become fearless, active, and free, the Belize will fast sink into insignificance, and be abandoned. Commerce will pass it by contemptuously, and even *Hanseaticated* San Juan will flap her wings and crow over it.

You will see by the note I enclose from Lord C., that he has got a late letter from Mr. Rowcroft, which entitles you to dismiss that gentleman's anxiety for a nol. pros. from your mind.

I have no misgivings about the Presidential canvass. We must succeed. The adversary has kindly submitted to as much division as was necessary to secure their weakness. It is quite plain, too, that, like frightened birds, they have lit on a twig too fragile to support them. Fremont is respectable enough *per se*, but he cannot carry the weight of a party. Besides, all who reflect must perceive that our failure would rock the Union to its deepest foundations, if not snap it in two. I dare say, that like all other free peoples that have ever existed, ours is destined to be mad some day; but the hour has not arrived.

Mr. Herran has this instant come and gone. In his interview at the Foreign Office on Saturday last, Lord C. said he would draft a treaty restoring the islands, and only bargaining that Port Royal should be a free port, except a small duty adequate to pay the police officers of Honduras. Mr. Herran is not the ablest of men, and may not be perfectly accurate; but of the main point, the restitution, he is quite certain.

The prorogation just over. The speech adverts to our negotiations on Central America, and the Queen wishes them a happy conclusion. That's all; but it is something.

Very truly and respectfully yrs.

---

## No. 43.—TO MR. MARCY.

London, August 8, 1856.

My dear Sir,—I have not been successful recently in efforts to continue and ripen the discussion with Lord Clarendon. Three several days have been fixed for conference during the last week, but each has had to give way to some peremptory call elsewhere of his lordship. The Queen last commanded him to Osborne, and, unless her Majesty release him for to-day, he will fail in his engagement to meet me at the Foreign Office at 3 o'clock. Mr. Herran has been subject to the same delays; and when he came to see me yesterday, he appeared worried at not having received the draft of his convention, promised for a week ago. Interruption and procrastination are, we all know, unavoidable incidents of high official station. They must be borne with due patience by those who have public objects in view. As to myself, I cannot undertake to be in a hurry, until, 1, Mr. Herran secures the Bay Islands, and 2, I am enabled to do something more than discuss, or theorize, or plan.

It is quite obvious that no single member of the ministry assumes to act, on a matter of moment, without consulting his colleagues. This is necessarily productive of endless postponement. Most of the cabinet have left London since the prorogation of Parliament, and are wandering in the Provinces. They can confer along the telegraphic wires, not otherwise. I believe I told you that Lord C. had requested me to treat as *private* his sketch of a scheme to abate the protectorate, because he had not had an opportunity to show it to his colleagues. That is an example.

The diplomatic corps is even more scattered than the cabinet. The French, Austrian, Prussian, Spanish, Turkish, Sardinian, and Hanoverian ministers are all on the Continent; indeed, I doubt whether there be a single "chef" except myself in London. It is often impossible to get a passport *viséd* at any office but mine. Holidays here are literally holidays all round.

"Order reigns in Spain;" but the stability of O'Donnell is by no means assured. He must either carry out his movement to its legitimate results, and let Christina return in triumph, or he must fall back upon the constitutional party and reinstate the Espartero influence. When the Pope, Christina, Isabella, and, *sub rosa*, Louis Napoleon, are making "a pull all together," at one end of the rope, O'Donnell can scarcely keep a steady footing at the other, alone. He will probably yield to the absolutists, and then they will soon get rid of him, or he will resist, and on the liberal side inaugurate another revolutionary struggle, when the French will intervene decisively. The "prestige" of this country, I consider gone, *fuit*, and no party on the Continent thinks her willing and competent to stand by and protect the cause of liberal government. She is essentially and practically chained to the footstool of a usurper more dangerous to the liberties of mankind, because more cunning to employ the vocabulary and arts of freedom than would be a dozen Russian Czars. Steam, too, has brought her into such close proximity with her neighbor, that she dare not oppose him without being, what she knows she never is, ready to repel a sudden invasion. She does not venture to remonstrate against Pélissier's new title of Duke of Malakoff, but is obliged to witness in silence this unmistakable and indelible claim to the monopoly of the crowning honor of the Crimean war. Lord Palmerston, in the heat of debate, uses loud words now and then, but his followers' stare in terrified astonishment, and he sinks silently back again into unavoidable submission. *Fuit! Fuit!*

I have just returned from the F. O., and after two hours' conference with Lord C., have only time to say that everything connected with the negotiation wears the most promising and satisfactory aspect. He told me, upon being asked how it stood with Mr. Herran, that he thought that matter of the Bay Islands quite settled; that he would send for Mr. Herran this afternoon; that he would draft the convention of restitution without delay; and, indeed, that there was nothing left to be done, except to agree upon some mode of indemnifying the English residents. I enquired whether he had kept steadily in view to avoid any stipulation for peculiar privileges. He replied that he had.

We have, as to the protectorate, one only remaining *snag* to get over, or to get round, and that is the condition of Nicaragua; and we are both to set our wits to work to remove it if possible.

Very truly and respectfully yrs.

---

## No. 44.—TO COL. PAGE.

LONDON, August 12, 1856.

MY DEAR COLONEL,—You must deal with me in mercy. I have been working hard and unceasingly, so that private correspondence became an almost prohibited indulgence. Mr. Marcy is a tyrannical monopolist, and exacts all my written ideas. In a little, I shall have finished my job, and may then take an airing among the friends who have kept me in mind.

All this part of the world is anticipating, hoping, and wishing the defeat of our democracy in November. It must not be. Col. Page, I say, it must not be! It is difficult to tell you how much of human liberty, right, and happiness is at stake; enough to make selfish and personal prejudices, were they a hundredfold multiplied, fly up and kick the beam. Alas! how much disinterested virtue the maintenance of a republic demands! but it *is* virtue, and *is* its own glorious reward.

* * * * writes me in a rather desponding tone. He should bustle more, and work off the megrims. A fling into a free fight is sure to stiffen the nerves and banish the blues. If he shirks fighting for himself, let him fight for what I think in greater peril, the Union. I say this to every one of the true men to whom I feel at liberty to address an honest exhortation. To myself individually it matters little whether the Union be saved or subverted; my own chapter of politics closed with the dead silence at the Cincinnati Convention; but it is natural to look somewhat after the happiness of one's children, and of the friends of well-organized liberty throughout the world. I pray and beseech all who care a fig about my opinion, to struggle for the preservation of the Union against the "dissolving views" of Eastern and Anglican abolitionists, until their tongues can no longer wag.

All, aye all, that I came here to do will be successfully accomplished, if indeed it has not been already achieved, in the course of a week. The two countries, five months ago, were at that critical stand of mutual and morbid defiance when a prolonged war might have sprung from a few more hot words, or the hasty discharge of a gun at sea. People watched with suspended breath the news of every hour. Americans, all over the continent of Europe; and in particular, Commodore Breese, commanding our Mediterranean squadron, awaited a signal from this office to hurry home. Well! it all changed in the lapse of a month or six weeks; and the change has advanced, step by step, until now, before the entire expiration of five months, they who understand the condition and tone of international relations, are satisfied that a sounder basis for mutual harmony and respect has not existed since the Treaty of '83. I cannot tell you how this has been brought about. There is the fact. I am, and always have been, just as ready to fight England as any man living, upon any adequate and honorable ground. Still, to have been accessory to the conversion of a ticklish state of reciprocal rage, springing from a mere bandying of diplomatic sentences, into calm and solid good-will, is destined to close my political life with entire satisfaction to myself. Wait a fortnight, perhaps a month, and you may then hear the finality.

I want you to do me the favor to call upon Judge Sergeant, and give him the warm assurance of my continued attachment. He has never recognized my appointment to this Court, and perhaps it was contrary to his sense of prudence. Write me often and "lengthily" as you can.

Always sincerely yrs.

---

## No. 45.—TO SENATOR G. W. JONES.

LONDON, August 20, 1856.

MY DEAR SIR,—It has taken me a little time to find the books which Judge Tuthill, in his letter to you of the 23d of June last, expressed a wish that I would apply the three pounds in my hands to purchasing for him. I now send you one of those books, "Memoirs illustrative of the History and Antiquities of Norfolk and the City of Norwich," and a single number of the reprint going on of the other, to wit, "The History of the Landed Gentry, with Index, etc." This last is in fact out of print, and can only be had by instalments, as it is reprinted in numbers. The "Memoirs" cost £1. 1. 0. and the "History," at —— a number, will probably run the judge some shillings in my debt. He need not worry himself about that;—when I am out of his funds, he shall frankly be apprised of it.

We have kept at peace, and I hope we may continue so. It is barely possible, however, that the late Congress at Paris intended their declaration abolishing Privateering as the groundwork of a coercive movement by a confederacy of European sovereigns against America. If so, have at ye all, my lads! Governor Marcy's letter to Sartiges is unanswerably conclusive, and is a fine platform upon which to fight till doomsday.

Faithfully yrs.

## No. 46.—TO MR. MARCY.

LONDON, August 22, 1856.

MY DEAR SIR,—You will perceive by what I send, as well as by the newspapers generally, that your letter to Count Sartiges, on the Declaration of the Peace Congress at Paris abolishing privateering, was not in London forty-eight hours before it appeared with an effective editorial in the *Morning Advertiser*. The *Times* reprinted it the following day; and it is going the rounds, attracting great attention, but no attempt at reply. Let us hope that European statesmen will not be so absurd as to attempt a concerted and combined movement to coerce our adoption of their absolute phrase "*Privateering is abolished!*" But there is no knowing how far their folly may carry them. In this piece of cunning, as in the case of African Slavery, they shelter their purpose behind a screen.

I had hoped to send you by this steamer the Central American Treaty. It is, however, not ready for transmission, though very little more is wanted to complete the job. It is thrown into form, and makes a longer document than it ought to be. Much space, however, is given to the details of appointing, qualifying, and instructing Commissioners for settling boundary, and adjudicating upon Land Grants.

Mr. Herran has not yet pocketed his convention about the Colony of the Bay Islands. No doubt he will have it in a day or two. The new Free State or Municipality may be some time in assuming the proper shape, and in getting fully under way; but it will rapidly assume importance after that, especially if, as will be quite natural, our enterprising traders squat on Ruatan; and it will be recognized as under the sovereignty (to be sure the empty sovereignty) of Honduras. There is a buzz circulating to the effect that the immense value and importance of these islands have only just been found out, and that it is well for us that the contract has been made! I believe the rumor to be unfounded; but, in twenty years, if all things go on steadily, they can scarcely fail to rise into an interesting relation with the commercial and political world.

Your private letter of the 4th instant reached me on the

18th, accompanied by six copies of the Sartiges communicatiôn, all exceedingly welcome. I regret extremely to hear of your daughter's illness. Mr. M. has repeatedly mentioned it as very severe : but I sincerely hope she has recovered.

You will have noticed that an outbreak in Naples is daily looked for. The proud and retaliatory manner in which the king has met the intervention and menaces of England and France rather raises him in one's estimation, in spite of his flagitious despotism; but it will advance the movement of reform by stinging the reformers. The critical state of affairs in Italy is, perhaps, at the bottom of this ministry's unusual conciliation towards America.

Spain, like a diseased horse, after kicking out famously has sunk again into forlorn resignation.

The eyes of all the world of courtiers are just now fixed upon the Coronation at the Kremlin.

Very truly and respectfully yrs.

---

## No. 47.--TO MR. GILPIN.

LONDON, August 19, 1856.

MY DEAR GILPIN,—Your letter of the 21st July reached me yesterday.

I left your introductories, with my cards, at Mr. G.'s and Sir C. F.'s. They are distinguished parts of the world, and, at present, all the world is out of town. In a very little while, even Lord Clarendon and I will feel at liberty to take a short trip beyond the range of F. O. servitude. I hope to send Mr. Marcy his quietus, that is a thorough settlement, by the same vessel that carries this. If I do, all that I expected or undertook will be accomplished. I am afraid the men who wanted a fight will not readily forgive me. War, a few months ago, was the favorite word; it is now never uttered, and with it have gone off the Bay Islands and the Protectorate, both beyond the sovereignty of her Majesty. *N'importe!*—when it is a man's duty to make peace, he must close his heart to belligerent popularity. Besides, as I have told Col. Page, the chapter of my political life closed with the dead silence at the Cincinnati Convention, and I am content to end with the reputation of having kept two bull-dogs from tearing each other to pieces.

I shall, one of these "calm summer mornings," indulge you with an exposition of the outside and the inside treaties, the principles, motives, and difficulties; but just now, time is too important to me.

Our best remembrances to Mrs. G. and to Mr. Van Buren, and to Mrs. Livingston. We are all well, and enjoying a small coal fire while you are melting under 100°! Vide Rochefoucauld as to the miseries of one's friends.

Ever faithfully yrs.

August 22, 1856.

I have had a little time to think on your question as to the cause of the present amicable tone towards us. It is impossible to answer it upon any but conjectural grounds. There may be serious anticipations as to the condition of Italy, and misgivings suggested by the extreme courtship between France and Russia, but they are insufficiently developed just yet. Judging from obvious indications, I am inclined to the belief that Lord Palmerston, at the moment of pressure upon him two months ago, bought the parliamentary representatives of the industrial classes to support his ministry, by pledging himself to change his whole course of action as regards America. The instant he performed his part of the contract by retaining me here, his majority became assured and overwhelming. This has proved to him on what a rock he plants his ascendency when he conciliates us; and from that day, it has seemed to be impossible to be too civil. There are, no doubt, other co-operative causes, causes which made it easy for him to bend to the policy of the position. I could advert to some that are singular enough, but the basis of the whole is, I am almost certain, what I have stated.

My treaty don't go by this occasion. Its formalities are delayed by official absenteeism.

Always yrs.

---

## No. 48.—TO LORD DONOUGHMORE.

London, August 25, 1856.

My Lord,—I have your lordship's letter of the 23d instant.

The distribution of intestate estates, in the United States, is a subject of State or local, not of national jurisdiction. The government of the Union has nothing to do with it. They have no right or power whatever to decide to whom the real or personal assets of a deceased shall go—they must go where the law of the particular State in which the deceased resided or in which the property is found at his death, directs that they shall go. Every State has its own law of Escheat, and on the demise of a bastard without children, wife, or will, his property would legally belong to the State, by whose functionaries, after inquest and verdict, it would be taken for public use.

Mr. Marcy's enquiry had for its object, I have no doubt, the payment to whomsoever might present himself authentically as "the personal representative" of Joseph Mansford, otherwise called Joseph Carson, and therefore entitled to receive it, of a balance of wages due to the deceased as a seaman in the American service; or it may be that the consul of the United States, at Shanghai, Robert C. Murphy, Esq., has taken charge of the effects and money left by Joseph Carson, and has requested Mr. Marcy to ascertain who are "the personal representatives" to whom these effects and money may be transmitted. This latter supposition is the more probable.

What then should Peter Carson do? He has *legally* as much right to claim the effects and money of the bastard as his father has, and that is no right at all. But he can acquire a right by becoming "the personal representative" of the deceased, in other words, by having himself appointed the *administrator* to his estate. If by having reared and educated Joseph, or in any other way, he can claim to be a *creditor* of the estate, he is entitled to be preferred as administrator to John Carson. If nothing gives him a preference, he can still claim the administration, provided John Carson has not got ahead of him and already taken out the letters. Mr. Marcy or the consul at Shanghai would probably pay the money or give the effects to any one who proved his character as "personal representative" by presenting a certificate under official seal and signature of his appointment.

And *where* and *how* is Peter Carson to have himself constituted the administrator to Joseph's estate?

Where?—The proper place is the city or county in the United States in which Joseph last resided before he entered upon his last voyage.

How?—Application must be made to the Register of Wills, or other proper local officer, the facts stated, the necessary surety given, etc.

If Peter Carson cannot quit home to attend to this matter in person, he can authorize some one else as his attorney in fact to have the thing done; to get the certificate of his appointment as administrator; to forward that certificate or a duplicate of it to Mr. Marcy, either for his own action or for transmission to Mr. Murphy at Shanghai; to receive the effects or money; and, after paying all expenses and settling all accounts in exoneration of his surety, to remit the residue of the fund to Mr. Peter Carson.

I believe I have communicated all the information your lordship desires to possess. Let me, however, add what my experience in similar cases has taught me to believe, that in all likelihood Joseph has not left behind him more than a few months' wages and a sea-chest of old clothes, the aggregate value of which would not compensate Mr. Peter Carson for one-tenth of the trouble and expense which he would necessarily incur in their pursuit.

I shall be happy at all times to hear, upon this or any other subject, from your lordship.

Very respectfully, your lordship's
Most obedient servant.

---

## No. 49.—TO MR. MARCY.

LONDON, August 26, 1856.

MY DEAR SIR,—The engrossment of the Central American Treaty is going on, and I have no doubt that I shall be able to send it to you by the Arabia on Saturday next, the 30th instant.

I had my last discussion on this topic at the F. O. yesterday. An attentive examination of the phraseology of the treaty and separate article will shew you that I have kept constantly in mind the principles of your instructions, and where their open recognition does not appear substantively, words are used which create for them a necessary implication.

Lord C. is bound to escort the Queen on her journey to Scotland. Her Majesty leaves here the day after to-morrow. She became very sick on her last aquatic excursion, and now forswears the sea. He has positively promised to summon me to sign our concocted instrument in the course of to-morrow.

I have just had a long, agreeable, and interesting visit from Count Kreptovitch, the new Russian Minister to this Court. I knew him at St. Petersburg in the time of my mission there. He is the son-in-law of Nesselrode, whom he described as in full health and vigor of intellect. He intimated that he had met with a rather cold reception here, owing he presumed to his dilatoriness in coming. He told me that the impression on the Continent is that the Emperor of France labors under some serious disease which he does not possess the constitutional strength to throw off;—"And then," he exclaimed, "what, in the name of Heaven, is to become of France!" He expressed in very strong terms his admiration of your letter to Sartiges on privateering; said that as the argument of a statesman, it was conclusive; and that his opinion was entirely with you. During the last three years, Count Kreptovitch has been minister at Brussels, a place that he regrets leaving.

I intend introducing to you Sir Henry Holland, who goes out by the Arabia. He is, in every respect, a most estimable as well as eminent person, and withal a court and nobility physician. He will hardly stop a day at Washington, if he get there at all. He returns to London in six or eight weeks. I wish him very much to see the President, yourself, and General Davis.

London is the depth of dulness and emptiness.

Always faithfully yrs.

## No. 50.—TO MR. MARCY.

LONDON, September 9, 1856.

MY DEAR SIR,—Your letter of the 22d August by the Canada reached me on Sunday the 7th instant, and we are all much gratified at your telling us of the improved condition of your daughter.

I notice in our newspapers a number of things said about the Central American negotiation and about myself personally, which are utterly absurd and without foundation. The invention about that intelligent Albino, Mr. Lowe, is one of these, as you have already found. He is quite too distinguished and respectable a gentleman to be supposed capable of having connived at his supposititious mission. Then, that nonsense about a letter to me from fifty or more members of Parliament:—all trash. You are entirely right in taking it for granted that nothing of this sort can be true which is not adverted to in my despatches or letters.

I am much relieved by the Canada's mail from the anxiety about our political extravagance, created by that of the Arago. It would seem almost certain that a congressional arrangement on the Army Bill has been accomplished.

I went to the great Cutlers' Festival at Sheffield on the 4th instant. You will see the account of it in the newspapers. The report of my remarks, though inaccurate in one or two places, is as a whole quite good enough to submit to. Some of the reporters, with Yankee cuteness, interpolate *Cuba* for *Oude*, and introduce the phrase "infinitely more praiseworthy," as applied to Texas and Cuba annexation! Small artifice! The speeches of the Duke of Newcastle and Mr. Roebuck are interesting as matters of political development and degladiation. They have given rise to numerous newspaper columns. Mr. Roebuck I found to be, in Sheffield particularly, in the enjoyment of an immense and boisterous popularity. He is universally praised for ability and independence; and yet he had accepted a day or two before a present of £1000, raised by subscription, headed by Lord Palmerston! Sheffield is ultra-American. On the arrival of your minister, the church-bells were rung, and the flag of the United States was floated from the public hall, and from where I took up my quarters. The first aspect of the town is that of Pittsburg, smoky, dirty, dingy, and noisy. The suburbs are beautiful, hills richly cultivated and adorned with handsome villas. I ran through their principal "works," cutlery, plate, and steel, and found the crowds of workmen just as ardently fond of us as their employers. The distance from London is about 170 miles, which I flew over in four hours and a quarter.

There is some activity shewn to remove the prevailing impression that the Emperor of the French labors under serious malady. Mr. B., who is a warm personal friend of his Majesty, whom he once went bail for when arrested by the police in this city, adverts to letters from Paris that deny the story. And yet everything indicates that there is something in it. Some shrewd folks hint a softening of the brain! So much depends upon maintaining his *prestige* just now, that, if he be really ill, we shall be kept ignorant of it as long as possible. He dances, it is said, with great animation every night at Biarritz; but for a month or six weeks there has been an impenetrable and mysterious cloud about his statesmanship. "*Mais, nous verrons*," as your old friend of '98 used to say. At the reception lately of a recently formed municipal council, he was "quite odd;" unable to make a rational address, and suddenly in a trembling fit breaking out with "*Vive l'Empereur!*"

Truly and respectfully yrs.

---

## No. 51.—TO MR. MARCY.

LONDON, September 19, 1856.

MY DEAR SIR,—It is "quite odd" (a fashionable English comment) that one should be living in London, and yet have nothing to send to Washington, more than three thousand five hundred miles off, in the shape of news political, social or diplomatic. Such, however, is my momentary status; and it is ascribable as much to the constancy and frequency with which I have written to you, as to the universal nap the world is taking. I'm exhausted, and I suspect your patience is in the like predicament.

The *Post* said a few days ago that if Russia were not faithful to the Treaty of Peace, England must bring her to her senses, and could do so *even though unassisted by another power*. So, so, says the *Constitutionnel*, you begin to doubt France! be it so. Russia is a great and glorious nation, her monarch and nobles worthy of all praise! and as for you, bah! you talk too big! There are occasionally apparent other symptoms which indicate the possibility of our seeing, one of these days, a revival of the Continental system against "perfidious Albion."

The Coronation at the Kremlin is certainly a very different display from our inauguration at the Capitol. The first appeals to the eyes, the second to the ears; so that if Horace be correct (*segnius irritant animos*), the Imperial pageant is more permanently impressive than the Presidential one. I should like to know the effect produced upon our republican representative, Mr. Seymour; —strongly suspected to have been one of intense fatigue. And yet, listen you great progressive nineteenth century! there are at least one hundred and fifty millions of bewitched bipeds called men, who think of nothing, read of nothing, talk of nothing, gaze on nothing, but the robes, the jewels, the bows, the holy oil, the illuminations, the serfs, and squadrons of the Czar! It gave me great pleasure to hear from our returning consul, Colonel Reilly, that you had spared Mr. Seymour the ruin of witnessing and partaking this orientally gorgeous display by assuming his expenses. Lord Clarendon is still in Scotland. Lord Palmerston flits backwards and forwards every day or two, between Downing Street and St. Leonards on Sea. The rest of the ministry are everywhere, or nowhere.

I have hinted to Mr. Alvarado, minister to the United States from Honduras, that he would act wisely if, now that the matter is over here, he were to present himself at Washington, for reception by the President.

Nothing yet about a successor to Mr. Crampton, except, perhaps, the speech of Mr. Baxter who, although very nearly an opposition member, singled out as eminently fit, Mr. Villiers, Lord Clarendon's brother. He would undoubtedly do admirably, as I think I have heretofore said.

John Frost and the Chartists! A more wretched exhibition, as they passed the legation on their way to Primrose Hill, it would be difficult to depict. Our mass-meetings, in town or township, are coronation crowds in comparison. When you stir the dregs or sediment of any European community, the show is saddening. Our almshouses would do better.

Always faithfully and respectfully yrs.

---

## No. 52.—TO MR. MARCY.

LONDON, September 24, 1856.

MY DEAR SIR,—It is hardly worth while, and yet it is perhaps best, as a matter of extreme precaution, that I should send you the two copies of notes that accompany this, especially as I have scarcely matter wherewith to fill a page.

You see, this business of passports exacts great vigilance and good humor from your representatives. There are touchy men even in frocks, who think they ought at once to be granted whatever they ask, and who misunderstand everything when kindled by a little scrutiny. Having carelessly neglected to provide or pack up the authentic proofs of character, they are angry with themselves, and snappishly vent themselves on others. The poor fellow in this case will, I hope, smooth down his indignation, and furnish me with some sort of apology for giving him the passport, even against the judgment of the Secretary. If not, and he wants to make a rumpus, why, you have the means of appreciating him.

The absence from London to which I refer was during a visit of a few days to Sir E. B. Lytton, at his residence about twenty-seven miles off. He kept me a day or two longer than I intended, to have me at the agricultural meeting of his county. The newspapers contain, as usual, reports of what was said and done, at least substantially.*

---

* DIARY: 1st October, 1856.—"The week before this last was spent by Mrs. D., Susan, Philip, and myself at Knebworth, the charming residence

Your old cabinet colleague and present diplomatic employé, Mr. J. Y. Mason, is here, and dined with me yes-

---

of Sir Edward Bulwer Lytton, the novelist, poet, and statesman, in Hertfordshire. A more interesting piece of antiquity (our bedroom and bedstead had been occupied by Queen Elizabeth when preparing to receive the Spanish Armada) I have not come across:—spacious halls, picture galleries, ancient armor, old oak staircase, and grotesque monsters numberless. It is seated within and domineers over some thousand acres of park, woodland, garden, and farm. No wonder this man writes so exquisitely, on the margin of his own lake, in a retired cottage, and with all the appliances of comfort, silence, and sweet air about him! I found him the very soul of hospitality, a republican in his philosophy, a polished gentleman, and yet made by domestic trials peculiar, if not somewhat eccentric. He has a son attached to the British legation at the Hague, already a remarkable writer. He pines over the loss of a beautiful daughter of 15; and his wife, reputed quite impracticably singular, though very talented, won't live near him. He is laboriously intent on high political fame and position, which, as an M. P., he cannot fail to reach. He persuaded me to accompany him to his county agricultural dinner in Hitchin, where they treated me '*en ambassadeur*,' and I briefly addressed five hundred farmers. The Hertford *Mercury*, reporting this banquet, said, *inter alia:*

"Mr. Dallas, on rising, was received with a perfect hurricane of applause. When the cheering had subsided, he addressed the assembly as follows:

"GENTLEMEN,—It is impossible for me to allow the flattering manner in which you have received the toast so kindly introduced by the distinguished gentleman who presides to pass without the expression of my warmest thanks. A stranger to you all, I deeply feel the hospitality of your welcome; though, in truth, my short experience in England has given me more than reason enough to expect it. (Cheers.) For the generous allusion made to the institutions, the progress, and the prospects of my country, let me also return, in my public as well as in my private character, the most cordial acknowledgments. (Cheers.) Youthful among nations, and perhaps, in the estimation of many whom I address, far from faultless, she has, nevertheless, undeniably achieved in the general cause of civilization, in science, in art, in mechanics, in human elevation and improvement, what may well justify encomiums from such enlightened, discriminating, and candid men. (Cheers.) In no sphere of social action are the United States better entitled to your esteem than in the very one with which this banquet is connected. They recognize their agricultural interest—their planters and their farmers—as their predominant interest—the interest that wields the power, originates the wealth, cherishes the manly freedom, and promotes the happiness of their entire people. (Cheers.) You can make no advance on that subject which will not meet with their sympathy and co-operation. In the vast valley of the Mississippi, amid measureless plains of exhaustless fertility, millions of my countrymen accept, as the noblest of human pursuits, the cultivation of their own soil. (Hear, hear.) With them their chief aim and delight is to stock their farms with cattle of the best breeds; and they hail, as more worthy of their gratitude and their applause than military exploits and political victories, every onward step in practical husbandry. (Cheers.) I wish, gentlemen, I felt competent and at liberty to engage a few moments of your attention in adverting to American movements similar to your own.

terday. I have not seen him since leaving Washington on the 4th of March, 1849. His health seems restored, and his vivacity as quick and agreeable as ever; but he walks awkwardly, and forbears the use of his left arm. We talked politics, home and foreign, until tired out; and, with the exception of his very exalted admiration of certain French personages, we chimed in sentiment pretty harmoniously. We agree in the belief that the success of Fremont is an unimaginable visitation of Providence. He returns to Paris to-morrow, having crossed the channel only to execute, with the formality required by Virginia law, a deed of Conveyance before the Lord Mayor.

It is rumored and understood that a small squadron of French and English vessels is about anchoring before Naples. The pretext is to be to protect the persons and property of their respective subjects *as soon as diplomatic relations are suspended.* In reality the purpose is to secure the Emperor L. Napoleon from the contagion of a violent outbreak in Italy, by being there as overáwing mediators between King Bomba and his people. The principle of non-intervention will be actually violated, but ostensibly avoided.

I suppose our cabinet is about as much dispersed as is the cabinet here, and that I may not hear the fruits of consultation as early as I should like; but I still flatter myself with hope of something by the Persia, due to-morrow. The condition of affairs in Kansas is, at this distance, and by the *Times*, monstrously exaggerated, and I wait for accurate news impatiently.

Always most respectfully and truly.

---

They are numerous in every separate State of our confederacy. Impelled, as here, by the highest intellect and the truest patriotism, their combined results might be regarded as an offering not wholly unworthy of your acceptance. (Cheers.) But I cannot venture so far; and, although I am really sensible that an interchange of agricultural repórts would constitute a powerful bond of national amity and peace, still I shrink, under the warning of one of your own venerable proverbs, to which my Lord Hamlet migh tapply his epithet of 'somewhat musty,' inculcating the folly or futility of carrying coals to Newcastle. (Laughter and cheers.) Gentlemen, I renew and repeat the expression of my thanks, and will now give you the only good thing which belongs to my address, in the shape of a sentiment: 'All honor and success to the Agricultural Society of Hertfordshire.' (Loud cheers.)"

## No. 53.—TO MR. MIDDLETON.

24 Portland Place, September 27, 1856.

My dear Sir,—Your note of the 19th instant would have had an immediate answer but that it reached me in the country, whence I have only just returned.

Of course, and I might have supposed without a moment's hesitation, you can refer any one to me upon the subject of your proposed publication. It will give me pleasure, as far as it may be in my power, to inspire those who do not know you, with the confidence of those who do.

I happened at the receipt of your letter to be among gentlemen whose works made me sure of their being experienced in regard to London publishers: and, without adverting to my purpose at all, I took occasion to enquire as to the best direction. They were unanimous in the opinion that a volume of about the size of yours, and on a speculative topic, would run the risk of falling still-born from the press, if put into the hands of a *City* publisher. I am no judge of the soundness of this opinion, but think it best to mention it. Mr. Murray, in Albemarle Street, was greatly preferred. In the present preposterously confident anticipation in England, that the knell of our Union has rung in Kansas, you may possibly find it difficult to get any one to give to your *subject* the zealous introduction it deserves. It really seems to me that the political structure and social temperament of our country are less understood by those who indefatigably claim to be our kindred than by any other people.

I am truly and respectfully yrs.

---

## No. 54.—TO LORD ELLESMERE.

24 Portland Place, September 28, 1856.

My dear Lord Ellesmere,—Many thanks for your indulgence towards my venturing on an effort to obtain admission at Bridgewater House for a specially recommended countryman of mine. I knew of your absence, but felt perfectly assured that his was a case which would greatly extenuate the liberty I took. He is an artist of uncommon merit. Some of his paintings, in their characteristics resembling those of the Russian Orloffsky, are exceedingly fine; and he gives every promise of reaching an excellence equal if not superior to that of his fellow-townsman, Leslie; for both are from my home, Philadelphia. His name is Rothermel, and he is travelling for the first time in eager pursuit of the masterpieces of his art. As he returns from Italy and Germany, for he cannot afford a long suspension of labor, I will make another attempt at your Gallery, under the encouragement your kind note has given.

Always faithfully yrs.

---

## No. 55.—TO MR. MARCY.

LONDON, October 3, 1856.

MY DEAR SIR.—The Roman Catholic clergyman, Mr. F., of whose angry missive about his passport I inflicted upon you a copy, cooled upon getting my letter, and very frankly came to beg pardon for his folly, and to make himself very agreeable by his vivacity and intelligence. I was not sorry to hear him say that the F. O., which never recognizes our naturalization of her Majesty's subjects, gave him a passport immediately as a native Irishman; for it was still impossible for him to adduce a scintilla to warrant my granting one.

You have narrowly escaped a formal despatch by this occasion; but you shall have it soon, I promise you. Lord Clarendon has written me a note respecting a Mr. Smith, our consul recently appointed to Londonderry, whose wild advertisement for "30,000 laborers" and for the sale of "millions of acres" in Iowa, seems to have "riled" the political economy of Downing Street. I have invoked explanation and defence from our splashing representative, and hope to tranquillize the "labor market" of her Majesty before any fresh dido is kicked up. You shall enjoy the entire muss, solemnly set out, on a future day.

Captain Pendergrast of the Merrimac, and his Lieutenant, Jones, dined with me yesterday. This noble ship, tell Mr. Dobbin, is attracting much attention. But (and make my apologies for venturing the suggestion) why is she to winter at Brest in preference to Cherbourg? Every national purpose would seem far more attainable at the latter than the former. I am extremely anxious to pay her a very formal visit; for in sober truth, I have "itching ears" for the booming of American cannon in British waters. The Captain, however, may be kept in London for a fortnight.

Every sunrise is expected to throw light upon the ministerial policy as to Naples. We are kept in quite an interesting state of suspense. Now we have the fleets in the Bay, and now we haven't. Now Austria intimates dissent, and now she don't. Then Russia backs up Bomba, and Prussia, but then again neither does. Some say Clarendon's dogmatic and pragmatic violence will push on to another war; but more hint that Lord Palmerston shews the white feather, and would back out if Louis Napoleon would let him. The leading men of the Opposition take courage and hope from this intervention, which, they say, will break down the administration, whether it be carried out or shabbily withdrawn from. In the meantime, the Ominous and Anonymous bulletins of imperial illness are still circulating in defiance of every effort to stop them; his Majesty is coming, but not yet come, to Paris:—he is in good health, goes to operas, concerts, baths, and reviews:—"*mais, en homme d'état, il se repose!*"

Lord C. has left the Queen, but is visiting about, and may not get to the F. O. for a week.

I hope to hear by the next steamer your idea of the Central American arrangement, and that your daughter is restored to health.

Always truly and respectfully yrs.

---

## No. 56.—TO MR. MARCY.

LONDON, October 10, 1856.

MY DEAR SIR,—Some of the suggested modifications of the *projet* underwent early discussion, were thought to enter into unnecessary detail, were not regarded as material enough to insist upon, and at all events were made to yield to the pressure of an anxiety to get on, before anything should occur to change the disposition to give up the Bay Islands. This surrender involved, as it appeared to me, so striking a triumph to the American cause and argument, that I was prepared to do, or omit doing, almost anything to secure its final accomplishment:—especially as I knew, that when once done it could not be undone, and that my own more direct work with Lord C. was a mere *projet ad referendum.* Had there been any serious delay, I now know that the apprehended mischief would have occurred. I don't despair of having your improvements incorporated, but there will be difficulty, grumbling, and procrastination.

That Londonderry consul! Poor fellow! he wants to make money and therefore made a noise. And the gravity with which disturbance in "*the labor market*" is predicated of such a puffing bulletin is really worthy of those circumlocution chambers, the Colonial Department and the F. O. A genuine rough and tumble and yelling hoosier, kicking up his heels amid the solemnities of office in this region of the globe, necessarily frightens all the red tapists, and makes every venerable political economist peer from under his eyebrows and shake ominously his theorizing noddle! I wish, however, that our wild functionary wrote better English, especially as he seems inclined to enter upon the patriotic labor of lecturing (on invitation! ahem!) upon America! Give the man a chance, my Lord C., and don't cut him down for a single exuberant caper. He is utterly unknown to me, though hailing from Philadelphia, and of a name belonging to a most extensive family there and everywhere.

The oscillating funds in Paris keep the mercantile community here in great anxiety. Some of the political quidnuncs, too, see in the Bank panic and its incidents, of an attempt to force paper and to prevent a premium on silver, an approaching revolution. The Emperor has at last got back to Paris, and certainly he seems already to have shewn that he has carried with him an unimpaired mind:—for he peremptorily objected to the Bank project. Still, the workmen are beginning to complain, and to press up to him! Nothing to do, high rents, and bread rising!

I think the symptoms indicate that the intervention at Naples will "fizzle" out, and leave the King at liberty to imprison, starve, and kill, as his fears or whims may dictate. Austria appeals the question to the reconvened Congress of Paris: that is plausible, will give time, will check Lord Palmerston, will reunite the three absolutist Emperors and Prussia, and will give Lord Clarendon an opportunity to explain and back down. The Lazzaroni are with King Bomba, and the appearance of the fleets in the beautiful Bay might produce a popular outbreak fatal to English and French residents.

Strange as it may seem, I wholly forgot, until reminded a few days ago, that I possessed by law the life privilege of franking!

Always truly and respectfully yrs.

---

## No. 57.—TO MR. MARCY.

LONDON, October 14, 1856.

MY DEAR SIR,—Our consular representative at Londonderry may be considered in smooth water again. My communication to the Foreign Office, of which my last despatch presented you a copy, appeased the ruffled plumage of the Colonial Department, and the matter drops. I have, however, taken the liberty to hint to Mr. Smith that his notices hereafter should be somewhat more measured and guarded.

It is quite extraordinary with what unanimity, and yet I must confess with what moderation of tone, the success of Fremont is here wished and expected. What good he is to do them, one cannot perceive; and, after all, unless assisted by greater rashness on our own part than can be reasonably anticipated, he will not be able, in the face of the Senate, to do his country serious harm.

I shall give myself henceforward and exclusively to efforts to carry your amendments to the *projet*, and you need not expect to be worried by my eye-straining penmanship until I am able to send the perfected treaty, or despair of it. I sometimes think that you have aimed at more perfection in the instrument than was practically important or necessary; but your points are undoubtedly improvements, and shall be pressed "until my eyelids can no longer wag." My father's favorite inculcation was "attempt the impossible, and you'll achieve the highly difficult." So, here goes!

I see that you and Sir. H. H. have been "nobbing." Pray, if you have still a chance, hint to him that he is bound to return home; for I have not been well for a fortnight, and was obliged to send for another physician.

Naples *in nubibus* still. The policy of "passivity"—that is, Louis Napoleon letting England do the job while he merely looks on, will probably prevail. The coalition of Russia, Prussia, and Austria to shield Bomba, only exasperates the ministry here to obstinacy and action. Soon, the ball will have rolled beyond their reach.

Always truly and respectfully yrs.

---

## No. 58.—TO MR. GILPIN.

LONDON, October 17, 1856.

MY DEAR SIR,—Two hours ago, under a Full Power received a week since only, I put my hand and seal to the Treaty which, if ratified by the Senate, must close, and with mutual honor, all strife between the two countries. Am I to be more applauded by the philosophers of Peace or reviled by the champions of War? *N'importe!* I have done what I conceive to be right, and will accept its consequences, be they what they may.

The upshot is that Great Britain withdraws from her Colony in the Bay of Honduras, gives up her Protectorate of the Mosquitoes, admits Greytown to be a Free City under the sovereignty of Nicaragua, pens up her Indian king and his subjects within a narrow and precise reservation, and promises never to overleap the limits of the Belize as they were when the Clayton-Bulwer Treaty was made. That will do, won't it? And what is more, the whole of it is perfectly compatible with the honor and dignity of this great nation:—for, although the Parisian scribblers have dubbed me "the wily diplomat," it never has and never will enter into my own sense of personal or public honor to get from political agents a dishonorable concession. That, too, I believe to have been the ruling principle of Lord Clarendon, of whose fairness and frankness, as well as ability, I cannot make too full an admission.

United and best regards to Mrs. G.

Ever sincerely yrs.

---

## No. 59.—TO MR. MARCY.

LONDON, October 17, 1856.

MY DEAR SIR,—The possession and communication of the Full Power so fortified my position that I was able to carry your modifications although several had been resisted before. The effect of having the authority, at all events in a measure, to decide instead of merely discuss, is that you prevent the other party from taking the chances involved in an *ad referendum*. At least it seemed to me that the exhibition of the Broad Seal had a most persuasive effect.

Mr. Buchanan once spoke to Lord Clarendon proposing a co-operation of the ministers of the two countries in favoring the union of Buenos Ayres to the Argentine Republic. Lord C. adopted the idea, and advised with the French government, who also assented. He is anxious now, in consequence of a letter just received from the British representative, to act; but he has never heard whether our government are disposed to carry out the suggestion. Mr. Peden, it appears, stands very high in general estimation, and his co-operation is much desired. Lord C. requested me, informally, to ascertain how the matter stood at Washington.

In my No. — I sent you certain bills made out against our government by her Majesty's, and requested attention to them. Have you forgot them, or are they paid without my being apprised?

Always faithfully and respectfully yrs.

## No. 60.—TO MR. MARCY.

LONDON, October 24, 1856.

MY DEAR SIR,—I have your Nos. 34 and 35, which will, of course, be promptly attended to and acknowledged in a formal despatch, as soon as there is accumulated enough matter.

Is it not rather singular and invasive that Mr. Guthrie should meditate building light-houses on British coasts? I rather suspect that Lord Clarendon will be puzzled how to answer the proposition. He has, however, got it fairly before him, and I hope will treat it less cavalierly than Spain did our offer to buy Cuba.

By the time you get this, the curtain will be lifted from the Presidential future. Perhaps, indeed, the result may ultimately turn upon the electoral vote of California, and you may be held in suspense for a fortnight. But I hope that you will send me a missive as soon as possible, so that I may have all the time that can be given for putting my house in order. I am perplexed about prolonging or renewing the lease of my legation. If Pennsylvania shall have proved false to her vows, I shall want to hurry up.

As I anticipated, the spirited retorts made by the Sicilian Absolutist, upon the treatment of Irish rebels and Cayenne convicts, have exasperated the policy of intervention into something like firmness and action. The embassies are to be withdrawn, and the squadrons to cruise within hail, though out of the Bay! How tenderly is the divine right to govern wrong dealt with!

O'Donnell, too, has taken already the direction of my vaticinations; and now even Narvaez is hardly servile enough for the reaction! The general impression here is that a very gloomy convulsion is at hand in Spain.

Always truly and respectfully yrs.

---

## No. 61.—TO LORD ELLESMERE.

LONDON, October 25, 1856.

MY DEAR LORD ELLESMERE,—Mr. Allibone, who is publishing "A Critical Dictionary of English Literature," in the city of Philadelphia, has confided to my care, for transmission to you, a specimen volume of his work, embracing only letters A, B, C. It seems to me admirable in plan, execution, and getting up, and I am desirous to hasten its reception by your lordship. Shall I send it to Bridgewater House, or is there a more direct avenue to you? It is something in shape between an octavo and a quarto.

Very sincerely and respectfully yrs.

P. S.—Has your lordship adjudicated the claim of Bacon to the authorship of Shakespeare's Plays?

---

## No. 62.—TO MR. MARCY.

LONDON, October 28, 1856.

MY DEAR SIR,—The result of the State election in Pennsylvania has just reached us by the Africa. I suppose it may be regarded as a conclusive proof of the victory that awaits us this day week. It would seem that the majority can scarcely be less than fifteen, and may be twenty, thousand. This is a nut which the London and Parisian editors must find it hard to crack.

Sir H. H. says he was delighted with Mr. Marcy, and I told him that Mr. Marcy was equally pleased with Sir Henry. In return for your kind expressions about him, he begged me not to omit conveying his best respects.

At last a significant step has been taken in the Neapolitan affair. The French and English Legations are withdrawn. The movement is accompanied, however, with so much hesitation, and with arrangements as to the fleets so opposite to intervention, that King Ferdinand must regard it rather as a triumph than a hurt. The breaking off of diplomatic intercourse is, after all, a blow not very difficult to bear. According to European sentiment, Bomba may perhaps not relish being *cut* by Louis Napoleon and Victoria; but then, his lair remains inviolate; he can consult his humor there, and he may smile at the "*brutum fulmen*" while he stands between, and arm in arm with, Russia and Austria. This may not be an actual "fizzle," but it so much resembles one, that it cannot satisfy any shade of political party in Parliament. Lord Palmerston has either lunged at too distant an aim, or has too readily recoiled. Most persons regard the present position as neither one thing nor the other—a sham for France, and a shame for England.

Talking of a lack of British diplomatic representation at Naples reminds me that you labor at Washington under the same deprivation. How do you bear it? Have any serious inconveniences developed themselves? Or do you begin to feel that there is a point at which farther delay would be uncivil? Not a whisper on the subject has come to my ears. I believe Lord E. would like it. I believe the Duke of N. would like it. I believe Mr. V. would like it. I believe Lord H. would like it. And I feel convinced that Sir G. O., who married a daughter of Gov. Vanness, would like it. And I am persuaded that either of these gentlemen would make himself quite acceptable. But the acid of Crampton's (I beg pardon, *Sir* John Crampton's) dismissal has not yet been neutralized.

Always faithfully and respectfully yrs.

---

## No. 63.—TO REV. DR. BINNEY.

24 Portland Place, October 31, 1856.

My dear Sir,—I fulfilled to the strict letter my promise to you about your friend, and have had, for some two weeks or more, the response in my pigeon holes. I hoped you might call in from day to day. It requires verbal explanation. When your engagements call you to London, I shall take pleasure in letting you see the matter in its real aspect.

Consider Mr. Buchanan elected to the Presidency on the 4th of November, by the overwhelming defeat he gave the adversary in Pennsylvania on the 14th inst. In my judgment, the indication is unerring, and makes doubt idle.

We all renew our thanks for the kindness and frequency of your invitations, and only regret that a sort of

American "manifest destiny" has prevented a visit to you, or Mr. W. Brown, or half a dozen others, whom we long to burthen with our presence.

Having accomplished to the entire satisfaction of the American government the adventurous and unpromising enterprise which brought me to England, namely, a restoration of amicable relations and feelings between the two countries, on terms honorable to both—a result which the fairness, frankness, and ability of Lord Clarendon reached directly and promptly—I am ready to resume my niche of obscurity at home, be our new President whom he may. Indeed, I begin to doubt whether I can consent to prolong my representative residence at a Court which does not esteem my doing so worth reciprocating. This you may consider democratic pride. Perhaps it is so. We are excessively touchy, I own, at anything construed to imply a slight from an aristocracy whose principles of personal or political conduct we do not perfectly understand. In the United States, the humblest citizen would deem it a sacrifice of self-respect to stop at a house whose owner notoriously declined returning the social compliment. I am only, of course, illustrating the political attitude of the two nations—not referring to private life—and to explain to you why and how it may be that my "continuance here may in no measure whatever depend upon the Presidential election." A long story you will say, in answer to a single phrase.

Always faithfully and respectfully yrs.

---

## No. 64.—TO MR. MARCY.

LONDON, November 4, 1856.

MY DEAR SIR,—Our last accounts of the State election in Pennsylvania on the 4th of October, have created here a universal conviction that the democrats must succeed in the struggle of *to-day*. Even the inveterately anti-American and anti-slavery newspapers—*Times*, *Post*, *Advertiser*, *Globe*—are beginning to hedge, and admit that England can get along without a quarrel, let who may be President. People are wise who accommodate themselves to a relation they cannot avoid.

The great alliance is loosening. Something on this score is due to the insinuating diplomacy of Russia, which began immediately on the meeting of the Peace Congress in Paris,—something to the under-current of contemptuous remark in which the French indulge against the military capacity of their English Crimean heroes; something to the unavoidable diversity of sentiment and policy as to the Principalities; something to the manifestly inconsistent attitude of the absolutist of 2d December, with thousands banished and perishing in Cayenne, towards his disciple Bomba; but more than either, or perhaps than all of these, will be due to the Napoleonic warning, given in the *Moniteur*, to the calumnious British press. Louis Napoleon put his hand, by this, literally into the lion's mouth, and the lion has been chafing, chewing, and biting ever since. That which touches the quick of the imperial sensibilities is the incontestably true charge of fraudulent speculation in the public funds. Private and personal aberrations may be imputed by wholesale and be disregarded, because in these regions of civilization such matters are turned into mere amusing gossip; but to swindle the masses, and especially "*les ouvriers*," by tricks in stocks, to become in office suddenly rich in this way, endangers the throne even with the army. Such an act must not be charged, if the alliance is to be continued. It is committed, but it must be concealed and indignantly denied. The spirit with which the editors confront the imperial scolding is worthy of all praise. I had cut out for preservation a fine specimen of this manliness and ability combined; but I will send it to you with this, as worthy to fill up an idle moment at your fireside.

London is refilling. Many of my colleagues are back. Dinners are beginning. But the full tide comes only with the Court and Parliament in February.

The Merrimac left Southampton three days ago, and without my being able to visit her. She was most hospitably entertained during all her stay.

I have not a scrap on hand worthy of an official despatch, and I dare say you have not failed to detect that this scrawl is more marked by a determination to write something than by a superfluity of matter.

My best compliments to your family.

Very faithfully and respectfully yrs.

## No. 65.—TO MR. EVERETT.

LONDON, November 4, 1856.

MY DEAR SIR,—"The Uses of Astronomy" reached me yesterday morning; and I read it last night with such real delight that I cannot restrain the wish to thank you most warmly for having sent it. Nothing has given me the same pleasure, since your refusal, as Secretary of State, to enter into the tripartite guaranty of Cuba to Spain. I cannot speak of your lecture on Washington, of which I have heard a great deal, but as yet have met no copy.

You have many ardent as well as distinguished friends here, who speak with pride of having known you intimately.

Always faithfully and thankfully
Your sincere friend.

---

## No. 66.—TO MR. MARCY.

LONDON, November 7, 1856.

MY DEAR SIR,—The Washington, which quitted Southampton the day before yesterday, and by which I intended to send letters, was given up at Mr. Miller's suggestion of her being a laggard in movement, and her mail reserved for the Niagara of to-morrow. I am, therefore, able to send you two newspaper cuttings, which you may find worthy special notice.

Lord Palmerston's speeches at Manchester are in place of what he might say in the House of Commons, were Parliament in session. I have invited your eye to certain passages by marks. They will attract attention. One of my diplomatic colleagues had with me a short conversation, whose bearings on two points may make it not wholly unworthy of repetition to you.

C. This is a very strange administration!

D. Why do you think so, Baron?

C. They are not harmonious:—they don't agree among themselves.

D. I can't perceive that: at least they hide their differences from the public.

C. Well, I will illustrate. I had, two days ago, a long interview with Lord Palmerston, in the course of which I told him I could not understand the policy of the cabinet about the Principalities. He said it was very plain and very direct. No, I replied, you are for preventing their union. Certainly, he observed, you are right there. But why? I remarked; their union would undoubtedly augment their power and prosperity. Perhaps so, said he; but then, Baron, our wish is to keep them weak and to increase the powers of Turkey. Mon Dieu! I exclaimed, that is not the idea of Lord Clarendon, his opinion is different. Very possibly, he replied; if Lord Clarendon has expressed to you a contrary view, it is his own private one; it is not that of the ministry. We have always entertained the policy I have avowed. The Principalities must remain feeble by being kept apart. In that way only can they be kept under the influence of Turkey and be a barrier against Russia. Consolidate their strength, and the Sultan would soon find them, under the magic of Russian diplomacy, ready to join the Czar in driving him out of Constantinople. Lord Clarendon has his own notions: but *we* have *ours*.

How odd these contradictory sentiments! and for the Premier to say Pooh! pooh! to the words of the Minister of Foreign Affairs!

D. Well, Baron, do you talk again to Lord Clarendon, and you may discover that he has modified his opinions, and brought them to harmonize with those of Lord Palmerston.

This question as to the union of the Danubian Principalities has greater depth and importance in its speculative futurity and in its immediate effects, than may at first be supposed. It is vastly interesting as bearing upon the relations hereafter to exist between Russia and the rest of Europe. But its present operation in producing a disagreement on a great principle between France and England, and tending to end the alliance in angry quarrel, cannot be overrated. The statesmen, politicians, and press of both countries are already by the ears in relation to it. It is more fundamental than the disputes about the Isle of Serpents, or the two Belgrods, or the Finland fortifications. There would seem to spring out of it at once, a new arrangement of European alliances: Great Britain, Austria, and Turkey antagonistic to France, Russia, and Prussia. The languor of the movement against Naples is a premonitory symptom.

Always faithfully and respectfully yrs.

---

## No. 67.—TO MR. EDWARDS.

24 Portland Place, November 11, 1856.

I confine myself strictly to your enquiries:

1. The Electors of a President of the United States are, by an Act of Congress of the 1st of March, 1792, "appointed in each State," and are in number equal to the number of Senators and Representatives to which each State is entitled by law.

Except in South Carolina, the *appointment* by the State is made through the agency of a popular election, within 34 days preceding the first Wednesday in December.

The election in each State is conducted under State regulations and officers; its result is certified to the State Executive; and that State Executive, by proclamation, makes the result known, and by communication to the elected.

2. The Electors, thus officially notified, are by law directed to meet wherever the Legislature of the State may appoint, and give their votes by ballot for a President and Vice-President, on the first Wednesday of December.

On meeting, they select their own presiding officer; they sign and seal *three certificates* of all the votes by them given; they send one of these certificates, by an officer of their own choice (generally one of the electors), to the President of the U. S. Senate, one other they transmit to the same person by the Post Office, and the third they deliver to the Judge of the United States of the District in which they meet.

3. On the second Wednesday in February, both Houses of Congress assemble in Convention, the President of the Senate presiding: the certificates transmitted from the several electoral colleges are opened, the votes counted, and the persons elected ascertained and declared.

4. If, on opening the certificates and counting the votes it appears that no person has received a majority of the whole number, then the House of Representatives alone proceeds immediately to choose by ballot, out of the three highest in votes on the list, the President:—and in making this choice, the votes are taken by States, each State having one vote. If the House fail to choose before the 4th of March then next following, the Vice-President enters upon the office, as in the case of the death of the President.

So as to the election of the Vice-President; only, that, if the certificates of the electoral votes do not shew a majority for any one, the Senate (not the House) choose the officer, and may choose immediately, without waiting the result of the proceedings in the House as to the President.

Respectfully yrs.

---

## No. 68.—TO MR. CHILDS.

LONDON, November 12, 1856.

MY DEAR SIR,—I am extremely obliged to you for your kind and interesting letters. In this, a sort of exile, they comfort and cheer me greatly.

Your last spoke of Mr. T. Buchanan Read, and of your wish that he should paint two portraits for you. I gave him a strong introductory letter to Lady Franklin, and enclose her reply.

Dr. Kane has left here, and is perhaps in Paris; but, continuing quite unwell and feeble, he was undetermined whether to go to Algeria or Cuba, and I sent him such letters as I thought might serve him at either place. His book has given as much delight here as with you. A thousand congratulations on its merited success.

Very faithfully yrs.

## No. 69.—TO JUDGE KANE.

LONDON, November 13, 1856.

MY DEAR JUDGE,—I am afraid you have reason to complain of my not writing to let Mrs. Kane know of the Doctor's arrival here and of the state of his health. The truth is, I waited from day to day, to see him improve in strength, and thought more of him than of you.

He soon made up his mind that the climate was unfavorable, and hastened over to France; undetermined whether to go to Algiers, or to recross the Atlantic and winter in Cuba. I made him promise me a line from each resting-place as he proceeded, but have not heard from him since he left.

Of course, he was received here with open arms. His book is rapidly circulating and gives delight to every one. The reviewers and critics will begin their notices as soon as they have had time to digest it. If they prove to be what they ought to be, I will use the scissors and send them. Enclosed is a slip respecting the proceeding of the Royal Geographical Society at their meeting three days ago.

We wait on tiptoe, expecting to hear of the Africa, on Saturday or Sunday, the 15th or 16th, what you did with the Presidency on the 4th instant. No doubt, however, is entertained that our noble Party has carried 21 out of the 31 States.

Present me most warmly to all your family.

Always faithfully yrs.

---

## No. 70.—TO COL. L.

LONDON, November 14, 1856.

MY DEAR COLONEL,—Judge Jones writes me word that you are suffering under the apprehension of a domestic deprivation. I sympathize with you too warmly to refrain from writing, though I am generally unwilling to draw your thoughts away from professional business.

Consolation it would be idle in me to attempt. Such calamities admit of none. Time, in its action upon a Christian spirit, administers the only balm. You and Mrs. L. have been sorely tried, and may have dark days still to encounter, but I fervently hope you will pass through them with sentiments of submission, resignation, and firmness. Such is my sincere prayer.

Since effecting all that my most heated ambition could desire in this sphere of public service, I have indulged in meditations somewhat selfish. Such is, perhaps, the unavoidable consequence of too much delusion as to the direction we seduce ourselves to take by calling it "devotion to one's country." After all, no individual person is wanted; if he abstain or withdraw, others by wholesale are ready to undertake and to execute any duty. We are taught this truth by a slow experience, too late to avoid the pitfalls of buoyant and blind patriotism. Perhaps, indeed, after being taught, the habit of risking every sacrifice in order to do some supposed service, would still work on. Is it not wiser and more virtuous to take care of one's own family and old age, leaving the general weal to others, unless Providence has placed you beyond the reach of want? It is easy, and it must be delightful, for a rich man to be patriotic; but when a poor one becomes absorbed in his country's affairs, he really naught enriches it, and only paves the way for his own "Vanity, Vanity, and Vexation!"

We anticipate hearing to-morrow, or the day after, the grand finale of the Presidential chorus of the 4th instant. We do not doubt, as we ardently pray, that our glorious Union may be again saved by our glorious democracy.

I remain as ever, my dear Colonel,

Your friend faithfully.

---

## No. 71.—TO MR. MARCY.

LONDON, November 14, 1856.

MY DEAR SIR,—I don't know how better to dispose of the accompanying grandiloquent petition from Corfu, than by sending it for adjudication to you. There may possibly be some reason in what the man says as to our vessels out there wanting a consulate.

I inadvertently omitted, in my last, calling your attention to the fact that Lord Palmerston, in his recent speech at Liverpool, almost entirely gave in to your proposed addition to the anathema against Privateering. He makes it a mere question of time, and seems to expect the time to be at hand. We are certainly on the confines of the Millennium. I enclose my slip.

In the Despatch Bag of to-day I send a somewhat formidable looking document addressed to the care of Senator A. G. Brown. It should be made to pay toll:—that is, I think it an article of such authenticity, clearness, and force, that it should be examined by Mr. Guthrie before leaving Washington. It is a Paper read by Mr. J. T. Danson at a meeting of the British Association for the Advancement of Science on "The Connection of American Slavery with the British Manufacture of Cotton." Not being in print, I requested a manuscript copy, and it has been most kindly furnished. Perhaps Mr. Brown might feel himself authorized, under the circumstances, to let the paper be read as it passes on its way to his constituent of Mississippi, Mr. John F. H. Claiborne:—perhaps not, and if not, I must try to get another copy.

Appearances in Paris are getting worse and worse. A financial panic seems inevitable. The Bank broods over a suspension of specie payments, and its chief directors insist upon its necessity. Napoleon remains firm against the measure. Scarcity, hoarding, high rents, placards, stock-gambling, and frightful licentiousness will, I think, soon give him an opportunity to prove the superiority of his arrangements over those of Louis Philippe to repress a movement of barricades. He has warily worked in advance, and under pretence of adorning beautiful Paris with perspective rows and colonnades "long drawn out," has opened for his artillery avenues into all the mutinous districts. He is beyond the reach of anything but assassination, and that he in a measure defies, for I am told that metallic underclothing does for him what was done for Achilles by the water of the Styx;—makes him bullet-proof. To be sure, one of these days, the army may desert him, and then, of course, down he goes. But no symptom of that yet.

The last received of our newspapers led me to expect the "Resolute" at an early day.

King Bomba, after laughing at his sulking and quitting guests, is getting more gracious, and the "complication" may be esteemed at an end.

You are all now in the bustle preliminary to a session, and I ought to be ashamed of this twaddling intrusion.

Always respectfully and truly yrs.

---

## NO. 72.—TO MR. MARCY.

LONDON, November 21, 1856.

MY DEAR SIR,—Your despatch No. 37, and private letter, both of 7th November, have just arrived by the Atlantic.

I am at a loss to fix the precise clause of the Convention in which you think a *clerical* mistake has been made in using the word "*within*" instead of the word "*without.*" If you allude to the preliminary declaration of Art. 4, you will on further examination perceive that every inch of territory *outside* of the reservation, or "*not included within it,*" south of the Segovia, is recognized as Nicaragua's. If you go north of the Segovia, you get into Honduras. However, I await your promised more formal explanation of this matter; although unable to see anywhere in the document a place in which it is possible, without destroying the sense, to substitute "*without*" for "*within.*"

There has been a rapid series of Cabinet Councils in Downing Street, and they are still going on. Quidnuncs speculate in vain on their objects. They may relate to foreign embroglios; or to projects of domestic reform; or to changes in their own personnel. There is a talk about exiling Lord John Russell into the House of Peers. Several judicial and episcopal vacancies have had to be filled. After all, I suspect that these frequent consultations are ascribable to the ticklish position of the alliance with France rather than to any other single cause.

The first Monday in December will have arrived a day or two before this reaches you; and as the steamer Niagara quits Boston on the 3d, I hope you may not have omitted to direct me to be supplied by her with the Message, and any other documents on hand.

Frauds and murders are the order of the day in these realms. They throw our wickedness completely in the shade. It is gravely mooted whether the revolver and the bowie-knife, those much vilified weapons, ought not to be carried by every honest and peaceable Englishman to protect his life.

London is fast refilling from the Counties and the Continent.

Always faithfully yrs.

---

## No. 73.—TO MR. MILES.

London, November 25, 1856.

My dear Sir,—Your kind letter, which circumstances prevented my answering sooner, has left a very strong impression upon my mind. Its incidents and sentiments cannot fail to be always and warmly remembered.

I do not know how long my stay in Europe may be protracted. Apart from the consciousness that I am not altogether now my own master, either to quit or to remain, I feel in doubt as to what, in a domestic point of view, it would be expedient to do. The public objects which were aimed at in coming are attained; my diplomatic job is finished; and, as I am somewhat insensible to the attractions of an idle post, and perfectly content with private life, the idea of resuming my Walnut Street home, not unfrequently becomes persuasive.

The distractions which, at this distance, appeared to convulse our country, ever since the Presidential nominations, have awakened within me sad and serious anxiety as to the fate to which we may be destined. This frightful sectionalism, dividing us into North and South, giving to the former the power of population and of fanatical fierceness, and to the latter the strength of constitutional right and of social necessity, presents an aspect of things which would seem, for the purpose of rescue and safety, almost to demand the interposition of Providence. How else is this Red Sea to be traversed? Where is the wisdom, where the self-sacrificing patriotism, the broad honor, and continental nationality of '87 and '89? I have never underrated the capacity of the President elect, and feel assured that the instincts of his high position will rally for his cabinet the ablest and truest men whose services he can command:—what I fear is, that no one will appreciate the imminence of the danger, no one will disengage himself from the sweeping torrent of the present and strike out boldly for the future, no one will sink the victory of the day in calm and laborious efforts to prepare the regeneration of fraternity in 1860. The two sections must not be permitted to drill their respective forces for four years, and then confront each other for a definitive fight:—*that* would be to risk our existence as a nation upon an issue of uncertain result:—to such a pass matters should not be allowed to go:—the whole term of Mr. Buchanan would be wisely expended in rendering sectionalism impossible at its expiration.

This subject goes deeper into my feelings owing to my being in the midst of those who show a profound incapacity to understand the federative structure of our government, and who keenly set on their Press, their Pulpits, their lecturers, their speakers, their novelists, their poets, and their historians to produce an overpowering chorus for the subversion of a Constitution which shelters the Southern form of African labor from their crusade. Our Constitutional democracy, if *unsectionalized*, is our only means of baffling them.

I am quite curious to know the effects, actual or anticipated, of the new order of things. This curiosity is not, indeed, confined to myself. Enquiries are constantly made as to the probable course of our new chief magistrate: and before his inauguration we shall probably have his whole future shadowed out in parliamentary speeches, editorial leaders, and political dissertations all over Europe. That great Western Republic is, just now, a mighty "*John Jones*" in the eyes of the world.

Remember me to Judge Jones, Phillips, M. C., Col. Page, Col. Lee, etc., etc.,—indeed, to all whom you know I value as generous friends. Present me especially to Mrs. Miles and your boy, also to your brother, and believe me

Faithfully and sincerely yrs.

## No. 74.—TO MR. MARCY.

LONDON, November 23, 1856.

MY DEAR SIR,—After sending off my last somewhat hurried note, I resumed my search for your "clerical error" in the Convention, and found it (!), after passing it over twice, lurking in the tail of a word, and constituting the well-recognized difference, both physically and politically, of *out* and *in*. When once detected, it is so obvious that you can see nothing else: like the cast in a man's eye. Two queries:—how did so palpable a mistake occur? and how put it right? Your instruction is faultless and clear:—and the wrong termination must have been committed by myself in copying from your original on to a separate paper for the benefit of the final draftsman of the Convention. Once crept into the text, it is of that attenuated and subtle character—like a particle of rust upon a needle's point, or of dust upon the glass of your spectacles, both excessively obstructive and subversive—which is readily overlooked. As to its remedy:—the finger once upon it, unlike the Irishman's flea, it cannot escape, and I should presume the Senate's Committee would, in briefly reporting a verbal amendment, yield to a natural desire of changing *out* into *in*. But be this as it may, I will lose no time in seeing Lord Clarendon, and in devising such form of rectification as may be deemed best. Perhaps a joint recognition of the slip of the pen, with a joint request to *scratch out and write in*, prior to final "advice and consent," would put you in complete command of the complication.

The American ultimatum about Privateering is winning its way. I must confess that, although the general principle is sound and philanthropic, I do not think we have yet reached that point of naval power which would justify our abandoning the great private means of public defence for any consideration whatever: and I am a little apprehensive that the Paris Congress, if it convene again, may take you at your offer. Lord Palmerston at Liverpool avowed a decided leaning in that way: and Mr. Cobden is out with a letter to the same effect. As you may otherwise not see this last promptly, I send you my slip cut from the *Globe* of yesterday.

Our excellent friend the Earl of Ellesmere is laboring under a fierce and protracted attack of gout.

Suppose you add to the list of those whom I have heretofore reported as probably ambitious of representing the Queen in the White House "The Man with the White Hat," now Sir Charles Elliott, Rear Admiral, etc., etc. I met him at the Premier's last night, and his exceeding amiability and politeness led me to do, what Dr. Dablancour would not do, *i.e.* "smell a rat." He was slightly disconcerted when I reminded him, jocosely, of the sobriquet he achieved in the United States. He is the only candidate, if candidate at all, whose welcome I should doubt:—and yet he may be *in petto* for us.

Always faithfully and respectfully yrs.

---

## No. 75.—TO MR. MARCY.

LONDON, November 25, 1856.

MY DEAR SIR,—The Austrian minister has requested me to forward a package addressed to the Imperial and Royal Legation of Austria at Washington. It is the Extradition Treaty recently executed between the Plenipotentiaries of the two governments, and the time within which it must be ratified is rapidly running short.

I have just got back from the F. O., where I *scratched out and put in*, and then drafted the note to you which I now send. Not a moment left.

Always respectfully and faithfully yrs.

---

## No. 76.—TO LORD SHELBURNE.

LONDON, November 29, 1856.

MY DEAR LORD SHELBURNE,—It may be observed that in the whole Treaty there is but one *letter D*, and that in Article 4. Our former missive of authorization to Mr. Marcy was not susceptible of misapplication, although, pursuing the erroneous description made by Mr. Marcy himself, it referred to No. 3 instead of No. 4. Still, after your lordship left me, I thought it best that every doubt upon the subject should be relieved.

I beg you to accept my apologies for the trouble this inadvertence has occasioned, and my assurance of high respect.

Very truly your obedient servant.

---

## No. 77.—TO MR. MARCY.

LONDON, December 1, 1856.

MY DEAR SIR,—The joint request that you would correct the "clerical error" in the Treaty, was forwarded in much haste, and very near losing the post, on the 26th November by the Atlantic.

Availing myself of the first leisure moment I re-examined the verbal irregularities, and lo! here is another, not in the treaty itself, but in our united authorization to you:—really unimportant, but still fit to be absolutely righted.

I had carried with me to the F. O. your despatch No. 31, to give to Lord Clarendon ocular demonstration, by shewing a single sentence, that the "clerical error" had been mine, not yours:—for your original contained the word "*without*" which, for purposes of engrossment, I had turned into "*within.*" Well! in drafting the paper to you to put this word with its proper ultimate, it was necessary to describe the *locus in quo* of the mistake in the treaty, and inevitably and naturally your description in No. 31, "*Art.* 4, *No.* 3, *letter D,*"—"staring one in the face with rapid strides"—was adopted.

Now, there exists in the treaty but one Art. 4, and in that Art. 4 but one *letter D:*—in truth there is not in the whole document another *letter D:*—to misapply the description was therefore impossible;—but the description is inexact, and the vindication of positive truth is a part of the duty (is it not?) of every genuine diplomatist.

Hence, you will perceive that the enclosed paper is simply and strictly a copy or repetition, designed as a substitute, of the one transmitted by the Atlantic, only the breastwork *numeral* 3 being made to yield to the pressure of *numeral* 4! *Fiat justitia!*

You will perceive by the newspapers that Parliament, again prorogued, is to meet on the 3d of February next "for the despatch of business." Her Majesty's consideration for posterity will probably prevent her engaging in the solemnities of the occasion.

I have at last some reason to think that the ministry meditate sending, early, if not immediately, a representative to Washington. I refrain, however, until something more definitive and explicit takes place. To me, Mr. Villiers appears the prominent and "coming man." He is not, however, in perfect health, and may shrink from the effects of an Atlantic voyage.

In conversation with the Prussian minister here, I could perceive that he had recently had his attention called by his government to the Abolition of Privateering question. I explained at large, and he seemed to approve, the views and final offer of the United States. I let him have, too, a copy of your letter to Mr. Sartiges. Count Bernstorff was at St. Petersburg during my mission there in 1837–39. He is a loyal, amiable, and attractive gentleman, inspiring confidence, but slow in exhibiting intelligence. Speaking of mitigating the calamities of war, by treaty stipulations, or by propounding, as at Paris, new articles of the laws of nations, he told me that I could form no idea of the depth of ill will which this government had inspired by its military conduct in the Baltic and Black Seas, especially at Kertch and Odessa. The sentiment pervaded all Germany, if not all Europe.

Always faithfully and respectfully yrs.

---

## No. 78.—TO MONS. MARCOLETA.

LONDON, December 1, 1856.

MY DEAR SIR,—Your letter of the 25th November has been received. Having very little faith in the utility of diplomatic secrecy in a case like the one to which your enquiries are directed, I should probably not hesitate to answer you fully in conversation. But the whole matter, accomplished and I believe entirely approved by the President, is in the hands of Mr. Marcy, and may be submitted to the Senate in a few days. I prefer, under these circumstances, to abstain from putting on paper anything upon the subject. Allow me, however, generally to say that as far as respects Nicaragua, nothing, if I remember aright, has been done or proposed which you have not, heretofore, as her representative, sanctioned.

I entirely agree with your sentiment as to Mr. Marcy. On my own score, having done the only business that induced me to come here, I am ready, at a hint, or moment's warning, to resume the private life which at my age is so much more desirable than the most glittering public employment.

With profound respects to Madame Marcoleta,

I have the honor to be very truly yrs.

---

## No. 79.—TO MR. MARCY.

LONDON, December 5, 1856.

DEAR SIR,—I wrote by the Hermann three days ago, though it is probable the present steamer will overtake her.

What I surmised in my note of the 1st instant turns out to be reality. I met Lord Clarendon at the Brazilian minister's dinner on the evening of the 2d (his sovereign's fête day), and in the course of conversation, apart from other guests, he suddenly referred to some former chitchat we had had, and said, "We shall send a minister to Washington without delay;—we shan't wait the incoming of the new administration." I quietly expressed my gratification, but forbore further remark. I received no hint as to the person. His manner, and other circumstances, impress upon me the conviction that the choice has been made, and that her Majesty's representative will be with you almost as soon as this letter. I perfectly well know, but deem it inexpedient and unnecessary to put on paper, the reason for this sudden ministerial decision. It has no relation whatever to the yet unarrived "Resolute;" none to the President elect. I hope they will send the right man. Of course, I most scrupulously avoid the indelicacy and impertinence of intimating a preference.

All your summer visitors from this country, Lowe, Holland, Delane, etc., have returned, loudly expressing their delight. The *Times*, under the influence of the last, is becoming almost fair and eulogistic. In a little while, a run to "the States" will supersede, with the rich and fashionable, the too crowded and vulgar, because close at hand, salons of Baden-Baden. Yesterday the *Times* published the best description of Niagara Falls and river I have ever read, from their correspondent, Mr. Filmore.

Very faithfully and respectfully yrs.

---

## No. 80.—TO MR. J. Y. MASON.

LONDON, December 8, 1856.

MY DEAR SIR,—Your letter of the 6th reached me this morning, and I hasten to answer it, though, owing to an inflamed eye, with the aid of one of my private secretaries.

Mr. Marcy has given me no official instructions upon the subject to which you refer. He sent me very early a copy of his admirable letter to Mr. Sartiges; and I caused it to be immediately published in the London newspapers, under a profound conviction that it was vastly too important to be hid under the bushel of diplomacy. In his private letter, he left me at discretion to do this, saying, that the British government not having addressed ours upon the subject at all, he did not wish me to open the matter to either of the Lords Palmerston or Clarendon, but only, in case I was spoken to about it, to be prepared to state the President's views. I have carefully conformed to this idea: and perhaps you will agree with me, now that I have stated it, that I had better not depart from it.

I had occasion, some week or two ago, in a private letter, to fix Mr. Marcy's attention on the very manly and liberal language uttered by Lord Palmerston at Liverpool; and I then ventured slightly to regret the offer of our government, and to fear that it would be accepted by the reassembled Congress at Paris. The qualified abolition of privateering—that is, the exemption of private property on the high seas from seizure by public armed vessels—is undoubtedly a great improvement upon the bald and naked proposition of the Parisian Conference: but I do not think myself that we have yet attained that point of national power which renders it expedient to yield the right of privateering upon any consideration whatever. If the navies of England and France combined, or the fleets of England alone, are to be relieved from the necessity of dispersion, in order to convoy and protect their commerce, there is not a point of our immense coast on which they could not land any amount of force which they might deem necessary in order to countenance servile insurrection or separate the States. The danger of such a thing may be distant, and on our own soil I should hope we could get the better of any alliance: but I must confess that, until by the vast increase of our national naval armament we become more equal antagonists in the *national duel*, I should prefer not to diminish the difficulties of our invasion. Public belligerent force is our weak point:—whether it be traceable to the nature of our institutions, or an unguarded policy:—this is perfectly well known to the statesmen of Europe, and when to this are added existing sectional animosities, should they conceive the project, as they may, of assimilating or subordinating the Western to the Eastern Continent, could anything be more flattering to their hopes than the fact of our having voluntarily enabled them to swallow at a single gulp our comparatively little navy and army?

I beg pardon for saying so much, although I could add a great deal more. Too much philanthropy is the vice of the age. The Absolutists despair of their millennium, unless they can somehow get the better of American peculiarities.

Always faithfully and respectfully yrs.

## No. 81.—TO MR. MARCY.

London, December 12, 1856.

My dear Sir,—Accept my thanks for your private note of the 24th ult. I can very well realize the business oppression to which you are all now liable, and to which you especially, in maintaining the reputation achieved within the last two years, are forced to submit. You must not suppose me so inconsiderate as to expect punctual replies to the private letters I write. I am quite satisfied in believing that they tend to keep you familiarly acquainted with political incidents and prospects, and the general tone of feeling prevalent here.

The "*Resolute*" has been in the newspapers for some days past. Of course, not having heard from you anything upon the subject, I can only speak of her departure and destination, in ordinary conversation, as they are represented in the American journals recently received. It is obvious that a disposition exists to regard the restoration of the alleged derelict (though in fact and in law no derelict at all) as something very extraordinary and handsome. Preparations to receive her are being made by the scientific sympathizers with her Arctic exploration, and her officers will, on reaching Portsmouth, find themselves objects of all sorts of public feasting and welcome. It is possible, however, that the continued stay in the country of the chiefs of the departments at this season of the year, may deprive the manifestation of its more formal officiality. It is somewhat agreeable (in a way you will understand) that the determination to send a successor to Mr. Crampton, which I communicated a week ago, was announced before the news of the sailing of the "Resolute" had reached here, and without any reference to it whatever.

I have felt restrained, by a paragraph in your private letter of the 4th of August last, from opening to Lord Clarendon the views of the President on the Abolition of Privateering. Great Britain has in no respect, directly or indirectly, imitated the example of the other powers who constituted the Congress of Paris, in consulting upon this subject the sentiments of the United States. She has maintained perseveringly and no doubt intentionally strict silence. I am a little at a loss how exactly to regard this: —but on the whole take it to indicate a consciousness that the proposition originated with her, and is thought to betray no friendly purpose. Be this, however, as it may, while she abstains from intercourse in relation to it, I presume I am bound to remain aloof. Circumstances have given me the impression—I believe I have heretofore referred to some of them—that your amendment will prevail, if the Conference reassembles, an event not yet *absolutely* certain. Quere?—would it be prudent, in advance, to have the entire programme of change in maritime law sanctioned by a resolution of the Senate? It is best to keep in mind that this Parisian Congress has not the character of a permanent body, and may be persuaded to doubt whether your amendment is not of uncertain result, or deficient in the full and definite constitutional obligation. Such a doubt might be advantageously played upon by those who affect to understand the structure of our government, reasoning with Prussia, Austria, Turkey, Russia, France, or even Sardinia. I ought to beg pardon for presumptuously poaching on Mr. Mason's preserve.

Great interest is felt to ascertain what you propose doing to maintain inviolate the security of the Panama route. I do not believe that any disposition prevails to adopt the newspaper slang, and to be uneasy about your cautionary measures in that quarter. The necessity of doing something is frankly admitted:—and if what you do be in the interest of general commerce, you will not be quarrelled with should you hold a tight rein over that inefficient, though possibly well meaning, State of Granada.

I send you, more as a curiosity than anything else, a copy of two memorials addressed to the Congress of the United States, and which I was requested, in all form, to transmit to the proper official authorities. It emanates from a self-constituted Committee at Sheffield, who have kindly undertaken the management of Foreign Affairs and the control of diplomacy everywhere. The felicitous ease with which they impute treason to the functionaries of their own government, and abuse a foreign one, is quite refreshing. I certainly could not become accessory to the presentation of any such alien document; and have therefore left them to seek a hearing through the channel of the post-office, frankly telling them that, according to prescribed rules, I did not feel at liberty to use the agencies of the Legation in forwarding their papers. This is a single illustration of very many attempts made to get countenance and importance by your minister's endorsement. The other day, a political enthusiast in the centre of Germany wrote me a violent philippic against Mr. Miller, our Despatch Agent, for not stuffing the bag with countless pamphlets addressed to all the Legislators and Governors of the Union, and coolly demanded that I should instruct Mr. Miller to transmit what he denominated his "precious discoveries" in political science. Of course, I answered him with an entire approval of Mr. Miller's conduct, gilded by the expression of a profound regret that the statesmen of my country should thus incur the hazard of remaining ignorant of his "precious discoveries."

Owing to an inflamed eye, I eschew for awhile the use of spectacles, and have been therefore obliged to employ the pen of one of my domestic secretaries.

By-the-by, have you noticed that Mr. Consul Matthew has been appointed to Odessa? Mr. Crampton being knighted, and Mr. Rowcroft dead, the only one of your victims remaining undisposed of is Mr. Barclay, in whose favor invention is fruitlessly racked.

Always faithfully and respectfully yrs.

P. S.—You will see by the enclosed slip just cut from the *Globe* newspaper that Mr. Cobden anticipates for your conditional surrender of privateering, an almost unanimous decision in the House of Commons in its favor. This is a sincere, and I believe a sound opinion, viewing the question as *an English one.* They will gain everything, first, for the security of their commerce, and, second, in the concentrative efficacy of their prodigious naval armament. War will not endanger their merchant ships or their manufactures, and thus, relieved from all care about these vital interests, they may send their fleets to bully and thunder where they please. Opposite results may be drawn from *an American view.* Losing the right of privateering, in other words, of assailing the vital interests of our adversary, our means of aggression are nil. Our navy must be docked; and we must be content with whatever terms the adversary in this national duel may prescribe for a peace, if indeed a peace would ever be desirable or attainable. You see, I have my misgivings on your great measure of change in the rights of nations at war. If our navy approached anywhere near to the power of the one displayed off Portsmouth last spring, I should be quite willing to let it take its chance in defending our coast:—but as it now is, and as I am afraid, by an unwise economy, it may be long kept, it is impossible to say at how many points of landing along our coast, a war would rapidly become one of invasion. However, you have no doubt considered all these matters with your accustomed sagacity, and your policy must be made to triumph.

G. M. D.

---

## No. 82.—TO MR. MARCY.

LONDON, December 16, 1856.

MY DEAR SIR,—Our steamers are rather disappointing us. The America which left Liverpool on the 6th December, and the Hermann which left Southampton three days before, have both been forced back by damage from tempestuous weather. I had mails in each: but I presume they will reach you by other vessels.

The arrival of the "Resolute" has created quite a sensation. Capt. Hartstene came to London on the afternoon of Saturday the 13th instant, and I at once prepared a communication, agreeably to your No. 36, to ascertain from Lord Clarendon, whether we might be allowed to restore the vessel to the British navy. This went to the F. O. on Sunday morning. Hartstene dined with me that evening: and at about 9 o'clock, while yet at table, I received a telegraphic express from our consul at Portsmouth, requesting me to apprise Capt. Hartstene that the Queen had intimated an intention to visit the Resolute on Tuesday morning, and to beg his return to the ship. Of course, the Captain started back to Portsmouth early yesterday morning, and by this time, her Majesty has graciously welcomed her new and gallant guests. At the time I wrote to Lord Clarendon the official letter I have mentioned, I also sent a private note requesting an interview in the course of yesterday, asking leave to bring Capt. Hartstene with me. He was out of town, and only received my communications late in the day at his country residence; sending me an answer on Monday that he would meet me and Capt. Hartstene at the F. O. to-day at 3 P.M. My object is, should I find that this government intend to accept the Resolute, of which no doubt is entertained, to have some understanding as to the preferred manner of having her formally made over to Sir Charles Wood's Board of Admiralty. Perhaps I may have time to add to this letter a short account of to-day's interview.

Always faithfully and respectfully yrs.

P. S.—Just back from F. O. His lordship had the answer to my letter tendering the Resolute lying before him unsigned, and said he would send it in the course of the evening. He is also to put me without delay in communication with the Admiralty, though he believes Sir Charles to be out of town.

Lord C. specially requested me to repeat to you what he had said at the Brazilian minister's dinner about sending you a British minister. His manner intimated some difficulty in choosing out of a number of candidates. But the cabinet were upon it, and would lose no time.

G. M. D.

---

## No. 83.—TO MR. MARCY.

LONDON, December 26, 1856.

MY DEAR SIR,—Putting myself in the Confessional, I should be inclined to think that I was bound to acknowledge having too hastily "acquiesced" in the return of Captain Hartstene and his associates on board of a British steamer. No matter, however:—second thoughts have prevailed:—satisfying reasons have been assigned for the change of mind: and these gallant objects of a boundless hospitality will speed their way back (as now intended by the Commander) by the packet which leaves Southampton on Wednesday next, the 31st instant. What, in the mean time, will be done with them, on the score of compliments, deputations, feasts, testimonials, photographs, and newspaper eulogies, it is impossible to conjecture. The enthusiasm does not yet seem to ebb, and it may take a fresh start. Lord C. writes me a private note, saying that her Majesty's government desire to present to Capt. Hartstene a Sword of Honor; and that the Queen had said to him (Lord C.) that she was much pleased with the Captain! The restoration of the Resolute has certainly been the happiest act of comity to a friendly power ever devised. The feeling it has excited would seem exaggerated:—yet there it is, eager, universal, and loud. I am told (though not by our officers) that some of those who left her in the ice shew mortification, and look askance at the restorers:—but they are few, and avoid attracting notice. The Washington, the steamer from Southampton, is a slow vessel, and our men may therefore have a long, cold, and disagreeable voyage. Capt. H. will of course hurry to Washington, and give Mr. Dobbin a full narrative.

The quarrel about the insurrectionists of Neufchâtel is rapidly reaching the war point. Prussia is openly and ostentatiously arming. Switzerland, with admirable composure, exhibits the unshaken resolution of conscious right. Her spirit is up, and her people seem unanimous. The Absolutists may deem it expedient to stop the matter in some way or other, because to allow the general peace to be broken merely to gratify a king's personal pride, or to assert a shadowy *suzeraineté*, don't suit modern notions, and might disturb all the elements of democracy. England just now appears inclined towards the Swiss:—but, in my opinion, she will join Napoleon in mediating, upon some plan which may ostensibly save the honor of both disputants and keep things quiet. The sturdy land of Tell will, by the force of circumstances, her position, the justice of her cause, the dread of subterranean fires, and the cool and manly attitude she has taken, come off the victor, or I shall be much mistaken. The thrones of Europe are all equally affected by the epidemic of a holy horror of agitation:—even the great spider in the centre of the web keeps a steady eye on popular commotion and has misgiving fits.

I should find it difficult to convey to you a correct idea of the effect produced on this side of the water by your departmental reports of the 1st December. Of these, the most impressive and appreciable is the Treasury. They, somehow or other, insinuate themselves almost everywhere, and are more read than is generally supposed. Some men receive them with frank delight:—but the prevailing feeling which they produce is of a different character, resembling that which we owned in the United States when the assault upon the Malakoff and Redan proved successful:—we could not deny the magnificence of the feat, but we did not relish it, and would have preferred its failure. Precisely so with the undeniable achievements, the wonderful prosperity and substantial power of our political system:—they can't be disputed, have even the eulogy of words, but they inwardly provoke dislike.

No one can say when the Paris Congress will reassemble. Its day has been sliding along through December, without settling yet. The talk is for the 29th instant: but I perceive causes for floating doubts still: and it would not astonish me if events postponed the matter until spring. Have you noticed that the ministerial press, unable since Lord Palmerston's Liverpool speech to make open fight against your offered amendment to the Abolition of privateering, are contriving modes of avoiding it? They say, it is vague in its terms, that you are insincere, that the President's message attributes to the European programme what it never meant, and so on. Now all this appears to me as merely preliminary to intriguing the Congress into a doubt as to whether the subject might not be wisely postponed to some indefinite future day. No doubt, however, you have armed my colleague of Paris with all the means and powers necessary to surmount these captious pretexts.

The East India Company's war with Persia has become a fixed fact, and of course involves, without regard to Parliament or People, the whole of the British Empire. What with this last movement, the quarrel with Naples, the growling with Russia, the stir about Switzerland, the jealousy as to France, and the approach of the session of Parliament, Lord Palmerston would seem to have his hands full.

Faithfully and respectfully yrs.

## No. 84.—TO MR. MARCY.

LONDON, December 30, 1856.

MY DEAR SIR,—Owing to the slow sailing of the Washington, I would decline writing by her and wait for the America on Saturday next, but as Captain Hartstene and his crew return to the United States on board of her, I wish the same vessel to carry a notice to you.

Although I will trouble you with a despatch by the steamer of the 3d January, 1857, there are a few topics worth adverting to in advance.

1. Mr. Villiers has, by the advice of his physician, after deliberating for a fortnight, refused the American mission. It is now at the disposition of a Scotch Peer, whose name I am not free to mention, who is distinguished in the diplomatic line for great intelligence, winning deportment, and ultra liberalism of opinion, who is about forty years of age, and was Secretary of Legation at St. Petersburg with Sir Hamilton Seymour before the recent war.

2. The minister from Greece, Mr. Tricoupi, with whom I am on sociable and kind terms, begged me two days ago, in consequence of instructions he had received, to ask whether it would not be agreeable to our government to change the officer who represents it at Athens from a *Commercial Agent* to a Consul. His reason for urging this is the real desire felt to draw closer the ties of intercourse between the United States and Greece. Nothing of negotiation or public attention can, by etiquette and usage, be extended to a commercial agent, even though the King and Court would wish to make an exception in favor of the American.

While on this subject, I take occasion to send you a newspaper published at Athens, *Le Moniteur Grec*, of the 9th of December instant. It contains Mr. Ranjabé's much celebrated delineation of the present social and political condition of Greece — which, if well translated, might be allowed to grace the columns of the *Union.*

3. The Sword of Honor designed by this government for Commander Hartstene will, I have reason to believe, be given this direction :—Lord C. will transmit it to me, accompanied by a letter of compliment, requesting that I would forward it to the American Executive, to be

handed, if compatible with law, to the gallant officer who has won the Queen's heart. Of course, I will do with it most cheerfully and promptly whatever the Earl may suggest, and I hope the Commander may find Congress disposed to let him wear his badge of courtesy.

4. Mr. Miller has brought to me, on deposit, a quarto-sized paper envelope, with the "Department of State" earmark on the north-east corner, and addressed to "J. A. Barnard, Esq., London and Port Stanley Railway Company, Secretary's Department, London." Both the man and the Company are, as the polished Parisian would say, *introuvable*, or, as the classical Floridian would call it, *non-comeatibus in swampo;* for I dare say it is some scheme which vanished in the making. Pray tell me what I am to do with it.

5. Your letter of the 12th December, whether "private," "strictly private," "confidential," or public, don't exactly appear, has reached me. It tells me that I should receive with it, what I have *not* received, to wit, a Cipher for our Minister Resident at Berne; and it omits to tell me that I would receive what I did, namely, a *bulkish* packet for the Austrian legation here, which I presume may be the ratified Extradition Treaty transmitted to you through me some month or two ago. I have delivered the *bulkish* packet, but feel anxious and discomposed about the Cipher.

It may amuse you for a vacant half hour to look over the slip I cut from the *Globe* of last evening on Maritime War. You are aware that this newspaper never contains an article repugnant to ministerial views. This is the *second* of the same sort—the *first* I sent hastily over to Mr. Mason. They lead me to suspect that the Premier, notwithstanding his Liverpool speech, will give your amendment a go-bye.

Always truly and respectfully yrs.

---

## No. 85.—TO MR. MARCY.

LONDON, January 6, 1857.

MY DEAR SIR,—Very severe storms have occurred at sea, and disasters are being constantly reported. The coasts, it would seem, on both sides of the Atlantic, are strewed with wrecks. I feel some anxiety about the America, which left Liverpool on last Saturday, the 3d, and must have been that very night in a perfect tempest. She bore to you my Nos. 35 & 36. Winter voyages are rather to be avoided.

Can anything, however, in the shape of physical violence, be as shocking as the bombardment of Canton? Talk of Greytown after that! The massacre of the innocents was comparatively heroic. Poor, harmless, unarmed, ignorant, and unconscious creatures, men, women, and children, by tens of thousands, butchered with shot, shell, and fire, to avenge a disclaimed insult to a fraudulent flag!

There would seem to be accumulating a heavy score against the ministry, for Parliament to force to settlement. The public sense is greatly shocked by Admiral Seymour's infliction, and it may be that the administration will disavow. Yet, there is the amateur Persian war: and the milk and water Neapolitan fizzle: and the fast and loose game about the Treaty of Paris: and the relaxation in the Gallo-Anglican ties: and the alliance with Austria: and the lack of sympathy for Switzerland: and the shabby trick about the Income Tax: and the Premier's off-hand blunder in meddling with the Southampton election: and so on, and so on. Then the Opposition are said to be secretly organizing under fresh leaders, Gladstone and Graham, and to be fatally bent on mischief. Still and nevertheless, to my calm and disinterested eye, Lord Palmerston steadily consolidates his power, and becomes more popular and more necessary every hour. He and his colleagues are strong, too, in their harmonious unanimity.

Statistical philosophers have suggested as one of their deductions that assassinations are epidemical. First, the King of Naples attempted:—now the good Archbishop of Paris slain at the very altar:—who next? and how many? Some self-exalted William Tell may be moodily prowling about the streets of Berlin; or, if the path of the disease be religious, why may not the Pope fall as well as his representative? Crimes in England are countless and frightful: but their incentive is not piety nor liberty; it is money, nothing but money.

I gave you some idea of Lord Napier, who is coming

over to you as minister; but in the *Times* of this morning is an article which on his subject you may as well read, and which I therefore cut out and enclose. The sole ground of objection is practically shallow; for a man of Napier's mind and character, instead of being deluded, is disgusted by absolutist absurdities, and the better fitted for republican simplicity and truth and reason, after passing through them.

Nothing yet about the law of maritime war. The Conference would seem to have finished its business, except as to fixing the time for final departure from the Principalities and Black Sea by Austria and England, which is left to be announced as soon as the rectified line of the Bessarabian frontier is actually surveyed and verified. What direction, then, have you given to your amendment? Will you offer it to each Power separately? and, having obtained the adoption of the majority, will you give it to the world by proclamation? I see no objection, but much to attract, in this course, except that Great Britain, who has somewhat suspiciously stood aloof from you on the whole business, may meet you at the close by saying she was no party to your modification.

The financial situation of this government, always excepting their debt, looks just now very prosperous. Their revenue has largely increased. Of a consequence, the popular demand is for a reduction of taxes and a return to the peace footing existing before the recent war. That demand will be gratified only to a limited extent. The military taste has been pampered unceasingly during the last six months, in all sorts of ways, shows, reviews, parades, feasts, speeches, etc., and now one is afraid to talk of such a process as ours in 1816, of *razeeing*.

I send a wooden box addressed to Mr. Dobbin. It is a lithograph-portrait of the Bark Resolute,—a vessel destined to outlive in history, in song, and on canvas, the one that bore Jason in search of the golden fleece, or Ulysses seeking Penelope, or even Cleopatra when fighting by Antony's side!

Always faithfully and respectfully yrs.

## No. 86.—TO MR. HUTCHINSON.

LONDON, January 12, 1857.

MY DEAR SIR,—Yours of 24th Dec. received.

I propose sending to your address shortly, for our City Library, a set of the Patent publications of this government. The despatch agent will manage their transmission for me, so as to incur as little expense as possible. What you have called Blue Books are valueless trash, and a collection of them might fill a 74.

I will send at the same time, and for the same destination, an antique daub, painted, as is believed here, in 1720, purporting to be "The South-East Prospect of the City of Philadelphia, by Peter Cooper, Painter." It is on torn canvas, some 8 feet long by 1½ wide. One of the members of Parliament, in peering among the rubbish of a city curiosity shop, picked it up and brought it to me. The principal buildings of the town of that day are pointed out, and twenty-four good old Philadelphia householders are named in a margin. Although worthless on every score but that connected with "auld lang syne," it presents at half a glance so striking a contrast to the "Consolidated City" of 1857, that it has its interest for a corner in Franklin's institution. If your colleagues repudiate it as unworthy, keep it for me.

Owing, I presume, to the tempestuous character of the season, we have been unusually long without news from home. I am not as sanguine as you appear to be about the Central American arrangement, and therefore desire to know the decision of the Senate. There are trifling points in it, at which a filibustering spirit may possibly carp. Indeed, in order to appreciate it correctly, much more study of details and bearings is necessary than will be given to it. If it be rejected, some of the rejectors should be required to devise and carry a better scheme. We are bound by the Clayton and Bulwer treaty of 1850, and, starting from that, any project that will remove the difficulties which have arisen from opposite constructions, may now be calmly discussed. If I have done anything by coming here, it is by bringing about a disposition to listen without losing temper, and honestly to contrive expedients to get rid of obstacles and avoid quarrelling on trifles. This state of feeling will, in the end, secure something effective.

Ever faithfully yrs.

---

## No. 87.—TO MR. O'SULLIVAN.

LONDON, January 12, 1857.

DEAR SIR,—Your letter of the 6th December, which was slow in reaching me, relates to an interesting subject on which I have felt myself somewhat restrained by the reticence of this government and my instructions. It has nevertheless entered into my correspondence with both Mr. Marcy and Mr. Mason. I believe England is the only one of the Powers represented in the Congress which announced the new programme of maritime war, that has abstained from presenting it to the United States. Quite explainable!

In the actual attitude of Nations, I entirely coincide with you in the opinion that Mr. Marcy's proposal to exempt private property on the high seas from capture, would work so advantageously for England that her statesmen ought at once to close with it. I believe they will. Mr. Cobden does not doubt that when understood it will obtain the unanimous sanction of the House of Commons. Lord Palmerston avows his theoretical approbation; but forbears to shew an exulting eagerness to catch at it.

But—how about the United States? Will they be benefited by abandoning the principle and practice of *voluntary* action, and by so doubling at a single stroke the already resistless power of Great Britain's naval means of invasion and blockade? Are they prepared and disposed for the national duel wherein the parties shall be a small squadron to the West, and a cloud of concentrated fleets to the East? Will they make safety secondary to trade? Or can they forego the simplicity and economy of their federal system, and ceasing to trust emergencies to the spontaneous movements of popular defence, enter upon the creation of large standing armies and great navies? I do not intend that these interrogatories shall be considered, *per se*, argumentative. They are only sent to you as evidence that my mind rather inclines, in the existing relations of America and England, and perhaps always jealous of an excess of philanthropy in public policy, to doubt the expediency of yielding the right to employ privateers, no matter how modified and upon any consideration whatever. To be sure, these combined potentates of Europe may try to force their international code upon us, and one of these days, with the joint condemnatory standard of "Abolition of Slavery and Privateering," they may put us on our mettle;—but the probability of such an attack is not to be avoided, need not be deprecated, and may not be lessened, by our voluntarily diminishing the weapons to repel it with.

I am truly and respectfully yrs.

---

## No. 88.—TO JUDGE KING.

London, January 13, 1857.

My dear Judge,—I agree with you, the ways of life are a labyrinth, and our two actual positions are striking illustrations. My peregrinations, to be sure, are nothing compared to yours. You have wandered almost the world through: I have (as yet!) only crossed the Atlantic. But it would have baffled, some thirty years ago, the most foreseeing prophetic vision to have traced us to where we now are.

I don't know that I am yet entitled to the praise you give me for restoring the pacific relations of the two countries permanently. It may possibly turn out to be but a deceptive truce. The scheme of arrangement is before the Senate, and, if sanctioned by that body, I verily believe it will put an end forever to all Central American difficulties, without the slightest departure from principle or honor, and secure in that region the most glorious field and highway of active and untrammelled commerce men have ever witnessed. The Senate may think otherwise. It is not impossible that in removing all the points of controversy under the Clayton-Bulwer treaty, I have crossed the grain of some who wished to get rid of that contract:—and it is very likely that, in both countries, I have provoked large bodies of turbulent spirits, by preventing them from coming to blows. These are incidents inseparable from such public measures, and must be philosophically foreseen as liable to take place. Still, Marcy and his colleagues have approved and adopted, and I cannot but hope the Senate may do so too.

Do you propose a trip to London? Or what are your plans? I send my notion on the legal proposition you have stated, separately.

I am truly and respectfully yrs.

---

## No. 89.—TO MR. MARCY.

LONDON, January 13, 1857.

MY DEAR SIR,—Since my despatch of the 9th instant, nothing of interest has occurred worth relating, unless it be the visit volunteered yesterday by Lord Napier.

He stayed for about two hours, and conversed freely. His personal desire is to reach Washington as early as possible, not later, he proposes, than the middle of February. He brings his wife and children with him, and is anxious to secure for them, in advance, a furnished and healthfully situated house.

There was peculiar and attractive frankness in many of his remarks. He said that he had no political position at home, and no fortune; and although he had a title, he was quite conscious *that*, in America, would avail him nothing, if indeed it would not do him harm. He was aware also that in England there was a considerable party who would not consider him the proper man for the mission, who appreciated its great importance justly, and desired the selection of such a statesman of acknowledged weight as Lord Carlisle, or the Duke of Newcastle, or the Earl of Elgin. These ideas made him uneasy. But he had been habitually and from conviction an admirer and student of American character, and he hoped *to get on* by promoting with his best exertions the friendly relations of the two nations.

Of course I encouraged his modesty, and assured him that success or failure in his mission, as far as our public men and society were concerned, would depend upon himself alone.

At first, this gentleman will seem to you cold, a little awkward, and disposed to silence, like all the best bred and best minded Englishmen I have yet met:—but I think it fair to say that, in the course of the two hours he gave me, notwithstanding his comparatively youthful appearance, I became aware that he was a man of remarkable ability, of sound unprejudiced judgment, and of elevated sentiments of morality and honor. I hope and believe that you will like him.

For the first time an intimation is given in one of the morning journals that the Queen may be disabled, from her early expectations, opening Parliament in person.

The Canada is in her 14th day, and not yet heard of! This goes to you by the Arago.

Always faithfully and respectfully yrs.

---

## No. 90.—TO MR. MARCY.

LONDON, January 20, 1857.

MY DEAR SIR,—Your private letter of the 5th January I received yesterday.

Your original suggestion, not to initiate officially with this government any interchange of views on the Privateering question, I have watchfully conformed to:—always, however, upon the slightest approach, prepared to shew the philanthropy, justice, and *generosity* of your offer. They have studiedly kept away from the subject, although many opportunities for opening and discussing it frankly have presented themselves. I suspect the existence of divided councils—indeed so equally divided as to prevent movement. We shall have it in the House of Commons shortly after the session opens, a fortnight hence.

Until within this last year, I had been accustomed to regard the perpetual untruths which disgrace our newspapers as rather the results of mistake or the discolorations of fancy, than as intentional falsehoods. My charity has lately been much shaken:—for I have seen so many utterly unfounded statements respecting myself, that I can find no mode of accounting for them but in a malignant invention steadily pursuing some unseen objects.

I need hardly say to you that the paragraphs which in our journals connect my name with the coming cabinet, are all, from first to last, false and flimsy. Since he left London in March last, not a syllable has reached me from our President elect;—and my correspondence to him has been confined to two letters, one relating to the sad drowning of a Lancaster gentleman, Mr. Witmer, and another, more recent, covering a congratulatory note from Lady Alice Peel, which, being addressed simply to "*the President of the United States*," exacted a short explanation from me, of my reason for knowing that it was intended, not for General Pierce, but for him. Nay, more; I have written to you much oftener and more freely than to any one else, and I am quite sure that nothing has escaped me respecting possible appointments that was not of the most general character. The stream of misrepresentation will probably be kept flowing until after the 4th of March.

Chess players are sometimes blind to the most powerful moves with which they can fortify their game. Those gentlemen who are unable to see the preponderating influence in Central America, and *all around* that region, secured, by the scheme of pacification, to the United States, her policy, and her citizens, had better give up the *rôle* of statesmanship, and confine themselves to the art of managing personal and prurient explosions of predatory violence. Your treaty does everything for the honor and interest of the nation, and for the independence and safety of the Central American States, in all future time; but these sages think nothing done because Walker is not patted on the back! Well, if the spirit of filibusterism can't see beyond the tip of its nose, and, like abolitionism, it increases in force, we shall ultimately have, I suppose, to submit to our "blind guides," and let them lead us to calamities which they have not the sagacity to provide against. If, however, they *will* go on in their own way, do, I beseech you, encourage them to appropriate, boldly and promptly, all the surplus revenue to fleets and forts.

The Chinese and Persian wars are daily becoming more substantial: the Prussian and Swiss one has *fizzled* out under the soothing assurances of England and

France:—and King Bomba is let alone. It is well for quidnuncs that Parliament approaches. Lord Palmerston will meet it in a spirit of exultation; and unless Lord John Russell be soured, the opposition will be faint. The effect of the Senate's declining to ratify will be worth watching.

I have taken it for granted that Mr. Fay has apprised you, as he did me, of his having safely received the Cipher.

You will have by this opportunity, the Baltic, the brother of your minister at Constantinople. He brings you a purely commercial treaty with Persia for ratification. He has been a good deal with us, and we have found him a very intelligent and agreeable traveller.

Though not as cold as with us, the weather here, for full three months past, has been raw, uncomfortable, and suggestive of suicide. Very little snow or ice, but much rain.

I received in the Despatch Bag yesterday a letter from *Paris*, of the 11th December, 1856, which had taken the circuitous route of getting to London by first going to the United States! It was from Mr. J. Y. Mason, and fortunately did not relate to anything of importance. Such a mistake, however, might, under other circumstances, cause great embarrassment.

Always faithfully and respectfully yrs.

---

## No. 91.—TO MR. MARCY.

LONDON, January 23, 1857.

MY DEAR SIR,—After having sealed the despatches and letters for the steamer of to-morrow, I have just received a note from Lord Clarendon, in which he seems much worried by the delay of Lord Napier's departure, arising exclusively out of domestic arrangements. He tells me, too, that he has written you a letter accrediting Mr. Lumley as Chargé, so as not to postpone any longer "the formal official renewal of our diplomatic relations."

How far, in all this loss of time, the reported non-ratification of the treaty may have had its effect, I cannot pretend to say. Of Lord C.'s sincere desire to do everything that can contribute to make by-gones by-gones, I am unable to entertain a doubt. Still, negotiators, like other parental personages, are not apt to be gratified by the crucifixion of their offspring. At least such is my opinion just now.

I send you to-day *three* swords, and all for naval officers.

The quarrel between Prussia and Switzerland is "a dead cock in the pit," and the prisoners are at large.

There are editorial hints of changes in the ministry:—the ejection of Sir Robert Peel, and a coalition with the Peelites upon giving appropriate places to Mr. Gladstone and Sir James Graham:—but I consider the whole rumor apocryphal.

Always faithfully and respectfully yrs.

---

## No. 92.—TO LORD CLARENDON.

24 PORTLAND PLACE, January 24, 1857.

MY DEAR LORD CLARENDON,—Your note of yesterday, though received at the eleventh hour, came in time to permit my writing to Mr. Marcy, and I did so.

I have always supposed that our scheme of pacification would encounter the resistance which was met by the Clayton-Bulwer treaty:—aggravated, perhaps, by the debility incident to a retiring administration. Opposition, therefore, does not surprise me. But the newspapers exaggerate it, on the principle of "fanning the embers." I have many private letters from gentlemen on whose information and judgment my reliance is implicit, and all unite in saying that the ratification is certain. Still, like yourself, I am anxious, and impatiently wait the next steamer, which will be due to-morrow. The secret sessions of the Senate are invaded by those only who cater to an appetite for new excitements; and the deliberations and prospects connected with a matter so important as the treaty, are sure to be falsely represented. Remember, too, that as the ratification requires two-thirds of the Senators present, there is always room for hostile speculation and prophecy.

I cannot think the enlightened and judicious body before which the plan is pending, will be unwise enough not to accept it.

Always faithfully and sincerely yrs.

---

## No. 93.—TO MR. GILPIN.

LONDON, January 30, 1857.

MY DEAR SIR,—Your letter of the 25th December came just in time to prevent my giving you up, as relapsed into that feverish antipathy to pen, ink and paper, for which more than a year ago I worried you with prescriptions. I heartily thank you for it. The contents were in every way kind and consolatory. The truth is, for the last five months the business of the legation has kept me hard and close at work, making it impossible to leave town, while all the rest of the world were away:—and, even during the hours of daylight, that is from 10 to 4, no time was given for relaxing and refreshing pursuits. Strange as it may seem to those who entertain the common notion as to the idleness of diplomatic life, although I have been more than ten months in London, and constantly anxious to visit objects worthy of attention, my feet have not yet crossed the thresholds of Westminster Abbey, St. Paul's, the Tower, and hundreds of other interesting edifices, made classical by recollections associated with them, or by the purposes to which they are now devoted. I have allowed myself to be perhaps too much absorbed by the substantial business undertaken a year ago, and which, while a vestige remains to do, jealously excludes all thoughts of other matters. I must confess that after so much systematic devotion to it, the prospect of the non-ratification of the treaty is not the most digestible thing imaginable. To be sure, the old hostility to the Clayton-Bulwer Convention would naturally spring up again, in the hope of ultimately so impeding the pacific execution of *that*, as to render a formal legislative declaration of its annulment necessary:—this I expected:—but the possibility of its even approaching to success never entered seriously into the account. I cannot help thinking that the scheme of adjustment is not properly studied in its details. Certainly it contains no pledge, direct or indirect, to sustain or encourage the individual Walker:—if that be deemed essential, another negotiator is necessary, both to make the proposal, and to bear its rejection:—but, as regards the expansive policy of our country, and especially the future opened for American enterprise and commerce in the Central American and West Indian regions, I am quite convinced and conscious that the plan far outstrips, though in a peaceful, just, and honorable manner, the crude, fitful, and unlawful projects of our filibuster-statesmen. If it fail of adoption, these gentlemen will defeat their own alleged objects because they are not permitted to carry them out in their own peculiar and unjustifiable way:—a way which is founded upon the great vice of our public men, namely, a restless want of confidence in the natural energies and persevering progress of American citizens. Under the stimulus of a safe and uninterrupted trade, the cloud of British naval armament dispelled, and one or more free cities as *appuis*, we should in less than five years exercise controlling influence on the Isthmus, elbow out the Mosquitoes, render the Belise a comparatively neglected and dwindling settlement, and possibly entertain volunteered offers from their respective owners for the purchase of Cuba and Jamaica. Walker, Nicaragua Walker, is, by habit, incapable of waiting this development, and may be excused if he blunder so egregiously as not to catch at the arrangement proposed; but that Judge D., Mr. S., or Mr. M. should fail to appreciate correctly the practical consequences of it, is marvellous and incomprehensible. Delay may have sharpened their sagacity:—if so, the treaty will be ratified.

I interrupt my Lord Napier's industrious preparations for his voyage by a diplomatic dinner (12 only) to-morrow; and this I mention to shew you my disposition to secure his favorable reception in the United States, by such endorsement as I can officially give. The young gentleman I propose introducing to you, and to Mr. Everett and Mr. Bancroft; he is of those tastes and attainments, of simple and unaffected manners, and, I think, of more intellect than Crampton:—his wife is said to be quite an agreeable person. He has published a book or two in the nature of travelling observations. He is of excellent Scotch lineage; his great-great-grandfather having invented Logarithms, and the Duchess of Inverness (now resident in Kensington Palace) being his aunt. There is in my office, hanging over the fireplace, Doo's celebrated engraving of Wilkie's picture of John Knox preaching to Mary Queen of Scots, and on his first visit to me, Napier pointed at the little boy standing near the desk under the pulpit, with his back to the spectator, and looking up as if riveted by the roaring speaker, and he said *that* was his renowned ancestor. Perhaps he may, but my opinion is that he will not, reach Washington before the inauguration.

I am convinced on reflection that, in a former letter, I told you of my having left the parcel you sent for Sir Charles Fellowes. It was done on the same day we visited Mr. and Mrs. Grote. The two last called in about a fortnight, having come in from the country for the purpose; the former has been content with the parcel. Your friend Bright is in Algeria or Italy, in pursuit of health. No one entertains a hope of seeing him again in public life, though his relish for it obviously lingers. Mr. Cobden will probably take an active part in the proceedings of Parliament, which opens on Tuesday next, and expects (naturally, from an English stand-point of view) to get a unanimous vote catching at Mr. Marcy's offer for the abolition of privateering. The ministry are likely to be stronger and more popular than ever. They derive wonderful security from the absence of men fit to take their places. The Queen foregoes reluctantly the ceremony she delights in of opening Parliament in person—odd enough! since writing the preceding line, I have been told that her Majesty has suddenly announced her determination to attend, *quand même.* Lord John says, *nolo peerifi.*

European politics have, just now, all the insipidity of a game of chess without a plan:—no great piece is called into action, and pawns are straggling over the board, surprised at their own progress. The affairs of Naples and Switzerland are by-gones. The system of confederating, for mutual support and security, all the monarchies, through the agency of Parisian Conferences, is I think firmly inaugurated. We have on hand, however, two pretty considerable wars, the Chinese and Persian:—and the condition of Spain promises an early explosion and imbroglio.

My despatch bag demands its food.

Pray remember us all most kindly to Mrs. Gilpin.

Always sincerely and faithfully yrs.

---

## No. 94.—TO GENERAL PIERCE.

LONDON, January 30, 1857.

MY DEAR SIR,—A highly respectable deputation waited upon me yesterday with the request that I would transmit to you a Memorial from the European and American Electro-Telegraph Company. They assured me that their only desire was to let Congress, now contemplating legislation upon the subject, be apprised, if you deemed it proper, of the advantages which they conceived their scheme to hold out. I promised simply to forward their paper, and do so now.

Since I left home, eleven months ago, Gov. Marcy has despotically monopolized through despatches and letters, all the thoughts worth sending from the legation. I beg however to say, that I have taken it for granted that what I wrote reached you with as much certainty as if directly addressed to you, and of course with less appearance of presumption on my part. In this view I ought perhaps to apologize for having so often intruded upon you the light, crude, and fugitive ideas and opinions of the current hour in this place. Nevertheless, I cannot permit you to renew your enjoyments and repose in private life, without once more, and that shortly, putting you to the trouble of reading a letter from, dear Sir,

Ever most respectfully and faithfully yrs.

---

## No. 95.—TO MR. MARCY.

LONDON, February 3, 1857.

MY DEAR SIR,—At the soirée of Countess G. last night, were a number of the Privy Council (in their gold embroidered suits), and one of them said to me that the Queen's speech to-day contained a sentence or two upon the United States. I am therefore anxious to be at the opening (which is by Commission) and hope to get home again before 5 o'clock, and make a brief report to you for the steamer of to-morrow morning.

Lord Panmure took me apart to express his sentiments upon the subject of the Report of *our* Secretary of War to Congress: and pressed me very warmly to convey to General Davis his grateful sense of the manner in which the courtesies shewn to our commissioners, Messrs. Delafield, Mordecai, and McClellan, had been noticed by him.

An expectation is prevalent that the ministry will be more severely tried than I had supposed. It is thought that they may founder on the sharp rocks of finance. The call for reduction of taxes is loud and general; and though this call is met by the new wars of China and Persia, those wars are themselves condemned as artfully predetermined in order to save the Income tax. The Chancellor of the Exchequer, an honest and able man, is prosaic: and in view of this characteristic, and of the emergency, it is foreseen that an effort will be made to bring in the brilliant oratory of Mr. Gladstone.

Lord Napier tells me that he has directions to proceed to Washington without delay. But he represents the difficulties of getting ready in a manner that satisfies me he will not reach Washington before the middle of March.

* * * * The Queen's speech, as read by the Lord Chancellor, contained as little as it was possible to put together. On our subject not a word but that she had been negotiating, and hoped all differences would be settled. A single *point*, the only one, is the adoption of the Canton massacre.

My diplomatic colleague of Lisbon, Mr. O'Sullivan, is expected here on a visit in the course of the present week.

Always faithfully and respectfully yrs.

## No. 96.—TO MR. MARCY.

LONDON, February 13, 1857.

MY DEAR SIR,—Europe would seem to be settling herself for another long spell of peace. Fresh negotiations on the Persian war are opened at Paris between Lord Cowley and Ferouk Khan:—though the Shah vents a measure of indignation on the abrupt capture of Bushire. If the quarrel be not arrested, Russia must obviously take her part in it, and is already approaching the frontiers of Persia, as an ally in case of need. A member of the cabinet told me recently that it would soon be settled.

The question as to the union of the two principalities, now that Bolgrad and the Isle of Serpents are disposed of, is looming up into the importance which I originally ascribed to it. One of its first fruits is to create a new division of cabinets: Russia, France, and Prussia on one side, for the unity:—England, Austria, and Turkey against it. The inhabitants are represented as disposed to form a single nation and to choose a foreign king. The *Moniteur* has avowed the imperial sentiment and policy. Qu.? Is he forecasting for a throne for Prince Jerome?

The affair of Neufchâtel is being arranged, as fast as *gout* or *grippe* will permit the negotiators to indoctrinate Louis Napoleon. It cannot possibly be allowed to disturb the serenity of European order again.

You will have noticed the "adjourned question of veracity," in the House of Commons, between the Premier and Mr. Disraeli, on the assertion made by the latter that "a secret treaty" was actually entered into, with the assent and approbation of this government, between France and Austria, by which the Italian possessions of the latter were guaranteed to her by the former, while at the same time the ministry were seeking popularity by a public affectation of desiring Italian nationality. Three passages of arms have come off; and, until the one of the last evening, opinion leaned in Palmerston's favor. His admission that, after all, such a *Convention* was signed in December, 1854, reinstates the discredited veracity of his opponent and leaves him nothing to stand upon but the general reasoning as to the nature and circumstances of the treaty not justifying the conclusions drawn from it. The *fact* which he pronounced a *romance* he finally concedes.

I told Lord Napier, who leaves in the Persia on the 21st instant, and therefore cannot reach you until after the inauguration, that he would experience no difficulty at our custom-house on arriving. But to obviate the possibility of embarrassment, may it not be expedient that special directions should issue?

The Queen came in from Windsor Castle to Buckingham Palace yesterday. Her confinement is expected early next month.

By the time this reaches you, the new cabinet will be known. Wherever I go, I am eagerly questioned as to its composition;—but I remain as profoundly ignorant as if, instead of being at the grand distributing office of information and news, I was immured in an Esquimaux hut, at or near the north Pole. I dare say, the good quidnuncs here disbelieve in my alleged emptiness and regard me as a sham. My correspondents, yourself among the number, have been singularly reticent upon the subject.

Your winter seems to have been unusually severe. Here, more frost than is common. But the last three or four days have been delightful weather; and the approach of spring is heralded by the appearance of bunches of crocuses and violets offered for sale in the streets.

My respects all round.

Always faithfully and respectfully yrs.

---

## No. 97.—TO LORD CLARENDON.

24 Portland Place, February 15, 1857.

My dear Lord Clarendon,—While impatiently waiting the result of Senatorial advisement (of which I have just received cause for entertaining less doubt than ever), it has struck me that your lordship might be pleased to see that there was one man at least in the United States who seems to have seized, in the midst of its details and complications, the essential spirit of our treaty. I enclose an editorial cut from a New York paper that reached me yesterday.

Always faithfully yrs.

## No. 98.—TO LORD CLARENDON.

24 PORTLAND PLACE, February 23, 1857.

MY DEAR LORD CLARENDON,—I received several letters yesterday from Washington. The prospect of ratification is very gloomy, but the finality not yet reached. It is barely possible that the vigorous exertions of the Chairman of the Committee may save the substance of the treaty: but I must confess, after what has been said and done, my hope, as a Yankee would say, has been whittled to the smallest end of nothing.

The end cannot be reasonably expected for a week.

Always faithfully and respectfully yrs.

---

## No. 99.—TO LORD CLARENDON.

24 PORTLAND PLACE, March 3, 1857.

MY DEAR LORD CLARENDON,—The treaty was again reported by the Committee to the Senate, with several really unimportant amendments. Forty-five members were present, and thirty votes, therefore, necessary to ratification. Its friends seem to have determined to avoid a vote on that final question, and to let the responsibility lie with the incoming administration. *Five* more votes would have been enough *to ratify*, but twenty-five were a majority and sufficient to *postpone* the consideration of the subject to the 5th of March, the day following the inauguration: that was effected by 25 ayes to 20 noes.

My letters do not warrant me to encourage a hope less attenuated than the one I described in answer to your former note.

Believe me faithfully and resp. yrs.

---

## No. 100.—TO MR. CASS.

(*Unofficial.*) LONDON, March 10, 1857.

MY DEAR SIR,—It may be important that you should have early the first indications of opinion among public men here on the Anti-Privateering question. This morning's *Times* contains the report of a debate last evening in the House of Commons touching that subject, and I have cut out the enclosed as worth sending to you.

At this particular juncture, when both political parties are preparing for a popular canvass, Lord John Russell seems to have more than usual influence and weight. He is averse to the proposal made by Mr. Marcy in the letter to Mr. Sartiges, and of course to the Convention I have recently submitted.

Mr. Cobden expresses an opposite sentiment.

The Chancellor of the Exchequer speaks on the point with great caution, and, I think, justifies an inference that we shall have no reply to the invitation until the elections are over.

I am very respectfully yrs.

---

## No. 101.—TO MR. WOLFF.

24 Portland Place, March 11, 1857.

My dear Mr. Wolff,—I send you, in reply to the memorandum which accompanied your note, some remarks and references, which, though themselves very imperfect, may be serviceable to Sir John Burgoyne, in his researches respecting the militia of the United States.

Very sincerely yrs.

### MEMORANDUM.

The number of the militia of the United States, as appears by the Army Register of 1856, is 2,421,163. The return for the present year will probably be about 2,500,000, as it will include what was omitted in 1856, the returns from the State of Iowa and the Territories of New Mexico, Oregon, Washington, Kansas, and Nebraska.

1st. The Constitution of the United States, Art. 1, Sect. 8, Cl. 16, vests in Congress the power to provide for organizing, arming, and disciplining the militia, and for governing such part of them as may be employed in the service of the United States, reserving to the States respectively the appointment of the officers and the authority of training the militia according to the discipline prescribed by Congress.

The following laws may be examined to show how this constitutional power has been exercised:

1. An act more effectually to provide for the national defence by establishing an uniform militia throughout the United States.—Passed 8th May, 1792—1 vol. U. S. Statutes at Large 271.

2. Act of 6th July, 1798. 1 St. at Large, 576.
3. Act of 2d March, 1803. 2 St. at Large, 207.
4. Act of 3d March, 1803. 2 St. at Large, 215.
5. Act of 10th April, 1806. 2 St. at Large, 359.
6. Act of 18th April, 1814. 3 St. at Large, 134.
7. Act of 20th April, 1816. 3 St. at Large, 295.
8. Act of 12th May, 1820. 3 St. at Large, 577.

2d. The enrolment in the militia is variously regulated in the different States, and is enforced by moderate pecuniary fines.

3d. The mustering, training, and service are gratuitous.

4th. The officers are generally elective, and commissioned by the Governor of the State.

5th. Arms, ammunition, and accoutrements are furnished by the several States, and deposited in arsenals under State militia officers.

6th. Clothing is not furnished, nor do the militia, unless formed into volunteer companies or called in the service of the United States, wear uniform.

7th. The acts of Congress already referred to will show the authority for calling out the militia; but a clear comprehension on this point may be formed by consulting the following cases decided by the highest judicial tribunal: Martin *v.* Mott, 12 Wheaton's Reports, 19; Houston *v.* Moore, 5 Wheaton's Reports, 1.

8th. Numerous public documents upon the subject may be consulted in the two folio volumes of American State Papers which are appropriated to "Military Affairs," and which, I presume, can be, as they ought to be, found in the Library of the British Museum, and perhaps in the Libraries of Parliament.

---

## No. 102.—TO MR. HUTCHINSON.

London, March 16, 1857.

My dear Sir,—I hope the five cases have safely reached you. One of the bills of lading accompanied them in the "City of Baltimore:" the other I have retained.

Mr. M.'s bill of charges is enclosed:—in all £5. 12. 0. The Library Company can either remit this amount, or, if they prefer it, I will pay Mr. M. and be reimbursed when I get home. The charges and the freight, £7. 7. 10,—say sixty-three dollars, constitute the entire cost of what I think may be esteemed one of the most valuable acquisitions. I owe you many thanks for having suggested to me this mode of being accessory to benefiting our city and State.

The ministry, outvoted on the Canton outrage in the House of Commons, dissolved Parliament, and are hastening their appeal to the country. They are confident of a triumph, and indications are thus far strongly in their favor. Lord Palmerston's personal popularity has some resemblance to that of General Jackson: his partisans concede his violence and his arrogance, but call them an excess of patriotism. Bluster seems, in all countries, to have its charms for the mass. The new Parliament will meet probably about the 25th of May.

Remember us all affectionately to your family.

Ever faithfully yrs.

---

## No. 103.—TO MR. DIXON.

LONDON, March 23, 1857.

MY DEAR SIR,—We were all gratified at hearing from Fitz that the Russian helmet, picked up on a Crimean battle-field the day after the head had been knocked out of it, was acceptable to you. Armor of this sort augments in interest in a collection like yours, and with the lapse of every year.

I think your beautiful work on Surnames is faultless in its new edition. Mrs. D., Phil. and I have many thanks to make for our respective copies. In speaking of it, by-the-by, some days ago, to an acquaintance, he said he had in his library a book upon the subject, which he regarded as a curiously labored production, and which he sent me to look over. It is in two small octavo volumes, and is entitled " An Essay on Family Nomenclature, Historical, Etymological, and Humorous." The author is 'Mark Anthony Lower.' It is probable that you know and have the work, as its third edition was printed in 1849.

I looked for his notices of our three names. Of *Dixon*, he says in his list of "*sonnames*, nurse names, and diminutives"—what you seem to agree with, thus "Richard, Richards, *Richardson*, Ritchie, Rickards, Hitchins (!), Hitchinson, Hitchcock (!), Dick, Dickson, Dixon, Dickens, Dickinson, Dickerson."

Of *Homer*—he ranks it in a batch corresponding with the designations of "the divinities and celebrated persons of classical antiquity, such as Venus, Mars, Bacchus, *Homer*, Tully, Horace, Virgil, Cæsar. These are doubtless derived from traders' signs. The former three would be appropriate for Inns:—the remainder for the shops of mediæval dealers in books or their materials. So recently as the last generation a celebrated publisher gave his establishment the name of the 'Cicero's Head.'"

Of *Dallas*—he places it in a class deriving the second syllable from "*House*." This, with your signification of Dall, would make the name purport "the house in the valley." I remember that my father used to sport, by addressing my mother with a quotation from Swift, "Mrs. Dal*housie*, great Goddess of War!" etc., etc.

Always most truly yrs.

---

## No. 104.—TO DR. DUCACHET.

LONDON, March 25, 1857.

MY DEAR DR. DUCACHET,—I send you an exceedingly interesting judgment, but now pronounced by the Judicial Committee of the Privy Council on points of church furniture and ornamentation, parts of which would seem somewhat applicable to our dear old St. Stephen's.

The suits began in the Consistorial Court, where decrees were given by Dr. Lushington broadly against the use of crosses, candlesticks, credence tables, and altars. Appeals were taken to the Court of Arches, and Dr. Lushington's decisions were affirmed. Finally, the cases were taken before the Judicial Committee of the Privy Council, and, after a protracted and able argument, have ended in the judgment I enclose, which affirms in part and reverses in part, and which is characterized by such deep research and sound sense that I presume it will be accepted as conclusive on the merits of the controversy.

It would appear to be distinctly adjudged that the Communion table should be of wood and movable:—and I am under the impression that ours is of white marble, and too ponderous to be stirred without machinery. How is this? If as I suppose, then I think it would be wise to consult upon the subject in vestry, and, under your controlling advice and wisdom, to have such steps taken as may prevent any charge of deviation from material forms. Of this, however, I am rather presumptuous in making a suggestion. You will excuse (won't you?) what springs only from an affectionate interest in all that relates to yourself and our temple of Protestant worship. Perhaps you know that many years ago, I assailed in verse the cross surmounting the steeple of St. Peter's:—Bishop Doane replied to my rhymes: and it is now authoritatively established that I was wrong and the learned Bishop right. "*Stare decisis*" is a rule alike orthodox and conservative.

Your disciples here are all in good health, and send their kindest regards to Mrs. Ducachet and yourself.

Always your faithful & sincere friend, etc.

---

## No. 105.—TO MR. CASS.

LONDON, April 2, 1857.

MY DEAR SIR,—Let me thank you for your two private letters of the 11th and 17th of March, which reached me at the same time three days ago. They have led me to think that the informal and unofficial correspondence which I kept up with Mr. Marcy may not be unacceptable to you. One prefers, in lounging or in writing, not to be in full dress.

I pity you all from the bottom of my heart. Nothing can be more deplorable than the harassing state of siege to which every new administration is subjected. Your description—which almost resolves the whole country into a heaving mass of Ins and Outs—reminds one of the recent *bon-mot* of the Duke D'Aumale who, speaking of the social state of Paris, said there were but three classes, "les fonctionnaires, les factionnaires et les actionnaires."

The elections here have absorbed attention. The whole operation has been effected with a sort of "*snap-judgment* rapidity,"—much faster than a debatable question would be brought to a vote in the Senate. John Bull can't bear being without his omnipotent Parliament for a moment. He fancies the whole social edifice at hazard, and he hurries blindly to manufacture a new one. Not one-sixth of the old body will undergo change:—and such changes as are made do not spring from calm consideration, which moves slowly, but from the personal passions of the moment, which are quick in striking. Two features of result are already quite obvious:—a great accession to the incongruous strength of what is called the Liberal party, and a decisive individual triumph to Lord Palmerston. The early scenes of the coming Parliament will be full of ministerial exultation; but in the belief of many astute politicians, this will be short-lived, for the elements of discord among Liberals are countless and impracticable. If Lord John Russell exhibit his usual tact, the city of London has re-endorsed him in a manner which may make him an early successor to Lord Palmerston. Much, but not everything will be indicated by the choice of a Speaker;—and it is amazing how few gentlemen of either party are admitted into the category of the competent.

Nothing worthy of a regular despatch. Not a syllable from the Foreign Office on the maritime war Convention. The attitude of Lord John Russell as to this will seriously tend to defeat the movement. Besides, Cobden and Bright and Gibson and Walmsley have lost their elections. Yet, it is worth while noting that a correspondent of the *Post* is laboring a series of essays, and with some adroitness leans to the *projet* of Mr. Marcy. I am quite in a fever to hear from *you* on the subject.

Somebody, it appears, finds access to the *penetralia* of your department:—for I find in the *Morning Star* of to-day, as extracted from the New York *Herald* of the 19th March, what *professes* to be a copy of the Central American Treaty, but what in fact is a copy of one of its *projets* subsequently altered. So that even your unperfected documents are, for some purpose or other, dug from their dormitories and paraded in the papers. I wonder whether the Senators may not have been perplexed with the several draughts, adapted to my several instructions, which I transmitted to Mr. Marcy? The mistakes in newspapers as to the provisions and phraseology of the instrument, are innumerable and to me incomprehensible. But fifteen days remain of the six months during which the ratifications are to be exchanged. I suppose they will complain here of the short time left them for deliberation on the amendments. They will have ten days, not more, should your final instructions come by the next steamer. Perhaps the whole period will be allowed to run out! As soon as it appears that the proper moment has arrived, I shall write you a special letter on a special topic as regards myself.

Ferouk Khan (pronounced here Cawn), the Persian ambassador, cottons singularly to your minister. He prides himself upon having made the Treaty with Mr. Spence: and proposes to remain here until he can exchange its ratifications. If he did not suffer dreadfully from sea-sickness, he assures me that he would visit the United States, and expresses a hope that the two countries may soon interchange diplomatic representatives.

Señor Don Bravo, the newly arrived envoy from Spain, is quite an agreeable gentleman:—a genuine black-eyed, black-browed, black-haired, black-moustached, sallow-tinted, short, and compact caballero. With a smattering of his tongue, fetched from the memories of fifty years ago, I get along with him tolerably well. They say there are shades on his past; but of that I know nothing.

The Greek minister, whom I esteem as one of the most intelligent and estimable of the Corps, was enchanted on my shewing him that by our new Tariff, *currants*, under the description of dried fruit, would be admitted at a duty of 8½ instead of the old 40 per cent. ad valorem. By-the-by, I wrote Mr. Marcy that this gentleman, in order to cultivate the intercourse between our and his country, had been instructed to suggest the expediency of our converting the *Commercial Agent* of the United States in Greece into a *Consul:* the latter allowing more public manifestation of regard from the Court. He has spoken to me again on the subject. I presume Mr. Marcy was preoccupied with arranging old matters, and avoided new ones, as he did not notice the idea.

The news from China, given out by the ministerial candidates at the hustings, to the effect that the Emperor did not approve the conduct of Commissioner Yeh, does not seem to have been well founded. Now that it has served its purpose, it is discredited. The electric telegraph is not the most reliable agency. I perceive prevailing here among official men a solicitude that the United States should join England and France in their proposed pressure against the wall of exclusiveness within which the Chinese choose to exist. I retain the opinion expressed in a former letter, that the two powerful allies meditate a serious aggressive movement, if not a military occupation, in the disorganized land of Tartars, Teas, and Junks. The moment is propitious. Neither Louis Napoleon nor Lord Palmerston is averse to maintaining tranquillity at home, by turning the public gaze to military proceedings at a distance. The merchants do not seem to apprehend, as a consequence, any important disturbance of commerce.

Allow me to enforce the suggestion made in my last despatch, respecting the Supreme Court's decision in the case of Dred Scott, by adding that if we do not, in some authentic form, let this prejudiced portion of the world have access to the *whole truth*, it is a hundred to one that the *dissenting opinions* of Judges McLean and Curtis will be represented and almost universally received as *the Judgment.* As to obtaining from the Press here, or anywhere in Europe, a fair and impartial exposition of the relation of slavery to our national constitution, so as to vindicate the principles and practice of our national democracy, no hope can be conceived more chimerical.

Parliament is to assemble on the 30th of this month. I am told that the swearing in of the members will consume a week, and no important business will take place before the expiration of that time. The Queen will not open it in person, as she will hardly have recovered the fatigue of dropping another pearl in the jewelry casket of her devoted subjects. Her Majesty still drives out every day, showing that if there be no royal road to learning in general, there is undoubtedly one to the multiplication table. Pray present my respects and regards to all around you, and believe me

Always cordially yrs.

---

## No. 106.—TO MR. MARKOE.

LONDON, April 3, 1857.

MY DEAR MARKOE,—Don't abuse me—though you have certainly a right to do so—for putting your kind energies under contribution to accomplish, if possible, two small purposes which I found it impossible to avoid undertaking.

Primero. Can the Secretary of War, under the statements of the two notes I enclose, be induced to spare poor Mr. W. H. B., who unwittingly enlisted in our army, and has incurred the penalty of desertion? His family is of high respectability, and I should be much pleased if they could be gratified by having their reckless kinsman sent home.

Secondo. Has there not been published in Washington a work entitled "Report on the Commercial Relations of the United States," Vol. 1? The Department of State ought to possess it for distribution among the foreign legations. I certainly ought to have a copy. But I specially want a copy for "The Statistical Society," and if your department can't order it sent to me, you must be kind enough to direct any one of the librarians on the Avenue to address it to me in the next despatch bag, letting me know the price and debiting me. Pishey Thomson, or his successor, I dare say has the book.

Let me say to you—of course in profound personal confidence—that the amendments made to the treaty by the Senate are a series of miserable little criticisms, doctrinal and verbal, utterly unworthy the dignity of the body and the gravity of the occasion. I can scarcely understand how, by the utmost excitement of filibustering declamation, such paltry picking should have occupied that great council for three months. In a little while the minority will have no resort but to laugh off their folly as well as they can. But two weeks left for the exchange of ratifications, and yet I have nothing on hand! Perhaps this beautiful exhibition of senatorial wisdom is to be rounded off by—but, *n'importe!*—the thing was satisfactory all round, to both Governments and both Peoples—conformed rigidly even as to phrases and terms to instructions, and was most flatteringly eulogized by Marcy "for *judgment and skill*" of negotiation, and eagerly sanctioned by President Pierce and Queen Victoria, and the Press on both sides:—but it got into a dark hole and has been nibbled at by rats in search of food for faction. Unless we go on sinking deeper and deeper in the mire of filibusterism, and encouraging the revival of the age of buccaneering—an ignominy not altogether impossible—the treaty, with all its faults, will, as John Q. said, "stand the test of time and talent." I especially think so, because, after being buffeted about by eminent men so long, its substance and spirit remain unchanged.

I am waiting to hear from Washington about two matters which must be definitively disposed of before the moment can arrive for adopting your hint as to the mode of acting on my own subject. I have no idea of a peevish and petty course:—and the instant all misconception of motive can be avoided and all imputation of idle pique, it may be proper to act frankly and finally. There has been "negative pregnant" enough not to be mistaken, and I am quite ready for what was thought not unlikely when I started on the mission. I find no fault anywhere.

Palmerston's star is in the ascendant for another *year* at least. His party, and his ministerial associates particularly, are flushed with victorious exultation.

My affectionate regards to all.

Ever faithfully yrs.

---

## No. 107.—TO MR. CASS.

LONDON, April 7, 1857.

MY DEAR SIR,—I have not had time to prepare a despatch since Mr. Evans came an hour ago with the Central American treaty, and your accompanying official letter of instruction. Yet I do not like to allow the Fulton to leave to-morrow morning without a word from me.

This matter will, of course, have my earliest attention; and, as I agree with you that the real substance of the arrangement remains unaffected by the amendments of the Senate, I have strong confidence that this government will, without much delay, pursue the wise example of the President. Varieties of opinion on an entanglement so complicated and so multifarious in its bearings, cannot be avoided. It is the fruit of the Clayton-Bulwer treaty.

I have yet ten days before the period for an exchange of ratifications expires. All the necessary copies will be prepared this evening, and the matter fully submitted to Lord Clarendon to-morrow morning. The only expunging on which it is possible they may hesitate is that relating to the grants of land.

Since my last, the result of the election in Middlesex has given a still loftier tone of exultation to the Palmerstonians.

Always faithfully yrs.

---

### No. 108.—TO LORD CLARENDON.

24 Portland Place, April 7, 1857.

My dear Lord Clarendon,—I shall be able to send your lordship, in the morning, official copies of the treaty, with the Senate's amendments, and the President's ratification, and the letter of instruction to me from Mr. Cass on the subject.

In the mean while, I have thought it might be agreeable to you to have the draft I prepared for my own use, by which the *locus in quo* and bearing of each amendment might be seen at a glance.

The temper of the President is most admirable:—his *acts* better natured even than his words. Your lordship need not be reminded that ten days only are left of our prescribed time.

With assurances of the highest consideration,

Ever faithfully yrs.

---

### No. 109.—TO MR. KNEASS.

London, April 9, 1857.

My dear Sir,—Your letter of the 19th ultimo reached me a few days ago.

I have procured and now transmit to you the Act of the British Parliament, 18 & 19 Vict. c. 120, which you think may be usefully added to the library of your Department of Surveys in the city government.

On the subject of Sewers and Drains, great activity and research have recently been manifested by the Board of Public Works, at the head of which is Sir Benjamin Hall, in order to effect a permanent purification of this vast city:—and it will give me pleasure to find myself, on taking the necessary trouble, able to send you something from this source of value to the future health and comfort of Philadelphia.

Very respectfully your friend and servant.

---

## No. 110.—TO MR. CASS.

London, April 10, 1857.

My dear Sir,—Although I have several irons in the fire, there is no business sufficiently ripe for a despatch.

I sent the whole Central American Record to the F. O. three days ago, and I saw Lord Clarendon yesterday. It is obvious that the amendments are not thought materially to change the original design and text, except as to the Land Grants. Some soreness is felt at the abrupt treatment experienced by the second clause of the second separate article, though substantially and practically it reaches the same end. His lordship, however, had not consulted his colleagues, and did not intend expressing any opinion before doing so. Some apprehension as to Parliament was intimated; and he reminded me that Mr. Gladstone had already attacked the ministry for aliening a colony without the consent of Parliament and without consideration. He said, too, among other things, that their treaty with Honduras remained yet unratified, and this broad handing over the Bay Islands bodily, contained in the amendment, to Honduras, though heretofore not asked by Honduras, might put her up to reject the treaty,—a far-fetched supposition to be sure, considering how immensely advantageous to Honduras that treaty was in respect to the railway. He wanted me to agree to extend the time for ratification:—the cabinet was scattered: and its regular meeting would not take place before next Thursday, the 16th. I said that was entirely out of my power:—the expiration of the time was prescribed in the instrument ratified by the President, and nothing could now suspend or change it. This conversation was casual, and apparently so unofficial that I am rather reluctant in repeating it. It certainly, however, involved nothing definitive, and had only a tendency to disclose the personal opinions and thoughts of Lord C. for the time being. They have left me under the impression, that, notwithstanding the rough handling of the Senate, the treaty will finally be ratified, and the ratifications exchanged this day week or sooner.

The spring is hastening on, with rich green turf, glowing flowers, and expanding shrubbery. The parks and gardens and terraces of London are already beautiful, and give great comfort to those who are kept in town. *Absente Parliamento*, fashion has flown back into the country:—to return about the 10th of May.

The new House of Commons, it is agreed on all sides, will have an unwieldy and unmanageable weight of Liberalism in it. If that weight can be solidified as a party, distinct and *prononcée*, and be once brought to move, it will rush into Reform in a manner to constitute an epoch in British history. The number of able, influential, and active men who think, talk, and act for sweeping political and social changes, is greater all over the country than in the United States is imagined.

Lord C. told me that Lord Napier had written home in the highest delight with his new residence:—that he was enthusiastic about everybody and everything:—and that in such a spirit he could not fail to please.

My best respects to all around you, and in particular to Miss Cass.

Always faithfully yrs.

---

## No. 111.—TO MR. CASS.

LONDON, April 17, 1857.

MY DEAR SIR,—Lord C.'s proposed *proviso* strikes me as much more open to the senatorial objections than was the clause as originally framed. It enlists the United States in favor of the ratification of the Honduras Convention, and so affects them with a full knowledge and approbation of all its terms:—it connects the two treaties by a direct and indissoluble link.

Now, the sole and declared object of the original provision was to express the fact which removed the Bay Islands from the category of differences:—that fact being one derived exclusively from her Majesty's Foreign Office, to wit, that they had ceased to be a British colony whose existence was irreconcilable with the purpose and in violation of the letter of the Clayton-Bulwer treaty, but had become, under the admitted sovereignty of Honduras, a free territory. All that *we* had to look to was the extinction of the British pretension to sovereignty there, and the retrocession of the islands to Honduras in any form or shape that she, Honduras, might be freely willing to accept them. We could, consistently with our public principles, interfere with the terms of a contract over which Honduras had absolute and rightful control, only by refusing to treat with England at all unless she announced the restoration of the islands to Honduras, and their voluntary acceptance as restored by that republic. As to the conditions upon which this bargain might be made agreeable to each other, either in reference to the actual inhabitants of the islands, or to the opening of an inter-oceanic railway, or any other measure of sovereign action, our intermeddling would be intrusive and absurd.

These were the views of my instructions. Hence the original provision in the 2d clause of the second Separate Article, with which Mr. Marcy expressed his approbation, as in fact he and General Pierce did with the whole *projet* when matured. But the Senate did not like the provision, and have substituted another more substantial and direct. And now comes Lord Clarendon with a *proviso* that means to assert, if it mean anything, that England had a mental reservation, not expressed in the original provision or in any part of the treaty, not to hold herself bound, unless the convention with Honduras was ratified, by her distinct, palpable, and positive engagement with the United States "to recognize and respect in all future time the independence and rights of the said free territory as part of the Republic of Honduras." What had the United States to do with the *ratification* of their convention? That was their own lookout. If they entertained a doubt about it, why not offer to refer to it in some way? If they entertained, as probably they now entertain, no doubt at all, then it is not surprising that they considered the mere making of the convention as equivalent to its ratification, and so at once, and without deeming it at all expedient to communicate its contents, they agree to start from its making, and make the stipulations for all future time which I have recited. Wait for ratification, indeed! Look to Honduras for the efficacy of our treaty with Great Britain! I can understand why Lord C. may shrink from doing what the Senate requires, but that he should hope to extenuate his shrinking by offering a *proviso* whose purport never would have been and never can be accepted is incomprehensible to me.

It is said to be useless to "cry over spilled milk." The philosophy is sound and practical. Nevertheless, in extreme anxiety to do nothing that may affect the public interests injuriously, I shall wait to hear from you on this finality to the year's efforts to adjust the Central American questions.

I have been obliged to write in great haste, and possibly with a looseness which will tax your indulgent kindness.

Always faithfully yrs.

---

## No. 112.—TO MR. KENNEDY.

LONDON, April 21, 1857.

MY DEAR SIR,—Your parcel addressed to the Bishop of Oxford arrived safely; and of course you know that I shall take pleasure in conforming to your wishes about it.

I furnished his lordship in July last some American experience on the execution of capital sentences in private:—too late for use in the then existing Parliament. He has the reform much at heart: but all reforms here are slow in gathering confidence, and their advocates omit nothing to strengthen themselves against resistance, before making the final push. The United States is a quiver full of arrows for them:—teeming with successful experiments in all practical improvements. It is really quite surprising, and certainly not disagreeable, to note the numberless ways in which the new world has turned teacher to the old.

I will not forget the Dean of St. Paul's.

The relations of the two countries are, I hope, independent of diplomatic formularies: as the Central American treaty returned here with only a single feather on its back that broke it down. The point of difference between the Senate and the ministry was whittled to the smallest end of nothing. It is possible, after swallowing a camel, to gasp at a gnat.

Pray present the best regards of Mrs. D. and myself to Mrs. K.

Very sincerely yrs.

---

## No. 113.—TO MR. CASS.

LONDON, April 24, 1857.

MY DEAR SIR,—You get by this steamer more of my writing than you will be able to tolerate.

Mr. E. was yesterday entrusted with a despatch which failed to go on Wednesday owing to an accident happening to the Hermann. He carries also back, in virgin purity, the unexchanged ratification of the Central American treaty. As bearer of a private letter from Mr. Buchanan to Lord Clarendon, he was most kindly and courteously treated by his lordship.

The *coup-de-grâce* given to the treaty has, as yet, been unnoticed in the newspapers. This I presume to arise from an uncertainty as to the most expedient course in reference to its effect on the new Parliament. Even the fact is unmentioned.

The foreign ministers at this Court are invited (or summoned) to be present in Manchester on the 5th of May next, at the opening of the Art Treasures Exhibition, destined, under the auspices of Prince Albert, to surpass everything of the sort ever undertaken!

Lord Lyndhurst sets us all a capital example. He is 85, and yet, as Mr. E. will tell you, at a crowded soirée two nights ago, he was the observed of all observers as well with ladies as gentlemen:—that too in the drawing-room of a Liberal, although he is an incurable Tory.

The Queen recovers more rapidly than would a farmer's

wife. It is even surmised that her Majesty may be energetic enough to open Parliament in person this day week. She is fond of going through that ceremony, which she is said to perform with peculiar grace and emphasis.

The imbroglio between Austria and Sardinia promises to disturb the serenity of European politics. Count Cavour overwhelmed Count Buol with too much united force and quiet:—the latter, of course, can't forgive. As to Switzerland and Prussia about Neufchâtel, the controversy is finally hushed up by France and England to the disadvantage of the Republic. She pays money, and permits a title derogatory to her territorial independence.

Lord Elgin is off for Hong-Kong. So are land and naval reinforcements, quite enough to plant a colony wherever they please among the distracted and decadent Chinese.

Cordially yrs.

---

## No. 114.—TO COL. MURRAY.

LONDON, April 28, 1857.

MY DEAR SIR,—Your packet for Mr. D. was received and forwarded to Mr. Mason in a despatch bag.

General Mercer is one of those clear thinkers who are not easily misled by mere appearance or sound. Our system constitutes, as the final negotiator of treaties, a popular body of 62 members! They amend such instruments with all the freedom they amend ordinary bills, engrafting each his peculiar notion, and indulging claptrap and bunkum without stint. This is diplomacy run riot:—and one must not be astonished at finding foreign powers occasionally restive under its operation. As early as 1794, our Senate struck whole clauses from Chief Justice Jay's treaty:—in 1824, they so mutilated one made by Mr. Rush, that this government refused, just as they have now refused, to exchange the ratifications. Whoever was the Senator to offer the amendment to strike out and insert the twenty words about the Bay Islands, he alone has the glory of killing the treaty:—as to all the other paltry picking, it was regarded with indifference:—*that* was esteemed an intolerable dictation, and, though with extreme reluctance, was visited with a tit for tat. Nothing was more perfectly innocuous than the clause as it originally stood; but its treatment has, I fear, given the adversary a very dangerous weapon to fight with. Whence came that truly valiant and filibustering amendment?—that, to us, is shrouded in senatorial secrecy—but *it is known here*, and will amaze us, they say, hereafter. An outside concoction?

The Cobden party committed a blunder, and dearly have they answered it:—not in moving against the Chinese war, but in, immediately upon success *there*, consenting to assume a *defensive* attitude against the charge of coalition. They found out their mistake at too late a stage of the canvass.

After all, *blustering* goes a mighty distance in practical politics—and of that Lord Palmerston employs no small a load.

Very truly always yrs.

---

## No. 115.—TO MR. CASS.

London, April 28, 1857.

My dear Sir,—I send a cutting from the *Spectator* of the 25th inst. It is, as you know, the best *weekly* published in London. This is the first and only notice yet taken of the non-exchange of ratifications. I do not doubt that the intimation in the last line is, in a certain sense, well founded:—and that the ministers prefer that the annunciation of their having rejected the Senate's amendment shall be made by them in reply to parliamentary "interpellations," accompanied by such justificatory and soothing remarks as they may think the occasion calls for.

The negotiation as to modifying the rules of maritime war has been formally suspended. I have reason to know that the answer to our proposal has been prepared in two forms, and was on the point of being laid before the cabinet and then sent to me. Both forms declined:—

one assigning reasons at length, the other merely saying that just now the *projet* was not expedient in the judgment of her Majesty's government. My belief is that Lord Palmerston favors it, and that as soon as he can reinforce his strength in the House sufficiently to beat Lord John Russell's opposition to it down, he will make it a cabinet question. Mr. Lindsay, a most intelligent and re-elected member, and a devoted friend of Mr. Cobden as well as of free trade, said to me the other day that this was *the second* time on which, in reference to surrendering the right to use privateers, we had *retracted* at the very moment when they were persuading the government to close with the offer. "To me," he added, "it is perfectly incomprehensible how you can think of giving up privateers, when you contrast the size of our two navies." He is amazed that Mr. Marcy's proposal was not instantly closed with.

The Speaker of the House will be chosen the day after to-morrow. Then the swearing in will go on for a week. And on Thursday, the 8th May, Parliament will be opened by Commission:—unless "the little lady" should, in the mean time, muster strength enough to go through a shewy ceremony in which it is said she acts her part admirably, and of which she is therefore naturally very fond.

You notice the assiduous and unremitting courtship of France and Russia. It will yet end in something *éclatante*:—especially if the British press perseveres in its recent labors to mortify and exasperate the self-esteem of the "degenerated race." The *Edinburgh Review* and the *Times* have forcible and humbling thrusts at the undeniable diminution of French numbers and "physique." The Grand Duke Constantine is now the Imperial guest at Paris:—and his Majesty the Czar is said to contemplate a visit in the course of the summer.

Your refusal to join the hunt against the Chinese is not relished. It is characterized as a cold, selfish, and isolating policy:—not actually disapproved, but extremely disliked. If they can't get your representative out there to combine with them, they will probably try their best to make his time unpleasant:—if he side with them in the remotest manner, that will be enough to produce upon "the ignorant Chinese" all the "moral effect" they desire.

With cordial respects yrs.

## No. 116.—TO MR. CASS.

London, May 8, 1857.

My dear Sir,—The oracular speech of her Majesty, delivered yesterday, through the Lord Chancellor and his fellow-commissioners, to Parliament, was sent to me from the F. O. late last night. I enclose it. You will note the 5th paragraph as amazingly precise, explanatory, and clear!

Observe also, that though Reform be allowed a place, it is only *Law* reform. *Expressio unius*, etc. For this session, then, the ministry are for that *only*. It is certainly important:—but a great deal more is expected, and the opposition will probably hurry to get in advance. Opinion is becoming every day bolder. At large public meetings, one hears not unfrequently "No State Church," "No legislative Bishops," "No hereditary law-makers," "No property franchise," etc., etc.

I cannot resist the impression that this government contemplate taking possession of a large portion of the southern territory of China. An adequate military force will soon be there, both French and English:—and our squadron will find it hard work to abstain from the general foray. If you have Mr. Reed still with you, tell him there is a capital article on the Chinese Question in the last, or April, number of the *Edinburgh Review*.

Always faithfully yrs.

---

## No. 117.—TO LADY MORGAN.

London, May 9, 1857.

My dear Lady Morgan,—It was my intention to seize the pleasure which your remark to Mrs. D. held out, although somewhat apprehensive of being an intruder. Your kind "*remind*" of this morning gives to the lunch on Monday an attraction not to be resisted, and as my countrymen say when wishing to make an impressive appointment, "You'll find me *thar*."

Always faithfully, your Ladyship's
Most obedient servant.

## No. 118.—TO MR. PISHEY THOMSON.

LONDON, May 9, 1857.

MY DEAR SIR,—Pray accept my very cordial thanks for your letter of the 2d instant. It would have been replied to at once, but that I was preparing for an absence of several days in Manchester.

I have been much interested in your account of the Memorial proposed to be erected to the Rev. John Cotton in the Chapel connected with the Church of St. Botolph in Boston, Lincolnshire; and I shall feel it a high privilege to attend at the contemplated ceremony in grateful remembrance of that eminent clergyman. Whether I shall be able, at the time that may be fixed upon for the inauguration, to quit London, I cannot at present say; but, as soon as apprised of the day's being finally designated,—which I understood the Rev. G. B. Blenkin to say might be at the close of July next—I will promptly determine that point and let you know. This reticence is in a measure dictated by my knowing that you desire to give to the solemnity a partly international aspect, which I am not quite certain that three months hence it will be in my power to aid you in doing.

Mr. Ingram was kind enough to offer to send me an account of your city, and I frankly accepted his offer, supposing that it would be in the shape of an ordinary pamphlet or guide-book. He has, however, sent me your really magnificent and costly folio of "The History and Antiquities of Boston, etc., etc." The work is truly beautiful:—but is it not too valuable for me to retain?

I remember you at Washington with much pleasure, and regret to hear that your health is bad. Should you visit London while I am here, I beg that I may have an opportunity to renew our acquaintance.

Very faithfully and sincerely yrs.

## No. 119.—TO MR. M.

LONDON, May 14, 1857.

MY DEAR MR. MARKOE,—A thousand thanks for "The Commercial Relations," one half at least of which I beg you to present to Mr. Flagg. The volume graces the library of the Statistical Society, and lies ready to be devoured on my table.

As many acknowledgments for your successful intercession with Secretary Floyd about young Bamping.

Indeed, I am very much in your debt for these and similar acts of assistance. So, to wipe off a score or two, let me amuse you with a reference to a recent symposium.

On Monday last, *Lady Morgan* (Sydney Owenson, the Wild Irish Girl, Ida of Athens, etc.) summoned me to meet a friend of hers *at lunch.* I went at half-past two. Her house is a small curiosity shop, crowded with interesting relics. She has Voltaire's writing chair, and a sketch of his study. The walls are literally concealed by likenesses and autographs. Everything, like herself, is "*en petit*" and antique, except the music she never fails to enlist. She is so short that when sitting her feet can't reach the floor. Her vivacity is boundless, and her intellectual attractions recognized, as you will see, by the first minds of the age. She dresses as you must imagine a discreet sylph would dress, that is, in a mass of light, many-colored gossamery stuff, with ribbons flying in all directions, and a fanciful coquettish cap. Well! she rouges highly, and, though turned of eighty, might under the magnetic mask of wit, were her sight and hearing not imperfect, pass for something over fifty. She placed me on her right at her little round table, and inquired in a whisper if I was aware of the celebrities present. "They were a cluster of brilliants, and I knew them all." Here you have them. Close on my right sat *Macaulay*, the fullest and fastest man in conversation I ever met with:—his only defect an uncontrollable effort, arising from excessive self-esteem, to monopolize the talk. On the left of Lady Morgan was Lord *Carlisle*, the Lord Lieutenant of Ireland (Morpeth). Then came *Hallam* (Middle Ages), a most interesting person in appearance and manners, suffering to such an extent from disease as to be unable to walk without help, and perhaps evincing a partial loss of mental energy. There too was that most excellent historian of Greece, *Grote*, whom I like and respect the more every time I see him. Near him and opposite the hostess twinkled away the pink eyes of Albino *Lowe*, the only highly gifted individual of that species perhaps in being: and we rounded off with *Charles Villiers*, a true, talented, and uncompromising liberal, I had almost said democrat, albeit the brother of Clarendon: *Monckton Milnes*, a poet, politician, parliamentary speaker, and ready converser:—and, though last far from least, *Lady Combermere*.

Now I won't indulge in repeating the numberless admirable things said at this cosey lunch, during about an hour and a half. The eagerness to talk far outstripped the eagerness to eat. At one time, I believe every man was leaning forward over the table and giving to the whole unlistening company his particular idea. The bursts of merriment were unceasing. If I were a bookmaking tourist, I am certain that I could expand the intellectual gold at this lunch through an octavo of leaves. Review the names, and realize its character.

I think it very probable that you would prefer a description of some geological cabinet, but I have no relish for that sort of thing. Sir Roderick Murchison now and then walks me through his rich collections of fragments of ores, spars, rocks, etc., and I take it for granted that they are all very curious, very valuable, and very instructive:—but, "*chacun à son goût*," and mine never ran in that direction, farther than to admire your drawers full of what I would scarcely be willing to allow house-room.

Did you get Guizot's study of Peel? That and Dr. Kane's book have aroused more *furore* among the ordinary run of readers here than any other new publications. Lever has just launched a new novel, "The Fortunes of Glencore," which can be read at a single sitting, though in three volumes, and is really full of strong pictures and capital notions of life.

I have a mind to rush you into the Art Treasures Exhibition at Manchester, whose opening I felt it a sort of official duty to attend. But the labor would be intolerable. You must wait until another appropriate fit comes over me.

We are all well. Your notion of Florence is too wise to last. It would benefit you, your wife, and the whole family:—*therefore*, I take it for granted you have long since given it up.

My best love to every one at home.

Always faithfully yrs.

---

## No. 120.—TO MR. CASS.

LONDON, May 15, 1857.

MY DEAR SIR,—The officers of the Niagara have crowded my despatch bag with letters, official and private. You will probably, therefore, have full accounts of her performance in crossing the Atlantic. Their representations are glowing in her favor. She was able to accomplish two-thirds of her voyage in six days:—subsequently she took it leisurely, and reached Gravesend on the eighteenth after leaving the Narrows.

I am afraid matters are not as advanced on this side as they seem to have been thought by Mr. Toucey. There is a difficulty, owing to her draft of water and certain unfinished dredging, in her taking the place in the Thames originally assigned, and, indeed, it was contemplated, a few hours before she entered the Downs, to have signalled and sent her to Liverpool. I cannot learn that the Cable is near ready: and when it shall be, the calculation seems to be that it cannot be stowed on board the ship at a rate more rapid than twenty miles of its length per day:—so that full two months will be consumed in shipping alone the 1200 miles. Should she begin to receive her cargo, which is a bold hope, by the 1st of June, she cannot finish loading before the 1st of August, even supposing no accident or delay:—and thus the most advantageous season for laying the wires must be lost. It would, I think, be imprudent to run the risks of September or October. On the whole, unless Captain Hudson, or Professor Morse, apply the screw effectually to the operatives here, and push them to a speed beyond all their habits, the grand consummation will be delayed till next summer. As in military, so in mechanical, exploits England always lags until the second or third campaign. The thing will be achieved no doubt: but not by any means so promptly or punctually as American goaheadness would exact.

Queen Victoria, in spite of the prevailing popular prejudice, has invited the Russian Grand Duke Constantine to pay her a visit. Of course such a summons brings him shortly to Osborne:—although it is gossiped as an unprecedented barbarism that, some years ago, when the present Emperor Alexander was here and at a ball, on being apprised by the Master of Ceremonies that her Majesty required him as a partner in the next quadrille, he very coolly and imperturbably answered that he was engaged, and declined the honor! Constantine is said to be fatally bent on the mischief of breaking asunder the Anglo-Gallican alliance. Success to the Imperial politician!

You must not let me worry you unreasonably with these letters. My aim is to keep you *au fait* to current yet unofficial topics in this maelstrom of intelligence and bustle. Stop me unhesitatingly as soon as you tire.

Very faithfully yrs.

P. S.—Mr. Marcy made some arrangement with the captains of the Cunarders, by which our despatch bags were confided exclusively to their control and care. I hate suspicion, and the plan may in the long run work well:—but when I look at your violated letter about New Granada, which came by the Arabia, and compare its contents with the speech of Lord Palmerston on the 15th inst., I feel as if I could not explain, without offence to some one, so singular a coincidence. If our negotiations become delicate, it would be well not to flinch from employing special messengers. Economy is an excellent aim, but it is possible to overshoot it.

G. M. D.

---

## No. 121.—TO MR. CASS.

London, May 26, 1857.

My dear Sir,—Mr. William Brown, of Liverpool, addressed to me the enclosed letter somewhat too late to be sent in the last despatch bag. He is so worthy of every consideration and respect that I am sure you will not object to hear his appeal for aid as to the survey of the railway route in Honduras, although it be informally made and may not obtain the least acquiescence.

I suppose we cannot have too many lines of Isthmian transit. Until some thirty years hence, when a direct communication with the shores of the Pacific shall run upon the surface of our own soil, it will not be wise to rely on a single road at Panama, or San Juan, or Tehuantepec. We cannot perhaps have too many strings to our bow. Still, the extent to which we will co-operate with others, either governments or companies, in projects for opening these passages, deserves careful consideration. I think it quite obvious that the commercial interest of England is contemplating an extensive settlement on the cotton-yielding lands of Southern China, and looks to hold direct and rapid intercourse across the Isthmus. As peaceable competitors, our merchants, with the advantage of location, would distance them in this trade, as they are fast distancing them everywhere:—yet it might not be prudent to facilitate their selling cheap China cotton to the manufacturers of Manchester.

Your private letter of the 5th instant reached me but two days ago. This slow progress may have an accidental cause:—but my despatches from the United States have recently so regularly been violated on their way, that I am really growing suspicious. I mentioned to you on a former occasion that your despatch about New Granada had been torn open;—and by the very next bag, a large communication, with the seal of the department, had undergone the same treatment. The apprehensions created by such a state of things destroy the unreserved character of correspondence. There is a mischievous Paul Pry somewhere between this and Washington.

Thus far the votes in Parliament indicate, to a casual observer, a large and firm Palmerstonian majority. Knowing ones, however, say significantly "wait a little:"—and they mean by a *little* a whole year at least. By that time, the strong infusion of Reform in the new House will have fermented, found its way to the top, and be prepared and able to shake the smooth surface of the ministerial caldron. It is astonishing how patiently they bide their time. The power to "wait" is a great one.

Of course quidnuncs affect great anxiety as to the relations between the two countries. The rejection of the treaty, which they now realize, and the spirited articles in our newspapers just received, have created a lively stir. The Press here still holds back; an abstinence which may be ascribed to a dread of provoking the Premier to exhibit his, at this moment, irresistible power in the Commons, and so committing the country to an extravagance which in a twelvemonth he will find impossible.

The Russian minister seems pleased with his news from Washington, and prophesies the abrogation by Congress of the treaty of 1850:—a proceeding quite unequivocally represented to Lord Clarendon when I read to him Mr. Marcy's No. 13, of 24th May, 1856, where it is stated as a resort to which we might be ultimately driven.

The difficulties about the Niagara rather increase than lessen. The officers, however, behave exceedingly well under the circumstances. They still hope not to lose the summer.

Very faithfully yrs.

---

## No. 122.—TO MR. CASS.

London, June 5, 1857.

My dear Sir,—The Whitsuntide Holidays dispersed the members of Parliament throughout the country:—and, under the influence of animal magnetism perhaps, I too went out of town for several days. It is impossible to imagine anything more beautiful or more perfect in all its details, *intra et extra mœnia*, than the rural life of a man of fortune in England. When the clear and comfortable weather of early June is superadded, a miserable devil emerging from the smoke, dust, fog, and odor of London, finds himself in Elysium among the hills of Hampshire. I came back yesterday.

Our good countrymen, in heavy battalions, are winding their way across the island, to spread themselves all over Europe and part of Asia. I found my table covered with their cards and introductories, and they are most cordially welcome. There are among them Professors, Chancellors, Bishops and Clergymen *sans nombre.*

The Niagara goes to Portsmouth to-day, to be so altered, as I understand, as may fit her for receiving the submarine cable. She will be put in one of the Royal Docks for the purpose. I am asked to give my official assent to this proceeding:—but, although willing to aid the great object in every possible way, I do not feel empowered, and must leave the matter in the sound discretion of Captain Hudson. The Susquehanna also is in the Thames. Captain Sands and his first lieutenant were with me yesterday. You will have noticed that, as a little lucky accident would have it, they were first in saluting the Russian Grand Duke Constantine as he entered the British waters on board of a royal yacht from France, on his way to the Queen at Osborne. You would be amused to see how this casual and light incident is remarked upon.

The French elections come off on the 20th instant, and inspire some interest:—though why, it is difficult to say. Great care has been officially and openly taken to secure to the Imperial government an immense majority both of representatives and votes. The suffrages are expected to exceed nine millions.

I enclose some papers which the Greek minister has put into my hands as explanatory of his great desire that something may be done in respect to the matter I have heretofore written about. He says that Mr. —— is really not entitled to act as consular representative, and that his informal authorization from Mr. Diomatari has expired many years ago; that as a missionary he is constantly provoking the public mind by *proselyting*—a course prohibited by the Constitution of Greece. Can you empower me to say a word to him? or is it necessary that the subject should assume greater formality?

I have nothing worthy of a regular despatch, and cannot have the means of enlivening you until some movement in the political atmosphere disturbs the existing serenity and dulness.

It is supposed that Parliament, which reassembled last evening, may continue in session till August and yet their proceedings be quite devoid of general interest.

Always faithfully yrs.

## No. 123.—TO MR. HUTCHINSON.

LONDON, June 12, 1857.

MY DEAR SIR,—I have yours of the 26th of May, covering the letter from the Library Company to Mr. Woodcroft, and have immediately forwarded the latter. It gives me great pleasure to perceive that the Directors justly appreciate the value of the Patent Publications, and have complied with the engagement as to binding them.

I have come across, in the possession of a fashionable widow, a Frenchwoman who married an Englishman, a painting which I wished were in one of the rooms of the Library. It is an admirable portrait of Franklin, when our minister in Paris, by a great contemporary artist ranking now as one of the masters, *Greuze*. He is taken in his morning wrapper of green velvet with fur collar. The widow has repeatedly and significantly called my attention to it as an object of historical art which ought to be in America. But I remain stupid to the hint, as it would be beyond my dilettanti zeal to encourage republicans to give a thousand guineas for a Greuze.

When you tell me that beef in the Philadelphia market is from 20 to 25 cents a pound, you describe a condition worse even than the one existing in this overcrowded and extravagant capital of carnivorous gourmands. You can get the choice pieces, from the butchers' stalls here, the tenderloin at 9 pence the pound, the ribs at 8 pence halfpenny. Our victuallers are making too high a profit on their business: but we are fond of good eating and seem willing to pay for it at any exalted rate. Some scheme should be adopted, of setting off one meat against another: of bringing beef down to reason by eating mutton alone for awhile, or by resorting to fish and fowl. As long as everybody covets beef, and permits the audacious butcher to run the price up-hill, we shall have shillings instead of sixpences for mouthfuls.

Politics are just now serene and quiet. Louis Napoleon waves a more powerful wand over all Europe than his uncle did, and has a better right than Nicholas to announce that Order reigns, not merely in Warsaw, but throughout the monarchies. Austria has an aspect of liberalism: — Prussia lets go of Neufchâtel: — Russia, France, and England (perhaps the U. S. too?) are creeping silently after the eggs of the Shanghais: and the only ripple to be discerned on the surface is in a pretty little flare-up against priestly encroachment and practices in the domestic legislation of diminutive Belgium. Can't we break the universal peace, by a row on the Isthmus? Why not monopolize all the transits?

The weather has been warm, for a day at a time:—but the general temperature is yet too cool to admit of the slightest diminution of woollens. I suppose you are sweltering under a fierce sun, or rushing to the sea-shore. By-the-by, be good enough not again to be tempted to try the treacherous waves of inland waters.

We are all in good health, thank Heaven, and hope to remain so, even in spite of the incessant entertainments and soireés to which we are obliged to go. Like good-natured eels, we are growing callous to this sort of martyrdom. The "season," however, will not last beyond the middle of July.

Present us all to your sons and daughters most affectionately.

Always faithfully yrs.

---

## No. 124.—TO MR. CASS.

LONDON, June 12, 1857.

MY DEAR SIR,—There is quite an uncommon serenity just now in the political heavens. Were it not for the far-off quarrel with China, the anti-priest excitement in Belgium, and the French elections on the 21st—all rather tame subjects—the quidnuncs would be utterly dumb. Parliament is coolly discussing domestic topics, the camp at Aldershott, the law of divorce, penalties on fraudulent trustees, improvement of parks, reformatories, etc., etc. The ministry appear wonderfully at ease, and my Lord Palmerston could yesterday mount a fine spirited horse at Windsor, ride to Ascott, in the Queen's train, stay to the races, and ride back again, without feeling the weight of duties or years.

Opposite to all this, I fear, from the statements in the newspapers just received, that the condition of things with you is much disturbed. I hope a great deal from Mr. Walker's ability and manliness in Kansas, from Harney's inflexible firmness in Utah, and from the force of the Supreme law in Ohio. In Granada, you will probably find little further difficulty, unless indeed the incredible story be true that England has got another Ruatan on the Pacific side of the transit at Panama. These really grave subjects, superadded to the oppressions, complications, and bitternesses, springing almost necessarily out of your official patronage, must tax your patience and philosophy not a little. God grant you a safe deliverance!

Please let Mr. Toucey know that Captain Hudson having apprised me of his intention so to change the Niagara as to fit her for the reception of the submarine telegraphic cable, at the expense of the company and without injury to the ship, I applied, at his request, to Sir Charles Wood for an order that the work might be done expeditiously, safely, and well by the operatives in the public employ at Portsmouth. Sir Charles telegraphed Admiral Seymour immediately. The alterations will probably be completed in two weeks. Everybody appears now sanguine that the cable will be on the bottom of the Atlantic in the course of the summer:—let us hope, with the two ends tight to Newfoundland and Ireland respectively.

The British Museum has recently had its attractions increased by the noblest room for a library now existing. It is an immense circle lighted from a lofty and beautiful dome. Our congressional apartment devoted to the same use is quite eclipsed by it.

You see how dull I am forced to be.

With my best regards to Miss Cass,

I am faithfully yrs.

---

## No. 125.—TO DR. SHAW.

LONDON, June 27, 1857.

MY DEAR DR. SHAW,—Pray excuse my delay in answering your note of the 24th instant:—it has been owing to absence from London and other causes.

The last session of Congress was the short one, that is, from December to March 4th. Still, the general subject to which you refer was not entirely neglected. Two handsome and adequate appropriations of $6760 and $25,000 were made:—the *first*, "for preparing for publication the surveys of the late expedition to the North Pacific Ocean and Behring's Straits, and for finishing the publication of the charts made by the late expedition for the exploration and survey of the river La Plata and tributaries:"—and the *second*, "to authorize the Secretary of the Navy to cause to be extended and completed the exploration of the Parana and the tributaries of the Paraguay river."

This, to be sure, is not much:—but it may help you out of a tight place.

I received about two months ago a ponderous quarto from the United States Coast Survey Department:—the Superintendent's Report of the proceedings during the year 1855:—it is an exceedingly elaborate and interesting *exposé*, aided by many admirable charts. Have you got it? My only copy was given to Dr. Whewell of Cambridge, Master of Trinity.

Always most respectfully and truly yrs.

---

## No. 126.—TO LORD CAMPBELL.

June 29, 1857.

My dear Lord Campbell,—I must beg you to run your eye through the enclosed letter received by me from the United States this morning.

It will shew your lordship that I have been anxious to fulfil my promise, and that probably the failure to do so must be ascribed to a mistake of memory in both Judge Rogers and myself. My correspondent is a member of the Bar, of established repute for diligent and accurate investigation.

With the highest consideration, etc.

## No. 127.—TO MR. THAYER.

LONDON, July 3, 1857.

MY DEAR THAYER,—You will see by the enclosed how very much your letter of the 10th June has gratified the Lord Chief Justice as well as myself.

By-the-by, talking of judges:—there is hanging in the gallery of the British Exhibition this year, a very large-sized and admirably painted portrait of Judge King. He is in full Turkish or Egyptian costume, with magnificent turban, sabre, shawls, and withal a fine flowing white beard reposing on his breast. The likeness is speaking:—and he ought never to appear in any other dress. It was sent over from Paris, where he now is, and where it was painted by Kellogg.

Love to all—ever yrs.

---

## No. 128.—TO JUDGE KANE.

LONDON, July 6, 1857.

MY DEAR JUDGE KANE,—The busts have only just reached me, and, in honest truth, our recollections are too vivid to allow us to like them. The artist has fallen short of justice to his subject. He has failed to delineate, as he might, the traits of thought, enterprise, vivacity, courage, and endurance:—these constituted the heroic original.* For my own part, too, I miss the beard which was the necessary consequence and companion of his greatest exploits. Still, we unite in thanking you warmly for the present.

I sent the copy intended for the Royal Geographical Society to Sir Roderick Murchison. If his acknowledgment come soon enough, it will accompany this.

With the best regards of all mine to all yours,

Faithfully yrs.

---

* Dr. E. K. Kane.

## No. 129.—TO MR. CASS.

LONDON, July 17, 1857.

MY DEAR SIR,—Observing in the newspapers that you have returned from your northern journey, I venture upon resuming my private missives.

Recent events have disturbed the political serenity on which I commented a month ago. The rebellion in India, the elections in France, the explosion and failure of the Mazzini scheme at Genoa, and renewed disturbances in Spain, are all very interesting in their details and probable consequences.

A grand drama seems preparing from one end to the other of Hindostan. Every effort is made to conceal or disguise the fundamental cause of the disaffection. May they not be playing over again the game of lordly redcoats and paltry provincials? The outbreak at Meerut has been expected somewhere by intelligent observers, for several years back. The Home government imprudently repelled warning and advice. The larded cartridge was merely the last feather on the camel's back. Proofs of a vast preconcert, requiring much time to mature, are manifest. The elevation of a King at Delhi is a measure of permanent bearing. The simultaneous mutinies of widely separated regiments of sepoys cannot be misunderstood.

Passion is in the ascendant here. Perhaps this is inevitable while their relatives and friends are being butchered, and worse than butchered, by the revolted slaves. Too much force cannot be sent out to execute a prompt vengeance. No money to be stinted. No mercy to be shewn. The "fanatic natives" are destined to a worse fate, by fire and sword, than our blacks undergo after insurrection. There are represented to be about 70,000 British, of all descriptions, military, civil, and mercantile, in India; and they are maintaining the sway of this island over 170 millions! The reinforcements in motion are said to be about 25,000 men: among which are counted the troops going out to China, but which the Governor-General, Canning, has intercepted and ordered to Calcutta.

It would seem that Cavaignac and Carnot have decided

on taking the oath of allegiance to the Imperial dynasty. Their constituents insist that it is a condition prescribed by irresistible force, and if they don't take it they abandon their country to her fate.

I hope you benefited by your absence for a time from the turmoil of Washington.

Always faithfully yrs.

---

## No. 130.—TO MR. CASS.

LONDON, July 19, 1857.

MY DEAR SIR,—There is a carelessly worded sentence in one of my despatches (No. 61, 10th July, 1857), which, if I had the power, I would like to correct. Fortunately it is of no importance, being a bald expression of opinion: but then it would seem to assert a sentiment of my own, which was not intended. It relates to Cavaignac and Carnot taking the oath of fealty, and begins, "They should not hesitate, for what is the obligation of an oath enforced by 500,000 bayonets?"—Had I merely used the words "*It is urged that* they should not," then my exact aim would have been reached. There is enough strength in the view to puzzle casuists:—but I am not prepared to adopt it, though powerfully enforced. Pray don't suppose me willing to treat official swearing lightly for any purpose.

The death of Mr. Marcy was announced to us by the steamer which arrived yesterday. The "inevitable hour" came to him in an enviable manner. No sickness, no debility, no pain, no disquietude. I presume it was a sudden stoppage of the heart's action. Being at the Premier's drawing-room last night, I observed that it awakened about as much interest as would the decease of any sepoy in India.

A fierce struggle getting up between the two Houses of Parliament on the Jew question. Lord John Russell moved a new bill, giving to a former act authorizing oaths to be administered to witnesses in the manner binding on their consciences, an extension to legislative oaths:—and if the Lords throw *this* out, he avows his readiness to call Baron Rothschild into the Commons, and to have him take his seat, omitting the clause "*on the true faith of a Christian.*" Such a course, if the Peers be firm, must bring on a most unseemly collision. Lord Chief Justice Campbell has frankly *prejudged* it as a violation of positive law. The truth is, the movement of Lord John is as clearly revolutionary as was the effort of the black republicans to compel or nullify the Senate on the Kansas question. Mr. Roebuck and many of the newspapers denounce the Lords with all the bitterness and contempt used by the old Jacobins of France against the nobles. If we examine symptoms closely I think we should come to a conclusion that the upper House is fast losing its prestige, and that its end may be looked for as soon as some five or six of its veteran sages are removed—Lyndhurst, Brougham, St. Leonards, Lansdowne, Aberdeen—I doubt whether our Senate has ever had so little hold upon popular respect. Still, a fondness for aristocracy and a subserviency to wealth leaven the whole lump of British society, and an attempt to extinguish or curtail the legislative power of the Peers is always in danger of reaction. The Crown too shields them by its popularity. If George IV. were on the throne, both would be in imminent danger.

We have here a number of distinguished Americans:—among them, Ticknor, Sparks and Sumner. The last is quite a favorite as the suffering champion of Abolition. Ticknor and Sparks have no politics, and are delightful. Doctors Mütter and Gibson of Philadelphia are also in London, the former very ill of the gout. A rally of American sojourners takes place on the 21st instant, the day after to-morrow, at Boston in Lincolnshire, to "assist" at the inauguration of a Chapel in honor of the Pilgrim father, John Cotton. I am bound to be there.

We cannot have farther news from India before the latter part of this week.

Always faithfully yrs.

---

## No. 131.—TO MRS. GALES.

LONDON, July 20, 1857.

MY DEAR MRS. GALES,—It is extremely provoking to be obliged in frankness to confess the entire failure of my efforts to carry out your suggestion as respects Miss Juliana May.

I reserved an answer to your letter in the hope that, before the season finally closed, something might enable me to write more agreeable prospects:—but the concerts and parties at the Palace are now over.

I cannot venture to say why the royal attention was not attracted to Miss May. Her Majesty and the Prince Consort justly take pride in selecting the most accomplished and skilful musicians and songsters for their concerts; and Miss May, under her engagement with Mr. Lumley, had publicly, though under some disadvantages, exhibited her fine vocal powers. The number of great "*cantatrices*" from which to select, has no doubt embarrassed choice: and there are obviously some personal friends, like Novello and Balfe, with whose uniform preference no competitor could hope for success.

I cannot say, for honestly I do not believe, that any prejudice exists against a voice simply because it is American: high art is too much cultivated, too ardently pursued, too triumphantly fashionable for that:—nothing so cosmopolitan:—but we have yet to achieve for our country the reputation of a land of song; and until that be achieved, and made undeniable, we must not wonder if even the excellence we know we possess fails to be sought for.

Had I been able to accomplish your wish, my being accessary to the happiness of Mrs. May and her daughter would have given me unalloyed pleasure; and certainly no one would be more eager than myself to contribute in any degree to your gratification, or to that of Mr. Gales, whom I can never regard in any other light than as an old friend of my father's and I hope of mine.

Always most faithfully yrs.

---

## No. 132.—TO MR. CASS.

London, July 24, 1857.

My dear Sir,—It has struck me to be expedient to send you the accompanying copies of *private* letters on the subject of handsomely inaugurating the wire which is to run under the Atlantic from Valentia to St. Johns.

I hope the President will approve my giving the note of preparation to Lord Clarendon. It was marked "private" because there is not absolute certainty that the enterprise may not be balked by one of the thousand accidents that are possible, and so the two governments be made to appear too confident.

One can scarcely yet credit the realization of this most vast, yet most delicate, conquest of science and machinery. The first spark that goes from Buckingham Palace to the White House will, like mercy, be twice blessed, securing immortality at once to giver and receiver, in more durable records than those of politics.

Mr. Huffnagle, our consul-general for British India, is now here. Nothing as yet from that region to allay the general anxiety. There seems, indeed, a prevailing impression that the mutineers at Delhi are numerous, strong in arms and ammunition, and skilful as soldiers: so that the siege may be a protracted one and encourage disaffection elsewhere. The rumor of defection in the army at Bombay does not seem to be well founded.

The course of the three leading republicans lately elected in Paris, Cavaignac, Carnot, and Godchoux, as to the oath of fealty, seems still undecided. The constituencies press the argument I have heretofore stated, and the general impression is that it will prevail.

The facilities and comforts of locomotion by railways are capital aids to the harmony and distinctive power of crowned heads. Continental royalty has fairly overrun England lately. Whether they come like shadows and so depart, can only be guessed. We have had from Austria, the Grand-duke Maximilian:—from Prussia, Prince William:—from Spain, the Duke and Duchess of Montpensier:—from Belgium, nearly the whole reigning family:—from France, Prince Napoleon:—from Holland, the Queen of the Netherlands (the Duchess of *Van Buren*):—and Louis Napoleon promises a quiet call at Osborne with his empress in the course of a fortnight!—*Jam satis terris nivis atque diræ grandinis!* When curiosity is once gratified, these personages are rather inconvenient to the corps diplomatique, at least to our portion of it. "To meet her Majesty," or "to be presented to H. R. H.;"—*hic labor, hoc opus est!*

The toast given at the banquet in Boston to the President of the United States was received with a cheering altogether vehement and remarkable, by a company of at least 300. It was prefaced by an elaborately prepared and really forcible speech from the historian of Boston (whose work, by-the-by, is a magnificent folio volume, got up with a superabundance of elegance in engravings, type, paper, and binding), Mr. Pishey Thomson, whom we all knew as an admirable bookseller for so many years on Pennsylvania Avenue. The learned and eloquent Bishop of Lincoln was there, and gave us a speech. So was our Bishop Smith of Kentucky, who did ditto. So also, Erskine, Dean of Ripon, son of the old first Lord. And so, too, a succession of members of Parliament. The Mayor presided. Our flag waved all day upon the topmost turret of the beautiful tower of St. Botolph, which is three hundred feet high.

Always faithfully yrs.

---

## No. 133.—TO MR. CASS.

LONDON, July 28, 1857.

MY DEAR SIR,—It is here next to impossible to procure authentic information of what is meditated at Madrid respecting Mexico. Don Bravo left London some months ago to meet the Cortes, and Comyn, the Chargé, is either unable or unwilling to talk on matters of public interest. The newspaper correspondents only invent and mislead. It is now alleged that the mediation of England and France has been accepted. It is, I think, rather to be suspected that the Spanish movement was from the first unreal, and meant more to cover Cuba from apprehended filibustering than to invade Mexico. At all events, just now the condition of Spain is too much disturbed and uncertain for an important military expedition to the other side of the Atlantic, which might furnish *us* a plausible ground of action. Spain will be very shy of doing what might possibly swell to overflowing the popular current in the United States. The mediation has, in all likelihood, been part of the original plan, and invited by her.

A moderated tone on the subject of Slavery is undoubtedly observable even in Parliament. How explainable? 1. The pressure of the truth as to their West Indies. 2. The pressure of the rebellion in Bengal. 3. The pressure of the China fight. 4. The shake recently given to the Napoleonic throne. 5. The annexation of Perim, protested against by Turkey under impulse from France:—and with all these, 6. The hourly increasing conviction that there is no safety for the ascendency of the Liberal Party except in honest friendship with the United States. It may be that this abatement in the crusading spirit is preparatory to aiding us to acquire Cuba:—for as they despair of stopping the trade from Africa, they may see reason to prefer the institution as it exists with us to the one on the Island.

The French ambassador urged me by letter, three or four days ago, to obtain for an Imperial hydrographic engineer, the privilege of accompanying Captain Hudson in the Niagara, during the voyage for laying the sub-Atlantic cable. The ship was on the eve of departure, and I had no time to correspond with her officers. I sent his Excellency a short note addressed to Captain Hudson, requesting, if no orders or rules were in the way, that he would invite and receive the engineer, a Mr. Delamarche, on board the frigate. I hope the President will approve what it was impossible to avoid or evade without extreme discourtesy. The correspondence on the subject I have thought it proper to send to Mr. Toucey.

You will see by the newspapers that the Jew's Oaths question has taken a more decided phase than ever. Mr. Horsman, an able and influential liberal, has twitted the Premier, in language to which that functionary is not accustomed, on his duties as the party leader:—intimating that the Earl of Harrowby, Lord Privy Seal, cannot be permitted, while a member of the cabinet, to withhold his vote in the House of Lords from the bill, and that the whole united and active power of the ministry must be given to the measure, on penalty of whig denunciation and disorganization.

Still no fresh news from India, though expected every hour. In the House of Commons last night Mr. Disraeli made a very tedious and elaborate speech on the causes of the disaffection and the proper course of government now that it had exploded. A worse picture of political administration could not easily be painted:—far exceeding, especially in its deep shades of usurpation and confiscation, the recapitulated grievances in our Declaration of '76. It fell, however, very flat on the ear, though I was a patient listener during the whole of it, from 5 to 8 o'clock. Lord John Russell, who just now resembles an inexpert swimmer trying to buoy himself with awkwardly entangled bladders, gave Mr. Disraeli's motion a patriotic direction.

I was earnestly assured, during the concert at Apsley House last night, by Lord Stanley, whom I think better informed as to the condition of the British colonies than any other man in England, that the whole affair was a mere military *émeute*, and would certainly be at once repressed. And yet an Indian Commissary-General, Col. R., very lately returned home, is anxiously in doubt as to the result, looking to the fall of Delhi before the besiegers as indispensable to the safety of the whole against the pervading discontent. One thing is quite certain:—that this country will concentrate all its energies against the insurrection, first to put it down, second to revenge its cruelties, and third to reform its causes.

Mr. Huffnagle, our consul-general in the East, is returning home from Calcutta, wholly unable to meet the expenses of his post by his salary. I have long known him, and believe him, as a public agent, to be eminently reliable for intelligence and integrity. At this interesting moment of Chinese and Indian perturbation, he will have a fund of valuable practical knowledge to lay before you. That region of the earth is looming up into so much importance that I should think it wise, rather than lose the public benefit of his skill and experience, if he were permitted his salary unencumbered by his actual expenses.

Those fierce and endless riots in New York make very disagreeable echoes in the ears of Americans abroad. We cannot vindicate or excuse them. I really hope they will soon die out.

My latest official Register is that of 1855; and I often want the Army and Navy Registers for the current year.

Always faithfully yrs.

P. S.—Your old assailant, Brougham, in his 80th year, was last night busy among groups of beauties, chatting and laughing as a boy long after midnight!

## No. 134.—TO MR. J. M. M.

LONDON, July 28, 1857.

MY DEAR SIR,—Although extremely indignant, I was not sorry to see the venom spit at you by the Yankee parson. I was sure of the rebound; and it has come in the best possible way and to the greatest possible effect:—subserving not so much the individual—for really he could not be harmed—as the cause with which he is identified.

You notice the progress of things here? China, India, Paris, Italy, Spain, Parliament? I thought the world going to sleep; when it suddenly, like a drowsy lion, stood up and shook itself all over. I am afraid, however, that the monster won't keep on his legs, but will sink into deeper slumber than ever.

Two or three things are worth noticing.

There's the wonderful readiness of the oldest and ablest men to mingle, night after night, and all night, in the light gaieties of life. Lyndhurst (85), Brougham (80), Lansdowne (77), St. Leonards (76), Palmerston (73), Campbell (78), Aberdeen (73), Combermere (77), Wensleydale, Baron Parke (75), etc., may be found wherever amusement, though it be in the form of mere show, is to be had. So with the very ancientest of ladies. The effect on society generally is salutary and obvious. To be sure, the very young are rather cowed.

There's also the busy and widespread eagerness to revive church ornamentation. I have recently visited a number of Cathedrals and Parish Churches, and, being a tolerably good Episcopalian, have trembled to notice the immense backsliding to Romanism in the crosses, altars, painted windows, symbols, mottoes, sedilias, piscinas, etc. They look more like niches in the vast St. Peter's, or even chapels in the Greek Kazan. A fierce controversy, to be sure, is waging on the subject: the newspapers and periodicals are full of it. I went into Wiltshire, and saw a church on which Mr. Sydney Herbert, the M. P., had spent a fortune: it had 754 pillars, big and little, no two alike! I went, in the opposite direction, to Lincolnshire, and there saw another on which its wealthy rector, called Barridge, was in progress of lavishing his money, making it, to my eye, a glittering temple for Catholicism rather than a house appropriate to Protestant worship. The religious archæologists are raking up and restoring, under one pretence or another, all the Roman abominations denounced by the Reformation.

Confound it:—I am in a garrulous vein, and here suddenly comes the necessity of a despatch!

Ever yrs.

---

## No. 135.—TO LORD CLARENDON.

LONDON, July 29, 1857.

MY DEAR LORD CLARENDON,—Definitive information may I think be expected as to the prospects of the sub-Atlantic cable in about two weeks from Monday next, the 3d August. In the mean while, I am promised a telegraphic despatch from the Niagara when she will have successfully laid three hundred miles of the wire:—and this shall be sent to you as soon as received.

The message from her Majesty it would seem prudent to have in readiness for transmission by the 10th of August; and I would respectfully suggest that it should be placed in a *sealed* envelope addressed to the President, to be opened only upon the instant the communication between Valentia and St. John's is certain. The envelope, in a letter containing this instruction, should, I am informed by Mr. Cyrus W. Field, be forwarded to "George Saward, Esq.—Secretary of the Atlantic Telegraph Company, Valentia, Ireland."

With sentiments of the highest respect,

I am faithfully yrs.

---

## No. 136.—TO MR. CASS.

LONDON, July 31, 1857.

MY DEAR SIR,—The news from India, which reached here the day before yesterday, has augmented alarm and affected the funds. Delhi holds out, with a force of 30,000 mutineers, against General Barnard; and sorties, though not successful ones, are made frequently and with spirit. It is admitted that all Bengal is disaffected. The "plot" was on the eve of exploding at Calcutta, and was only stayed by a sudden disarming. The King of Oude has been arrested and imprisoned. A large body of revolted sepoys are encamped, and yet, it would seem, unattacked outside of the walls of Delhi. The loyal profession so much magnified and relied upon by the native troops, was ardently repeated by a regiment which on the next day massacred all its officers and dispersed. Christian missionaries are being mercilessly slain. Madras and Bombay, though agitated and anxious, have yet witnessed no overt acts. These are the leading traits of the telegraphed news. When we get the details, by the correspondence on its way here, it is supposed the picture will be much more gloomy.

Troops are forwarding as fast as they can be got ready. Large inducements are offered to those whose terms of service have expired, to re-enlist. Some intimations are given of French assistance:—but there is an instinctive jealousy of that. It may, however, be confidently expected that for two or three years to come, England will think of nothing but India. Even if she puts a prompt close to the present insurrection, she will have to increase her European forces there immensely, and inaugurate an entirely new system of government. She has, for more than a century, been arrogant, cruel, rapacious, intolerant, and mercenary, and yet she expresses surprise at the rebellion!—thinks she has nursed the Hindoos into civilization as an affectionate "mother" would train her children! and now finds in the monstrous ingratitude she meets a justification for dooming the race to a dreadful retribution. Barré's portrait of her parentage to us is no doubt true in application to her colonies in general. She is the reverse of Rome.

I have heretofore referred to the question of the Moldo-Wallachian Principalities as one calculated in its progress to disturb existing combinations. You perceive that it is now working. France, Russia, Prussia, and Sardinia are on one side: England, Austria, and Turkey on the other. Their representatives have reached the point of angry rupture.

You have probably had your mind recalled to the question of the Right of Search by the case of the Panchita. Does not that case, and the actual position of this government present a most favorable conjuncture for quietly putting an end to that pretension?

Pray say to the President that the Queen of the Netherlands specially enjoined it upon me to express her pleasure at hearing of his complete restoration to health, and to say that she remembered with much gratification his visit to Holland, where he had left many agreeable recollections. Her Majesty speaks English like a book.

There can be no doubt that every effort will be made to break up the refuge which the unhappy continental democrats find in this country. Sovereigns are, for this purpose, in their turn "conspiring." The failure at Genoa, and the implication by arrested men in Paris of Mazzini and Ledru Rollin in a design to assassinate Louis Napoleon, furnish the pretext. The Press here will resist gallantly: —but it will not surprise me if, as one of the possible results of the actual predicament of England, the visit of the Emperor to Osborne on the 5th proximo were to be followed by some harsh measure against aliens.

To-day, it is thought, will realize the recent giving out of Lord John Russell, and see Baron Rothschild sworn in by resolution in such form as he may deem obligatory upon his conscience. Such a course promises to be the initiation of a protracted contest.

Always faithfully yrs.

---

## No. 137.—TO MR. CASS.

LONDON, August 4, 1857.

MY DEAR SIR,—Lafragua, the Mexican minister in Madrid, is reported as gone to Paris, but it is believed in order to facilitate the accepted mediation of England and France. Were anything serious and critical impending, Mr. —— would not keep it from me. As it is, nobody anticipates a belligerent course from Spain. There is, however, great difficulty in getting at the truth.

The recognition of the free navigation of the Danube,

and the extinguishment of the Sound Dues, have very naturally brought into question another kindred matter,—the tax levied by that great potentate the King of Hanover upon commerce on the Elbe. Goods crossing a line running from the mouth of the Schwinge, a small Hanoverian river, nearly due east across the Elbe to the opposite Holstein shore, are subjected to a toll ranging from $\frac{3}{8}$ to $\frac{1}{4}$ and $\frac{1}{8}$ per cent. ad valorem. The exaction is enforced even though the vessels are merely passing up the river, and do not stop in the Hanoverian sovereignty, which does nothing to preserve or improve the channel. Is it not worth while inquiring how far our trade is affected?—perhaps it has been done already—and whether it be worth while to make the stand against the "Brunshausen Toll," which you took the lead in making against the Sound Dues?

I send you a fat parliamentary volume in the nature of a Blue Book. Lord Clarendon was kind enough to let me have two copies:—one will adorn the library of your department, the other that of this legation The contents are valuable and interesting.

The contest about the Jew's Oath waxes warm. Lord John Russell has again shifted his ground, and now relies upon the general language of a forgotten and disinterred statute of William IV. He has got the Attorney-General, Sir Richard Bethell, to agree with him in its interpretation, and so may find his position strong notwithstanding the clear and powerful dissent of Sir Frederick Thesiger, certainly one of the ablest, if not the very ablest, lawyer in the House. A committee to construe the Act, to consult, and report, will probably be appointed this evening. Lord Palmerston reserves himself for their interpretation

The details of the news from India are frightful:—but they do not attest that disaffection among the people out of the ranks of the army without which the military mutiny must soon fizzle out. Delhi has probably succumbed to the army of General Barnard, say about 12,000 to 13,000, though we have no authentic account of the fact. The zeal here is unabated:—their empire in the East must be saved at every cost: the sentiment is common to all shades of party.

Do you notice the peremptory violence of the French minister at Constantinople on the Danubian Principalities question? *A la Menschikoff* he threatened to quit, and the frightened Turk changed his cabinet to prevent his departure. How Lord Stratford will stomach this remains to be seen. This political arrangement of the Treaty of Paris always struck me as having in it the seeds of great controversy.

The Queen, in person, will probably prorogue Parliament about the 23d instant, and proceed the next day to Balmoral. Everybody that can will imitate her example in hastening out of London. I propose, after having endured city confinement continuously for 16 months, to give my family a swallow of sea air, on the eastern point of the Isle of Wight. The heat has been trying for a week past, the mercury sometimes at 90°.

Always faithfully yrs.

---

## No. 138.—TO MR. CASS.

LONDON, August 7, 1857.

MY DEAR SIR,—At Lord Palmerston's, the night before last, I had a short dialogue with Mr. Comyn, the Spanish Chargé.

D. I notice in the *Post* that your *Chef* is coming back. When will he be here?

C. He intends returning, but has not yet left Madrid.

D. He will probably be able to tell us how your controversy with Mexico gets on.

C. Oh! for the present, and perhaps finally that is disposed of. We have accepted the mediation of France and England. But, Mexico is impracticable; and it is difficult to say how we are to get a guaranty that she will not repeat her barbarities.

D. Her domestic politics are very much distracted, and her government took no part in the injuries of which you complain.

C. May be so.

D. And, after all, an attack from you might do her an essential good. You would rouse her to union and action:—as to reconquering her, that, of course, you know is an impossibility. Where is Mr. Lafragua?

C. I believe at, or on his way to, Paris.

The French sovereigns arrived at Osborne yesterday morning. Prodigious pains are taken by military, naval, and police to secure their personal safety. Nothing was allowed, on the water, to approach within two miles of them. A body of Parisian detectives forms a cordon round them at a distance. And yet the eagerness of his Majesty to greet Prince Albert, when near the landing, led to his stumbling down the paddle-wheel and falling heavily on the deck, thereby, as it is said, "grazing his face and shaking himself considerably." Mazzini should provide a Roman augur to make the most of the Omen!

Parliament will remain in session some two weeks longer. A general desire prevails to hear something definitive from India before adjournment:—and the grouse can wait a fortnight.

Lord Carlisle fastened the European end of the sub-Atlantic telegraph wire to its place at Valentia yesterday morning, and away westward steamed the little squadron! I am hourly expecting a message from Mr. Field, who is on board the Niagara, and who promised one when the expedition has prosperously got 500 miles forward.

I send you the copy of a letter which I received yesterday from a leading commercial house here, one of whose partners, Mr. G. Moffatt, is a member of Parliament. It complains of what it calls "an anomaly" in our recent reduction of the tariff, passed March 3d, 1857. Tea was a non-enumerated article in the schedules of the tariff of '46, and therefore by a special clause made subject to a duty of 20 per cent., "*when imported direct from the place of its growth or production in American vessels*, or *in foreign vessels entitled by reciprocal treaties to be exempt from discriminating duties, tonnage, and other charges.*" The object of the discrimination is obvious: and yet, perhaps, while the Chinese market is affected by political difficulties, we should find benefit in suspending its operation. What thinks the President, or Mr. Cobb?

Always faithfully yrs.

## No. 139.—TO MR. SAWARD.

London, August 9, 1857.

Dear Sir,—I enclose a sealed letter addressed to you from "Osborne," and must beg you to apprise me of its having reached you safely.

Trusting confidently in the success of your great enterprise, notwithstanding the croaking prophecies of failure,

I am very respectfully yrs.

---

## No. 140.—TO MR. EVERETT.

London, August 11, 1857.

My dear Mr. Everett,—Your volume of Cushing's Lex Parliamentaria Americana for Speaker Denison has reached me just as I was preparing the despatch bag for to-morrow by the steamer City of Baltimore. I will take care that it gets to him immediately.

Your letter accompanying this book evinces an apprehension that I may be overwhelmed with letters of introduction. Pray dismiss it. My countrymen come over in shoals, and are all heartily welcome, especially those who bring me a line from esteemed friends. I can be of little service to any of them, farther than to receive them frankly, and give advice if need be or an occasional official facility. As a general rule, they appreciate the matter correctly: if some do not, they might as well.

Rest assured, my dear sir, that a note from you always gives me pride and pleasure. I am quite sure of my visitor, and feel entirely at ease, if so vouched.

You see what was done at *mother* Boston, for the rehabilitation of old John Cotton. The Church is a noble one. The new Chapel small but neat, and admirably set off by your tablet.

Always faithfully yrs.

## No. 141.—TO MR. CASS.

LONDON, August 13, 1857.

MY DEAR SIR—The arrival of Gov. Wright in the steamer Atlantic took me by surprise. Mr. Vroom has left Berlin, and will reach Paris to-morrow or the next day. He proposes to embark for the United States on board the Arago which leaves Southampton on the 26th instant. Gov. Wright, who has been with me all the morning, is worried at not having got to his post before his predecessor quitted it, as he very naturally hoped to get the benefit of his local knowledge on modes and means of life. Hence he hastens across the channel.

You observe that Lord John Russell's Committee on the Statute of William IV., after complying with the decencies of consultation for two or three days, put a negative upon the hoped-for construction which would apply the words "*body corporate and politic*" to the House of Commons, and Baron Rothschild is again put off. This failure of Lord John will, I think, strengthen the position of the House of Lords, and, with the help of the Church, set the current against the Jews.

Louis Napoleon managed matters on his recent visit with singular adroitness. He has obviously carried his present, if not his ultimate, point as regards the Principalities, and induced Lord Palmerston to confess in the House of Commons, with some disingenuous distinctions, a change or surrender of policy. The truth, however, is that India, and India alone, is the predominating and controlling thought;—nor should I wonder if the offer of a regiment or two of Zouaves had proved more attractive than the mere abstract theory of bolstering the independence of Turkey by keeping Moldavia and Wallachia divided. *Nous verrons.*

You know how impossible it is for an Englishman to understand and apply the limited nature of our federal constitution and system. They all hope and believe here that you are about to extirpate the Mormons, and rejoice as much at the prospective overthrow of that fanaticism, as at the cherished expectation of the triumph of another in 1860. Perhaps (according to a favorite form of speech) you may not gratify them on either point.

One of the Parisian correspondents of a daily journal here invents the idea that Mexico has taken the stud at Spain's backwardness to accept her proffered hand, and has instructed Lafragua to make not a step farther in conciliation. If Mr. Comyn spoke truth to me, and I cannot doubt it, the mediating powers, having got the matter in charge, will soon end it.

I am sending my family for a short period to the Isle of Wight:—a distance which I can conveniently run over on the railway in four or five hours.

The ministerial white-bait dinner, precursive of parliamentary prorogation, has been announced for the 19th instant.

Always faithfully yrs.

---

## No. 142.—TO MR. CASS.

LONDON, August 18, 1857.

MY DEAR SIR,—The failure as regards the electric cable is a sad affair. It would not appear to be relieved by any promising or remediable symptom. The sudden rising of the ship, in obedience to the swell, must necessarily test the strength of the wire, and may be more or less violent:—a rise which does not jerk might be harmless notwithstanding the weight already immersed: but even a momentary pause in paying out would risk a snap. However, a great result is rarely achieved by a first experiment, and we have many reasons for confidence in the power of mechanism scientifically directed.

The Niagara and Susquehanna went into Plymouth. They will probably remain on this side of the Atlantic until their officers have had opportunity to consult with their associates in the enterprise, and the prospects of the future as well as the facts of the past are capable of being embodied in a report.

Mr. P. reached here on the 14th instant, and has brought me letters from yourself and Governor Wise. I have not yet had the pleasure to see him, and, of course, do not know the aim of his mission except very generally. The American demand for English capital is increasing and almost unlimited:—but I should hope that the timidity of money-lenders would subside in sight of such security as the State of Virginia can exhibit. The letter printed by Governor Wise a short time ago, and of which he was kind enough to send me a copy, put the resources of the Ancient Dominion in a striking light. All our States, however, are still suffering, more or less, the disrepute inflicted by the caustic and undiscriminating pen of Sydney Smith.

Parliament will close with this week, and the world of official business and of fashionable toil will immediately disperse to the four quarters, not to be reassembled before late in February, unless the Indian rebellion assume a size—*dignus vindice nodus.*

I have recently obtained for our worthy historical compiler, Dr. Jared Sparks, the permission of Lord Clarendon to rummage through and extract from the diplomatic correspondence in the State Paper Office carried on during our revolutionary struggle, between the ministry here and their representatives in Spain and Holland. He goes to the Hague, too, to see if Mr. Belmont can obtain for him there the like opportunity. He is a slow, pains-taking and honest compiler, and, as we have a vast deal of this sort of work to do before the foundation of our national history can be thought fairly and securely laid, it would be a wise measure in Congress to authorize his permanent engagement for the purpose.

I hope your eyes are less enfeebled by use than mine:—if not, I am afraid that you must regard the deciphering of my cramped handwriting as rather more troublesome than satisfactory.

Always faithfully yrs.

---

## No. 143.—TO MRS. BACHE.

BONCHURCH, ISLE OF WIGHT, August 18, 1857.

MY DEAR SISTER,—We have got ourselves temporarily ensconced at one of the most picturesque points of this beautiful island. Facing south, we have immediately below us a hidden cluster of houses:—beyond these a lower cliff, with a precipitous fall of some three hundred feet, and then, all open to the eye, the wide sea rolling or glittering to the Bay of Biscay or the coast of Spain. Just in our rear frowns the first of a succession of cliffs north, on whose side we have ventured to clamber a little, but whose top has thus far proved inaccessible to us. Our cottage rests, amid trees and flowers, on one of the platforms, as it were, of this mountainous stairway called the undercliff:—we have no neighboring houses in sight, except the belfry and cross of an old chapel far below us, although elegant villas are numerous all about and their sites may be guessed at by the curling smoke from their kitchen fires. We are said to be in the village of Bonchurch, to have the town of Ventnor on our right, to the west about a mile off, and the City of Ryde nearly due north, distant a two hours' stage. This is *said*, for unless we journey away we are actually able to see only the ocean at our feet or the broad green cliff in the clouds.

So far for position, to which my description necessarily fails to do justice. Our home is what a man of fine taste and adequate means would adapt to such a *locale*. It is the perfection of a Swiss cottage, in exterior architecture, and its interior is inimitably arranged for hall, parlors, dining-room, six chambers, kitchen, servants' apartments, and so forth. The furniture is exceedingly neat, and everything in the highest order of English cleanliness. I have rented it for six weeks for forty-two guineas, say $220. The principal incidental expense of this delightful rustication is that of moving to and from London:—for, of course, my presence at the legation must not be suspended, if there be the smallest occasion for it. The jaunt by railway to Portsmouth, thence across the Solent to Ryde, is three hours:—and to *Cliff-Den* by coach an hour and a half more.

A favorable wind, like the one which began two days ago and still continues, gives us the finest imaginable marine panorama. All the harbors of Holland, Belgium, France, and the eastern front of England, disgorge their ships and steamers for the western and southern voyages. I have counted as many as 36, 46, and 48 vessels in full sail, and visible from the piazza. Sophia and the girls have been enchanted by a short absence from the London heat, smoke, and dust, to which they have clung continuously for sixteen months; and I sincerely hope it may brace them to bear another of those delirious "seasons" two of which have gone roaring by.

While thus writing, don't think that I am forgetting whom it is for. The good accounts latterly received of your improving state induce me to suppose that I may amuse you and beguile a few moments of slow recovery.

We are just now expecting a visit from two ladies of Philadelphia, Mrs. E. and Mrs. J. And here in fact they are! Mrs. E. says she has come on purpose to be able to report faithfully the character of our cottage when she gets to the U. S. by the steamer Baltic early next month. They will honor us for two days, and then travel through the little isle on their way back to London.

Ever most affectionately yrs.

---

## No. 144.—TO MR. CASS.

LONDON, August 25, 1857.

MY DEAR SIR,—No city can be imagined duller or more repulsive than London during the hot season of August and September, when Parliament, public functionaries, club frequenters, the Court, and fashion have all sped away as if flying from pestilence. Everything becomes insipid, languid, and listless. The resorts, the libraries, the galleries, the shows, are shut up. The great thoroughfares are thinned. The crowds of equipages have vanished. The Squares are without life or light, every house deserted, and the four blocks of buildings staring vacantly over the area with doors and shutters tightly closed. To be sure the summer's sun treats most towns in this way: —but the effect is worst in London, because of its vastness, and because of its multitudinous swarms at other times.

I have adverted to this matter, because the *genius loci* seems to have dried up the springs of these private letters to you. I can hear nothing, see nothing, read nothing, think nothing, worthy to be written to a Secretary of State, even had he not the superadded dignity of being on the other side of an ocean, four thousand miles off. It's a sad dilemma. A diplomat without a topic! An envoy without food for a despatch! and that too in this huge "*poluphloisbos thalassa*" of intelligence and news! One consolation:—you will certainly not regret the absence of what must be so vapid and empty.

All eyes, all hearts, all heads are fixed on India. The accounts, since my despatch of last Friday, are gloomy and heavy. Butcheries, savage, indiscriminate, and fanatical, are pouring in. The climate, too, takes sides with the natives. Generals Barnard and Lawrence dead: all Oude up: the circle of mutiny and murder widening every hour. The 1500 men intended to back Lord Elgin in China have found their way to Delhi. At farthest by the month of November—and they could not stand the heats earlier, there will be in Bengal thirty-one thousand British soldiers:—a force quite ample to reconquer Hindostan, if properly commanded: and I must confess that my personal intercourse with Sir Colin Campbell, the new commander-in-chief, has inspired me with great confidence in his military capacity and qualities. If he fail, or sink under the climate,—to which fortunately he is partially accustomed,—the prospect will be dark.

Suppose the rebellion put down, as it may effectually be by this time next year, then comes the problem what, under the new circumstances, will be done with India? An indifferent stranger almost shudders to think what *may* be done. The population is so great, so ignorant, so superstitious, so vindictive, so cruel, so utterly unprincipled, that, with the zealous counsel of missionaries, no government will be thought capable of lasting six months which is not preceded by overwhelming strokes of vengeance and accompanied by a system of inflexible and unrelenting oppression, political, religious, and social. It will require all the exertion of all the ablest writers and statesmen of England to prevent this consummation, so inconsistent with her humanity, toleration, and justice.

The accident to the sub-Atlantic electric cable is by no means regrettable. Such a thing is natural enough at any time and in any hands:—it is not discreditable. But, had it not happened—had they gone on depositing at the rate they did,—they must inevitably have developed, "not a crime, but something worse, a blunder." For, only think, notwithstanding the several voyages, the soundings, the calculations, the consultations, the experiments,—their cluster of scientific and mechanical experts had actually provided a cable five hundred miles too short! Captain Hudson tells me that the length payed out exceeded expectation 25 per cent., owing to depths, currents, etc., and that no doubt they would have fallen several hundred miles short of reaching St. John's:—one mile of which would have been just as fatal as one thousand!

A project of a Red Sea electric telegraph is much talked of:—the India difficulties make it exceedingly desirable; and there is great probability that the East India Company will purchase the Atlantic cable at its cost, and apply it to their more urgent purpose:—leaving the Atlantic Company to construct a new one by next spring.

Parliament may be prorogued to-morrow or the next day, or it may linger on for several days. The Queen will not be kept waiting, and so it is given out that the prorogation will be by commission. One cause of uncertain delay is the Divorce bill, now gone amended back to the Lords: another is the expectation of receiving something decisive from India by Thursday next, when parliamentary votes of supply for a great military effort may be required. Lord Panmure said, while I was in the House of Lords last night with Mr. Preston, that they had out upwards of 550 recruiting parties, and had enlisted in one week about 1600.

I bade Governor and Mrs. Vroom good-by on Saturday last. They were leaving for Paris and will join the Arago at Havre to-day.

Always faithfully yrs.

---

## No. 145.—TO MR. CASS.

LONDON, September 1, 1857.

MY DEAR SIR,—These missives of mine must be regarded with indulgence. I am quite aware that they must often be vapid and flat. That is unavoidable in a correspondence continuously kept up at brief intervals. It is impossible to find the supply of news always equal to the demand. Still, I am unwilling that you should be long without at least a line from me.

1. Lafragua, the Mexican Envoy to Madrid, is "*in nubibus.*" No one can say where he is, or what he is at. The last theory represents him as having gone to Cadiz, to embark for home, in a pet: a theory on which no reliance can be placed.

2. The affair of the steamer Cagliari is being exaggerated by quidnuncs and newspaper scribes into a ground of war between Piedmont and Naples. She was the vessel seized by certain of her Mazzinian passengers and employed in reaching Sicily. Having been taken into custody, the King declines restoring her to his brother of Sardinia:—and so the seed of quarrel is fresh planted in the soil of old grudge.

3. Vogorides has had all his electioneering trouble and squabbling for nothing. He is obliged to repeat the same game, as the Sultan has consented to cancel the former result. The Union party in Moldavia is strong, but not believed to be in the majority. The management of Vogorides tricked and overwhelmed it. Wallachia will probably remain steadfast to the principle of Union:—backed by the potent influences of Russia and France. Austria is particularly and angrily averse to the Union, and the Porte dislikes and intrigues against it. England has cooled in her zeal about the matter, under the shadow of the India revolt and the sunshine of the Imperial visit to Osborne. The chances are not bad that we shall witness the creation of a new Monarchy and a new Royal Dynasty.

4. The world of London is dispersed. The rush abroad and into the country preceded the prorogation and left scarcely a "Corporal's Guard" to do the ceremony. Locomotion will soon be the pastime of all the sovereigns. Queen Victoria has gone to Balmoral, taking Lord Clarendon in her train. The Empress Eugénie has had her Sunday sport at bull-baiting, and is off to Plombières. Louis Napoleon is whisking from one town to another, and, it is thought, after the review at Châlons, will contrive to meet the Czar somewhere in Germany.

Always faithfully yrs.

## No. 146.—TO MR. CASS.

LONDON, September 14, 1857.

MY DEAR SIR,—I have availed myself of a few days in the country to draft a letter to Lord Clarendon on the Panchita business. It rather grew under the pen as I analyzed the papers you sent me. His lordship is, however, in attendance upon her Majesty at Balmoral, and I may not get an answer these two months.

Fresh news hourly expected from India. In the mean time, the old dishes of insurrectionary atrocity are rehashed and daily spread in the newspaper columns. They certainly are shocking. The *Weekly Press*, Mr. Disraeli's special puffer, told us on Saturday, the day before yesterday, of a suspicion that government had received further accounts so disastrous that they kept them back until well ventilated. This is mere party coinage.

The populace are becoming irreverent. The ministry are assailed for absenting themselves on grouse plains, stalking moors, and watering-places, at a moment when the empire is shaken to its foundations. Even the Queen is thought to fall too easily into the bull-baiting track of the Empress, when she celebrates the massacre of her subjects in Bengal by festive sports in Scotland.

The quarters whence men receive help in life are sometimes very hidden and odd. You perceive that Macaulay has been made a Peer. Well, I ascribe his promotion as much to Horace Greeley, of the New York *Tribune*, as to a real sense of his merits. For, you must know that just as the public were discussing "a creation" of Lord John Russell, Lord Robert Grosvenor, Lord this and Lord that, out from over the Atlantic came a caustic and dogged article in a number of the *Tribune* on the discomfiture of Thackeray as a candidate for Oxford, and dwelling with gnashing teeth upon the indifference shewn even by the liberals to ability when contending with family and title. It had no look towards Macaulay:—when it was penned, the great historian had not been thought of:—but its drift touched a sensitive spot, and, in true Palmerstonian style, without a word said, what was meant as a practical disproof brought up Macaulay. "There's more in heaven and earth, *Horatio*, than is dreamt of in (even!) your philosophy."

The two Emperors, of Russia and France, design to meet and embrace at Stutgard on the 25th or 26th instant. *Cui bono?*—unless to swear eternal friendship as their predecessors did at Tilsit, and then straightway fall to fighting, it is hard to say. Perhaps, Louis Napoleon, assuming the character strongly hinted for him in the last *Edinburgh Review*, of the Roman Augustus, being a nephew of another Julius, meditates the golden era of universal peace, as the sequent of his uncle's everlasting wars. If India permit, I think Palmerston or Clarendon will meet Walewski there. Suppose the world parcelled into tranquillity by a national triumvirate which will secure China to the Czar, Egypt to Octavius, and Hindostan to Vernon Smith!

My theory about the Spanish menace against Mexico is merging into reality. The dread of our seizing the plausible opportunity to acquire Cuba has put them into fidgets to prevent the quarrel. All over Europe just now, there is a disposition to regard the United States as a sort of "*John Jones of the War Office*"!—a belligerent individual to be encountered wherever there is a muss, and who cannot be put down;—when he looms up the alarmed gaze at him, as Alpine travellers watch the impending avalanche, which a single musket-shot may bring crashing down upon them. You'll say, this is flighty figure: I insist that four-fifths of it are positive matter of fact.

Always faithfully yrs.

NOTE.—The note addressed to Lord Clarendon, referred to in the first paragraph of the foregoing letter, was printed in a Blue Book furnished to Parliament six or eight months after its date. It is extracted from the Blue Book.

*Inclosure* 1, *in No.* 580.

MR. DALLAS TO THE EARL OF CLARENDON.

LEGATION OF THE UNITED STATES, LONDON,
September 16, 1857.

MY LORD,—It has been made my duty to call to the notice of her Majesty's government, certain proceedings of Commander Fairfax Moresby, of the Royal Navy, on the Western Coast of Africa, in the early part of May last; and to avert, if possible, any unfavorable influence which those proceedings might have upon the relations of the two countries, by inviting from your lordship such early and distinct disclaimer and assurance as may be esteemed adequate. No doubt is entertained that the acts of Commander Moresby were unauthorized; that, however plausibly pursued, they were the suggestions of his own discretion, not of his official instructions, and that all danger of their repetition will be promptly removed.

The barque "*Panchita*," Frederick B. Sladden, master, owned by citizens of New York, with an American register, and trading under the flag of the United States, was, on the 9th of May, 1857, lying at Punta de Lenha. At the same date, in the river Congo, was her Majesty's sloop "*Sappho*," commanded by Commander Moresby, one of the British squadron then stationed off the African coast to prevent the Traffic in Slaves. The "*Panchita*" had, in some manner, awakened suspicions as to her objects in the mind of Commander Moresby, who (agreeably to his own narrative) with "the pinnace and gig" of his armed vessel, proceeded to Punta de Lenha "for the purpose of examining her." Meeting Captain Sladden, Commander Moresby "expressed" to him "a wish to muster his crew," and "no objection being made," went, accompanied "by Mr. Frederick Wells, master of her Majesty's sloop under his command, on board the '*Panchita*;'" mustered the crew; asked, and was refused, permission to look into the holds; became confirmed in his "opinion" of her being "engaged in the illegal Traffic of Slaves," and was thus "induced to inform" Captain Sladden, that he should "detain him," with a view to give him over to the first American man-of-war he could meet. Finally, the "suspicions" of Commander Moresby being "by the vast quantity of fresh water" aboard "still further corroborated," he took "upon himself the great responsibility of sending" the barque to New York "for the decision of the United States authorities," detailing for that purpose, Lieutenant C. D. J. Odevaine, with a party of seamen, and giving special and prudent directions for their conduct.

It may be added that the "*Panchita*" duly arrived at New York, was transferred to the custody of the Marshal of the United States for that district, and was libelled in the proper Court of Civil and Admiralty jurisdiction as a forfeiture. The question whether or not her voyage was, either in fact or intention, connected with the Traffic in Slaves will ultimately be determined in that still pending judicial proceeding; but its decision, one way or the other, can have no bearing on the violation of sovereign right now brought to your lordship's attention.

This statement of Commander Moresby's conduct is made, as already intimated, almost exclusively in his own words: nor is it deemed necessary to the design of the present communication that the striking discrepancies of detail between his statement and that of Captain Sladden should be drawn into relief by comment. They illustrate, it is true, the conflicts to which a course of action like that of Commander Moresby necessarily leads, so liable to exasperate popular sensibilities on either side, and, in the end, to endanger the friendship and peace of nations. But I am unwilling to mix with the public aspect of the subject the coloring of individual imputation.

The Earl of Clarendon will, then, perceive that Commander Moresby, on the occasion described, impelled by "suspicion," actually effected a visitation, search, and seizure of the "*Panchita*:" that he knew her to be an American vessel; that, for predetermined "examination," he went to her, accompanied by a show of force, namely, the master of the "*Sappho*," and two boats' crews from his sloop-of-war; and that, excited by discovering what he construed to be badges of a criminal employment, he assumed the responsibility of disregarding the flag she bore, and of wresting her from the control and possession of her American captain.

Against each leading feature characterizing this transaction—the visit, the search, the seizure—the government of the United States has uniformly, on all appropriate opportunities, for more than fifty years, openly and effectually protested, as inconsistent with the laws of nations, sanctioned by no Treaty, subversive of the separate rights and derogatory to the honor of independent communities. It was not the exercise of any fancied privilege of war, for profound peace prevailed; and yet, without the pretence of belligerent necessity, in respect to contraband or blockade, the property and citizens of a friendly Power were invaded and arrested, and the protecting presence of their national symbol irreverently slighted.

The flag of the United States has a meaning which should not be hastily overlooked. Like that of Great Britain, or of any other civilized country, no matter how distant the sea, or humble the lorcha on which it floats, it implies a pledge of a nation's power and honor to shelter what is beneath it from invasion or wrong. All flags are but hoisted emblems asserting the national presence and jurisdiction. Commander Moresby, even while recognizing the genuineness of the "*Panchita's*" flag, failed to appreciate its real dignity and inviolability.

The reasons assigned for this extraordinary proceeding are certainly as distinctly confessed as they are frivolous. They are found in the report of Commander Moresby to his superior officer, Commodore John Adams, of her Majesty's ship "Scourge," dated the 15th of May, 1857. They do not call for much elaboration of analysis or remark.

Commander Moresby "suspected," say, confidently believed, that the "*Panchita*" was engaged in the illegal Traffic of Slaves.

I need not remind your lordship that since the United States led the way, by their Federal Legislation, to the abolition and penal proscription of the African Slave Trade, they have manifested, in every manner deemed compatible with their fundamental institutions, the fixed opinions of their people, and considerations of the highest moment, the utmost determination and sincerity in carrying out that policy of philanthropy and justice. But the United States, although they went far, stopped at the line which the reckless zeal of Commander Moresby overleaped. Though often persuaded, they have invariably declined to concede to any nation, upon any terms, for any object, a right irreconcilable with the perfect immunity of their mercantile marine from foreign interference. Without their previously obtained consent, no visit, or search, or seizure, of an American vessel can take place except with defiance and insult to their flag. The Convention of the 9th of August, 1842, signed at Washington by its negotiators, Mr. Webster and Lord Ashburton, with the principles and provisions of which your lordship is familiar, arranged for a small squadron of the United States Navy on the coast of Africa, in order, first, that their public force might co-operate with that of her Majesty in extinguishing the Slave Trade; and, secondly, that their merchant vessels, if suspected, or even flagrantly guilty, should, nevertheless, be liable to visitation, or search, and seizure, by the officers and seamen of their own country only. Eagerly, even at great cost, as the suppression of the noxious Traffic might be sought, it was still not an aim to which the United States would consent to sacrifice the more dearly valued exemption of their own citizens from coercion by strangers. *I may be pardoned for here adverting to the language used on this very topic, by one of the brightest and most authoritative ornaments of English judicature: "No one nation has a right to force its way to the liberation of Africa by trampling on the independence of other States, or to press forward to a great principle by breaking through other great principles that stand in the way. The right* *of visitation and search on the high seas does not exist in time of peace. If it belongs to one nation, it equally belongs to all, and would lead to gigantic mischief and universal war.*"*

It is hardly worth adding that the mere "suspicion" or belief of Commander Moresby of the illegal occupation of the "*Panchita*" cannot be accepted as the slightest possible basis for his proceeding, when the open avowal or the living proof of the supposed fact of guilt is not itself admitted, by compact between the two nations, to be a justification of search or seizure.

Some difficulty is naturally felt in adverting to the remaining reasons with the respect due to an officer honored in the possession of the Queen's commission. But I feel assured that Lord Clarendon will understand me as only desirous to bring out the true lineaments of the transaction.

Commander Moresby informs Commodore Adams that in sending the "*Panchita*" across the Atlantic, in charge of his lieutenant, to New York, he was "incited by the unfortunate fact of the total absence of anything like an American naval authority, and that in consequence the '*Panchita's*' detention may be prolonged for an indefinite period."

It would, perhaps, be harsh and invidious to scan too closely the statement that the sending the vessel to New York was regarded as the step which involved him in his alleged "great responsibility." In the chain of his acts, that one is the only link not liable to objection, at least on the part of the United States. The American government is outraged, not by the subsequent misgiving and politic device of a reference to its own tribunals, but by the violation of its flag at the outset, the unwarranted intermeddling with the property and pursuits of its citizens, the "examination" and "detention."

Actual trial for a number of years has, perhaps, demonstrated the inadequacy of the squadrons on the Western Coast of Africa to accomplish the great end contemplated by their respective governments. The vessels are, probably, too few; necessarily distant from each other; and occasionally disabled by the diseases incident to climate, or the disasters of weather. They certainly cannot be ubiquitous, and yet without that attribute they are no match for the wary and covetous slave-traders on that extensive shore. Such difficulties, if remediable at all, are to be remedied, not at the discretion of any one, or all, of the naval agents in both services, but by the concurring action of the two governments. Commander Moresby alleges "the total absence of anything like an American authority;" but such absence (in one aspect, rather fortunate than otherwise) justified, as regards the flag of the United States, and the lives and property over which it waved, no arbitrary substitution of himself in the stead of the American absentee, for the purposes of visitation and search. An American authority might, very possibly, upon receiving from Commander Moresby a revelation of his "suspicion" of the "*Panchita*," have done precisely what Commander Moresby did; but Captain Moresby could under no circumstances or pretext whatever do it, without usurping a supervisory function, not only not confided, but expressly forbidden, to him.

It would seem as if the imposed restraints, and the purposed omissions, of the Treaty of 1842, were not in harmony with the speculative opinions, and chafed the eager spirit, of this subordinate officer. He entertained "a firm conviction that if some steps be not taken, there is nothing whatever to prevent the American flag from sanctioning any vessel, openly in the eyes of the world, equipping and trading with slavers in any part of the African coast;" and he proceeded to take the reformatory steps of

---

* Lord Stowell.

visitation and seizure of the "*Panchita.*" This may be one mode by which the Gordian knot of the "consuetudinary Law of Nations," "great principles that stand in the way," and even precise conventional stipulations, can be cut. But Commander Moresby has to learn from your lordship that it is an absurd and indefensible mode. It is absurd, as having a tendency to alienate and detach from the united undertaking a powerful people who first legislated to abolish the Trade; who first, by municipal enactment, made that Trade punishable as piracy; and whose armed force has been perseveringly stationed to watch and prevent it. It is indefensible, as placing the matured policy and peace of nations at the mercy of their rash and presumptuous servants, and as "leading to gigantic mischief and universal war."

It would be unjust to ascribe to Commander Moresby the mistaken impression that, because the Criminal Code of the United States denounced as piracy the Traffic of which he suspected the "*Panchita*" to be guilty, he was, therefore, at liberty to search and seize that vessel and her crew as "enemies of the human race." He puts forward no such erroneous reason for his conduct. Ignorance of the wide distinction between the Law of all Nations, and the Municipal Law of a single one, cannot fairly be attributed to him, or to any British officer. The protection or rescue of the American flag from prostitution to illegal aims, still rests exclusively with the American government and people, whose will and ability to enforce their own statutes cannot, or need not, be questioned. On one or more occasions, the Secretary of State, by direction of the President—both of them ardently disposed to combined movement against the Trade, and stimulated by a Resolution of the House of Representatives—proposed to her Majesty's government a scheme for the extirpation of that condemned commerce, to be incorporated, by universal consent, into the Law of Nations, and involving mutual concessions of the right of search. The discussions, perplexities, and obstacles encountered by that proposition need not be recalled; it is enough to say that its ultimate failure left the Law of Nations, which it was designed to modify on the point referred to, unaltered.

I trust I am not too sanguine when anticipating that her Majesty's government, aware how occurrences such as the one on which I have thus animadverted grate upon the sentiments of an independent people, and how rapidly they become unmanageable causes of estrangement and quarrel, will promptly mark the act of Commander Moresby with just reproof, and otherwise render its repetition extremely improbable.

Copies of the documents transmitted to me from Washington, and which have been observed upon, accompany this communication.

I have, etc.,

(Signed) G. M. DALLAS.

---

## No. 147.—TO MR. CASS.

LONDON, September 17, 1857.

DEAR SIR,—I had scarcely closed my letter of the 14th instant under the impression that it would go in the steamer of the 16th, when I found that fresh Indian news had arrived.

Nothing more auspicious, however;—perhaps a still farther sinking in the morass of rebellion. Another general forced by ill-health to quit the siege of Delhi, which has made no progress. The Bombay Presidency disaffected and doubted. The rainy season, with all its difficulties and diseases, fairly set in. Yet Havelock has marched from one victory to another, has probably relieved Lucknow, and possibly terrified Nana Sahib into suicide. Sir Colin Campbell had reached Calcutta. I shall be mistaken if he do not hasten to attempt Delhi by assault.

More will be made of the Imperial coincidence at Stutgard than is generally supposed. It will probably originate a Congress.

Lord Clarendon has been relieved of his attendance on the Queen in Scotland, and may give attention to my Panchita despatch within a reasonable time. I suppose Commander Moresby will, for his reckless zeal, be ultimately rewarded with knighthood.

Always faithfully yrs.

---

## No. 148.—TO MR. CASS.

LONDON, September 28, 1857.

MY DEAR SIR,—I am somewhat exercised to determine which conspiracy against common right will be the less injurious to the United States, the existing one between France and England, or the one concocted at Stutgard between Alexander and Louis Napoleon. That the Emperors contemplate an alliance which will affect the relations and policies of all the European governments, no one doubts: that it must ultimately embarrass, perhaps endanger, this country, is gloomily anticipated:—but its power to extend its influence across the Atlantic nobody believes. The course of British cabinets, in the constant snarling and arrogant tendency to alienate America, has perhaps accomplished its natural result and rendered it impossible to bring our people to sympathize, much less co-operate, with John Bull in his contests with continental despotisms.

The effect to be produced on the domestic politics of England, by the measures of the new alliance, is dreaded by some, and exultingly foreseen by others. It is said, the ministry must be changed: that Palmerston, though very well for ordinary times, is not competent to a great national crisis: that he cannot enact the wonders of Pitt. I think this impression of his capacity is very general. But what then? Is there a stronger man to be had? Certainly not among the Whigs, properly so called. Clarendon? Granville? Lewis? Panmure? Labouchère? Vernon Smith—? No, no, no! But can't better be extracted from the Tory ranks? Derby?—not relished. Disraeli?—very respectable as subordinate, preposterous as Prime. Ellenborough?—ditto. In sober truth, the eye ranges over the whole field without encountering a single mind up to the mark of command. Perhaps we might, as the best of a bad bargain, pick up Lord Stanley.

I have a perfect horror of Mormonism. It is a sort of carbuncle on the body politic, which will get worse and worse every year, and inflame the whole system unless resolutely extirpated. I know the Constitutional and legal difficulties in the way:—but sincerely hope that you will seize the first fair opening for a decisive swoop. The subject is one for conversation here almost constantly. Within the last few weeks some of the Elders, roaming for converts, have held meetings in London, and inspired extreme disgust.

A dread prevails as to what may be the character of the hourly expected news from India. It is feared that the cholera may have compelled an abandonment of the siege of Delhi; that Lucknow Fortress may have fallen before Havelock reached; that he may be surrounded by an overwhelming force of sepoys and annihilated; that there may be a preconcerted rush, during the Mohammedan Festival, from Delhi all along the Ganges to Calcutta; and that Madras and Bombay will be unable to withstand the torrent of insurrection. It is said that no substantial succor can arrive until late in October, by which time irreparable mischief may be done.

It is a curious fact that there is a considerable party in Ireland, headed by the newspaper *The Nation* and not a little countenanced by Cardinal Wiseman, which takes sides with the Hindoos, against the *English filibusters*. It would be difficult to find a stronger illustration of the liberty of the Press as it prevails here.

Of course you notice that Lafragua has received instructions authorizing him to accept the proffered mediation. By the latest hypothesis (for facts are unattainable) the arrangement will be negotiated in this city.

Not a single member of the ministry is in town; unless he have casually strayed in for a few hours to or from scenes of social enjoyment.

Always faithfully yrs.

P. S.—September 29, 1857. Last night's telegram (a newly coined and most convenient noun) of events in India, although not as bad as was supposed possible, gives additional shades to the picture. Havelock had been unable to advance for the relief of Lucknow as late as the 12th of August, and the gloomiest apprehensions prevailed as to the fate of the thousand English, men, women, and children, who had taken refuge there, but who had estimated their provisions to last only to the 6th of August. Delhi as heretofore. General Nicholson had reached there with reinforcements, though not sufficient to justify an assault, say 2000. The spirit of mutiny seems spreading:—to the southwest of Delhi, at Judpore, at Belguum, in the Bombay Presidency, and in Bombay itself, where they were disarming particular native corps; and in Madras. Lord Canning is the object of much attack, as inefficient and too forbearing. It is said that he and Sir Colin Campbell had had serious differences, and that Lord Elgin took sides with the latter. Nothing short of prompt vindictive cruelty towards the sepoys will go down now. John Bull doubts the capacity and patriotism of every man who is not implacable; he exacts torrents of black blood, and razed cities. Canning will probably be recalled because he don't play the part of a British Nana Sahib. Lord Elgin may be summoned from Hong-Kong, whither he has returned, to assume the Governor-generalship. Nobody, just now, cares for China.

Lord Clarendon has appointed a new consul-general at New York, Mr. E. M. Archibald, the brother of the gentleman who has been lately actively soliciting the place and who is known I believe personally to the President. The consul was formerly the attorney-general of Newfoundland; and had retired on a pension. He was preferred to his brother because younger, being within 50 years of age, the maximum of consular appointees, agreeably to the rules of the Foreign Office.

Always faithfully yrs.
G. M. D.

---

## No. 149.—TO MR. CASS.

LONDON, October 5, 1857.

MY DEAR SIR,—It is said we need expect nothing farther from India for a fortnight. During that period anxiety will work itself into fever.

I think I perceive much effort and dexterity in preventing really bad news from striking too suddenly upon the public mind. One of these finds facility in the little known geography of Hindostan, and the unpronounceable nomenclature of its towns and districts. As an instance: A mutiny of 20,000, with a Rajah of Akulkote at its head, is announced as having occurred at or near Shulapore: well, it produces no special sensation, because few are able to separate it from the general mêlée in Bengal between Delhi and Calcutta. But if you once turn to the map and gazetteer and discover this formidable outbreak to be in the Bombay Presidency, about 250 miles southeast of the city of Bombay, then you perceive it tells an ominous story of the extension of the rebellion some seven or eight hundred miles from its place of origin, far in the interior, and in a region whose order was still matter of boast. Perhaps I ascribe unmerited importance to this fact; but on carefully hunting up its locality, it appears to me terribly significant. One immediate effect of these sporadic outbreaks is to render a concentration of the British forces sent out quite impossible.

The large expenditures incident to the exactions of this "servile war" will bring the skill of Sir George C. Lewis, Chancellor of the Exchequer, into play. Government is more earnest and lavish now than in the Crimean war. Yet, by an official abstract it appears that the receipts in the Treasury during the quarter ending 30th September, contrasted with those of the corresponding quarter of

1856, shew a decrease of £900,000: although comparing the entire years, that of '56 surpasses '57 by only £170,000. Now the principal decrease has been in the Excise and property tax, amounting jointly to upwards of £500,000: and it may well be predicted that the reductions effected last fall will have to be undone, and that the Income tax, with such modifications as will prevent its becoming unpopular, which it certainly ought not to be, will be re-established and possibly increased beyond any rate it has yet attained. The amount of taxation which this people will bear is wonderful. Their capacity to borrow on emergencies is the only more wonderful thing:—their credit being literally inexhaustible, as the annual profits of their industry are enormous.

Your Nos. 80 and 81 by the Europa came this morning. Now do, pray, attend to what I have to say about *the die* from which you send a gold medal for Captain De Gruchy. So many have passed through my hands that I am almost ashamed of having been accessary to inflicting so much discredit upon the artistic taste and skill of the country. Nothing can be worse imagined or worse executed. We formerly had die-sinkers who produced beautiful medals. In the Mint at Philadelphia there are some that do credit to American art. But this! ye gods, it is frightful! Gold cannot make it tolerable, although it burnishes and recommends everything else. In silver, worse. Now, in this dilettanti age, we are snubbed at the sight of such specimens from the government studio. If the stamp is worth having at all, it is worth having such as will stand criticism. "Reform it altogether."

I send you what I think rather an interesting and tell-tale slip just cut from a newspaper. It shews the troops sent to India, vessels, and dates: and you will perceive that the greater portion can hardly be expected to reach their destination before November. Hence, no doubt, it has been resolved to try the shorter cut by the Isthmus of Suez and the Red Sea.

Always faithfully yrs.

## No. 150.—TO JUDGE WOODWARD.

LONDON, October 6, 1857.

MY DEAR SIR,—I had not supposed that it would take Lord Clarendon so long to deliberate upon the expediency of allowing me to have a copy of Major Butler's report. It is near a month since I wrote to him, and his answer came last evening. You will observe too that he has thought proper to omit some portions. Of the nature of these suppressions, it is useless to conjecture, though one can hardly avoid thinking that they might possibly have exhibited the combined forces of savages and English as committing equal, mayhap greater excesses than are now fiercely denounced as unpardonable barbarities by the "black fiends" of Bengal. This sensitiveness to national character is rather laudable than otherwise, but had better not be indulged at the expense of historical truth. The Earl is himself so excellent and amiable, that I am not surprised at his shrinking from disclosing how worse than wild Indians his countrymen sometimes are or have been. Copies of the letters which passed between us are enclosed for your private information.

Very faithfully yrs.

---

## No. 151.—TO MR. CASS.

LONDON, October 13, 1857.

MY DEAR SIR,—There is a great likelihood that the King of Prussia will shortly die. I presume we shall all be bound to go into mourning for his Majesty, especially as the marriage of his nephew with the Princess Royal has made so much stir in Parliament and elsewhere. By-the-by (even the d— is entitled to his due), I have been assured most positively that the alleged intemperate habits of the King were the false inventions of English travellers, that he is uncommonly abstemious, drinks nothing beyond wine and water, but that he has a silly trick of lowering his eyes and shaking his head, which suggested the notion that he was *vinum guzlando potens.* His intellect is fast yielding, and he now fails to recognize his oldest friends. When he is finally off, I suppose there will be an immense *rapprochement* between the Courts of Potsdam and St. James.

The Queen will honor the southern section of her dominions by returning from Balmoral to Windsor on Saturday next the 17th. Her Majesty stops a day, in the royal progress, at Haddo House with the Earl of Aberdeen. I take it for granted that this great dull town will feel the influence of regal vicinity, and be restored to the life so essential to sustain these private letters of mine.

Your idea of improving our foreign diplomacy by having each minister apprised of the principal objects pursuing at every Court is excellent. I urged something analogous to it upon Mr. Forsyth, while I was at St. Petersburg, and I pressed it upon Mr. Webster when Secretary of State. It is the great practical advantage enjoyed by the diplomats of Russia. It produces a harmony of action and *inculcation* that, in a long run, tells conclusively. Mr. Webster's difficulty was in the great labor which it must throw upon somebody in the department, already overtaxed. How that may be, I can't pretend to say:—but if there be any use at all in having missions dotted over Europe, they might as well be made to co-operate in the general policy of the government as run the risk of impeding it by a want of information from the fountain-head. Take an instance somewhat illustrative. I had been here but three or four months when, at an interview in the Foreign Office, Lord Clarendon suddenly asked me whether a treaty had been made between the United States and Persia, by which we had engaged to lend some naval squadrons to the Shah, and were to be indemnified by the possession of certain trading stations in the Gulf:—and he produced two or three long articles extracted from the instrument. What could I reply? There was no practice of communicating from the department on which I could rely, and I had never heard of the treaty. Fortunately, I took a strong impression that his lordship was making, rather hastily, a ground of complaint against us as a set-off to Crampton's affair, and that the alleged treaty was absurdly unconstitutional. I pondered over the paper he put in my hands for a minute or two, and, aware that his eyes were fixed with suspicion on my face, I slowly relaxed into a smile, and then exclaimed, laughing, "My lord, you are *hoaxed:* this is a document which no American statesman would dream of making: —some one has played upon what he believed to be the readiness of the ministry to think the United States capable of any enormity."—Now, this was little more than good luck, and certainly was not founded on any positive knowledge of facts, one way or the other. It struck his lordship forcibly, but did not convince him, and at his special request I wrote to Mr. Marcy inquiringly upon the subject. The hoax was proved:—but the risk run in denouncing it, at the outset, weighed upon my mind for some time.

Lord C. has just sent me two large Blue Books, purporting to be official correspondence on the Slave-Trade up to March, '57. Do you want them? I have not yet had time to open their pages. Indeed, I look upon these compilations, laid upon the parliamentary tables with exceeding regularity, as mere sops to Cerberus, intended to gorge the anti-slavery appetite, so keen throughout England, and to take from the Opposition one of the popular themes of declamation and attack. It is hard work to wade through them.

There is heavy sighing on the London Exchange and Paris Bourse. The calamitous panic in America, and the financial confusion in India are creating mischief everywhere, and the end is not yet. Consols, in one day, yesterday, fell near 1½ per cent. This was accelerated by the unlooked-for action of the Bank of England, in raising her rate of discount, before 10 A. M. to 7 per cent. Private failures are beginning to pour in, among the Scotch-American houses particularly. Some anticipations are gloomy enough to embrace a stoppage of the bank in paying specie. Gold and silver are flowing westward, across the Atlantic. A million of dollars, it is said, will be shipped to-day from Liverpool. The French funds underwent a rapid declension. The newspaper accounts from the United States are exceedingly distressing:—but, unlike any derangement of credit or currency we have heretofore experienced, it would seem that the present one is in no manner whatever ascribed to, or inflamed by, politics. Hence, I am inclined to augur an earlier recovery.

I should doubt whether the Central American Treaty will receive the attention of this government until they are relieved of anxiety about India. My impression is that, rather than quarrel, they will yield their interpretation of Mr. Clayton's unhappy Convention:—but they will be extremely reluctant to do so in a direct manner, or at a moment when it would seem extorted from their national embarrassment. When they do it, they will want it to appear a concession to amity. Perhaps, too, at this moment, the sore is a little too fresh.

The rage is for Imperial Conferences. These dignitaries are just now all three comparatively young men, and are naturally disposed to scan each other's figures. Austria and France meet next:—time and place not yet determined. As to my predicted Congress, to come out of the Stutgard "embraces," it is getting along slowly but surely.

Always faithfully yrs.

---

## No. 152.—TO MR. CASS.

LONDON, October 13, 1857.

MY DEAR SIR,—My Bag has gone, and I have only a moment to say that Sir William G. Ousely will be sent out, as a Commissioner of some sort, to settle the Central American question.

He comes to Washington first, and then proceeds to Central America. He leaves here in about a fortnight.

Always faithfully yrs.

---

## No. 153.—TO SIR W. G. OUSELY.

LONDON, October 18, 1857.

MY DEAR SIR WILLIAM,—Pray receive two packages, one composed of official documents, which I beg you to keep, and the other of two volumes, being Squier's work on the region you are about visiting, and which, as a gift from the author, I am bound not to part with.

If, on farther rummaging, I find anything more that can possibly be serviceable, I shall do myself the pleasure of sending it.

Begging you to make my best compliments to Lady O. whose prospect in the coming month I cannot help envying, I am,

Very faithfully yrs.

---

## No. 154.—TO MR. J. M. M.

LONDON, October 16, 1857.

MY DEAR SIR,—There is great difficulty in forming a satisfactory judgment on the actual state of things in India, or the prospects. So much is exaggerated, so much concealed, and so much thrown into confusion by endless repetition. My opinion, however, is that the rebels have done their worst, have leavened nearly all Hindostan with their spirit of mutiny without being able to produce a general explosion, and will now be rapidly reduced to subjection. The great body of the forces recently levied will reach the field of action before the 1st of November. They may find the country already nearly restored to tranquillity, by Sir Colin Campbell, Havelock, and Nicholson:—if not, their own numbers are abundantly sufficient to effect that end. England has exhibited more than usual military vigor and capacity, at this crisis. The beastly butcheries of women and children have stirred the blood in the lowest depths of John Bull's heart. So too, the British soldiery in Bengal have exhibited admirable courage and endurance. To be sure, everything has been made to give way before the resolution to save, at every cost, the Indian empire. They will soon begin to discuss the principles on which to refound their government there. The Bishop of Oxford and Mr. Gladstone have opened the theme with some impressiveness:—the former is for giving Christianity "*fair play*," by which he means proselyting: the latter is rather too much of a statesman and philosopher for that. I am, on the whole, inclined by the signs of the times to think that, after the subject has been well buffeted between parties, and hammered to death in the journals, it will gradually lull into silence, be forgotten, and the old course of proceeding resume tranquilly its march. To be sure, this will lead to future outbreaks periodically, but what of that? In politics, as in monetary affairs, panics, though momentarily frightful, have their permanent advantages.

The King of Prussia threatens to die. His brother and proper successor meditates renunciation or abdication (at least so your excellent friend Mrs. E. just from Paris told me she had heard), and then Prince William, with his British bride, the Princess Royal, mounts the throne. Victoria gets ahead of Louis Napoleon by this family arrangement.

Spain is at a loss to get men willing to assume the responsibilities of governing her. That race, so renowned some centuries ago, is fast sinking, indeed already sunk, into wretched impotency. Queen Isabella, sick of all the factions around her, musters character enough to insist upon presiding at the Council!

Our yellow fogs have begun, and her Majesty has come "frae Scotia:"—so London will be rapidly repeopled.

Ever faithfully yrs.

---

## No. 155.—TO MR. CASS.

LONDON, October 20, 1857.

MY DEAR SIR,—The Bank of England yesterday raised her rate of discount to 8 per cent.:—a rare, if not the single, instance of its being placed so high. Of course Consols fell:—they are 84¼, and all stocks are affected. The continental banks are taking the same steps. A feverish anxiety pervades the mercantile classes. The danger is attributed to the disruption of credit in the United States, and particularly to the lawless course of our banks. These institutions seem subject to periodical epidemics; and as the respective States have, over and over again, shewn their incapacity to control them, could Congress apply the constitutional power to better purpose than by enacting a bankrupt law for their exclusive benefit? It is quite clear that while they are at liberty when a storm comes to find shelter in suspending payment, they will never take in sail, or fasten the hatches down. They should be forced to forecast:—when the fit is actually upon them, measures of mitigation, compromise, and relief seem unavoidable:—the only plan is to prescribe, while they are sound, a rule which will keep them so. Hang the birch on the wall of the school-room.

This India convulsion will more or less affect the political attitude and pretension of England for some years to come. Hence it may be important to us that its real bearings and perpetually shifting phases should be distinctly understood. Is it to weaken her? Is it to tone her down? Will her relations with Persia or Russia become complicated with it? What branches of trade, or supplies for her manufactories, are put in jeopardy? These and many other questions naturally spring up, and I am inclined to think that Anglo-Hindostanee study might be very useful to our politics, if not now, at least soon. The Press is teeming with publications of great interest and authority upon the subject:—and I have sometimes wished that I had it in my power to send them to your departmental library, and add them to that of the legation. Here are some twelve or fifteen works—among them, that mine of exact and useful information of all kinds "*Thornton's Gazetteer of India*," without which a practical statesman's shelves are imperfectly supplied. What say you?

A continental and no unfriendly paper warns Englishmen not to be too sanguine in the expectation of repressing the rebellion, and points significantly to the Sikhs, as a probable source of great danger, though at the moment friendly. The warning is rather late, be its foundation what it may. John Bull thinks he has already strangled the tiger. The *Globe*, a few days ago, chanting the invincibility of the Anglo-Saxon, declared that even the American Revolution would have been crushed had not France lent her aid!

Isabella of Spain has at last a new ministry, of which Admiral Armero and Mon are the chiefs. The rest of the component members as yet unannounced.

Prussia will probably follow the example of Sweden, and have her Regency. From regent Prince Oscar, we are to have a new member of the diplomatic corps at this Court,—Count de Platen, in the place of old Baron de Hochschild.

The Queen and Court ensconced themselves at Windsor on Saturday last.

All Americans abroad recur with pride to the heroism of Herndon and his companions. An act which illustrates and dignifies national character should, somehow, receive national notice.

Always faithfully yrs.

---

## No. 156.—TO MR. MARKOE.

LONDON, October 23, 1857.

MY DEAR MARKOE,—Oh! for some sassafras, or slippery elm, vegetable simples apparently unknown to the pharmacopœia of this Babylon!—for the very act of putting on my specs reminds me that the rebellious eye of which I complained about this time last year, has come back to worry and disable.

The money mutiny, like that of the sepoys, is slowly but surely yielding to the force of metal. Consols closed yesterday at $88\frac{5}{8}$, a shade better than the day before. All the world here is engrossed by two possibilities; universal bankruptcy and the loss of India: one just as likely as the other, and both mere air-drawn daggers.

I have omitted to thank Mr. Chilton for his few beautiful lines on Herndon. Pray do it, and most cordially, for me. This incident is unequalled in moral beauty. The case of the British frigate Birkenhead was like it, but inferior in the fact that the saving of the women and children was the result of military discipline, and not of purely voluntary heroism. I hope the subscription for the family will succeed: but I look at the act in another point of view. It is a great event, illustrative of, and tending as long as remembered to mould, the national character. Our history has some, though few, of such significant and immortal utterances of high-souled humanity:—the clodhoppers rejecting André's bribe is one, and Miller's "I'll try" another:—but nothing so calm, so utterly unselfish, so simultaneously good *and* great, has yet been recorded. It should live and speak forever. Perhaps it is unsuited to the cold material of the sculptor:—but ten or twenty thousand dollars appropriated by Congress for a vigorous effort of Horace Vernet's brush, to be hung in the Capitol or the White House, would secure an everlasting discourse upon the glories of a subject far exceeding any military achievement on which we habitually expend folios of 4th of July Orations. I should like to enlist Mr. Pearce, of the Senate, and some such high-feeling and bold-speaking man as Governor Wise, in the House, for this.

But my eye is furiously angry, and threatens if I go on to burst—into tears.

Our countrymen are hurrying home in shoals, terrified at what the panic has done or may do.

Ever truly yrs.

---

## No. 157.—TO MR. CASS.

LONDON, October 23, 1857.

MY DEAR SIR,—The despatch on this occasion will bring you a formal notification of Admiral Seymour's blockade of the port and river of Canton. This may possibly interfere with our trade somewhat seriously. It puts a stop to the chuckle I have seen in some of our papers to the effect that we might reap a harvest while they were quarrelling.

This war is one between Sir Michael Seymour and Commissioner Yeh, or between England and Canton, not between the two Empires of Great Britain and China:—and certainly no declaration of war has yet appeared. I suppose therefore we are to regard it as an imperfect or limited war, though it looks more like a "Plug Ugly" skrimmage than a national war.

The panic in the United States acts upon our travelling countrymen like the "rappel" or beat for a retreat. They are fast thronging homewards. Mr. —— told me that on one morning, after the receipt of disastrous failures and suspensions the night before, one hundred and fifty had departed from the Hotel du Louvre at Paris to get on board the Vanderbilt!

Consols were yesterday a scintilla below 89. This is slight but perceptible improvement. The great effort is, if possible, to prevent the shipment of gold and silver to the United States. Such consignments are so immensely remunerative just now, that the Bank of England repels by an 8 per cent. discount notes designed to draw out her coin. She has succeeded, it is thought, quite sufficiently to avert the danger.

We can expect no news from India short of a week hence. Boys in the streets are, to be sure, every night shrieking out, "Delhi fallen," "Havelock defeated;"—but their newspapers contain nothing of the sort.

An inflammation in my left eyelid, engendered by a fierce midnight lamp and the intolerable types of the New York and Philadelphia journals, absolutely compels me to stop short. I dare say you will breathe a "thank gracious!" for if the members of your diplomatic ménagerie throw at you such heaps of paper pellets as I do, it is not in human nature to avoid a sense of patience overwhelmed.

Always faithfully yrs.

---

## No. 158.—TO MR. CASS.

LONDON, October 30, 1857.

MY DEAR SIR,—The last news from India, although accompanied by the storm of Delhi, is of a mixed character, and scarcely justifies the exultation expressed in the Press here. The capture of the city was not attained except with immense comparative loss, especially of officers, and it proved an almost empty acquisition, as the great body of the rebels, with their new King at their head, had skilfully managed to evacuate the place, to cross the Jumna by a bridge of boats, and to effect a compact and safe retreat. The details of the assault, if allowed to appear, will probably be frightful; as it was protracted for six days, during the greater part of which the fighting was conducted in the streets. Such disastrous and inconclusive successes, in a civil or servile war, ought not to be vapored about. The escape of the King and garrison, which requires explanation, makes the whole siege measurably abortive.

It is also quite obvious that, instead of being overawed and checked, the disaffection is becoming wider and bolder. The son of the deposed King of Oude, but 15 or 16 years of age, has been hoisted into the throne of his father, and his ministers have organized a force to impede the march of Havelock and Outram to the relief of Lucknow. Several sepoy regiments heretofore relied on have mutinied. The English battalions, to be sure, seem invincible where they stand:—but their power is confined to that "*possessio pedis*," and they do not put down the insurrection. By this time, however, the new levies have reached the scene of action, and we may expect to witness something definitive.

The question as to the union or *status quo* of the Danubian Principalities is rapidly ripening into what may prove a quarrel after the approaching Conference at Paris. France, Russia, Prussia, and Sardinia favor the consolidation, with a new King chosen from the western dynasties: England, Austria, and Turkey are averse to anything of the sort. The Principalities themselves have recently by large votes in their respective divans pronounced for union. The difficulty will not be removed when the Powers come to consider the Treaty of Paris (or of Peace) of the 30th of March last:—on the contrary, it will be augmented. For it is clear that by Article 25, if the Sultan alone holds aloof and refuses to agree to any proposed definitive organization of these provinces, he is at liberty to do so, and his "suzeraineté" remains unimpaired. But he has done so already, in advance of the Conference:—he has formally repudiated the new monarchy scheme as one to which he will never assent or submit; and while apparently silent, both England and Austria vigorously back him up in this stand. The majority of the Powers in conference, sustained by the regularly ascertained sense of the Principalities themselves, will not readily or cheerfully submit to the Sultan's veto. Hence it is not impossible that the consulting physicians may disseminate an opinion that "the sick man" is, after all said and done, pretty much as Dr. Nicholas thought him, and that depletion, drenching, and straight-waistcoating constitute the only promising treatment.

By this occasion, you have consigned to you Sir William Gore Ousely and his charming American wife, whose transmission by her Majesty to Central America (pray where *is that* government?) I apprised you of in my note of the 13th instant.

I had the pleasure to welcome Secretary Cobb's Commissioner on International Coinage two days ago. Professor Alexander shall certainly have the benefit of all the aid I can give him in getting access to the officers of government to confer on the interesting subject intrusted to his care. The topic, however, is not one to which attention can, just now, be turned.

Prussia, you will have observed, *has* lapsed into a Regency. The King, confiding everything to the hands of his brother, proposes travelling southwards to Rome and Naples. He will hardly get through the winter, and may be regarded, like the generality of patients whom their physicians recommend to travel, as a rapidly "*dissolving view.*" The circumstances connected with the event seem, somehow or other, to interfere with the programme of the marriage of Prince William and the Princess Royal:—a postponement to the spring is already hinted.

The alarm excited here by the monetary panic in the United States is subsiding. Few failures:—among which only one Bank, the Borough Bank of Liverpool.

Always faithfully yrs.

---

## No. 159.—TO MR. CASS.

LONDON, November 6, 1857.

MY DEAR SIR,—The commercial fright, which seems generally swelling into terror, is the only thing which might possibly be beaten up to an importance sufficient for a despatch. Everything else since the fall of Delhi was announced is flat and fugitive. England has rather a heavy load upon her back at present, and this last monetary pressure threatens to make her stagger. Every fresh steamer (the Vanderbilt last evening) brings gloomier accounts from the United States. All the merchants and manufacturers connected with American trade are startled and trembling. The Bank already appeals to the forbearance of her depositors and customers, and tells them that if they act upon their fears and ask her bullion, she cannot stand it. Her interest is raised to 9 per cent., and another puff of the western sirocco will lift it to 10. What then? Why, then she must cry out to Lord Palmerston and Parliament, "help me, Cassius, or I sink!"—What if they refuse? Why, then I should be disposed to remember that the population of this Babel might become feverish and excitable under the influence of an infusion of some hundreds of thousands of discharged operatives, and that it might be prudent to have the Stars and Stripes ready for exhibition from one's balustrade! Bread riots, however, are not famous for discrimination.

The failure to lay the Atlantic electric cable has been followed by the failure to launch the Great Eastern, or, as christened, "The Leviathan." An attempt on the 3d instant, to permit the monster to slide sideways down an inclined plane into the Thames was frustrated by some of the workmen mistaking a signal shewn by Mr. Brunel from his elevated position on the deck:—the effect being, that one part of the ship obeyed the signal and moved some three or four feet, while the other part remained stationary. It was accompanied by some sad accidents. Still the operation might have proceeded, and it probably would have proceeded, but that the river was densely thronged by crowded steamers and boats, and the mishap already experienced made it not impossible that another might occur, and precipitate the vast unmanageable bulk to overwhelm and deluge everything within two or three miles of her. She is now resting on the inclined plane, and it is feared that as that is constructed on piles, her enormous weight, say 14,000 tons, may gradually settle down and become immovable by any known mechanical force. The second of December is given out as the day for another trial:—but it would not surprise me to hear, that, in order to avoid the obvious and imminent dangers of a multitudinous collection, distracting and intimidating those engaged in managing the machinery, she had been safely launched without public notice.

Parliament has been prorogued to the 17th next month, and will probably, as usual, be again prorogued to the beginning of February.

The United States frigate Niagara, Captain Hudson, left Plymouth yesterday morning, homeward bound.

Always faithfully yrs.

---

## No. 160.—TO MRS. EDGE.

London, November 9, 1857.

I regret, my dear Mrs. Edge, that consistently with truth I am not at liberty to confirm your hope of our relationship. Judging exclusively by the intelligent and frank tone of your letter, it would have afforded me great pleasure to do so.

My father's name was not Joseph, but Alexander James: my own name is not George Mills, but George Mifflin.

My grandfather, somewhere in the middle of the last century, was a physician in Edinburgh, Scotland:—he married a wealthy lady of the Island of Jamaica, and had numerous sons and daughters, all born in that colony. His name was Robert Dallas. The estate upon which he lived and died was known as "Dallas Castle." His widow subsequently married a Mr. Sutherland: and these two, in some way or other dissipated all the family property, and threw my grandfather's sons upon their own energies. All of them became eminent, but none except one called Charles Stuart, or Stuart Charles, accumulated fortune.

My father, after marrying in County Devon, a daughter of Major George Smith, of the British Army, sought his future in the United States in the year 1783, when about 25 years of age. I was born in 1792 in the city of Philadelphia, Pennsylvania.

This short narrative shews you that, although our branches of lineage may have a common trunk, somewhere in distant times, they have extended far apart, and it would be impossible to trace their connection beyond the name.

Of the name, I knew there existed, during the last fifty years, in America, several very respectable families:—but enquiries have always ended in failing to prove that any one of them was of the origin of my own.

Very sincerely and respectfully yrs.

## No. 161.—TO MR. CASS.

LONDON, November 10, 1857.

MY DEAR SIR,—The worst apprehensions are fast seizing upon the merchants. The Bank of England raised her interest on discounts to 10 per cent. yesterday. Several heavy failures have been announced, among them the great firm of Dennistoun, of Glasgow; and others are hourly expected. Not a ray of sunshine breaks upon the gloom from any quarter as yet. Men look as if they were beneath an impending avalanche and scarcely dare to breathe. This applies to the great banking houses without exception, whose names I will not trust to paper, but whose deep anxieties are manifest.

Dr. Peter Parker, our late Commissioner in China, arrived here last evening, and has just paid me a protracted visit. Mr. Reed, according to the doctor's calculation, will arrive at Hong-Kong at about this date. He seems to regret that he was not left, like his colleague, Dr. Bowring, to aid the minister whom the condition of public affairs rendered it expedient to send out. His purpose is to proceed to the United States in about two weeks and to visit Washington without delay.

I have written only because of my wish to send you a line by every leading steamer, for I really am left by the extreme dulness of the times, without topics for letters.

Always faithfully yrs.

---

## No. 162.—TO MR. CASS.

LONDON, November 13, 1857.

MY DEAR SIR,—The panic proceeds:—leaving deeper vestiges of its march on this side of the Atlantic than with you. Yesterday, the cabinet took a step which cannot fail to be impressive, for good or evil, and which may produce serious discord in the approaching Parliament. They determined to throw the government as an impediment in the way of the spreading commercial embarrassment:—and the *Globe* of this afternoon contains the letter of Lord Palmerston and the Chancellor of the Exchequer addressed to the Governor and Deputy Governor of the Bank, authorizing a violation of the Charter by extending their issues beyond the limits prescribed by Sir Robert Peel's great and approved Act of 1844: and this, though with deprecatory language, at their discretion! The ministry pledge themselves to ask from Parliament a bill of indemnity, to save the Bank harmless, if it will break through the fetters of law, and give the merchants an unlimited supply of its notes:—And they omit the slightest provision calculated, if that be at all possible, to prevent the depreciation of the paper. After such a measure, it is quite time that the English journals should pause in their prolonged attacks on our Bank suspensions and their legislative legalizations.

Not all yet. An early meeting of Parliament is to be summoned, probably before the close of this month. Having taken the irrevocable step, the Premier resolves to face the music at once. To this conclusion the government would seem to have been hurried by two things:—first, by the violent disorders menacing Glasgow, on the stoppage of the Bank of that city, which demanded the presence of a military force: and second, by the example of Louis Napoleon, who, the day before, to wit Wednesday the 12th, came out in the *Moniteur* with a letter addressed to his Minister of Finance, stigmatizing the panic as a creature of the imagination, disclaiming any design to employ empirical measures, and counselling simple and temporary measures of prudence. The simple measures were immediately adopted by the Bank of France, and the interest on discounts made to rise according to the length of the note to 8, 9, or 10 per cent.

The vice of all this is governmental intermeddling. It depreciates the obligation of law, intimidates trade, and tampers with currency. Men struggle boldly and successfully, amid commotions incident to the natural elements of their business:—but if these are to be changed or controlled at the will of government, results cease to depend on individual energy and sagacity. When the fermentation is under way, abstinence is the true wisdom: wait till spontaneous, self-creating clarification takes place.

The last news from India has caused much relief and

exultation. The reconquest of Delhi and the complete success of Havelock in his movements on Lucknow are undoubtedly pregnant facts. The old Mogul King (90 years of age) and his old wife, with their three sons, have been pursued and captured: the superannuated couple spared, the rest executed. Still, the confessed loss in hard fighting, especially among the officers, has been immense. Two generals, Niell and Nicholson, among them. There is more disaffection reported:—a new and younger King has been proclaimed: the rebels of Delhi have gone in masses to other places to maintain and encourage mutiny: the cholera rages: and General Wilson has been driven from his command by ill health.

I am informed by one acquainted with him and his family that General Havelock has had, during all the time he has been pressing so gallantly forward, a daughter among the besieged at Lucknow!

The new ministry in Belgium is of advanced liberalism; so, it is said, is the new ministry in Madrid: Rogier and Mon are the respective vital spirits. I look to see, at an early date, the finger of Napoleon in both of these pies, disturbing the crust and displacing the plums.

Please say to Mr. Cobb that his Commissioner on International Coinage, Professor Alexander, after a short delay, accompanied me to-day to the Foreign Office, was introduced to the Earl of Clarendon, and received every necessary direction as to putting himself "*en rapport*" with the "*proper functionaries*" mentioned in the Act of Congress. The subject occupies many of the first minds in this country, and I think the time may come when the two governments will mature it into practice. At present everything financial and commercial is too dislocated and disturbed to allow the necessary attention to be given to the project.

Always faithfully yrs.

---

## No. 163.—TO MR. BATES.

LONDON, November 15, 1857.

MY DEAR SIR,—Your proposal as to Christmas is too kind and cordial to be resisted, notwithstanding our consciousness of the multitude it embraces. We anticipate great pleasure in conforming precisely to your programme, and in being with you and Mrs. Bates at Sheen on the 23d to the 28th December.

I am given always to doubt the virtue of nullification of law, whether it be executive or popular:—but cases of sudden necessity may arise which excuse, if they don't justify, a government in assuming the responsibility of doing it. The precedent set in 1847, of suspending the operation of Sir Robert Peel's Bank Act, was very seductive at this crisis; and the manner in which that bold breach of positive legal injunction was treated may be fairly regarded as equivalent to a legislative modification or relaxation of the terms of the Charter. No ministry can hereafter, under the same circumstances, venture to hold on to the law inflexibly. One position, "*ita lex scripta*," must yield to another, "*communis error facit jus*."

I hope what you say of *the storm* here may be true also of the storm in the United States, though you perceive that our Secretary of the Treasury recoiled from doing what is somewhat analogous to Lord Palmerston's proceeding:—he would not throw the doors of the sub-treasury vaults open, in face of an Act of Congress, although extremely inclined and tempted to do so. My letters are still full of sad foreboding, but I think a streak of sunshine returning here and there breaks through the dark cloud. We shall revive in sixty days, but we shall miss from the herd many a noble animal who carried veteran and magnificent antlers but two months ago.

Pray offer to Mrs. B—— our warmest regards, and believe me always

Most faithfully yrs.

---

## No. 164.—TO MR. GILPIN.

LONDON, November 16, 1857.

MY DEAR GILPIN,—It puzzles me to find excuses for your long protracted silence. I hear and sincerely hope that Mrs G. has perfectly recovered her health. If not, then to be sure the puzzle is explained.

Mr. Cobden brought Mr. Bright to see me about a week ago. The latter looks the type of florid health; but I doubt its entirety and permanency. He, several times in the course of an hour's talk (for visits here are very prolonged), put his hand to his head as if to aid the process of thought:—once, perceiving that I remarked the gesture with a slight sympathy, he said that he still felt a remnant of his complaint in being unable to push vigorously to concentration the course of his ideas:—that he was apprehensive he would find it hard, if not impossible, to take his old position in parliamentary debate: that in other respects his restoration was perfect. I told him that in convalescence, the mind, like the body, required *gradual* exercise; that his had been idle for nearly two years, and, though perfectly sound, was relaxed; and I exhorted him not to postpone exertion to the House of Commons, but to try himself first among his friends after a public dinner, and then at one or two political meetings. I added, that one of my chief inducements in consenting to come on this mission was the opportunity of hearing Mr. Cobden and himself in full blast on the free trade topic, and I did not want to be wholly disappointed. These gentlemen carried their Manchester Peace principle to an extreme, at a moment when the nation was irrevocably committed to war, and, as a necessary consequence, their popularity waned. Mr. Cobden lost his election last spring, only because of his constant opposition to vigorous measures against Russia. I do not yet perceive a prospect of his regaining his ground. His friend is younger, less dreaded or disliked, promised not to carry his Quaker notions into the Indian struggle, is re-elected, and if he will only surmount, by the regimen I have prescribed, his diseased want of self-confidence, must become the leading spirit of the House of Commons. Of course, I took the occasion to speak of you, whom he remembered with obvious pleasure, and to place in his hands the package of books you sent for him a year ago. No doubt he will acknowledge to you their receipt.

The very last accounts from India create extreme anxiety for the fate of Generals Outram and Havelock and their army about 3500 strong. They reached Lucknow and relieved the European men and women besieged in a fortress:—but they can't themselves get out again: the masses of Mussulmans in the city of Lucknow itself are watching an opportunity to overwhelm them; the road back to Cawnpore is infested with small armies of mutineers; Nana Sahib, with thirty or forty thousand men and munitions in abundance, is surrounding them; and a month at least must elapse before adequate reinforcements could reach them. After all the suffering endured and gallantry exhibited by Havelock and his men, their sudden destruction, by Nana Sahib too, would be as severe a blow upon the heart of this country as could be struck. It looks at this moment to be almost inevitable. Havelock will no doubt sustain the character he has achieved by a most desperate defence: but the odds are too great. Men argue here that the fall of Delhi and the capture of the Mogul King will dispirit the rebels at Lucknow:—perhaps so, and perhaps not. The city was a barren conquest:—it was kept with acknowledged courage and skill by the sepoys for months: it was abandoned by them when no longer tenable: and they have escaped to rally and continue the war elsewhere: the superannuated monarch was a mere effigy, though a cherished one, and the treatment shewn him, with the execution of his sons, may possibly produce more exasperation than fright. Nana Sahib, with all his atrocities exaggerated, is yet admitted to possess talents, bravery, and resources:—he may also see in the extirpation of the King's family, an opening for the establishment of a new dynasty: he may be a Spartacus, and yet hope to avoid the fate of Spartacus.

Parliament will meet in the first week in December. It is hurried up by the government to pass an Act of Amnesty for the benefit of the Bank, which, at the instigation and request of the ministry, openly violates the express restrictions of its Charter in issuing an unlimited amount of its notes and retaining its coin. There is precedent for this;—in 1847:—and the nullification of positive law not only does not create surprise, but seems to receive unanimous approbation. The panic has made its own law. I am told by the first city merchants that the "storm is over," that the breath of Lord Palmerston has stilled the agitation, and arrested an explosion on the brink of producing widespread ruin. The "Omnipotent" Assembly, whose past decrees are thus slighted, will register a new one with very little if any demur. It will continue in session for a week or two, and then be prorogued, probably to February. It will only take time to utter a few speeches about India, China, and perhaps Central America.

The book of the day is Livingstone's Africa. Read it. Don't be repelled, as I was on the point of being, by the first fifty or sixty pages. You will come to curious and interesting details of natural history which will abundantly delight you.

We all unite, nem. con., in sending the kindest regards to Mrs. G.

Ever faithfully yrs.

---

## No. 165.—TO MR. CASS.

LONDON, November 17, 1857.

MY DEAR SIR,—The meeting of Parliament will precede that of Congress by four days. It was prorogued to the 17th of December, but the Queen has by proclamation yesterday hastened it a fortnight. *Officially*, the object is "the despatch of divers urgent and important affairs:" *generally*, it is understood to be the passage of an act to amnesty and guarantee the Bank:—*really*, it is for these purposes, and specially perhaps to authorize a loan for the relief of the East India Company's finances. This last point will be a sore matter, notwithstanding the military glory which is represented to have been gained in the rebellion;—for John Bull thinks that the expense of the struggle should all be extracted, by the East India Company and the local government, through confiscations and fresh taxes, out of the natives, and not be wrenched from him.

It is doubtful whether the Queen will open Parliament in person. And why? You will be surprised to hear. The reason is that if her Majesty does open Parliament, she must, of necessity, advert to the gallantry exhibited in Bengal by the British generals, and particularize them by name. Public feeling will not be satisfied with cold comprehensive praise from her:—and yet she cannot step out of a dull formality without stirring the hot embers of an established feud in the India service, the feud between those called "*Queen's men*" and those called "*Company's men*." I have the disclosure of this covert but practical embarrassment, of which I was not before aware, from a highly distinguished and intelligent gentleman in office. How the difficulty bears upon Wilson, Lawrence, Havelock, Nicholson, Niell, and Outram respectively, it will be curious to enquire, and may be a key to explain future honors or slights. Thus far Havelock has borne off the palm, and he is even compared with Wellington:—although a morning paper, in view of his actual danger in Lucknow, denounces his advance to that place as the precipitate mistake of the campaign. His popularity here is unbounded, and may extort from Majesty a F. Marshal's baton.

There are philosophers everywhere who think themselves peculiarly competent to cure all existing evils. Such no doubt is the gentleman who wrote the accompanying pamphlets on monetary matters, pamphlets which he is anxious to administer, as a sort of homœopathic dose, to Brother Jonathan, in the convulsive crisis of his affairs. He has begged me (by the letter enclosed) to send them to the President, a courtesy to him which I cannot pretermit:—but, as I am averse to call attention from vastly more important affairs to the lucubrations of Mr. John M. Knott, a perfect stranger, I must, even, with a thousand apologies, transfer the burden to your broad shoulders.

There are puffs of news from China. Lord Elgin had greatly benefited his health, which was assailed by fever, by his voyage to Calcutta: but he ascertained, on his return to Hong-Kong, that he would have to remain in Southern China, until at least the next spring. The blockade had been pushed up to Canton itself. Several skirmishes had occurred, and, in the main, the English, under Commodore Elliott, came off second best. The French Embassy had reached Singapore. The Russian envoy had managed to communicate with the Imperial government at Pekin, and had then gone to Shanghai to wait reception and presentation, but it was believed that he had received information of the Emperor's unwillingness to accept his visit. With the exception of Canton, commerce with all the ports of China is as lively and tranquil as ever. "How very odd!" Commodore Tatnall, who arrived here a week ago, will proceed on his voyage to relieve Commodore Armstrong, in the course of a few days.

We are called upon by the Court official to mount mourning for the deceased Duchess of Nemours, as cousin of her Majesty! that is, I believe, she was the daughter of the personage who *first* married the Queen's aunt, and *secondly* married her mother!—well, according to the regulations of your department, our suits of sable are always on hand, and always "full dress."

Very faithfully yrs.

---

## No. 166.—TO MR. CASS.

LONDON, November 20, 1857.

MY DEAR SIR,—The progress of commercial disaster does not appear to have been arrested by the ministerial intervention. The Bank, to be sure, lends more freely, but the list of daily failures gets longer and longer. Unless the grand panacea of governmental guaranty prove effective soon, I don't see what is to prevent a general break-down, attended by great social disorders, far worse than any we need fear in the United States.

The ambassadors from the First and Second Kings of Siam, with their presents of rich barbaric gold and jewelry, were received by the Queen (upon the throne!) at Windsor yesterday. I met these illustrious mulattoes at the dinner of the Lord Mayor in honor of the Duke of Cambridge. Wretched, squat-faced, inexpressive, animal-looking creatures! in every possible trait inferior to our Indians. Strong and sinewy, with teeth stained jet-black, hair equally dark and cropped close, and tight-fitting gowns of thin cloth of gold:—admirable laborers for a Southern cotton-field.

Yesterday, too, Mr. Brunel made a second failure with the Great Eastern. He attempted to move her nearer to the water and applied a force which made the piles supporting the rams give and break without budging her. This trial was a private one: and no doubt all future ones, until the huge fabric is afloat, will be conducted without public notice.

Very faithfully yrs.

## No. 167.—TO MR. CASS.

LONDON, November 24, 1857.

MY DEAR SIR,—Stillness precedes a stir:—and by that reflection I account for the silent smoothness with which political affairs are gliding to the meeting of Parliament on the 3d of December, and of the Congress at Paris shortly after. Nothing agitates the air but the fall, actual or prophesied, of some great commercial house, or the learned declamation of an "Oxon." on the duty of making a Christian demonstration against Juggernaut in Bengal, so that future divine judgments may be averted. Two parliamentary, or rather ministerial, dinners are formally announced for the 2d of December:—one by Lord Granville, the other by the Premier.

The Reform party, headed by Mr. Roebuck, think the moment propitious for a fresh movement, and have issued a sort of manifesto which may be characterized as a cowed utterance of Chartism. I think Mr. Roebuck one of the ablest, he is universally admitted to be the most independent, of the members of Parliament:—but the country is, at this moment, tamed by two wars, by the alarm-bell of the Exchange, and by the prospect of popular commotion and suffering excited by augmented taxation. The period is unwisely chosen. Although Lord Palmerston explicitly pledged himself to introduce a Reform Bill at the present session, no one expects him to do it, and already the matter is treated, in conversation and in the press, as indefinitely postponed. Mr. Roebuck's followers are sufficient neither in number nor moral weight to make head against the quiet *overslawing* current of the time.

The death of Cavaignac was thought to be the knell of the French Republican party:—yet the fact that Carnot and Goudchaux have refused to swear allegiance to the Empire indicates very strongly the reverse. I am told that, owing to some yet undeveloped cause, the popularity of Louis Napoleon among the Parisians is perceptibly waning. This may be tested by the new election ordered.

You will receive this at about the opening of Congress, and I cannot repress an entreaty that I may be promptly supplied with 1. the President's Message, 2. the Report of Mr. Cobb, and 3. the Congressional Directory.

Always faithfully yrs.

---

### No. 168.—TO MR. CASS.

LONDON, December 8, 1857.

MY DEAR SIR,—The Arabia brought me, late yesterday, your interesting Nos. 85, 86, and 87. Their tone implies a policy which has my zealous sympathy, and which I am eager to see distinctly announced in the President's Message. At this moment, public opinion all through Europe is prepared for the new American Executive's cutting through all the protracted and complicated cobwebs of controversy which it has been the pleasure of England to spin out of the fruitful womb of the Clayton-Bulwer Treaty. Lord Napier's letter to you of the 9th October looks very like a deliberated effort to lay the foundations of another series of batteries for arguments long drawn out. Your reply of the 20th probably created a flutter, a suspension of works, and an appeal for further instructions.

If the Message be what I have thought likely on our Foreign Relations, Parliament will reassemble (it adjourns on Monday the 14th) after the holidays in a temper very different from the quiet and passive one it now exhibits. Not a word given to the United States, or Central America, in the Queen's speech!* a fact commented

---

* DIARY: *December* 3, 1857.—"The opening of Parliament by the Queen in person this morning was altogether a handsome and suggestive ceremony. Here, in a vast and rich hall, was in fact concentrated the government of a widespread Empire:—Royalty, Princes, Peers, Nobles, Bishops, Law-Judges, and Commons. Her Majesty wore a crown of brilliants, and jewels sparkled over her person. Her principal garment was a glittering skirt of striped golden stuff, and she removed from her shoulders the weight of a cloak of crimson velvet bordered with ermine. She was preceded into the House of Lords, from the corridor, by high officers, who bowed to the yet vacant throne as they passed it. She was handed up to the throne by the Prince Consort. On her immediate right stood Lord Winchester, holding a gold stick surmounted by a large red velvet cap, with gold tassel, termed the Cap of Maintenance. On her immediate

upon by the *Journal des Débats*, and deemed significant of disturbances behind the scenes. And a representative of France, Mr. Belly, has proceeded to join Sir W. G. Ousely, in order to realize Lord Clarendon's old declaration as to the universal bearing of the Anglo-Franco Alliance. Very well! There is nothing so impressive upon the majority of the House of Commons as decided language from the chief of our "fierce democracie," and Lord Palmerston may find himself suddenly unhorsed by the influence of terrified manufacturers already tortured by the panic. It is an epoch at which the very questionable opinions and interpretations of a Premier will not be sustained by the popular branch of Parliament at the hazard of reviving the hostile feelings of the two countries.

I went last night to both Houses. The Lords were on India, the Commons on the Bank:—but the benches were almost empty while Lord Derby was speaking in the one, and a Scotch member in the other. It is understood that the ministry have their way on both questions; and the opposition, after a few speeches, retires listlessly from contest.

I hope you have noticed that the great English historian, like a wise man chary of fame already acquired, has retained his name and taken the oaths in the House of

---

left was Earl Granville, grasping and keeping erect, with fixed solemnity of look, the huge decorated Sword of State. The Lord Chancellor, Cranworth, was next to the Marquess of Winchester, and held in his hand the Address, which he subsequently gave, kneeling, to the Queen, to be read. Lord Lansdowne carried a Crown upon a cushion. The Princess Royal and Princess Mary of Cambridge, seated themselves in front on the Woolsack, with their faces to the Queen, their backs turned necessarily to the crowd. The chamber was full of elegantly dressed ladies:—the Peers present were few. As soon as the obstreperous rushing in of the disorderly Commons to the Bar, headed by their Speaker, had subsided, the Address was read by the Queen, still sitting, and was well read:—her Majesty manifesting a slight and attractive agitation at first. There was much to gratify in the whole performance:—but it seemed to me that its charm arose from its being headed by an exemplary lady not yet old enough to have lost beauty, grace, and sweetness of voice. Her husband occupied what might be regarded as a secondary throne, on her left beyond Lord Granville. The Address read and returned to the Lord Chancellor, the Queen rose immediately, and, handed by the Prince Consort, bowed to the audience, who all stood up, and left by the door and corridor through which she had come. The Prince of Wales was not present. Prince William of Prussia was."

Peers, with the title of Baron Macaulay. If he choose it, he will carry great weight with his new associates.

You have doubtless heard that we are in the middle of the Nineteenth Century. What a mistake! The illustrious ambassadors from Siam, on being introduced into the presence of the Queen, actually and in a group fell upon their faces, crawled on all-fours to the foot of the throne, and presented her Majesty with the right royal and magnificent present (among others) of a spittoon! Shade of Basil Hall, and Genius of Trollope! what think ye of this intrusion by the representative of "the filthy practices of Americans" into the very sanctuary of transcendental refinement? I wonder if these eastern savages are given to practical jokes, or have in their wit a spice of sarcasm.

Commercial skies are slowly brightening. The reported failures are becoming few and far between. The example of the Bank of France will probably be soon followed, and the Dame of Threadneedle Street begin to lower her interest on discounts. At Hamburg, however, and it is feared at Copenhagen and Stockholm, the financial asphyxia threatens universal ruin. How singularly similar to the progress of an epidemical cholera has the advance of this monetary derangement been! only it travels in an opposite direction, from West to East.

Mr. Brunel has not yet got his Leviathan into her element: unless she rushed down in the course of last night. One half of her journey homewards is not yet accomplished. All things, however, inspire confidence, and very soon the astronomers in the Moon will rejoice in the discovery of a great spot upon the Earth's disc.

I ought to make—and therefore I do make—a thousand apologies to the Secretary of State for this mixture of incongruities:—but, as Monsieur Crapaud says, "*Que voulez-vous?*"—my notes are as musical as I can make them.

Always faithfully yrs.

## No. 169.—TO MR. J. M. M.

LONDON, December 11, 1857.

MY DEAR SIR,—The President's Message is eagerly awaited. Misgivings as to its tone are prevalent. It may rouse an opposition in Parliament which, disposed to anything rather than quarrel with America, will oblige Lord Palmerston to quit the helm. The administration, say rather the President, has a glorious opportunity for inaugurating a grand international clearing-house.

The French scheme for reviving the Slave Trade, ostensibly a mere license to a firm, Regis & Co., to ship from Africa large numbers of negroes, *as free laborers*, for the West Indies, will probably be abandoned. Some people think, though I do not, that the functionaries of this government would have connived at the project had it remained *sub rosa*:—but the keen-sighted and loud-tongued abolitionists gave the halloo, and now Lord Clarendon, when waited upon, gives positive and impressive assurances that their great and faithful ally beyond the Channel will effectually prevent the mischief. The conception of the plan is a proof of the straits to which they are reduced, as to labor, by their fanatical humanitarianism. Observe, the English statesmen and editors have had a measure of rationality infused into their doctrine of universal emancipation by their fight with the Indian sepoys:—for though, like the scrupulous framers of our Constitution, they sink the word slaves, they in reality inflict a servitude more abject and galling than is known to our Southern States.

The House of Lords will this afternoon dispose of, by passing, the Bill of Indemnity to the Bank and the ministry for violating its Charter. That proceeding certainly seemed to lull the commercial tornado which threatened universal break-down. Until the government cried "let go and hawl," the vessel, in general opinion, was upsetting:—that spell righted her, and she has ever since, on an even keel, been slowly getting into smoother water. Failures, to be sure, are almost daily announced of houses connected in business with distant continental places, Hamburg, Copenhagen, Berlin, Vienna, Constantinople, and St. Petersburg, to which the tempest has pushed and where it is expending its expiring force. But the worst is over, here; as I fervently hope it is with you.

It is curious to observe how popular sentiment *will* force its way in this country through all sorts of aristocratic finesse and obstacles. I have noticed many instances:—but here is a new and signal one. General Havelock, by a series of gallant exploits, made himself the favorite of the day, and the people called lustily upon royalty for his reward. Well, they first settled upon him a wretched annuity of £100. Pish! cried John Bull, that will never do! Then, they made him a Baronet:—Bah! grumbled John, that may do for Sir William Williams of Kars, but here's a soldier of a dozen victories! Then, the Queen, by special message, graciously hoped her Parliament would vote, and her Parliament has voted, £1000 per annum during his life. Still the heart of John Bull is swelling and dissatisfied, and he is demanding something like what was done for Marlborough or Wellington—for John solemnly believes Havelock to have saved the British Indian Empire—and he now insists upon a peerage and a fortune to maintain it. Success to him! and succeed he will, if he but stick obstinately to his demand. Havelock's present position at Lucknow, however, renders it extremely doubtful whether he will survive to wear his honors. He is beleaguered by 70,000, and wants food; and though Sir Colin Campbell may rake together a force of 5000 to go to his assistance, a deep dread prevails that he will be too late.

Always faithfully yrs.

---

## No. 170.—TO MR. CASS.

London, December 15, 1857.

My dear Sir,—Parliament has adjourned to the 4th of February next. It was in session nearly nine working days. The Lords met on Saturday last the 12th, merely to receive the Queen's assent to the act relieving the Bank. Little positive legislation beyond that was attempted. A Committee of broad investigation as to currency was reappointed: General Havelock was voted a pension of £1000 per annum for life: and a pretty distinct intimation was thrown out that the government would be obliged to go to the relief of the funds of the East India Company. As to Reform, explicitly promised in the Queen's speech, the Premier merely added in debate, "you must wait till after the holidays for our plan: --we have no notion of allowing the critics to brood over it during the recess." One thing was too obvious for doubt: on none of the existing public measures is the opposition capable to make a stand. It is difficult to imagine a British ministry more unchecked in pursuing whatever course they like, than that of Lord Palmerston. Nor can any change be anticipated as the fruit of some measure of domestic policy. Even a ridiculously small instalment of reform—a wee bit—will fail to exasperate a serious resistance. There may possibly spring up a foreign question to disturb this smooth ascendency, but it is not easy to designate the quarter whence it can come, or to say how it will divide parties when it occurs. The practical power wielded by Lord Palmerston would make me anxious lest, to attain some sinister purpose, it should be exerted against the United States, but that I feel assured that he and his cabinet are too sagacious voluntarily to run the risk of the only national quarrel which their countrymen cannot and will not uphold. His lordship's theory of administration certainly leads him to keep open an issue of war, as a vent for the humors of John Bull: and if he closes the Indian struggle, as appearances indicate that he soon will, you may expect to see Canton sacked, and Pekin menaced. But he must be very tightly cornered before he will aim at America, and so revive the swarming of the hosts of manufacturing hornets upon his head.

The solicitude about Outram and Havelock, cooped up in Lucknow with an extra train of women and children, continues, although somewhat less desperate owing to recent accounts. The contending forces are converging to that point, and the result of an assault by Sir Colin Campbell will probably close the insurrection. He was near being captured on his way to take the command. Travelling *en courrier* without an escort, in order to be quick, he pounced suddenly upon a considerable body of mutineers, and narrowly escaped by the fleetness of his horse.

In the course of next month the marriage of the Princess Royal is to attract hither an immense flight of crowned personages, their families, or representatives. Her Majesty has not palaces enough to accommodate her guests, and is obliged to engage public hotels in advance. The chief theatres will, in the same service, be thrown gratuitously open for several weeks. Every effort at brilliant éclat will be made. You probably experienced and remember the effect of such whirling court festivities upon a republican minister.

The money crisis seems to subside quite as fast as the monster steamer:—both are, however, still *upon the stocks*.

Always faithfully yrs.

---

## No. 171.—TO MR. CASS.

LONDON, December 22, 1857.

MY DEAR SIR,—The Message reached London at about 5 A.M. yesterday. I read it in bed and composedly. It appeared, in pretty large fragments, in most of the morning papers. It is frankly and distinctly praised, except in that portion which deals of the Clayton-Bulwer Treaty. The *Times* and the *Post* of to-day contain comments; and perhaps these, better than my impressions formed in so short a space of time, will enable you to see the reception it has had here; and although I know you have files of these papers sent to you, it may be convenient to have the slips I now enclose. By the interference of Terence's play at the School of Westminster with the free agency of one of my guests at dinner yesterday, I missed the opportunity of being told the sentiment of Lord Clarendon, who had in the early part of the day talked fully to him on the subject. I got my copy before sunrise, by virtue of an arrangement to expedite it from Liverpool on the arrival of the Arabia.

Commercial matters appear to be improving. They have not been as bad in France as either here or with us. They are still deplorable in Germany; and some intelligent merchants anticipate that the failures in that quarter, especially the north, will react upon France, and make matters worse than they have yet been. Consols have run up to within a shade of 93:—but the Bank still exacts 10 p.c. interest.

The town is deserted and dull.

Always faithfully yrs.

P. S.—The Message is printed at full length, not in fragments, in to-day's *Times*, partially disfigured by the headings to the several topics, originally devised by the New York *Herald*.

---

## No. 172.—TO MR. CASS.

LONDON, December 29, 1857.

MY DEAR SIR,—It occurs to me as possible that the many interesting subjects which are hourly demanding your attention in Washington may make you give less welcome than heretofore to these desultory letters of mine. I hope you will not hesitate, if so, to tell me to relax the stream.

It is quite apparent that the two leading topics for parliamentary disposition, in February, will be representative Reform, and a modification of the government in India. The minister will, after all and possibly very unwillingly, be obliged to offer his bill. A scheme novel in its character has been recommended to him, in a formal Memorial, by a large number of influential persons headed by the Archbishop of Canterbury. After the fashion of thinking which prevails here, the plan has its plausibilities. It rests upon the idea of creating a new and distinct constituency, to be composed of those who have been "*liberally educated;*"—that is, according to English common parlance, of the professions—of lawyers, physicians, and parsons. These, throughout the Empire, are designed to be jumbled into a separate mass, and to send their representatives from specified localities to the House of Commons. It is calculated that this constituency will furnish about seventy members, contributed in pretty nearly equal proportions by the Bar, the Faculty, and the Clergy. It is *class* representation, intended and avowed, according to some narrower examples already existing. Much attention has been awakened to it, and it may not be entirely excluded from the ministerial project. In discussing it the other day, at a dinner table, before some Judges and Members of the House, I took the liberty to characterize it as a sop thrown to Cerberus, oiled with conservatism, which, instead of satisfying, would only sharpen appetite: and that, after all, if they wanted to do justice to their fellow-men, nothing was so conservative as universal suffrage, the very opposite of such class preferences.

You notice that Baron Brunow returns to this Court, which he left when the Crimean war broke out. I hear through a diplomatic colleague that Count Kreptowitch, owing to some unexplained cause, went back to St. Petersburg somewhat under a cloud. *Sed, de hoc quære?*

Count and Countess Platen, who succeed, from Sweden, Baron and Baroness Hochschild (the former dead), are plain, unpretending, and attractive persons. The Count told me he had begun life in the British navy, had been in the Swedish ministry, but had retired many years ago from public affairs. He is owner of a large fortune. They knew intimately my old friend Mr. Christopher Hughes, whose daughter married Senator Kennedy of Maryland.

The Spaniard, Bravo, is off again to Madrid. He left here on the 21st instant. The very nice young gentleman whom he leaves Chargé d'Affaires, Conti, says that the minister is a leading member of the Spanish legislature, and that his presence in the Body is occasionally indispensable. Nothing need be apprehended against Mexico. The movement of General Walker may possibly revive a little alarmed bustle—for Spain regards all filibustering as ultimately destined against Cuba—but the President's Message effectually secures her good behavior.

The vestiges of the commercial panic are fast disappearing. The Bank suddenly dropped her rate of interest from 10 to 8, and will shortly lower to 6. She does but conform to the street rate. The storm is, however, growling as it retreats on the Continent. Everybody eulogizes Mr. Cobb's report, and the tendency to American investments will before long be greater than ever.

Sir Colin Campbell has done his job handsomely, with only such an amount of wound as would attest his personal activity and exposure. The details of his relieving

Lucknow have not yet arrived. He is conjectured to have returned to Cawnpore, there to organize an overpowering force for the subjection of the kingdom of Oude.

Can it be possible that while the case of the "Panchita" was being disclaimed and apologized for, the same thing was going on with dozens of our vessels and flags?

Many happy returns of the season.

Always faithfully yrs.

---

## No. 173.—TO MR. MARKOE.

LONDON, January 5, 1858.

MY DEAR MARKOE,—Your letters are full of interest to me, of one sort or another, and I thank you heartily for them.

General Cass has been, I honestly fear, palled by the ceaseless stream of those I have written to him. During the active labors thrown upon him by the session of Congress, he can hardly have leisure to break their seals. Miscellaneous and transient as their topics are, the desire to keep them up as long as they can prove, in the remotest degree, useful or agreeable, has kept me watchful of all the minor incidents of the day, and constantly on the *qui vive*. They cost me a great deal more in attention and thought, than the routine of official despatches:—and yet, I have a misgiving lest they oppress the General and be really valueless. Tell me the bald truth, without a mincing word.

I think I drew your curiosity before I left home to "Christie Johnstone," one of Reade's first novels. Well, now get his last, "White Lies." It is written with the same boldness of conscious power, is thoroughly and designedly French, and has a noble tone of domestic virtue and of moral.

Tell M. that the general inclination here is to disbelieve in the Leviathan. Another failure yesterday almost extinguishes hope;—but it arose from an outside piece of carelessness: a bark ran into and disturbed one of the barges essential to the operation: and so *I* keep a stiff upper lip of confidence in ultimate success.

Always sincerely yrs.

## No. 174.—TO MR. CASS.

LONDON, January 8, 1858.

MY DEAR SIR,—Yesterday's telegram of Indian news announces the death of General Havelock by dysentery, a few days after his leaving Lucknow, and the defeat of General Wyndham near Cawnpore by the Gwalior contingent of sepoys. This last force of mutineers was, about ten days subsequently, attacked and routed by Sir Colin Campbell. It is difficult to understand the defeat of Wyndham: but its effect must be greatly to reanimate and encourage the rebels. Explanatory details will not reach here for a week or ten days.

The necessity of Parliament's authorizing the East India Company to effect a loan in England of about £8,000,000, seems generally conceded. It will probably precede, and not embarrass, the fundamental change contemplated in the mode of governing "the Eastern Conquest." That change will mainly consist in bringing the political sovereignty of the Empire, passing by the "Company," to bear, in name and in reality, upon all Hindostan as a national conquest: in founding a new ministerial department exclusively devoted to the supervision and control of that immense region: and in fact, at the expiration of more than sixty years, to take the defeated scheme of Mr. Fox, and abandon for it the disproved one of Mr. Pitt. This important topic of legislation will go far to elbow out of the coming session every other, and may help especially in still farther putting off definitive action on Parliamentary Reform.

I can't avoid thinking that the present moment is peculiarly favorable for relieving our country from so much of the Ashburton Treaty as calls for the constant presence of an American squadron on the Western Coast of Africa. 1. The plan is, confessedly on all sides, a failure. 2. The whole system of British emancipation is combated. 3. The demand for black labor in the West Indies is loud and imperative. 4. France is obviously reluctant to yield up her cunningly devised method of reviving the trade by seeming to pay wages to ignorant brutes eager to exchange the actual servitude under their barbarous chiefs for the prospective and ameliorated one under white masters. 5. Is it not an "entangling alliance," of a nature to make us, ostensibly in pursuit of a common object, always play a secondary and equivocal part? 6. The press here, so long and so energetic in the negro policy, is backing before the logic of experiments and facts;—not a little perhaps affected by the consciousness of a glaring inconsistency in the two crusades, one *against* African slavery, the other *for* Hindoo slavery, both black!

Two great institutions, the Bank and the Leviathan, are nearing smooth water. The former lowered her interest to 6 p. c. yesterday; and the latter has become so tractable that she has gone on her ways rejoicing at the prodigious velocity of eighteen feet in forty-eight hours. Eheu! These monsters, nevertheless, are very differently actuated. One shuns, the other seeks, liquidation!

A German paper suggests the probability that the Prince of Prussia, now vested with the powers of Regent, will, on the death of the deranged King, carry into effect an often declared purpose of abdication:—so that the Princess Royal of England, having married his son, may first put her foot in Berlin as Queen of Prussia.

Our steam communication is becoming less frequent, irregular, and uncertain.

Always faithfully yrs.

---

## No. 175.—TO MR. CASS.

LONDON, January 15, 1858.

MY DEAR SIR,—The *Times* of this morning contains a telegram from Paris, dated at 10 o'clock last night, announcing that the Emperor had been shot at as he was entering the Opera House. Some few features of personal display and of popular sympathy are stated, but we await the details. You may have noticed that, during this lively season of the year, his Majesty has, with much ostentation, seemed to give himself confidently to his subjects, to walk about the streets in plain dress and without attendants, and to talk occasionally with a lively "*boutiquière.*" This was done, I think, twice, and duly noted in the newspapers. Whether the vigilant agents of the police, as at Osborne, encircled the Imperial person and gave him the ease of perfect security, no one knows. Suddenly, in the darkness of night, and without being touched, he is fired at: what next? All history tells how such incidents are used, to avoid an impending danger:—how can a generous people allow a chief who shews such free and confiding trust in them, to be victimized by conspirators and assassins? So, then, body guards, spies, and the army! Besides, is it not well to divert men's thoughts, in the profound tranquillity of politics which now prevails, by initiating a fresh series of arrests and of "*causes célèbres*"? The worst interpretation which can be put upon the event, is precisely that which best harmonizes with the character of its principal personage.

The Bank of England, yesterday afternoon, lowered her rate of discount to 5 per cent., and thus I think has discharged the farewell volley over the grave of the departed panic. She may reduce still farther:—but that will be owing to the plethoric fulness of her vaults.

Walker's capture by Paulding, and his subsequent alleged enlargement, are variously commented upon. Lord Palmerston's organ rails like a very drab. Generally, however, the arrest is regarded as a lucky thing, though accompanied by a violation of a foreign territorial jurisdiction. Nicaragua is clearly the only authority offended and entitled to complain, but will she be absurd enough for that? In converting into pirates those who offend our neutrality laws, and so making them like slave-traders seizable under the statute anywhere, it would seem to me that the Commodore has not manifested the discrimination of a criminal lawyer. Perhaps he remembered Porter's pursuit of pirates to Foxardo, and Jackson's following the Indians across the boundary into Florida:—if so, I am afraid he has confused extremely dissimilar cases. My curiosity is up to know exactly what you propose to do with this little complication. Perhaps, having the breaker of the law actually in your power, you will send him to a jury, and then appease Nicaragua by disclaiming the act of taking him on her soil. If you don't deal with him, his security in New Orleans will probably hasten to take him on a bail-piece.

Col. P. of Virginia, who tells me that he has succeeded

in effecting an arrangement with a French Railway Company, and Mr. John M. B., who has been visiting Russia, are both here on their way homeward.

Always faithfully yrs.

---

## No. 176.—TO MR. CASS.

LONDON, January 21, 1858.

MY DEAR SIR,—I was not far out of the way when, in my last, some of the philosophy of history was hastily applied to the recent escape of Louis Napoleon from assassination. He has hurried onward, while the explosions of the bombs were still echoing, to destroy every vestige of freedom. His address to the legislative body, written with uncommon ability and beauty, is simply a declaration of absolute despotism in maintenance of his dynasty. Repression must be the order of the day, to silence opposition and establish safety:—national prosperity can only be permanent when all resistance to him, as "*the just,*" is extinguished. Already, two journals, *Le Spectateur*, and *Revue de Paris*, are suppressed. The Ordinances of Charles X. were nothing to this:—and yet all Paris, under the excitement of an abortive conspiracy, is showering upon him enthusiastic congratulations as the protected of Providence, and assurances of devoted allegiance! How far this country connives at this "conspiracy" to rebuild the edifice of arbitrary power, it is not difficult to perceive. Telegraphic messages of sympathy stream between the Tuileries and St. James: and in all the court circles, and special court papers, the moment and the man are avowed to be propitious for chaining down the monster democracy. "*Laissez aller!*" While the army remains at his beck, he can go on: but let that falter for an instant, and France will spring up more anti-monarchical than in 1789. The faster he goes, the sooner will return the dawn of liberty.

The vehemence with which the Parisian orators and editors demand that England shall cease to be the sanctuary for refugee contrivers of revolution, may lead to important consequences. The cabinet is unprepared for a decided stand either way. The impression is that the topic has created internal dissension, and that the Premier is disposed to measures which will enable the government to order away whomsoever the French Emperor may desire to be so treated:—but he is alone in that opinion. This subject is connected in common conversation with another which is supposed also to threaten the "*entente cordiale*," and that is, Napoleon's private determination to adhere, for the benefit of Guadaloupe and Martinique, to the policy of the Regis contract. He is said to insist that it involves no violation of treaty, and that the interest of France demands a supply of black labor for her West Indian islands. The other night at a state ball, the Hanoverian expressed himself as anxious and apprehensive that "these contrarieties would make them very angry at St. Cloud!" To avert such an appalling danger, we shall probably witness all sorts of propitiatory attempts and speeches in the Parliament, which reassembles on 3d proximo.

We have a new member of the corps, in the person of Mons. Van Dockum, who succeeds the President's ardent friend General Oxholm, as minister from Denmark. The subject which engrosses that kingdom, and may involve a war, is the controversy with the Duchies of Holstein and Lauenburg. The army is being increased.

Spain has had another spasm or "crisis." Armero and Mon have thrown up, in view of their defeat in the election of a President of the Cortes, and we have, for perhaps a brief spell, an Isturitz ministry. The old mother Queen Christina is still anxious to augment the value of her large investments in Cuba, and her Court influence at Madrid is perhaps greater while she is absent. Your plan of communicating to our foreign legations the outline of what is designed and doing at each Court, would have told me your intentions as to the ultimately inevitable island. Of course I am scrupulous of touching, without some sort of authority to do so, any diplomatic purpose outside of Great Britain. But might I not lubricate a little wheel or two in casual conversation? As I understand it, the mountain which impedes our progress and through which we have to tunnel with care is the hurt feeling of national and really false pride. Such an obstacle may prove impenetrable and insurmountable; but, all circumstances considered, I doubt whether you can have a fitter moment than the present for undertaking it. The ruffled sense of honor is soothed by the sentiments of the Message on filibustering, while it is by no means easy for the pinched and disordered treasury of Spain to meet the amount of our just reclamations. There is, too, just now, among *some* who could aid your purpose, an opinion which, though adverse to slavery in general, deems it to be less reprehensible under the laws and morals of the United States than elsewhere, and would feel rather philanthropically employed than otherwise in being accessary to its transfer from Spain to us.

The *Almanach de Gotha* is enjoying its triumph in London. The hard names, complicated pedigrees, and endless titles of German royalty, are exercising the oldest and best of us. The palace swarms with the kindred of the Queen, actual and contemplated, for the wedding festivities:—and I must frankly own that these continental foreigners, both male and female, are very conspicuous for refinement of manners, delicacy of look, and absence of affectation.

Always faithfully yrs.

---

## No. 177.—TO MR. CASS.

LONDON, January 26, 1858.

MY DEAR SIR,—It is difficult while in the rapids of *wedding festivities*,* to stop and gather sober thoughts and facts

---

* DIARY: *January* 26, 1858.—"Queen Victoria's eldest daughter, Victoria Adelaide, was yesterday married to Frederick William, the Prince Royal of Prussia. The ceremony took place in the Chapel Royal at St. James' Palace, and in the presence of a comparatively small number of persons. The diplomatic corps were provided with seats as advantageous and comfortable as the building afforded, in the gallery facing the altar. The Archbishop of Canterbury and the Bishop of London performed the service:—the Bishop of Oxford and another being in the background, on the '*haut pas.*' About three hundred people in all witnessed the proceeding, which was as brilliant and effective as such a spectacle could possibly be. All the appropriate royalties, appropriately disposed, and making appropriate movements at appropriate moments, executed their respective parts in the interesting show to the general satisfaction. The appearance of the Queen, surrounded by her brood of children and seemingly flurried by natural excitement, inspired the kindest sympa-

for a Secretary of State. In truth, since I wrote by the Canada on the 23d instant, nothing of political bearing has occurred or, at least, caught my attention. I have, to be sure, a few items for a formal despatch, but they are incomplete, and I shall not trouble you with them until by doing so I am able to dispose of them finally. They are quite unimportant.

The President is doubtless well acquainted with Lord Overstone, formerly Samuel Jones Lloyd, created peer in 1850. He is, as I conceive, the highest financial authority, theoretically and practically, now living in England. At the state ball, a few nights ago, I expressed to him the gratification I had received in reading in the *Edinburgh Review* of the present month some comments upon his monetary and banking papers. He immediately insisted upon sending me his two volumes published last year. They came to-day, accompanied by the note of which the enclosed is a copy. I enclose it because of its reference to the President's Message and Secretary Cobb's Report, as the opinion of so competent and fair a judge cannot but have its interest to those gentlemen.

The diplomatic illuminations of last night were exceedingly dazzling. That with which your representative contented himself was a simple and brilliant star.

Always faithfully yrs.

---

thy:—the bridegroom's gallant and graceful kissing of the ring as he put it in the hand of the Archbishop:—the beautiful group of eight bridesmaids uniformly dressed in white, with their hair encircled by a wreath of pink roses: the 'abandon' of the embraces and felicitations among the newly created kindred after the marriage was finished:—the joyous aspect of the couple as they left the chapel '*man and wife*:'—the rich and regulated music: the gorgeousness of the toilettes:—all these striking features combined to invest the first wedding in the family of Victoria and Albert with a charm I had not expected. We went to it at 9½ A.M., and were at home again at 1½ P.M. At 10 at night a monster concert in the great ball-room of Buckingham Palace."

## No. 178.—TO LORD OVERSTONE.

LONDON, January 27, 1858.

MY DEAR LORD OVERSTONE,—Allow me to thank you for the very welcome present you sent me yesterday of the two volumes of your excellent tracts on metallic and paper currency. They are a mine of thought, experience, and logic, whence I propose to draw much instruction and conviction.

The monetary science has a wide field to explore and watch in the United States. Although the Federal government has, by the Constitution, the exclusive power to coin money, regulate the value thereof and of foreign coin and fix the standard of weights and measures, and although the respective States are expressly prohibited from emitting bills of credit or making anything but gold and silver coin a tender in payment of debts:—yet by an early judicial construction given to these provisions, the right of each State to create banks of issue and discount, and to manage its own currency, was recognized. This "State Right" decision, though often argumentatively controverted and deplored, has, for half a century, continued unreversed, and I fear must be deemed irreversible. Hence the control and operations of the currency are, practically, not in the single general government, but in the local legislatures, who are of various intelligence and motive, and who have deluged the country with separate floods of paper from more than twelve hundred banks. I mention this in order to shew you how deeply interesting to the statesmen of America such productions as your *Tracts* must be; and at the same time to intimate how really powerless and irresponsible our President and Secretary of the Treasury are, notwithstanding the soundness of their views.

This latter gentleman will, I am quite sure, be highly gratified should you determine to send him a copy of the *Tracts;* and it will give me much pleasure to forward them, with a note from you, in the despatch bag of this legation.

Reiterating my acknowledgments for your kindness, I have the honor to be,

My lord, yours faithfully.

## No. 179.—TO MR. J. R. McCULLOCH.

LONDON, February 4, 1858.

DEAR SIR,—Allow me to express the very great pleasure you conferred by sending me a copy of the Treatise on Money and Banks.* It is now many years since a work on political economy first introduced me (if I am not mistaken) to a name which has been held thenceforward in high estimation.

I am happy to find that the sound views on Banking contained in the President's first Message to Congress have your sanction. They are undoubtedly those maintained by experienced and enlightened statesmen throughout the United States. But, in carrying them out, we are encountered by difficulties such as, in a different system of government on this side of the Atlantic, you can but partially appreciate. The constitutional power to create a national bank is denied to the Federal legislature:—while, within their respective limits, the separate States charter money corporations, privileged to issue and discount *ad libitum*. Hence the channels of circulation are crammed with paper which loses nearly all value the instant any derangement of business creates distrust. Under such circumstances, the Federal authority is powerless over the currency, except so far as, within its own spheres of collection and expenditure, it maintains the solid superiority of its gold and silver coin. Something is achieved by keeping the government at Washington "*a hard money government:*"—and yet, until in the several States a reform of ideas on banking be thoroughly effected, the country in all its departments of trade and labor must continue liable to the shocks and mischiefs of redundant and inconvertible currency. It is no easy matter to correct perverted theories as they exist or arise at the thirty-one birthplaces of more than twelve hundred banks:—but I trust that even this is not impossible under the steady inculcations of our executive state papers, and of such authoritative treatises as that with which you have honored me.

Repeating my sincere thanks,
I am with the highest respect yrs.

---

* Treatise afterwards printed in the *Encyclopædia Britannica.*

## No. 180.—TO MR. CASS.

LONDON, February 5, 1858.

MY DEAR SIR,—There are two volumes in the Bag of to-day for Mr. C——. They are the "unpublished" (that is, printed for private circulation only) tracts of Lord Overstone on Currency, collected by the political economist, Mr. J. R. McCulloch. Of these papers, an article in the January number of the *Edinburgh Review* says, "As literary compositions, they are master-pieces:—as contributions to monetary science, they rank with the congenial and analogous productions of Adam Smith, Horner, and Ricardo." "As regards the investigation of questions peculiarly relating to the regulation of the circulation, and to the theory of Banking, Lord Overstone is in some respects superior to his illustrious predecessors." The author has been extremely pleased with the financial doctrines of the President's Message, and with their elaboration in the Report of the Secretary of the Treasury. Hence, as a mark of high respect, he has begged me to be the medium of conveying this compilation.

The two houses of Parliament had a reasonably short session yesterday, and the leaders of the opposition, Messrs. Derby and Disraeli, made their customary opening proclamations. By the reply they received, it is obvious that, under the pretext of only doing what is just, the ministry is prepared with a bill on the Refugee question by which to deprecate the wrath of the new Cæsar and his menacing legions. On this delicate point, the state of excitement throughout the country, in the press and among the people, has been such that the course proposed will be as severe a blow upon the pride and pretension of John Bull as he has ever experienced. Disguise the concession as they may, it will be ever adjudged an undignified and frightened retreat from the very citadel of their own most boasted laws, before the threats of Louis Napoleon. See, how just after vaunting their prowess in repelling, on behalf of Europe, the approaches of the northern Colossus of Absolutism, they connive at and cower to a fiercer and more proscriptive military tyranny in their ally!

The active measures of repression and precaution taken by Bonaparte are generally construed to betray great alarm founded upon the knowledge of some facts not yet publicly known as to the extent and resources of the conspiracy against his throne. He has gone farther than can be otherwise explained: as, for instance, in not merely dividing France into five military districts with a Marshal resident in each, but chiefly in authorizing each of these officers, on any supposed emergency, to act with his whole force without waiting the orders of the Emperor.

The wars in India and China are exacting reinforcements, and great exertions are being made to get recruits. It is understood, however, that the operation is flat and unproductive. From India we have no recent news of importance. Appearances indicate a protracted and exhausting struggle. From China, news is hourly expected of the bombardment and capture of Canton. Of course no one dreams that the assault of English and French forces combined can be repelled by the refractory Yeh. Some of "our own correspondents," to be sure, have repeated a rumor that the principal streets had been mined, with a determination that the city and its invaders should be destroyed together. That's the Russian mode of action;—not the Chinese.

The East India Company has been both industrious and spirited in resisting the transfer of her government to the Crown. The directors and proprietors have held a number of public meetings:—and the speeches and addresses have made out a better defence of their administration than was thought possible. A lively essay in *Blackwood's Magazine* for this month, entitled a letter from John Company to John Bull, gives a familiar and pretty fair view of the controversy.

The vacuum created in public solicitude by the Leviathan having floated safely to her moorings at Deptford and the Bank's weekly reduction of her interest until she has sunk to 3½ per cent., is being refilled by fresh movements preparatory to laying the Atlantic telegraphic cable.

All the festivities of the royal wedding having been brought to a close, and the young couple being ensconced in their Berlin home, we are suddenly called upon to don our suits of sable for the Grand Duke of Baden, who died pending the marriage ceremonies.

Always faithfully yrs.

## No. 181.—TO COL. MURRAY.

LONDON, February 8, 1858.

MY DEAR SIR,—I have lots of thanks to hand you from Mr. H. and myself for your kindness in procuring the information wanted respecting our coinage.

It might be supposed that so important and interesting a state paper as the Annual Report of our Secretary of the Treasury must have been transmitted to this legation from the State Department long before now. Alas! no—we *foreign agents* of the government must be contented with what we can pick up in the newspapers as to *current* matters:—by-and-by, when they have become antiquated and stale, then we are deluged with floods of Executive and Congressional volumes which the public printer furnishes for the benefit of his own finances. I am yet without a document of national manufacture since November last.

You observe how incontinently the great allies are getting by the ears. Louis Napoleon seems to have been somewhat upset by those hand grenades of Orsini, and is pursuing measures of tyranny "hand over hand"! He has the talent of *looking* cool:—but his acts betray supreme terror for his person and his dynasty. A man who usurps power with the incidents of the *coup d'état* should be conscious that millions are, at every minute, aiming to "hit back again," and become callous to *attentats*. He, however, seems surprised; and he encourages a blustering attack upon England by his officers of state, his army, and his press, as the sheltering den of miscreant assassins. Well! all England bristles up with indignation, talks back the libel, reviews "the Little" from top to toe, and hurls the phrases "murderer" and "conspirator" in his teeth. A pretty little quarrel as it stands! But old diplomatic heads will take care not to let the skrimmage go too far. Already the Premier has interposed a soothing draught in the House of Commons. It may be discussed this afternoon. Like a bread pill, it may make the Imperial patient believe he is taking something very composing and satisfactory, while in fact it is inoffensive nothing.

Ever faithfully yrs.

## No. 182.—TO MR. CASS.

LONDON, February 9, 1858.

MY DEAR SIR,—No preparations were made for sending anything to you by the Arago from Southampton to-morrow:—but as Mr. Pierce, the secretary of legation at St. Petersburg, being on his way home, has offered to take charge of a Bag, I have suddenly determined to send one.

The tempest of excitement against Louis Napoleon for having "insulted and threatened England," after raging in the Press, has found its way into both houses of Parliament. Mr. Roebuck, last night, in the Commons, and Lord Lyndhurst, in the Peers, exhibited great feeling and vindicated the public clamor. The attempt to appease indignation by an equivocal apology for the publicity given in the *Moniteur*, did not produce the success anticipated. The debate, which arose on a bill offered by Lord Palmerston to change the criminal law so far as to make a conspiracy to murder, in or out of England, instead of a *misdemeanor* punishable by fine and imprisonment, a *felony* liable on conviction to the minimum of five years, and the *maximum* of perpetual imprisonment, and to *transportation*, continued for several hours and was postponed without conclusion till to-day. It is curious to note that the *Times*, while advocating in its editorials the passage of this measure, supplies in the letters of its Parisian correspondent the most sharp and powerful weapons employed by its opponents. Thus,—that correspondent dwells upon the unquestionable fact that the present Emperor has hunted up and paid to Cantilo the legacy left to him by Napoleon I. as a reward for having attempted to assassinate the Duke of Wellington: and thus, too, he points out that the Colonels, who have in their addresses been especially abusive of "the den of assassins," have received the cross of the Legion of Honor, and promotion!

This subject absorbs the attention and feeling of the public. My opinion is that the ministry, aided by a large number of Conservatives, will carry their propitiatory measure.

Always faithfully yrs.

## No. 183.—TO MR. CASS.

LONDON, February 12, 1858.

MY DEAR SIR,—Enclosed are copies of two "*Private*" notes between Mr. H. and myself. I applied some ten days ago for the surrender of a man who was charged with murder on the high seas, on board of an American vessel. They seemed dilatory at the Foreign Office, and I addressed a "remind" to Lord Clarendon. Hence these epistles. I cannot conceive that the broad terms used in the extradition treaty will receive from the Crown officers the restricted or qualified construction which has suggested itself to the mind of her Majesty's principal Secretary of State for Foreign Affairs. Novel interpretations of the plainest international engagements are, however, a little too much the order of the day. This one, if persisted in, is so palpably wrong, that I should be disposed to regard the treaty as fit for the category of the Clayton-Bulwer, that is, fit for abrogation.

When I receive a formal communication from the Earl upon the subject, it shall become a part of a despatch, into which *private* notes from under-secretaries should perhaps not be introduced except on extraordinary occasions.

Lord Palmerston's bill, on the Refugee question, was allowed to be read a first time by a very large majority, in the House of Commons. It will, however, be attacked in committee, and be strenuously opposed at every stage. I was last night told by a Peer, that neither this measure, nor the Premier's India Bill (which he offers this afternoon), nor his Reform Bill, can pass in the Lords; and that he might cease to be the head of the government before the present session closed. These representations I suspect to be the offspring of party feeling, for I can perceive no diminution in his popularity or power.

You will have noticed fresh successes by Sir Colin Campbell in India, and the capture of Canton by the allied forces.

Always faithfully yrs.

## No. 184.—TO MR. HAMMOND.

LONDON, February 12, 1858.

MY DEAR MR. HAMMOND,—I can entertain no doubt as to the construction heretofore put by the government of the United States upon our Extradition Treaty of 1842.

The point arose when a similar treaty was negotiating by Mr. Webster, Secretary of State, and Baron Gerolt, the minister from Prussia, at Washington, in 1852. The language used in the Xth article of our Treaty, "all persons," was perceived to be too comprehensive for the powers of the King of Prussia, and of a large number of the German States (parties to the treaty) as restricted by their respective constitutions and laws:—and so in the preamble was specially recited the limited sense given to the general phraseology, and its cause.

I think, indeed, that owing to the constant employment of the seamen of each nation on board of the other's vessels, an extradition treaty which left either at liberty to decline the surrender of its own citizens or subjects, would lose more than half its value to both.

Very truly and respectfully yrs.

---

## No. 185.—TO MR. CASS.

LONDON, February 23, 1858.

MY DEAR SIR,—The despatch of to-day tells you of the sudden downfall of Lord Palmerston. It is possibly like that of the Son of the Morning, irreparable. The ground upon which it was achieved is undeniable as a fact, and as a sentiment irresistible. He *neglected*, is the charge, to maintain the national honor when it was assailed in the insolent and exacting letter of Walewski. This is the point on which he has heretofore, and justly, plumed himself for promptness and boldness, the lack of which at Vienna kept another statesman for some years under a cloud. Certainly nothing could be more insufferably offensive than the French tone; and John Bull has suddenly awakened to the conviction that his old hatred is as bitter as ever.

Among the rumors of the day, I have been told that the French minister, Mr. Persigny, while the Conspiracy Bill was pending, visited Lord Derby, and in the course of conversation, impressively urged its early passage. Well, said Lord D., it may get through;—but it may not, and what then? What then? exclaimed the ambassador,—"*la guerre!*" Ah! was the cool reply, you had better go and tell that to Clarendon! His Excellency left for Paris the next day:—the papers report him gone to a country seat; and it is conjectured that he may not return to London.

One of Lord Derby's earliest calls, after being invested with the power to construct a ministry, was on Mr. Gladstone. That accomplished gentleman expressed a readiness to join him, on one condition, however, namely, that his political associates, the principal of whom are Newcastle, Herbert, Grey, Graham, and Cardwell, would go with him. All of these, when asked, flatly refused.

On the day of the ministerial resignation, Saturday last, I dined at the Palace, and met at table, among a number of guests, two of the retired secretaries, Lord Clarendon and Sir Charles Wood. Their happy exhilaration was quite unusual and striking. No doubt, they felt personally the relief of having thrown off an immense weight of complications, commitments, and responsibilities. Such loads as the Conspiracy Bill, the India Bill, the Reform Bill, the war in China, and the Sepoy war, are not easily carried.

At the dinner, when my turn to receive a gracious word from her Majesty arrived, she informed me that she intended writing to the President on the subject of her daughter's marriage, and to send him a medal which she had had struck in commemoration of that happy event. These medals are of three descriptions, gold, silver, and bronze; and they are represented as exceedingly beautiful in design and execution. Of course, I made the proper assurances of the high gratification with which such a remembrance from her Majesty would be received by the President.

Always faithfully yrs.

## No. 186.—TO MR. CASS.

LONDON, March 5, 1858.

MY DEAR SIR,—The "inaugural" speech of the Prime Minister in the House of Lords on Monday was faultless in manner, and in general tone becoming. It was, however, impossible not to perceive that Lord Derby was oppressed by a consciousness of party weakness, and of his being at the mercy of the Liberal majority in the Commons. He enunciated no distinctive policy, assumed no elevated stand, but on the contrary seemed to deprecate the antagonism of those he had overthrown, by generally adhering to their recent measures, and by some instances of special compliment. He would go on with the India Bill:—he would continue the war in China; he would conform to the advanced state of public opinion by maturing a Reform Bill: and for the first time, he relaxed the rigid character of his conservative party by defining it as ready to introduce safe improvements of every sort. He eulogized the management of the army by Lord Panmure and the Duke of Cambridge. On the ruling topic of the day, the Imperial demand that the English criminal law should be made more stringent, he was puzzled how to shape his course differently from the one pursued by his predecessors. The French alliance was of incalculable value; and yet his countrymen were justly indignant at the libels and menaces which had been vented by certain official and military functionaries, and which had been crowding the Parisian papers headed by the *Moniteur*. He would take the vote of the House of Commons on Mr. Milner Gibson's motion as the voice of the people of England:—he would make that the groundwork of his action; he would, by a paper already prepared by Lord Malmesbury, answer appropriately Count Walewski's despatch of the 20th of January, and he should receive in reply such disclaimers of injurious meaning as would satisfy British honor and preserve the alliance.

At the close of this address, Lord Clarendon vindicated his forbearance in not at once answering the offensive letter, by a speech unusually lucid and able. But there was this obvious misapprehension of the gist of the matter running through the whole:—namely, he treated Walewski's letter, not as a *national act* but as an indiscreet ebullition of personal excitement, an imprudence that might be easiest got over in conversation between Lord Cowley and the Count. Every one must have felt that this secret mode of adjusting a public point of national honor would not do:—the affront should be repelled and disclaimed as it was given.

I have been struck by the series of incidents which led to this sudden change of the government. It is difficult to ascribe the immediate resignation of Lord Palmerston solely to the equivocal, and by no means impressive, censure of Milner Gibson's resolution. Perhaps I regard it from an American point of view:—but I cannot help thinking that, had not the roar of the angry and approaching masses been heard, the retirement would have been less precipitate. The plain truth is that on this point of conceding to foreign dictation and menace, the hearts of the people were in advance of the heads of their representatives of both political parties:—a case we have often seen illustrated in our own history. After all said and done, there *are* special occasions on which it may be accepted as Gospel that Vox populi *est* Vox Dei. The roar is less loud for the moment, that Lord Derby may have a fair chance:—but let him tamper for an instant with this deep and deaf popular sentiment, and he will have to follow the footsteps of his illustrious predecessor.

In the midst of all these grave proceedings, one cannot help being amused at some few manifestations of harlequinade. Almost in the same hour, some score of ponderous politicians invade the Palace, hand their seals (supposititiously?) to the Queen, kiss her hand, and bow backward into the grave of private life: and then advance an equal score among whom the seals are re-distributed, who kiss hands, and who stream like eagles, from the presence of her little Majesty, to the pinnacles of power! Observe, too, that the change in government exacts other more visible changes, as for instance, whereas the former score of functionaries sat, in either House, on long benches at the right of the presiding officer, Chancellor or Speaker, and the present score sat on similar benches on the left, *now* they must cross hands and front each other from exactly opposite quarters. And, as their chiefs do, so must the whole body of each of the political parties do: thus placing the ministry for the time being always on the right and the opposition always on the left. No doubt there is practical convenience in this conventional course of action, but it reminds one comically of the dancing among the Shaking Quakers.

You observe that Changarnier declines returning to France, until her population is "in possession of laws protecting their dignity and safety." This is throwing the glove at the foot of the throne, and, connected with subterranean rumors which have reached me, has much more than its apparent significance.

The new ministers are rapidly getting re-elected to their seats in the Commons: and I presume all will be ready by the 15th instant, the day to which Parliament adjourned.

Always faithfully yrs.

# LETTERS FROM LONDON.

---

VOLUME II.

# LETTERS FROM LONDON.

---

## No. 187.—TO MR. CASS.

LONDON, March 12, 1858.

MY DEAR SIR,—Two things are just now overshadowing the India and China wars, and intently engaging attention: 1. the uncertain tenure of the new cabinet, and 2. the critical relations with France.

Lord Derby is undertaking to do what has never been done before, that is, to conduct the government with a large majority against him in the House of Commons. That majority, however, is itself divided into Liberals, the greatest faction,—the Radicals—the Lord John Russellites —and the Peelites; and it will require some address to start a measure of leading importance which will concentrate enough of these subdivisions to outvote the ministry. Of course much speculation is indulged as to the advance by which the opposition will find it politic to bring on the decisive contest. I received a hint last night from an eminent member that I had better be in the Commons this evening, when Parliament reassembles, as some demonstration is expected whence it may be possible to foresee the fate of Lord Derby. It will be too late for your enlightenment by this opportunity.

The alliance with France is fast taking the aspect of "a dissolving view." Very bitter feelings have seized the populations of both countries. France would seem to go with her military chiefs in pursuit of some external quarrel whose effect at home will be the consolidation of the Imperial dynasty, and a succession of fields of glory. Nothing more in harmony with prevailing passions, or more promising, than a war with England. I think it a mistake to suppose this state of things to be the sudden creation of recent events. It has been long brewing;—and, as the Hindoo mutiny found its vent in greased cartridges, so this is rounded by the grenades of Orsini. You will see in the newspapers a remarkable paper, obviously emanating from the Napoleonic bureau, the tone of which is quiet and deprecatory, but the real influence of which is to prepare the French mind, by insidious allusions to Waterloo, St. Helena, and the Crimea, for an explosion of the alliance. On the other hand, Lord Derby, in the existing mood of his countrymen, in and out of Parliament, will find it hard to pursue steadily the policy of peace. The *Times* of to-day says they are "drifting into a war," and speculates on the facility with which they can protect the island from invasion and demolish Cherbourg at a blow! Should the Premier exhibit the spirit and faculties of a war minister—and he has already shewn some symptoms of the kind—he may become master of the political-party position, and through the ruling interest of the day greatly augment his popularity.

I must add to these views and impressions the undoubted fact that disaffection to Louis Napoleon is becoming wide-spread and menacing. Arrests have been multiplied:—spies, informers, and police swarm all over France: generals are planted in civil posts: Changarnier and Bedeau reject, rather contemptuously, the imperial invitation to Paris: Châlons, not far from the capital, has been the theatre of an *émeute*, during which was heard the ominous trumpet call "Vive la République!" and I was read parts of a letter from a highly distinguished and reliable source, two days ago, which depicted France as "*honey-combed*" with secret and affiliated societies. I think I perceive in my general intercourse, the existence of that vague and undefinable expectation of some coming events which is said to precede a convulsion.

All this may blow over:—it would seem hardly possible, and yet it *may*. But should it not, what then? We have vast interests, material and political, involved in the measures which it may please the two great European belligerents to take against the commerce and possessions of each other. The violence which followed the rupture of the treaty of Amiens may be revived under fresh Berlin decrees and Orders in Council: perhaps impressment! but I suppose we are not yet near enough to the catastrophe to render forecasting necessary.

Colonel Williams is here, on his way to Constantinople. He will probably remain for a week or ten days.

The Turkish Embassy to this Court express great gratification at the manner in which you have welcomed their High Admiral.

You will much oblige me by saying to Mr. Toucey that I have been earnestly requested to intercede on behalf of the Atlantic Telegraph Company for another steamship as a consort to the Niagara:—but I forbear troubling him, because quite sure that he will do what is right.

A gentleman just in from Paris states the universal dread of something impending as prevailing there: that the funds have gone down and are still sinking: that the railways are nearly all insolvent: and that business and movement are completely arrested. This is the very latest picture of that metropolis: what will be the next?

Always faithfully yrs.

---

## No. 188.—TO MR. CASS.

LONDON, March 19, 1858.

MY DEAR SIR,—I cannot permit the Persia to go tomorrow without a line, although I have really nothing worth communicating.

Since my No. 94 of the 17th instant, everything (always excepting the spiteful degladiation of the London and Paris presses) has been quiet. A few symptoms indicate that neither country is quite satisfied with the manner in which their respective governments have closed the discussion on the Refugee question. After some subterranean fermentation, it is not unlikely that there will break out a fresh stream of hot lava.

You will have heard from Madrid that the actual ministry discountenanced war with Mexico: that Zuloaga has recalled Lafragua and promised another envoy: and that the prospect is fair for an amicable settlement under the mediation of France and England.

Everybody is anxiously gazing on the military movement against the Sultan of Utah. When you have dispersed the Saints and their seraglios, it is possible that the Church of England may proclaim a special thanksgiving.

Mr. Disraeli constantly and fervently begs for quarter. There is a beseeching character about his whole manner in the House of Commons which really begets a generous sympathy and forbearance.

I was a guest—the only intruder—at a consultation dinner caucus the other day, about 20 in all. They were maturing a plan for abolishing light-house duties, following our example therein. It has to be managed with great caution and skill to avoid corporate and vested interests. It will, however, be soon stirred.

A telegraphic despatch from Naples announces that his Majesty has released the poor insane engineer Watt, though he retains unrelaxed his clutch upon the other Englishman. Public feeling is more excited here on this topic than it has yet been. "*Civis Romanus sum.*"

Always faithfully yrs.

---

## No. 189.—TO MR. CASS.

LONDON, March 26, 1858.

MY DEAR SIR,—Count Persigny withdrew from the French Embassy here, and we are expecting his successor in the person of the Duke of Malakoff. There are very many causes to which this change is attributable:—the simplest is perhaps the effective one, to wit, the personal rivalry and ill will between Walewski and Persigny. The former did not feel the extreme solicitude to preserve the alliance felt by the latter, and suppressed or mutilated papers elaborately prepared to attain that end: he treated his subordinate as too English; and preferred, at any cost, to maintain in the Refugee controversy, the "dignity of France" and her position. Persigny saw, or thought he saw, that this was not the Napoleonic idea, and has thrown up in disgust. He is said to be resolved on private life, or at most to restrict himself to the duties of a member of the Council of Regency. He has been devoted to the Emperor; is at heart, like most of the French absolutists of the hour, a republican: possesses independent landed estates: and is hardly fifty yet. His lovely and pleasure-loving wife, grand-daughter of "le brave des braves," is weeping her eyes out at the prospect of quitting her London throne of fashion for a rural *isolement.*

As far as I have yet been able to learn, the Duke of Malakoff is fitter for an Algerine Arab hunt than to hold the reins of diplomacy. Some regard his mission as a threat, or as a reply valiant to the manner in which the British Parliament and press have been lately dealing with the "cock-a-doodle-doo" loyalty of the French colonels and army:—others, on the contrary, and this is the construction most favored, esteem it as the highest possible pledge to preserve unimpaired the fraternization of the Crimea. *Nous verrons.*

I thought myself yesterday on the eve of another of those wretched pouts about Court Costume with which, as an intermittent, every Master of Ceremonies is liable to be afflicted. The new functionaries did not exactly understand or quite relish two suits of sable with which two of our countrymen shaded the brilliancy of the Levee on the day previous; and one of these functionaries very civilly called at the Legation to enquire the particulars of the understanding between Mr. Buchanan and Sir Edward Cust which might authorize the appearance of those "*bêtes noires.*" I frankly told him all about it, assumed the responsibility of the Yankee wardrobe, asserted its entire conformity with all the essentials of etiquette, and then told him he had better see Sir Edward Cust, and dive into the mysterious depths of the great subject, before he formed any conclusion, or said anything farther on the subject. Fortunately for the pacific relations of the two countries, my visitor was a gentleman, a gentleman in manners, sentiments, and ideas, Mr. Ponsonby, once in Washington with Sir Richard Pakenham, and he went away to investigate. On his return, after a long consultation, he declared my view to be entirely right, that he would make an official record of his decision, and that henceforward there could be no doubt or difficulty about presenting American citizens to her Majesty, from the General Circle, in the very dress of their diplomatic representative. *Laus Deo!*—for I think this will enable our ministers here to walk, on this treacherous element of dress, as on thick ice, not as heretofore on what boys call "kiddly benders." Now that this 4th of July equipment has reached the zenith of its triumph, I am tempted to shew that it has its injurious as well as its beneficial influences. But I won't. Let me only say that when worn amid a thousand embroidered red coats, it produces a peculiarity which necessarily gives the very distinction it professes to avoid, and so cultivates in the wearer anything but a plain republican spirit. *Crede experto.*

*Both* the English engineers are released by the Neapolitan monarch:—a fact which may be esteemed preliminary to his being readmitted to fellowship with France and her ally. Sardinia is, however, very emphatic in demanding the Cagliari, as yet without success.

Parliament has got along with the present ministry thus far pretty well. Prodigious efforts to propitiate members by the attentions and blandishments of private intercourse are obviously unremitting. They will have their effect:—and probably that will be first seen in the care with which a test question will be avoided by the extreme Liberals. There will be an adjournment, possibly to-day, to the 12th of April next.

At the Marquess of Salisbury's last night, Sir Charles Lyell informed me that General J. A. Thomas, recently Assistant Secretary of State, had suddenly died in Paris from the effects of a neglected influenza.

Always faithfully yrs.

---

## No. 190.—TO MR. CASS.

LONDON, March 30, 1858.

MY DEAR SIR,—The India bill, introduced by Mr. Disraeli on Friday last, as a substitute for Lord Palmerston's, absorbs attention. It is ascribed to the eccentric talent of Lord Ellenborough, and may be described as a brilliant specimen of imaginative statesmanship:—various, complicated, and incongruous. Some of its features are decidedly republican. It obviously aims to propitiate all sorts of interests, prejudices, and theories. The government is that of a representative council, under a minister of the Crown:—and the constituencies are executive, popular, financial, and municipal. A scheme so odd and intricate can hardly commend itself to the gravity of Parliament, and its failure will be the knell of the Derby ministry. As soon as the Easter recess is over, this bill will be treated as *the* great cabinet measure, will be picked to pieces, and probably condemned by an overwhelming vote. Lord Derby will then determine whether to hand the seals quietly back to Lord Palmerston, or appeal to the people by dissolving a refractory legislature. Either course can be sustained by peculiar reasons.

Nothing not military floats now in France. The Duke of Malakoff, even as ambassador here, will be encircled by his aids-de-camp. The English press tries hard to contemplate this aspect of things graciously:—but winces in a manner prophetic of early distaste and alienation. It is impossible to be blind to the war-footing on which Louis Napoleon is hastening to place his Empire, or to be deaf to the doctrines preached by his five Marshals at their respective divisional headquarters. There are gloomy forebodings among the City merchants. Austria characterizes the course of the French Emperor, in his repressive laws, his numberless arrests, his stringent system of passports, his ubiquitous espionage, and his filling civil posts with soldiers, as dangerous to the peace of Europe.

Sir Colin Campbell is besieging Lucknow with a force of about 50,000, and we are in daily expectation of news of the downfall of that great capital of Oude. It will probably be accompanied by immense slaughter.

It is said from China that Mr. Reed has joined the other plenipotentiaries in moving upon the Emperor at Pekin. I am often questioned about our policy in that region:—but you have not yet carried out your plan which would enable me to shape an answer.

I have just received the President's letter to the Queen:—also the draft in favor of Mr. F. L. Campbell. By-the-by, the Danish minister has been empowered to receive the money payable on account of the extinguishment of the Sound Dues, and is on the *qui vive* to hear of its arrival.

Always faithfully yrs.

## No. 191.—TO MR. LINDSAY, M.P.

London, April 5, 1858.

My dear Mr. Lindsay,—You must not suppose that because I have delayed answering your letter of the 30th inst., I am insensible to its admirable object, your meditated "History of Shipping." On the contrary, I have been thinking how I could most effectively throw in a mite of assistance as to that portion of your labors which will relate to the United States. Were I at home, in the midst of my own books, I should find no difficulty:—but here, I want the familiar instruments of action, and am unwilling to rely on memory.

The British Museum ought, I think, to possess in its library a volume published some forty or fifty years ago, entitled "Seybert's Statistics of the United States." If my recollection be accurate, the author devotes several chapters and tables to merchant shipping, bringing down his narrative to a date subsequent to 1800. I knew him personally and well as a friend and associate of my father, and am sure that he enjoyed a high reputation, as a painstaking, discriminating, and trustworthy compiler.

The legislation of the United States immediately after the adoption of the Constitution in 1789, may usefully be consulted. We then had, at the head of our financial department, one of those leading and powerful minds that never fail to send their practical wisdom down to a distant posterity, Alexander Hamilton. He was indefatigable in putting the new government into operation, especially as to the machinery for the "regulation of commerce" exclusively vested in Congress.

In our principal ports, Boston, New York, Philadelphia, Baltimore, New Orleans, there are committees or boards of trade, emanating generally from the active shipping merchants, who would, I cannot doubt, take pleasure in collecting such local information as you might desire to have.

But I reserve myself for another note after I shall have heard from the United States. In the mean while, I beg you to be assured that I shall take great interest in your arduous enterprise.

Always faithfully yrs.

## No. 192.—TO MR. CASS.

LONDON, April 6, 1858.

MY DEAR SIR,—The Arago, which quits Southampton to-morrow, is a favorite steamer, or I should be tempted to leave you without a line until Saturday:—there is so little worth saying.

Indications are strong that an effort will be made on the India bill to cut short the ministry of Lord Derby as soon as Parliament reassembles. The Palmerstonians have had frequent private meetings:—and the "extreme left" or radicals strongly denounce the scheme of government proposed by Mr. Disraeli. The success of the movement may be doubted, for thus far the cabinet has rather gained ground than otherwise. Observe, however, that they who want to return to office cannot safely allow their adversaries to be gradually creeping into public favor. A general impression prevails, without any decided cause for it, that an election is not far off. Candidates are being put in train. Should Lord Derby be in a minority on a division in the House, it seems agreed that he will march to the last Tory pitched battle—the Waterloo—by a dissolution.

The fondness of the good Queen Victoria for her handsome and irreproachable husband remains unabated; and I think it may enter into the propitiatory policy of the present ministry to gratify that conjugal feeling by proposing to Parliament that the former Prince Albert, the present Prince Consort, should be hereafter recognized as King Consort. What her Majesty takes to heart, her devoted subjects, however they may temporarily grumble, will not long withhold:—and, as a mere piece of tactics, Lord Derby, as champion of the Queen's private wishes on this score, would not find his strength at the hustings impaired. A petition to Parliament, the natural start of an appeal to popular sentiment, is drafted and seeking signatures. The Prince is not as universally liked as he really deserves to be. He has exhibited great discretion in a very trying position for many years:—but he is a German, and much jealousy is cherished as to his absolutist principles and his secret affiliations with the continental Courts. At this particular juncture, his known and busy liaison with Louis Napoleon is regarded with disfavor.

The French Emperor, although his diplomats are sufficiently soothing, takes care to keep alive among his subjects those reminiscences which invigorate their hatred of England. Waterloo, St. Helena, Libels on his great uncle, are common topics. By-and-by he will find it impossible to keep his throne without yielding to the "*vis a tergo.*" In allusion to the mission of Pelissier to London, one of his newspaper wags has remarked that at the beginning he said, "*L'Empire, c'est la Paix,*" now, by the slightest modulation of tone, he converts it into, "*L'Empire, c'est l'Épée!*" I am told his ambassador will bring in his suite some six or eight of those redoubtable colonels whose recent figures of valiant loyalty so exasperated John Bull.

News from India is daily expected to announce the bombardment and fall of Lucknow. It is, however, but one of a hundred strong fortresses in Oude. The Chinese demonstration, though successful against Yeh, looks, in other and broader aspects, very much like a "fizzle." The Cagliari affair has ceased, by the discharge of the two engineers, to have any English interest:—but between Piedmont and Naples it is rankling into bitterness.

Always faithfully yrs.

---

## No. 193.—TO MR. CASS.

LONDON, April 16, 1858.

MY DEAR SIR,—Now that we are officially and formally told that the extinction of the Clayton-Bulwer Treaty will be followed by no discontent or protest, might it not be well to effect the abrogation, if possible, by convention? It would seem best to avoid throwing this complicated subject into the House of Representatives for endless debate, as must be done to obtain a statute of abrogation: and I do not see but that a treaty, although the supreme law of the land, may be rescinded by the *modus operandi* in which it was created.

This subject reoccurs for reflection, in consequence of a short conversation had with Lord Derby at his reception on the 14th instant. He expressed a wish to know how soon they would be likely to hear of the result of the legislative movement to abrogate; for, said he, "though we make no objection, we should like to be apprised, as soon as it takes place." Of course, I could not say when: perhaps a month hence, perhaps more, perhaps less.

You are the best, and indeed the only, judges how far it may be prudent to precipitate the annulment of the treaty. There may be something in the actual relations between this government and the Central American States, and in the amount of British naval force present at San Juan or Panama, which may suggest the expediency of at all events not immediately relieving England from the obligation not to acquire dominion in that quarter. The effect of a sudden push might be inconvenient: and, although I can perceive no just reason to apprehend anything of the sort, yet no harm can be produced by treating it as imminent.

The arrival of the Duke of Malakoff, although publicly attributed to other causes, has been delayed by a lady's being obliged unexpectedly to keep her chamber in the hotel of the Embassy. He is now in London.

At the Levee on Wednesday, Baron Brunow said to me that he intended calling on me, with a view to a conversation respecting Russian and American policy towards the Chinese. Here again I experience the disadvantage of not knowing the objects Mr. Reed may have been instructed to pursue. The Baron will doubtless be very communicative, but he will get nothing in return, for I am in the safe position of having nothing to give.

The desire to monopolize the commerce with the western coast of Africa, under the guise of philanthropy, betrays itself more and more every day. They are quite convinced here, by their explorers, geographers, and lecturers, that they are opening a new India in that quarter. The coast will soon be too hot for any trade but their own. Spain is making reclamations like ours, for honest and legal voyages harassed, impeded, and broken up on the slightest pretexts. No merchants can stand this:—and in less than ten years, if these obstacles continue, all but the English flag will have disappeared. Monrovia may enjoy the benefits of a British protectorate.

You can see in the newspapers of this morning the

debate in the House of Commons on Light-house Dues. I suppose it a result of the dinner caucus of members to which I referred in my letter of the 19th of March last. We are largely interested in the success of the movement. Lord Clarence Paget exhibited great research and ability in his opening speech. Lord Palmerston, though when Foreign Secretary in 1850 he resisted the diplomatic notes of Mr. Lawrence, seemed yesterday a convert.

Always faithfully yrs.

---

## No. 194.—TO MR. CASS.

LONDON, April 23, 1858.

MY DEAR SIR,—We are now in the enjoyment of the Duke of Malakoff's presence. He is an undersized, chunky, compact, white-haired figure, with a fine dark eye, black and arched eyebrows, jet moustache, and a manner at once tranquil and impressive. Efforts are obvious to give his advent the appearance of popularity. At his residence yesterday, on his return from the Queen's Drawing Room, a crowd assembled and cheered him. He will doubtless accept the compliment as an ample amende for the acquittal of Dr. Bernard.

This verdict cannot be misunderstood. It has no connection whatever with the evidence on the trial. It is John Bull's natural protest against an excess of gallicism in the government and at the palace. Had the proof been ten times as pungent and cumulative, the "Not Guilty" would only have been pronounced with tenfold emphasis. A great Law-Lord ascribes it to the republicanism with which the mass of the people are becoming thoroughly imbued. And, notwithstanding all this, the mere mention of the verdict, no matter in what circle it be made, is accompanied by a smile of secret satisfaction!

I think the ministry are gradually getting firmer in their seats. Their movements have, thus far, had lucky results. They have raked Watt and Parke, the engineers, out of the Neapolitan fire. They have adjusted satisfactorily the vexations of the passport system. They have dodged an open breach with France. They have steered their India bill, piloted by Lord John Russell, into smooth *no party* waters. And now Mr. Disraeli, in a speech of clearness and ability, has introduced his Budget, which is praised and accepted by the practical financiers of the City. To be sure,. parliamentary reform may almost at any moment rise to alarm them:—and if the Brights, Roebucks, and Milner Gibsons can content themselves with what, on that subject, Lord Palmerston or Lord John Russell is willing to concede, then the Derby cabinet must disappear like a whiff of smoke:—but there lies the perhaps insurmountable difficulty of the opposition. The extreme Liberals whom I have named want manhood, or universal, suffrage, and regard the ballot as a *sine qua non*. Besides, they begin to look proudly on the ministry themselves, and I doubt whether any effective reconciliation between the disjointed sections of the Liberal party which does not make Bright and Gibson members of a new government, be at all possible.

The Greek minister, Mr. Tricoupi, has repeatedly begged me to say to you that the gentleman whom the President has appointed consul in his country occupied that post some years ago:—that he will undoubtedly be received and treated with the respect and confidence due to the United States:—but when he was there before, he did something which obliged the Greek government to complain; and on the present occasion, nothing more is wished than that he should be instructed not to intermeddle in the politics of Greece.

Always faithfully yrs.

---

## No. 195.—TO MR. CASS.

LONDON, April 30, 1858.

MY DEAR SIR,—There is a current of conversation among politicians leading me to think that a decisive effort will soon be made by the Liberals to eject the present Conservative ministry. The rank and file within, and the editors without, are beginning to reproach Lord Palmerston and his colleagues with too easy an acquiescence in the exclusion of the party. More vigor and readiness to rescue the government are called for. The practical embarrassment in effecting the necessary understanding among the sections of the opposition is the claim of Lord John Russell to the Premiership. Lord Palmerston will not be restored while his restoration requires votes from the Bright and Gibson division:—but if this rivalry of the whig chiefs could, in any way, be surmounted, say by adopting another leader, as Granville or Clarendon, the doom of the Derby cabinet would be immediately sealed.

You will have noticed that Mr. Disraeli, though unexpectedly and admittedly successful with the Budget, has greatly damaged the position of the ministry by his management of the India bill. That measure was timidly sacrificed to a menace from Lord John Russell, and now, this very evening, Sir Harry Vane proposes to move, and with every prospect of success, that the subject of a new government for India be postponed to the next session. The directors of the East India Company may thus, as I have expected they would, triumph by the quarrels of their assailants.

It is difficult to say in what way the issue will be made up for the final struggle. The gentlemen in power are so concessive, as to make a positive conflict upon a cabinet question hard to bring about. Their adversaries may be obliged to introduce a motion of a want of confidence. Room for such a step is afforded by 1. The weakness shewn on the India topic: 2. The implacable spirit against the admission of the Jews into Parliament: 3. The bungling in the War Department as to military commissions: and 4. The general inability or reluctance, springing from internal dissension, to assume and avow a distinct line of policy on any subject.

It is not believed that a disposition exists, either in the two countries themselves or elsewhere, to push the controversy between Piedmont and Naples about the Cagliari to extremities. The point of international law, as to the right of capturing the vessel, is knotty enough to divide professional men of the highest ability and repute. King Bomba will continue to be gracious, as in the cases of Watt and Parke, and liberate the steamer: or the dispute, now the cause of bold and loud words, will be permitted to "fizzle" out, in subdued tones, at the Paris Conference.

Sir Edward Cust, the Queen's Master of Ceremonies, who carries the warlike title of Major-General, has just put to press a military work to which he is paternally anxious to draw attention. He has begged space in the despatch bag for two copies, one addressed to the President, the other to General Floyd, and you will please to ensure their prompt reception.

Always faithfully yrs.

---

## No. 196.—TO MR. CASS.

LONDON, May 7, 1858.

MY DEAR SIR,—Lord Palmerston in opposition is singularly different from what he was as Prime Minister. He has become patient, discreet, and even conciliatory. He helps, with his whole following, Mr. Disraeli, whenever that gentleman is supposed to be in a tight place. He did so to the overwhelming discomfiture of Lord Harry Vane's motion against any present legislation on India government: and only the night before last, he repeated the movement, by planting himself and forces under the walls of the cabinet, against which Mr. Gladstone and the Peelites, with Lord John Russell and the Radicals, were briskly aiming an address to the Queen in favor of the union and independence of the Moldo-Wallachian Principalities! The tendency of this course of party action is to strengthen the roots of dissension among the Liberals. Recently, a caucus of these in number about 120, convened in a committee room and coolly denounced, as unsatisfactory or treacherous, all the whig leaders of late years:—resolving that until the Liberal party could be organized upon a broader and firmer platform, it would be unwise to oust Lord Derby.

The "Niagara," with more than 1400 miles of an electric cable on board, will be ready to begin the experimental trip by the close of this month. Captain Hudson goes to Paris this afternoon, and will ascertain what Russian or French guest he is to have with him. He and his officers are all sanguine that the improved machinery will secure success. The melancholy condition of the

"Susquehanna" will, it is concluded, prevent her participating in the exploit.

Consider me, my dear sir, as saying all that a modest man ought to say, in acknowledgment for the kind words in your letter of the 15th April, just received.*

Always faithfully yrs.

---

## No. 197.—TO MR. CASS.

LONDON, May 11, 1858.

MY DEAR SIR,—We have a second youthful Queen at Buckingham Palace, who received the homage of the diplomatic corps on Saturday last. Her father, here also, is of the multitudinous secondary shelf of royalty, the German House of Hohenzollern-Sigmaringen. Some few years ago he abdicated, being too poor to maintain the dignity of independence, and ceding his position, whatever it was, to the King of Prussia, that sovereign dubbed him "Highness," and made him a Prince of his royal family. His daughter, "Stéphanie," married by proxy to the King of Portugal, is on her way to Lisbon, and very naturally stops here to make her curtsy to Queen Victoria, the central link of the marriage compact uniting Prussia, England, and Portugal. She is just twenty-one, looks like an unaffected modest American girl, and probably is a little perplexed in thinking that, if the recent attempt to poison her morganatic better half had succeeded, her position as Queen and yet no Queen, as *civiliter* wife and yet *religiose* not wife, would have been rather anomalous and embarrassing.

The struggle between the Lords and Commons on the Oaths bill—properly called the Jews' Admission bill—is

---

* The "kind words" alluded to were the following, and they are extracted as the stimulus and apology for the present publication:

"I thank you very much for your graphic letters. I read them all to the cabinet, where they are listened to with great interest. Your facts and speculations are just what we want, and what we can get nowhere else. I will say to you what I have said elsewhere, that since the days of Horace Walpole I have seen no more successful effort of this kind than is furnished by your lifelike correspondence."

ripening to coercive legislation. Lord John Russell, last night, seconded ably and sternly by the late Attorney-General, Sir Richard Bethell, threw the gauntlet of defiance by moving the disagreement to the Peers' amendment of his measure, and his motion prevailed by a heavy majority. There will be a conference: and it is believed that some expedient will spring out of it to enable the hereditary wisdom to succumb gracefully to the elective. I doubt that. Lord Derby and his new Lord Chancellor have taken their stand "*inter apices juris*," and will I think inflexibly wait the "hazard of the die." If so, then will the Commons be invoked to rush into the illegal, and therefore unconstitutional, step of seating the wealthy Jew by a mere resolution of their own, dispensing with the phrase "*upon the true faith of a Christian.*" At that point the fight may flag. Men, however disposed to urge into practice the principle of religious toleration, may recoil from the uncertain consequences of a really revolutionary step in parliamentary action. They are not ready to set the precedent of a *single* House of Legislature.

A new and grave topic of political contest has arisen. The Governor-General of India issued, on the taking of Lucknow, a somewhat ferocious proclamation, confiscating the territory of Oude, with certain exceptions in favor of loyal chiefs and inhabitants. It has been disapproved by the India Directors, and by the President of the Board of Control, Ellenborough, in a manner highly offensive to Lord Canning and his friends. The first effect is a meeting of Liberals at Cambridge House, Lord Palmerston's, on Sunday, the day before yesterday, who seem to have seized upon the occasion as a peculiarly fortunate and promising one for an onset to overturn the ministry. Something will be attempted to this effect on the 13th instant. If it be shewn, as vehemently asserted in conversation, that, owing to local ideas, Lord Canning is right and Lord Ellenborough ruinously wrong, then the cabinet ignorance of the true policy towards India, connected with the terrible break-down of their India bill No. 2, may make very dangerous a resolution of want of confidence on the great subject of their Eastern Empire now uppermost in the thoughts and feelings of the nation. Here is a battery suddenly and indiscreetly provoked to open its deadly fire on an administration already tottering!

I have received a perfectly reliable letter, which has not been sent to you simply because you are worried more than enough already by unimportant matters, complaining that owing to some irregularities or neglect of the agents you employ, the books intended by the government for the British Museum very often fail to reach their destination. This is a waste or a misappropriation which perhaps a word from you might arrest.

Our quondam friend, Sir Henry Bulwer, functus as Commissioner to the Moldo-Wallachian provinces, has gone to the Porte, successor to Lord Stratford de Redcliffe. This appointment is deemed a good one, and may, in a measure, be traced to the connexion of Sir E. Bulwer Lytton, his brother, with the party in power. I have had the good luck to form a pleasant acquaintance with Lord Stratford, and to find that he has agreeable recollections of his stay in the United States as well as an exalted estimate of the ultimate destiny of our country.

Always faithfully yrs.

---

## No. 198.—TO MR. CASS.

LONDON, May 14, 1858.

MY DEAR SIR,—The specialty of the moment is the ministerial crisis. Mr. Cardwell's resolution, decidedly equivalent to one of a want of confidence, so accepted indeed by both sides, was postponed from yesterday and will be discussed in the Commons to-night. Lord Shaftesbury has a corresponding motion, though less comprehensive and pungent, with which the Lords will be occupied at the same time. I don't think hereditary wisdom will be excited to censure by this last, because Lord Ellenborough, against whose indiscretion in giving publicity to his despatch disapproving Lord Canning's proclamation it is particularly directed, has suddenly, obviously to save the cabinet, resigned. But Mr. Cardwell in the Commons is "an ugly customer." He has moulded his missile into a deadly shape:—if it hits, it must kill. I had an opportunity last evening, at the Admiralty, to ascertain the forecastings as to the result. All admitted the "tight place" of the ministry. Some affected to regard the self-immolation of Ellenborough as an adequate atonement. The great hope, however, seemed to be in the extreme difficulty if not impossibility of combining a sufficient number of Radicals with the Whigs in the vote. Mr. Bright and Mr. Milner Gibson are, for the emergency at least, in "*entente cordiale*" with the cabinet:—but Lord John Russell, though not immovably fixed, is deeply committed against. Gossip says that a perfect reconciliation would be immediately effected between Lord John and Lord Palmerston, and the Liberals at once disperse the Tories, but for certain in-door rivalries, each Lady's conjugal pride claiming the premiership. Those most intimate with the eminent quartette are profound, though probably deluded, believers in that article of secret history.

Possibly to-morrow's *Times* may take you the *finale* of the great debate in the very steamer to which I am obliged to send the Bag by 5 P.M.:—but I doubt its ending so soon: and if it be adjourned beyond Sunday, it may be prolonged to Wednesday the 19th instant. If beaten by a large majority, Lord Derby will probably acquiesce, and retire as promptly as he went in: if the majority be small, or in other respects equivocal, he will resort to a dissolution of Parliament, *should the Queen consent.*

Have you noticed the contemptuous manner in which the Commons treated the amendments made by the Peers to the Oaths bill? A precedent of 1715 has been disinterred upon the strength of which Baron Rothschild, the Jew bone of contention, without having qualified, but simply upon his electoral return, is sent as a member of the Committee to confer with the Lords! Lord Chelmsford, being a *parvenu* on the woolsack, and full to overflowing in zeal for his new Order, can scarcely articulate his offended dignity.

I sincerely congratulate our whole country, and yourselves especially, upon the news which reached London yesterday of the final votes on the Kansas question.

How odd, that you are still, after the lapse of seven months, as much at a loss to see the special and definite purpose of Sir W. Ousely's mission as I was when announcing it immediately subsequent to a personal interview with him! Diplomacy brings reproach upon itself by whatever looks double and disingenuous. Lord Napier labors very hard, and probably controls his real nature, in his explanatory and excusatory note of the 26th April last.

The opposition in Paris have carried their man: and thus, of that representation there are two to one against the Empire.

Always faithfully yrs.

---

## No. 199.—TO MR. CASS.

LONDON, May 18, 1858.

MY DEAR SIR,—As soon as my despatch bag had been forwarded to Liverpool on the 14th instant, with my letter to you of that date, I hurried to the House of Commons, and sent an aid to witness and report the proceedings of the Lords.

The truth is that more than the usual interest is felt at this legation as to the result of the vote of censure on the present ministry, proposed by Mr. Gladstone in the Commons and Lord Shaftesbury in the Peers. This arises from a strong impression that the gentlemen in power have in twenty various ways manifested towards the United States a more just and conciliatory disposition than was shewn by their predecessors.

The debate in the upper chamber closed on the evening it began, with a division of 9 in favor of government:—a small majority, which would have been smaller had Lord Aberdeen, with two proxies in his pocket, remained to vote. The announcement was cheered by the opposition, who expected a worse defeat.

In the Commons, the discussion is unfinished, and may be protracted beyond to-night. It was opened with measured care by Mr. Cardwell, who was poorly seconded by Mr. Deasy, and was fortified only when Mr. Lowe and Lord John Russell spoke. The weight of the last against the cabinet was the greater, as his course was ascribed, more or less, to a definite understanding with Lord Palmerston about the future. An adjournment to yesterday was agreed to after midnight. The defence has been marked by great ability and eloquence. Certainly the best speech I have heard in England was delivered by Cairns, the Solicitor-General, who was vigorously aided by Lord Stanley. Yesternight the debate continued until half-past 12, the principal advocates of the censure being Sir Charles Wood, and Sir George C. Lewis, and against it Whiteside, Roebuck, and Sir Robert Peel. It was again adjourned, to be resumed this afternoon.

The question *may* be taken to-night, as the Races are attractive: possibly it may be suspended till Friday next:—but what is expected to be the result? Judging from the sentiments expressed by the innumerable experts whom I have conversed with, the result may be considered doubtful:—but on the whole I incline to think that Lord Derby must sink under the united pressure of Liberals, Peelites, and crotchety Radicals. Let us hear, however, Palmerston, Gladstone, Graham, and Disraeli. The physiognomical expression of the last, in his seat on the Treasury Bench, imports the agony of crucifixion.

Our grand, full-dress, diplomatic, annual, Birthday dinner came off at the Foreign Office on Saturday last. Everybody, not excluding Mr. Cobb's Commissioner on International Coinage, was in appropriate costume. The *Turkish* ambassador, seated on Lord Malmesbury's *left*—not the *French* on his *right*—toasted the Queen: and shortly afterwards a little epigram in action made me and others smile. Our host had to embrace in one sweeping responsive sentiment the national constituencies of all his guests. He rose, hemmed repeatedly as Englishmen invariably do when about to speak—"*Messieurs, buvons à la santé des* SOUVERAINS (here his eye became fixed on mine, he paused, hemmed again, and suddenly added) *et aux* ÉTATS *dont les honorables représentants sont présents!*" Of course, you remember that at such a table, even in London, no tongue can be admitted as either "*à la mode*," or universal, except the French. The Duke of Malakoff, I understand, *can* but *won't* speak the language of this Court.

Lord Derby, if censured, will resort to a dissolution:—in doing which I am satisfied that, considering the condition of parties, he will act as a leader most unwisely.

Always faithfully yrs.

## No. 200.—TO MR. CASS.

LONDON, May 21, 1858.

MY DEAR SIR,—The difference, in respect to us, between the Tory cabinet of Lord Derby and a Liberal ministry selected and headed by Lord Palmerston, is perhaps distinctly illustrated by the slip which, cut from the Money Article of yesterday's *Times*, is enclosed. Contrasting the recently expressed sentiments of Lord Malmesbury, as to all the southern portion of the North American continent and as to the Clayton-Bulwer Treaty, with the tone of this piece, it is not difficult to see that whereas the *ins* are frankly favorable to the maintenance of the most pacific relations, the *outs*, now vehemently struggling for restoration, are disposed to pledge themselves to an opposite course. In the existing attitude of things, I cannot wish success to the pending motion of censure upon the government.

That motion is still under animated debate. Its fate will, no doubt, be decided by 2 o'clock A.M. to-morrow morning, and be carried as the latest telegraphic news from Liverpool to Halifax by the present steamer. I have heretofore thought that it would prevail by so large a majority as would make it idle for Lord Derby to resort to a dissolution. Just now, appearances and impressions run in the other direction; and one cannot help thinking that there is a great probability of Mr. Cardwell's resolution being rejected, or, if carried, carried by so small a majority as would entirely justify an appeal to the people. The defence has been conducted with a striking superiority of boldness, fairness, and ability on the side of the ministers. Two important men, one a Peelite, the other a Radical, Sir James Graham and Mr. Bright, threw their weight into the scale of the government last night. Mr. Roebuck states in private that the censure will be negatived by a decisive vote:—but he is a sanguine mutineer in the ranks of liberalism. Lord Palmerston, who exhibits quiet confidence in the result, reserves himself apparently for the final onset of this evening, and will rally his whole party with his accustomed skill. But, "lying low," ready for a spring, is Disraeli, and "keeping dark," to shock by a surprise, is Gladstone.

The electoral triumph of Migeon, in the Haut Rhin department, against the open and peremptory injunctions of the Imperial functionaries, Canrobert, Espinasse, the Minister of Police, and the Prefects, is a manifestation strongly resembling those which first developed the existence of our secret Know-Nothings. The candidate had neither character, capacity, nor influence:—but, without a symptom of organized effort, he is suddenly, as a sign, lifted to alarm Louis Napoleon on the score of his favorite pretence as to universal suffrage. This "portent" occasions much remark.

Always faithfully yrs.

---

## No. 201.—TO MR. CASS.

LONDON, May 25, 1858.

MY DEAR SIR,—The motion to censure the ministry broke down on the very day it was expected to triumph. The adjournment for two days to enable members to attend the Derby, gave just time enough for the arrival of explanatory documents from India, which were of a character to make the motion too palpably unjust to be farther pressed. Its withdrawal was loudly called for, and finally took place early in the evening of the 21st instant. Perhaps it might still have been urged to a division, but that there was a grim lion in the way to which the young members were unused and whose aspect, the more it was looked at, the more terror it inspired. The dissolution of Parliament, positively resolved upon by the Premier, if the attack prevailed, was fraught with so much uncertainty, expense, and trouble, that a large number, elected scarcely a year ago, could not bear to risk its possibility.

The effects of this abortive impeachment may, I think, be regarded as threefold. 1. It permanently splits, and so kills, the Peelite party. 2. It postpones for a considerable time any farther assault, and will probably involve in that postponement any definite legislation as to India. 3. It goes very far to produce throughout the country an impression that the men at present at the helm understand steering a little better than their opponents, and may be safely permitted to command the ship until some ruder emergency occur. Lord Derby will not be disturbed for a year to come; and the condition of the Liberal party will have to be vastly improved by the sacrifice of personal aspirations and antipathies, before it can disturb him at all. I repeat what I have before said, that I do not perceive as yet the slightest reason why the United States should regret the ascendency of the existing phase of conservatism here.

At the request of the Royal Geographical Society, I attended their session of yesterday, and received for the Superintendent of your Coast Survey, the great Victoria Gold Medal, awarded to him by those learned pundits. It is transmitted in the despatch bag.*

Always faithfully yrs.

---

## No. 202.—TO MR. CASS.

LONDON, June 4, 1858.

MY DEAR SIR,—You must bear with all due patience my *douche* of despatches by to-day's Bag. If I could only

---

* On the delivery of the Medal, the following remarks were addressed to Sir Roderick Murchison:

*Mr. President*,—I receive with much gratification, on behalf of my eminent fellow-citizen, Professor Alexander D. Bache, this mark of the approbation of your learned society.

The fame of her sons in the noble brotherhood of science is a most cherished part of my country's wealth and strength; and, as her national representative, I thank you, gentlemen, for thus adding to her store.

Professor Bache has for many years discharged elevated, interesting, and arduous duties under the government of the United States. He was specially fitted for these by academical training and successes, by educational labors, by an intellect at once lucid, profound, and persevering, and by an aptitude, not too common with reserved students and philosophers, for practical method and administration. Without adverting to a rich series of prior and of accessary performances, I speak with entire certainty in saying that his chief work (though yet uncompleted), the Survey of the American Coasts, Sounds, and Estuaries, in all their expansion, intricacies, and characteristics, admirably delineated as if daguerreotyped in charts of extraordinary perfection, has earned for him a solid and enduring reputation in this, as in our own, hemisphere.

I believe him, Sir, in every respect entitled to the high honor you confer by awarding this Medal, and am happy in being made by your distinguished association the medium of its safe transmission.

effect thereby a perfect *water-cure*, that is, a perfect relief of the Seas from the constipation of visitation and search, it would rather please me than otherwise to pour out a deluge by every opportunity for a month to come. Pray, be enduring. A little while, and that word "*discontinue*," if quietly but steadily used (*à la Poplicola*), will put into the President's bonnet something worth a whole "forest of feathers." The issue has been impudently forced upon us by the sudden and simultaneous spanking of our skippers, and that too under our very nose:—and now let Jonathan keep a flock of starlings to iterate and reiterate, at every point of the compass, the cry of "*discontinue*," in every note of the gamut, "*advient que pourra*,"—not "war"! but "*discontinue*"*!*

You will possibly think this a light mode of treating a grave topic, and not precisely ambassadorial. Well, you are entirely right:—but I seek a temporary relaxation from the oppressive solemnity of remonstrance at the Foreign Office, and I cannot but feel how gloriously right you are.

That sweeping search of our shipping at Sagua ought to be, as the French say, *constaté* with greater amplitude and authenticity. It is the grand climacteric, at which every independent nation will startle and mutter "Shame!" The informant of our consul may be mistaken, and the act is so transcendently outrageous as scarcely to be credible from the lips of one man only.

I have a fine group of compatriots here just now:—the Aikens, the Fishs, the Fishers, the Sparks, the Tottens:—but, alas, like an ill-omened bird whose shadow deepens the blackness of the storm, onward comes flying the perturbed Senator! This advent is regarded as most unfortunate. Will your minister be countermined? If so, have we not a penalty in the Criminal Code? What says your Attorney-General? If I had a modicum of secret service money, this mole's underground activity might be watched and thwarted. However, a good cause, like good wine, needs no bush. Surveillance is almost as mean as treachery.

Sir Edward Bulwer Lytton has entered the cabinet and taken the Colonies from Lord Stanley. The latter is transferred to the Presidency of the Board of Control. Both must be re-elected: and I tremble for my friend the great novelist. His nerves are strung to the trial, and his address out. Mr. Gladstone, after nibbling at the bait, peremptorily darted off.

While your representative was yesterday distilling his brains to form a decoction at once powerful and palatable for Lord Malmesbury, the Prime Minister of England was dashing away, indifferent to the cares of Empire, at the Ascott Races!

Mr. Locke King succeeded, the night before last, in the House of Commons, in carrying the second reading of his resolution for abolishing the property qualification of members, by a majority of 126. A pretty broad and flat "vestige" or footprint of republican progress! The old fogies of the close-borough genus, especially of the German order, are stupendously aghast.

Always faithfully yrs.

---

## No. 203.—TO MR. CASS.

LONDON, June 11, 1858.

MY DEAR SIR,—While I was sending my last despatch on the afternoon of the 8th instant by the Vanderbilt, the Foreign Secretary, on an interpellation by Lord Clarendon, was giving the House of Lords a very cautious insight into the arrangement I had effected with him that morning. This, I presume, you have seen. All right, *as far as it goes.* It made me, however, rejoice to remember that his lordship had himself made a *written minute** of the

---

* The "*Minute*" is as follows:

"*Minute of Conversation between Mr. Dallas and Lord Malmesbury, June* 8, 1858."

"Her Majesty's government are not prepared to justify or excuse such acts on the part of their officers as have been complained of by the United States government, if they are truly reported.

"Her Majesty's government recognize the principles of international law as laid down by General Cass in his note of THE 10TH OF APRIL, '58, and that nothing in the Treaty of 1842 supersedes that law.

"Her Majesty's government, however, think it most indispensable, in the interest of civilization and the police of the Seas, that there should be

agreed points. Had these points been less full and distinct, there would have been no agreement at all. His speech bears marks of an apprehension that he will be attacked for having yielded. Our old Palmerstonian haters are said to be already on his track:—but they will be kept at bay by the threat of exposing the orders issued to British naval officers by the former government, which are hinted to have involved not merely a search against slave-traders, but one also against William Walker and his associate filibusters. At the royal ball, the night before last, I was, assured, with emphasis, by one of the ministry, that he positively *knew* what had caused and motived the sudden outrages upon our vessels:—he did not feel at liberty to communicate it: but it would come out. The men now in power had nothing to do with it. He rather thought too much had been conceded, but, he added, I am content, as, rather than bring our two countries into collision, I would concede a great deal more.

My colleagues of the diplomatic corps have, one after another, expressed their congratulations. They seem to regard with pleasure every check given to the maritime arrogance of England. Even Malakoff said he supposed I was now in good humor, or softened. There is no country in Europe which does not look upon the Right of Search as a weapon in the hands of a single bully:—especially since your famous letter which stopped Louis Philippe's signing the Quintuple Treaty.*

---

a power of verifying the nationality of a vessel suspected on good grounds of carrying false colors.

"Her Majesty's government would wish to learn from the United States government their views in detail on this point, in the hope that some mutual arrangement, by way of proceedings to be executed by our respective officers, may be found effective, without being offensive.

"The French have lately proposed and laid down this rule, viz.: that a boat may be sent alongside of a suspected ship and may ask for papers, but not, unless invited, board the vessel. Such is our arrangement with France.

"Lord Malmesbury has given Mr. Dallas a copy of our instructions to our officers. Pending our negotiations on the above point, orders will be given to discontinue search of American vessels."

* DIARY: *July* 17, '58.—"At 11 o'clock P.M. went to General Peel's. Here met for the first time Mr. Guizot. A small figure, white hair and crowning scratch, dressed in black, with large star on his left breast, and much activity of manner. His eye remarkably fine and expressive. He boarded me at once with a compliment for having removed the last source of quarrel between this country and the United States. He said he had tried the same thing while here as French Envoy, but could ac-

We have apprehended some contest with the vessels you have ordered to the West Indies. Although far from afraid to measure swords the third time, I hope, as disclaimer and discontinuance have promptly followed your demand, that we shan't be embroiled just now.

The Niagara left Plymouth yesterday, on the final trial to submerge the cable and unite the two continents. I have my doubts:—as the experimental trip had its accidents. We shall know the result in three weeks or less.

Always faithfully yrs.

---

## No. 204.—TO MR. CASS.

London, June 22, 1858

My dear Sir,—The two principles of the Manchester men—peace at any price and anti-slavery—came into conflict on our subject, and you will see by the debates that the latter has been made to kick the beam. Mr. Bright, their leader, will not consent to force philanthropy down revolting throats at the point of the sword.

You will have noticed that the ministry of Lord Derby has continued in the groove of good luck. They obtained, on demand, £3000 for Watt and Parke, and, without any demand, the Cagliari for Piedmont. This sort of fortune imparts a prestige which is often equivalent to actual strength. Lord Malmesbury in addressing Carafa seems to have taken a leaf from our book.

English ill-will on the subject of the slave-trade takes a strong direction against France. In the recent discussion of the Lords, language of bitter blame was not spared. It will farther concentrate there, when the letter of Mr. Cobb to the Collector of Charleston becomes known. The press here is in the habit of saying that we secretly import slaves through Cuba:—the Secretary nails the falsehood

---

complish nothing. It was a great '*résultat*,' and would be felt everywhere. Enquired about the President's health:—he had seen him in Paris about two weeks before his final return to America. I shall probably permanently regard this accidental meeting with Guizot as among the most agreeable incidents of my mission to London. However debatable he may be, he has made a strong mark on his times as a statesman and an author."

on the front, and I shall try to have it generally seen. "No admittance here!"

Much is printed, and more spoken, about the quiet armament of France. In private circles anxiety and suspicion are apparent. Each neighbor is on the look-out: Belgium, Austrian Italy, and England.

Nothing yet from the squadron engaged on the sub-Atlantic cable. Indeed, as they start the submerging in mid-ocean, we cannot hear anything with certainty before the way is completed by attaching one end at Valentia. The Foreign Secretary and I have interchanged notes preparatory to the transmission of messages. If it succeed, however, this will be rather late notice to you.

There is a vague rumor that the Emperor is somewhat dissatisfied with his Ambassador in London:—that this great functionary has shewn towards the Duke d'Aumale too warm a sense of Algerine reminiscences, quite an inconvenient explosion of old companionship: — that, besides, his *brusquerie* among the ladies of the Court has occasioned some extravagant scenes; and, in fine, that he himself feels like a fish out of water, and longs to return to his Parisian element. "*Se non è vero*," etc.

The heat has been more oppressive than any I have before known here. Thermometer in the shade 91 and 92. The effluvia from the Thames alarms Parliament and threatens disease. There is, however, enough unfinished public business to keep the session going for at least another month. Lord Derby has been incapacitated by illness for attendance during a week past.

Always faithfully yrs.

---

## No. 205.—TO MR. SAWARD.

LONDON, June 22, 1858.

SIR,—I will thank you to present to the Directors of the Atlantic Telegraph Company my cordial acknowledgments for the case of specimens of the component parts of their cable which you were kind enough to send me yesterday. It is a most interesting and highly appreciated memorial of a vast undertaking whose success will be hailed with exultation by all civilized humanity.

Accept the assurance of my sincere esteem.

Most respectfully yrs.

---

## No. 206.—TO MR. CASS.

LONDON, June 25, 1858.

MY DEAR SIR,—The Bishop of Oxford's hereditary horror of slave-trading has drawn the House of Lords as it were to the confessional, and they have made a clear breast of it as respects the coolies. The middle passage was nothing worse than the accurate exposures of Lord Carnarvon. Here was a vindication of America for you! Here was something with which Walewski might unanswerably twit the expounders of the "modern requirements of a higher morality"! Nothing was left to the magnates but to get angry with themselves and the rest of mankind: and certainly the language of Earls Grey and Malmesbury, of Brougham, Clarendon and others, exhibited unsparing and undiscriminating rage. It is quite interesting to note the ferocity of the attack upon the great ally whom their post-prandial eloquence is apt to make an idol of. The British Peers and the Parisian press are interchanging a brisk fire of "*falsehood*," "*infamy*," "*hypocrisy*," "*barbarity*," "*murder*," and other equally courteous accusations. Of course, an occasional shot strays to the United States: but, like eels, we are used to skinning; and, on the whole, the two new targets, Spain and France, have been much worse riddled than we. That affair of the "Regina Cœli," in which the *fettered free laborers* rose upon the crew and butchered all but the surgeon, is not without its parallel on our record. Lord Brougham, like Mr. Adams, thought the "killing no murder." Notwithstanding all this, the Duke of Malakoff, the day before yesterday, at the Lord Mayor's dinner to her Majesty's ministers, was embalmed in unguents of flattery and applause! There is an inexplicable subserviency to the alliance, which may possibly outlive fanatical anti-slavery; rival pretenders just now.

The horrible condition of the Thames, aggravated by

unusually hot weather, is the universal town talk. The parliamentary windows, overlooking the widespread flats of poisonous filth at low tide, have to be tightly closed; and so the heat becomes in its turn insufferable. The sickening odors, however, cannot be excluded from the passage ways and committee rooms, and these furnish a second-hand supply to the Lords and Commons. Perhaps the matter may be exaggerated by those who want to adjourn.

Nothing yet from the Atlantic Telegraph Squadron. We ought to hear in a week. I reminded the Foreign Secretary by note of the preparation made last year for inaugurating the cable by messages between the Queen and the President, and, at his request, sent him a copy of what Lord Clarendon had intended should be first transmitted. He will probably use it, if he have a chance: and of that you will be apprised before receiving this letter.

Always faithfully yrs.

---

## No. 207.—TO LORD MALMESBURY.

LONDON, July 2, 1858.

MY DEAR LORD MALMESBURY,—Your message of last evening will be forwarded to Valentia without delay.

I *hope* it may be in time to inaugurate the work, and yet I *fear* it will have to wait another year or two. Shoals of my countrymen, arrived by the last steamers, represent the weather to have been very unpromising, if not unmanageable.

Always faithfully your lordship's
Most obedient servant.

---

## No. 208.—TO MR. SAWARD.

LONDON, July 2, 1858.

MY DEAR SIR,—Conforming to the course intended to have been pursued last year, I transmit to you the enclosed from the Foreign Office, containing the message which it is desired may be the *first* or inaugurating one sent across the Atlantic to the President of the United States, as soon as the communication is established. Pray let me hear of its safely reaching your hands:—and should any unexpected circumstances prevent the attainment of its object, you will oblige me by returning the package unopened. Ardently wishing success to your great undertaking,

I am very faithfully yrs.

---

## No. 209.—TO MR. CASS.

LONDON, July 6, 1858.

MY DEAR SIR,—I put into the Bag to-day a long narrow box addressed to Mr. Cobb, which I will thank you to have sent to the Treasury Department. It contains drawings of the life-boat preferred in this country, and which the Duke of Northumberland, on behalf of the Society over which he presides, wishes to engage the attention of our government. I enclose also copies of the two letters written upon the subject.

They are still fashioning upon the parliamentary anvil a government for India. Perhaps, as the bill was last night ordered to be reported to the House, it will soon be adopted and sent to the Lords. That job accomplished, there will be great anxiety to adjourn, as the Thames continues to throw out a most disturbing effluvia.

Her Majesty has gone to Osborne; and, as soon as Parliament disperses, designs visiting Germany, expecting to meet her daughter the Princess Royal at Cologne.

I am hoping to receive by the steamer which will be due the day after to-morrow, a despatch from you on the subject of the "*Minute:*" for although I have been apprised of its safe arrival, my solicitude is not quite extinct, and will not be until I hear from you.

Always faithfully yrs.

## No. 210.—TO MR. CASS.

LONDON, July 16, 1858.

MY DEAR SIR,—The Queen must, of course, keep her engagement with the Emperor, to grace the festivities at Cherbourg, by a short stoppage on her way to Cologne, and so, perforce, Parliament *must* adjourn before the 4th of August. It is easy to create a necessity, when the moors are attractive and the Thames offensive. You hear a grumbler, now and then, like Mr. Charles Villiers, while he throws an angry glance across the Channel towards the frowning fortification, ask, "Why *does* her Majesty go rejoicing *there?*" but such rough notions and suspicious jealousies are injurious to the alliance; and, though deeply felt in honest humbler classes, are repudiated by Court and ministry.

It is difficult to avoid seeing how closely the ties are drawing between Russia and France. The meeting at Stutgard is fructifying fast. The night before last, while "assisting" at a ball in the hotel of the Russian Embassy, I stood for five minutes ruminating before two magnificent full-length portraits, just put up, of Louis Napoleon and Eugénie! *Ex pede Herculem.* Nothing in themselves; only, going back for a couple of short years, one thinks of the ants in amber and wonders "how the devil they got there." The recent flagrant massacres of Christians at Jidda, and in Candia, by Mussulman mobs may give rise to a fresh enquiry about the condition of "the sick man," under a new combination of the consultative faculty.

You will have noticed how exceeding angry, indeed irrepressibly furious, Spain has been at the language used in the House of Lords, and especially by the Earl of Malmesbury, on her slave-trade connivances. A word, said the *Times* in reply, from his lordship, would give Cuba to the United States. The Thunderer, indeed, seems so exasperated that he has been known to insist in private, as well as preach in public, that the fanatics against the traffic can best and easiest extinguish it by transferring the jewel of the Antilles to the zone of Columbia. Mr. Cobb's letter, prohibiting the desired clearance for a vessel avowedly destined to bring a return cargo of Congo free laborers, has produced an agreeable surprise. It could scarcely at first be credited as anything but an elaborate and ingenious hoax—like Locke's wonders of the Moon—but it crept into the *Globe*, and is producing much sober thought.

Accounts from India are bad. The mutiny is spreading through all the Central districts. The numbers and resources of the rebels seem constantly on the increase. The scorching heat is decimating the European forces. A speculation admits as far from impossible that their armies may be driven for refuge and be besieged in Calcutta, Madras, and Bombay:—there finding safety in their inexhaustible navy. It would be a curious fact, if, as the Lords finish the Government of India bill, they perceived that there was no India to govern! Yet, it is within the range of possibilities, or, as gamblers say, "within the cards." Their total effective strength has dwindled to 26,000 men.

The President has failed to receive the sub-Atlantic message of the Queen. The fates are averse. All the elements, above and below, combined against it. A more fearful storm than that which separated the vessels and enraged the sea, cannot well be imagined. It is a miracle that the Agamemnon survived. And yet the tempest is not the gloomiest occurrence of the abortive effort. There is a sad sense of a mysterious and unfathomable agency of some sort in the "lowest deep," which takes the liberty, at discretion, to treat the cable as a thread of sand:—separating, perhaps dissolving it, without any kind of warning and at the most promising moment! Here is a problem which may baffle even Lieutenant Maury, unless some modern Empedocles will do the world the favor to engage the Nautilus, and dive three miles to verify the subaqueous facts. It is a terrible lion crouched in the pathway of the spark.

No doubt you are suffering from incessant toil and a burning sun: and I would not have my solicitude relieved at the cost of a single additional grain to your heap of troubles. Only bear with me while I say that you have had that little "*Minute*" about visit and search ever since the 21st of June, or twenty-five days, without a word to say what you think of it. Mr. Fitzgerald, to be sure, has eased me off in some measure by reading to the House of

Commons Lord Napier's official narrative of his interview with you on the subject. But I had rather get a monosyllable from yourself than a quarto from his lordship. I have a faint hope that the Persia, due to-morrow, may be freighted with a line for me.

Always faithfully yrs.

---

## No. 211.—TO MR. CASS.

LONDON, July 23, 1858.

MY DEAR SIR,—The day after the departure of the Europa I received, as was expected, your welcome letter of the 1st July, by the Persia.

The generous notice you take of my course in bringing about the abandonment of the vexed and vexatious pretension of visit and search, is most valued because it assures me of your continued friendship. I did my best, in seizing the occasion:—but what would that have availed, without the firm attitude and language of the President, and your overwhelming letter to Lord Napier of the 10th of April? Armed with such weapons as these, almost self-acting, it was enough to follow the injunction "*Carpe diem*," and point them at the adversary.

I do not think it enters into the policy or character of this government or people ever to resume an international doctrine which they have once formally surrendered. They fight to the last for a false position which props a bad practice, but the instant they give it up, they rather hurry to deny they ever took it. This is a result of an exorbitant self-respect, the rivalry of political factions, and a quickly detective press. Hence, I did not anticipate that the "*Minute*" of what was settled at the interview between Lord Malmesbury and myself on the 8th of June, could occasion doubt or misgiving. When those big fates, commonly called big wigs, the "law officers of the Crown," harmonized with Lord Derby's policy, and made a clean breast by honestly and frankly avowing the soundness of your public law, visit and search fell dead, and went to that bourn whence no mere expedient subtleties ever return. Peaceful resurrection is impossible. As to war, its chances, instabilities, and vainglorious fruits are proverbial:—and were force ever resorted to to restore a disclaimed principle, all we could do—and that is the *ultima securitas*—is to invoke Shakespeare and cry "lay on, Macduff, and d—d be he who first cries hold, enough." England will never try our mettle again; and least of all on this confessedly untenable pretence.

The Atlantic Cable Squadron are out again on their desperate enterprise. None but enthusiasts look for success. They left Queenstown on Sunday last, and we may hear of them again in ten days.

The Queen's visit to Louis Napoleon at Cherbourg, like that of Sheba to Solomon, will be an affair of much ostentation. Her Majesty proposes to have a train of ministers, peers, and members of the House of Commons, flounced off by a fleet of some twenty ships of war! Newspapers affect great indignation at her going, and have urged a "town meeting" to stop her. When Victoria once announces her purpose, after accepting an invitation, all that's left is to shrug one's shoulders and make the best of it. A resolution against her Majesty would be hooted down even in "Rag Fair."

Always faithfully yrs.

---

## No. 212.—TO MR. CASS.

LONDON, July 30, 1858.

MY DEAR SIR,—You will have noticed that Lord Lyndhurst, in asking for the production of papers on Monday the 26th instant, prefaced his capital speech by quoting from the *Times* report of my remarks at our 4th of July celebration here.* Those remarks *had* their purpose, and

---

* The report in the *Times* of the 5th of July, '58, was as follows:

"His Excellency MR. DALLAS rose to acknowledge the toast, and was received with loud cheers. He said,—Mr. Chairman and Fellow-Citizens, I had promised myself, in consequence of continued ill-health for some time past, to abstain from anything so exciting as public speaking; but it is, unfortunately, the 4th of July (laughter and cheers), and I find it impossible to remain silent on such a day after you have received the mention of my humble name so kindly and so cordially. A few years ago it would have been thought discourteous and intrusive had one or

have attained it. The slight doubt hinted in some newspapers, as to the extent of the renunciation on the board-

---

more American citizens ventured upon the celebration of the 4th of July, 1776, in the great city of London. The old wounds were still fresh, old feelings still survived, and the citizens of the United States who were here had the good taste as well as the forbearance not to do that which might have been misconstrued so as to be disagreeable to those among whom they were residing. (Hear, hear.) But now, gentlemen, we feel much more at ease. The principles of the American revolution have gone on conquering and to conquer. (Cheers.) They have received the approbation, cordially but certainly, of all the wise and good in England as well as in the United States. They have become perfectly well understood—they have beaten down the impressions of hostility which, being misunderstood, they originally created. The principles of the American revolution are acceptable here as they are at home. (Cheers.) The men of our heroic days—our Washingtons, our Jeffersons, our Madisons, and our heroes in the battle-field, are known now in England almost as well as they are in the United States, and are honored as much here as there. (Cheers.) The progress, then, of the principles of the Revolution of the United States has been striking, and has produced that to which I have already adverted—the propriety of our meeting to celebrate the origin of those principles in London as well as elsewhere. (Hear, hear.) Do not for a moment suppose that I am availing myself of a detached part of the toast just given in order to draw the conclusion that the recognition of those principles has been brought about in any degree by the diplomacy of the United States. ('Hear,' and a laugh.) The truth is—and you are, perhaps, not aware of the fact—that we have no American diplomacy. (A laugh.) In England and on the Continent diplomacy is a lifelong career. With us it is nothing of the sort. American diplomacy, compared to European diplomacy, may be likened to the militia as contrasted with the regular army. (Laughter.) To be sure, in the United States, from the outset, we have always had a partiality for the militia. (Hear, hear.) Our first military achievements were gained by men among whom were some of the rawest possible militia. ('Hear,' and a laugh.) And it has so happened, probably by accident, that our militia has over and over again proved equal to the best regulars of Europe. (Cheers.) It is in that way, perhaps, that the diplomacy of the United States has been able to do something towards giving expansion and popularity to the principles of the American revolution. Although our Ministers abroad have been drawn from the ranks of private and professional life, on very many occasions, at the most distinguished Courts of Europe and throughout the world, in conflict, or rather in argument, with the most refined diplomatists of any country, those militiamen of diplomacy have achieved remarkable success. (Hear, hear.) I might refer, if I were disposed to empty upon you the archives of the American Legation here or elsewhere (a laugh), to many striking instances of this kind; and as I propose to conclude my remarks by suggesting a particular name to your approbation, it may be proper to say that the list of our American diplomatists, beginning with Benjamin Franklin, Thomas Jefferson, James Monroe, and William Pinkney, includes a long array of illustrious 'militiamen diplomatists,' who have left behind them a record of the most glowing and gratifying character. (Cheers.) At this very Court some of my predecessors may be compared to the very best of the drilled cohorts of European diplomacy. There is one little comment, which is to a certain extent connected

ing question, and the reticence of ministerial M. P.'s when interpellated, seemed to make it important that the exact character of what had been done should be fixed before Parliament adjourned, and before the possible contingency of a change from Derby to Palmerston could take place. The post-prandial device worked to a charm:—and Lords Lyndhurst and Malmesbury have left nothing to desire in their public and precise avowals. The same thing as to the press. And now England, through her omnipotent Wittenagemote, through all her leading journals, specially the *Thunderer* and Lord Palmerston's organ, as well as by table oratory, is made to know the identical pretension her government has finally withdrawn from as illegal. After-claps, such as followed the Clayton-Bulwer Treaty, are impossible. By a lucky accident, Mr. John Y. Mason and myself were in the diplomatic gallery when Lord Lyndhurst addressed the Peers. I felt personally a little awkward at being present to hear my own name mentioned:—but the gratification of your Parisian representative at the force and lucidity of the Sage of 87 years was unmeasured. It was, indeed, a rare realization of Homer's Nestor:—and it beat down the assault of mere party.

---

with American diplomacy, on which I will say a word. You know that we have recently had some little difficulties on the coasts of the United States and in the West Indian Sea (hear)—a matter with which, as one of the militiamen in the diplomacy of the United States, I was lately charged. Now, without referring to that question more closely, it is a point which is essentially connected with one of the fundamental principles of the American revolution,—that principle being the necessity of maintaining on behalf of the great American people, as a great community, the independence of their flag. (Cheers.) Well, I am not going to argue the question as to visit and search. It has been over and over again, for years back, argued and re-argued. But I should like on the 4th of July to announce to my fellow-countrymen that visit and search in regard to American vessels on the high seas in time of peace is frankly and finally ended. (Tremendous cheering, the whole company rising and manifesting the liveliest enthusiasm.) While, gentlemen, I am able to announce this gratifying fact, I think it ought also to be accompanied by the assurance that the termination of that for which we have struggled for nearly half a century has been brought about with a degree of honorable candor and fair dealing on the part of the British government which is worthy of every acknowledgment on our part. (Loud cheers.) With a view to draw these remarks to a close, I beg leave to offer you as a toast the name of one of the earliest representatives alike of the principles of the American revolution and of the Constitution of the United States—I mean Thomas Jefferson, the author of the Declaration of Independence. (Loud cheers.)

"The toast was drunk in solemn silence."

Cherbourg will throw into shade the Field of Golden Cloth. But her Majesty will not, as has been erroneously rumored, be escorted by a large fleet:—nor will her subjects cease to grumble or soon forget this her first omission to uphold their national pride. Lord Derby did not foresee or he would have deprecated an invitation. As it is, "there's nothing left for it!"

The American horse "Charleston," running for the Goodwood Cup, has been terribly beaten, coming in only 7th. The Niagara and the electric cable are unheard of since leaving Queenstown for a re-trial. The driving current of American travellers to the Continent knows no abatement. It is a social phenomenon.

Always faithfully yrs.

---

## No. 213.—TO MR. CASS.

LONDON, August 6, 1858.

MY DEAR SIR,—The salvos of artillery at the meeting of the Sovereigns yesterday in the basin of Cherbourg were drowned by the sudden and unexpected annunciation that the Atlantic cable was laid! All London is in a tumult of surprise and exultation. The stock, which two days ago stood at £200 or £300, has with the quickness of its own electric fluid, risen to £800 or £1000. New Columbia (Frazer's river) is, at once, to the great relief of Sir E. B. Lytton, brought within hailing distance. I hope the Secretary of the Company, to whom it was specially confided, has not failed to transmit to the President the inaugurating message of the Queen. The reply ought to reach us to-day!*

---

* The telegrams here referred to were the following:—they were undated, but were interchanged on the 18th and 19th of August, 1858:

1.—*From her Majesty the Queen of Great Britain to his Excellency the President of the United States.*

The Queen desires to congratulate the President upon the successful completion of this great international work, in which the Queen has taken the greatest interest. The Queen is convinced that the President will join with her in fervent hope that the electric cable, which now already connects Great Britain with the United States, will prove an additional

I received on Sunday last an exceedingly interesting letter from Mr. W. B. Reed, written on the very day, the 20th May, of the taking of the Chinese forts at the mouth of the Peiho by the allied squadrons. He appears to have acted with great judgment and forbearance:—and yet perhaps the vigorous movement of Lord Elgin and Baron Gros in pushing nearer to Pekin may break down oriental form, and incline the brother of the Sun and Moon to be as courteous and kind to the Earth as are his relatives. Mr. Reed kept pace with the advance, a mediating pacificator always at hand. The complication is delicate and very interesting; and our representative expresses a doubt where it will end—possibly in territorial acquisition by one or the other of the allies.

Was there ever any paper so wretchedly devised and penned as the speech on the prorogation? And yet there are in the ministry Bulwer Lytton, Disraeli, Stanley, and Cairns! It must have been left to the bewildered cookery of a Law-Lord.

Mr. Miller, our Despatch Agent, whom I had desired to keep a sharp look-out for the Blue Book promised by Lord Malmesbury on the boarding question, informs me that he has ascertained it will not appear before the next session. There is an habitual, and often an inexplicable, fondness for procrastination:—they don't think it the *thief* but the *physician* of Time: possibly, on this occasion, dis-

---

link between the two nations, whose friendship is founded upon their common interest and reciprocal esteem. The Queen has much pleasure in thus directly communicating with the President, and in renewing to him her best wishes for the prosperity of the United States.

2.—*The President of the United States to her Majesty, Victoria, Queen of Great Britain.*

WASHINGTON CITY.

The President cordially reciprocates the congratulations of her Majesty the Queen on the occasion of the great international enterprise accomplished by the skill, science, and indomitable energy of the two countries. It is a triumph more glorious, because far more useful to mankind, than was ever won by a conqueror on the field of battle. May the Atlantic Telegraph, under the blessing of Heaven, prove to be a bond of perpetual peace and friendship between the kindred nations, and an instrument destined by Divine Providence to diffuse religion, civilization, liberty, and law throughout the world. In this view will not all the nations of Christendom spontaneously unite in the declaration that it shall be forever neutral, and that its communications shall be held sacred in passing to the place of their destination even in the midst of hostilities?

JAMES BUCHANAN.

creet views of party popularity suggest the expediency of extending the record.

You have no doubt remarked the interest attached to a recent and absorbed interview between the French Emperor and the Sardinian Prime Minister, Cavour. The general impression forecasts a breach with Austria and the Unity of Italy. As this country may probably side with Austria, hence the expediency of having Cherbourg in the rear, more as defensive and a refuge than a measure of invasion.

Lord Stratford de Redcliffe returns to Constantinople. *Pourquoi vient-il, l'enragé?* asks Thouvenel. His lordship says, to take leave of the Sultan:—others intimate, to teach, as privy councillor, the Divan how best to act in existing difficulties. *Perhaps*, Sir Henry Bulwer has missed a figure somewhere, and made the temporary presence of De Redcliffe necessary.

Always faithfully yrs.

---

## No. 214.—TO MR. CASS.

LONDON, August 13, 1858.

MY DEAR SIR,—Nothing exceeds the desertion of London—except the crowds in the streets. The heat, the odorous Thames, the Royal Highnesses in Prussia, and the whirring grouse of Scotland, are fast depopulating all the great Squares and abandoning the Parks to the million. The clubs are vacant. The theatres slam to their doors. Science closes her lecture rooms, and Art wraps her galleries in muslin. Even the Press, the Metropolitan Press,—unheard of thing! is somniferous and stupid. In such a state of affairs the affairs of State are apt to sympathize, and the despatch of a diplomat takes irresistibly a turn of tameness. I doubt much whether this my weekly missive don't fall sound asleep.

It would seem that Lord Elgin and Baron Gros have a fair prospect of demolishing the Great Wall. They are comfortably seated at Tien-Tsin, about sixty miles from Pekin, in daily communication with a new Grand Commissioner clothed with the indispensable full powers; they have propounded their ultimata; and they give infinite persuasion to these by the display of 2500 European soldiers before 300,000,000 of Asiatics! Mr. Reed and Count Putiatin follow the belligerent Admirals in a Russian vessel called the America, with their respective flags flying, steadily prepared to join the triumph and partake the gale! It is difficult, with our "western" habits of thought, to realize this extraordinary invasion of the oldest and hugest existing empire on earth. And yet there they certainly do go—winding their diminutive cavalcade through river and canal towards the Imperial palace, with that sort of audacious indifference to the Chinese that Cortez exhibited to the Aztecs!

Parties here are at odds about the character which the parliamentary and official measures of the ministry ought to bear. Well!—as a stranger, a mere looker-on, I can judge impartially. Lord Derby has shewn wisdom, tact, and statesmanship, far beyond what was expected from him, and the natural result is a corresponding triumph over public opinion. The spirit of exterior conciliation is quite distinct. He soothes and satisfies everywhere: France, United States, Naples. At home, he has ceased to fight with the age, concedes more liberally than he ever promised, accepts the Jews, abolishes property qualification, contemplates manhood suffrage if not the ballot, gives a government to India, and makes an acceptable budget! Surely, there is nothing equivocal in these traits of a six months policy:—shewn, too, in the midst of difficulties, which might have provoked their angry relinquishment without exciting surprise. I have no tendencies to what is called Toryism (perhaps you know that without my telling it!) and I may rather fall short of than exaggerate the merits of the Premier and his colleagues. If—as some anticipate, especially since that passage of the Queen's speech read on prorogation, which refers to the exercise of members' *influence* during the recess—a dissolution be attempted in the spring, it would not surprise me to find the new House of Commons more disposed than the present one to sustain the existing government.

We are having hourly messages from the Niagara, but none yet from the Office on shore.

Always faithfully yrs.

## No. 215.—TO MR. CASS.

LONDON, August 27, 1858.

MY DEAR SIR,—Note, that Marshal Pelissier is about marrying. At Cherbourg the predestined couple met for the first time. "*Mons. le Duc,*" said the sovereign, Eugénie, "*prenez la main de la Comtesse Paniéga pour le souper;—eh! pourquoi pas pour la vie?*" and so, we shall have a Duchess added to our corps in less than a fortnight. Malakoff is affectedly pitied as a victim though 62: his intended being 30 and surpassingly lovely.

Count Persigny deems it necessary to spread more sail. He would probably like to regain his diplomatic residence in London. So he has made a long speech at the Council General of the Loire, in which he reminds the world that he was among the first to attach himself to the fortunes of Louis Napoleon, and that the French and British alliance is essential to the interests of both nations. Although he used some very offensive words in addressing the Lord Mayor after Orsini's attack in February last, yet, take him for all in all, he is rather a favorite here.

Royalty has periodical fits of peripatetic restlessness. Just now, the great thrones are vacated. France, Russia, England, Prussia, Spain, Holland, have their monarchs wandering. Queen Victoria returns from her trip to Potsdam during the next week, and will hold a Privy Council at Osborne on the 2d September.

Lord Elgin has effected his objects:—opened China to commerce and Christianity, got an indemnity of $6,000,000, and made Pekin a residence for foreign diplomats and consuls. Such at least is the credited news from St. Petersburg. It is understood that the quiet Putiatin has dexterously managed to obtain great advantages for Russia. France claims a large half of the "glory" of the enterprise.

The Conferences at Paris have closed. The details of the arrangement respecting the Danubian Principalities have not transpired. Generally it is said the Suzeraineté of Turkey is maintained: Wallachia and Moldavia are each to have a Hospodar elected for life and a separate legislature: on what points a junction is effected, whether ecclesiastical, judicial, or electoral, don't appear yet. It is strongly illustrative of the irresistible tendency of the age that these consultative agents of despotic powers could come to no result but one essentially republican.

Doubts are whispered as to the state of France. The steadily continuing transportations of squadrons of "suspects" to Cayenne, indicate a widespread discontent, and must aggravate, not repress it. Your old assailant Lord Brougham, in the course of a long call with which he honored me, expressed serious anxiety as to what might soon follow. By-the-by, after all his termagant fury against your defeat of the Quintuple Treaty, he has come round to your letter of the 10th April last, and says that visit and search are the same, both against the law of nations, cannot be forced, but he hopes a succedaneum may be devised by negotiation. A few firm phrases in the President's message will place "The Police of the Seas" beyond the reach of the hand of resurrection.

Lord Derby obtained the prompt consent of her Majesty to the publication of the telegraphic messages between herself and the President. They appeared in the *Times* and other journals of the 23d instant. The contrast between the manner in which the success of the cable has been treated here and in the United States, is very marked and strange. Except at the first surprise, and in the rise of the company's stock, nothing symptomatic of enthusiasm has broken out: not even a dinner! Some hyfalutin articles got into a paper or two:—obviously, however, more inspired by pique against the glorification at Cherbourg, than by joy over the wire. What is the cause of this difference? Is it that your ecstacy arises from an instinctive consciousness that the cable will be a medium for propagating quickly and directly your swelling thoughts?—of indoctrinating this old continent with your principles and aspirations? There is vastly more in it, rest assured, than trade, and peace, and fraternity. If not, why is the lion tame and tranquil, while the eagle is huzzaing in the clouds?

I am meditating a short visit to Tunbridge Wells with my family, to give opportunity for certain repairs and improvements in the house I occupy. If I do not write as often as before, ascribe it to this and to the intolerable dulness of everything in London.

Always faithfully yrs.

## No. 216.—TO MR. CASS.

LONDON, September 10, 1858.

MY DEAR SIR,—An annoying uncertainty lingers about the Atlantic cable. It has stopped speaking:—and Whitehouse, the electrician who has heretofore taught it speech, ascribes its present dumbness to some injury inflicted upon the small line of wire by the violence of the sea off the Irish coast. He applied a remedy once, and can, he thinks, apply another:—but, then, men of science are akin to poets, the *genus irritabile*, and the cluster around the telegraphic instruments have got squabbling. The physician who cured the disease was dismissed as soon as he succeeded:—but now comes a fresh attack, and he won't stir unless soothed by ample reparation. If the Professor be not promptly propitiated the mischief may get beyond the power of repair:—and then, how idle the conflagration of the City Hall!

The cable's rival, Cherbourg, the "*standing menace*," seems to have won the day. John Bull is still loquacious about the splendor of that spectacle, and harps, at political meetings and dinners, about its incidents and meaning. He comforts himself, under the warnings of Roebuck and Lindsay, by preaching faith in the alliance, by mounting a few enormous cannon pointed in the direction of the French fortification, and by frequent iteration of "forewarned, forearmed!" But the old gentleman cannot divest himself of uneasy feelings: and a stern determination is everywhere evinced that Parliament, at its next session, must not lose an hour in strengthening the defences of the country. In connection with this, observe that Paris is flooded with anti-Anglican pamphlets, fostering and augmenting every sort of national prejudice:—and remember that the completion of Cherbourg places a weapon in the restless hands of the metropolitan blouses which they will long to try. Should the army, to whom Louis Napoleon has undoubtedly pointed the way to England, become infected by the same popular yearning, nothing is left for it but a trial, either with or without his Imperial Majesty. You may have noticed that a wag, during the magnificent pyrotechnics, construed the initials

N. E. (Napoléon, Eugénie) and V. A. (Victoria, Albert) as an implied compliment to the Czar on the NEVA. Who knows?

The news from China is not yet definitive. No doubt, however, is entertained that Lord Elgin has accomplished all that mere treaties can secure. I have just received an interesting letter from Mr. Reed, dated at Tien-Tsin on the very day, the 18th June, on which he signed his own treaty, which he describes as entirely satisfactory. I should judge from what he says, that he and the British Plenipotentiary have not harmonized. Some supercilious flings have already appeared in the newspapers here, against the American mode of getting honey without working for it, which are perhaps distillations of diplomatic ill-humor.

Much noise is just now occasioned by a Protest or Remonstrance against the intolerance of Sweden for having driven into exile some half dozen converts to the Roman church. The paper, signed by the great body of ecclesiastical dignitaries, headed by the Archbishop of Canterbury, was formally sent to Count Platen, the Swedish minister at this Court:—and his reply to it is at once curious and dignified: curious, as it explains the intolerance to be the law, which the legislature will not, though pressed by the Sovereign and Court, change: and dignified, as his Excellency plainly intimates the impropriety of one country meddling with the institutions of another.

Permit me to offer to yourself and your daughter my sincere felicitations upon the event which I see announced in the public papers.

Always faithfully yrs.

---

## No. 217.—TO MR. CASS.

LONDON, September 17, 1858.

MY DEAR SIR,—My despatch by this Bag will lead you to speculate as to what may be the possible objects of Lord M's. sudden eruption. It may go farther than it has gone. Whether the deficiency of party capital be felt and must be made up:—or whether it be conceived necessary to "tack ship and about," on the visit question: or whether the everlasting dripping of fresh reclamations for "outrages" has wrought what the French term "*un accès de fièvre:*" or whether the atmosphere of Potsdam exerted an unwholesome influence: or whether, after all (for Oxenstiern found the world very contemptible), there be at bottom meaner promptings than these,—let us leave the future to disclose. As for my own action, it lies plainly before me, and I have to make it clear by quietly repelling encroachment, preserving both temper and dignity.

Mr. Rücker, the minister of the Hanse Towns, who, by-the-by, has greatly lifted his mission by marrying an exceedingly pretty and most fashionably toiletted wife, has once more begged me to intrude the "Stade Dues" upon your notice. Europe is not unwilling, on some topics, to *feel* us on this side of the Atlantic. The House of Commons has had its committee, a copy of whose report I send you. Is it worth our while to take, as respects our treaty with Hanover, the course England is taking with hers? One word in reply, to assuage the solicitude of the Hanseatic diplomat.

Russia has, with sly insinuating softness, nestled herself at Villafranca with Sardinia. She has bought a steam-navigation depot on the shores of the central sea:—and already England foresees naval rivalry and is, of course, vehemently excited. Lord Derby will be interpellated to explain how he happened to be thus outwitted. But the step was, it is said, accompanied by political engagements of much significance:—Russia promising to aid Piedmont should she be assailed by Austria.

Another letter from Mr. Reed, dated at Tien-Tsin 1st July last. The airs played off by the British Peer among the effeminate Orientals are approvingly described in the *Times:*—Mr. Reed speaks of them in a wholly different strain.

The Cable don't speak:—the cause is yet undetected, not "*in nubibus*" but "*in profundis:*" and the electricians are at loggerheads. Everybody looks blank, and croakers are beginning their bull-frog songs with, "Well, you know I always doubted!" The absolutely perfect isolation which it is necessary to secure for the wire through the whole 2000 miles may remain for a short time:—but can it, in reason, be expected to last amid the lashings, grindings, abrasions, and corrosions of our stormy sea?

Always faithfully yrs.

---

## No. 218.—TO MR. CASS.

LONDON, September 23, 1858.

MY DEAR SIR,—Nothing more from Lord M. after the lapse of ten days:—so I suppose he may be considered as persuaded that "Her Majesty's Captains who visit suspected vessels" may sometimes be handled without kid gloves, and yet no offence be justly taken.

Mr. Bradley, our consul at Ningpo, who accompanied Mr. Reed up the Peiho, passed through London to Galway, bearing with him our Chinese Treaty. He must reach you some days before this note. Lord Elgin is much eulogized, no doubt deservedly, but he has obtained nothing which does not enure to the equal advantage of the United States, and there are stipulations in Mr. Reed's treaty which they are here congratulating themselves will, under the most favored clause, enure to the benefit of England.

Lord Brougham has made a most elaborate and unreadable speech on the occasion of inaugurating, the day before yesterday, at Grentham, a statue in bronze to Newton. He exhibited his own familiarity with the highest ranges of science:—but he does not appear to have, by effective words and generalization, brought into any stronger relief the creative genius of Sir Isaac. There are some fames, such as Johnson considers Shakespeare's, whose adamant nothing can strengthen or impair.

The Premier, apparently sacrificing his stud to his studies, tried a sale by public outcry:—but his heart caved in, and he fixed such enormous prices upon his favorites—on one, Toxopholite, 15,000 dollars—that all the really good nags are left upon his hands. He will be obliged to retract his abjuration of the turf. Why, indeed, should a man affect to be what he is not, even though he be prime minister?

Every day gives rise to some new theory as to the cause

of the Cable's failure. The last is the least hopeful:—it is in the shape of a report from an enquiring electrician, appointed for the purpose by the Company. He seems to think that an injury may have been inflicted when the Agamemnon, overrunning her log, unconsciously quit the submarine plateau of Maury:—or, as he intimates, the excessive force with which the fluid was impelled at each extremity may have transcended the ability of the wire to hold it, and so ignited the contiguous coating to a considerable length:—at any rate, he doubts whether the fatal wound was given short of 300 miles from shore, and, since it was given, whether it was by fire, or water, or rock, it may have spread its coils several hundreds of miles. I hope you quite understand this, although it be too erudite for me, partaking as it does of the wild invention and incomprehensibility of Southey's Curse of Kehama. *Vates ambo!*.

You must not find fault with the subjects on which I write. At this season, I grasp at whatever has any sort of interest. The Atlantic Cable has, besides, risen to be a great political institution, and its flaws have a tendency to check international intercourse and universal civilization! Ask Mr. Cyrus Field if that be not so. The wits of Paris, after long calling by the name of "canard" any piece of false news, have now christened immortally, every signal failure "a cable."

Always faithfully yrs.

---

## No. 219.—TO MR. CASS.

LONDON, September 28, 1858.

MY DEAR SIR,—I avail myself of the steamer "City of Baltimore" in order to beg your attention for a moment to the subject of the enclosed copy of a letter from solicitors long connected with this legation.

It is quite clear that a sharper has been for some time at work defrauding many of our too credulous countrymen by pretending to have discovered property in this country to which they are entitled: and inducing them to transmit small sums of five or ten pounds to meet the fees and costs of preliminary enquiry. The expediency of a short and prompt notice is suggested: and I submit whether something of the sort may not with propriety be inserted in the *Union* and *Intelligencer*.

The dumbness of the Cable seems alike incurable and inexplicable. Every day brings out a tedious rigmarole of imaginary causes:—but as yet no positive action to fix the distance or character of the mischief.

The Queen of Greece has resolved upon restoring the Olympic Games:—not, Mr. Tricoupi tells me, on or near Mount Olympus, nor exactly in their ancient simplicity:—but on an estate left for the purpose by a private millionaire, near Athens, and much in the form of modern industrial exhibition!

The *very* last *on-dit* about the Prussian crisis seems to be that the Prince has become permanent Regent, the King incurable. When his Majesty dies, it is not improbable that the Regent will abdicate and permit his son, who married *our* Princess Royal the other day, to take the crown.

Always faithfully yrs.

---

## No. 220.—TO MR. CASS.

LONDON, October 8, 1858.

MY DEAR SIR,—The rumor of the day is that apology and reparation are to be made for Captain Pullen's bombardment of Jidda! How different this from what would have taken place had Lord Palmerston remained in office may be seen from a characteristic anecdote which I know to be true. His Ex-premiership recently met Fuad Pacha, the Turkish plenipotentiary in Paris, who complained to him bitterly of the cruelty of firing upon a defenceless town, especially as the offence given was in train of diplomatic enquiry and reparation. Very harsh and very sad, was the reply:—but as the fanatic massacre at the consulate was incontestable, had I been minister I would have ordered the immediate destruction of the town. This goes a little farther than the precedent set at San Juan.

Another long and able report from the electrician Henley on the Atlantic Cable. He permits a scintilla of hope to survive that, by the use of *his* instruments, the mischief may be gradually remedied. He leans, however, to the opinion that the fault was in the cable when laid, and that it would have been discovered had a proper series of experiments been previously made. There are some subjects on which scientific men seem to delight in theorizing fancifully: the two most attractive just now are the deepest in earth and the loftiest in the heavens—the Cable and the Comet. I am told that the Earl of C. has written a book to prove that this latter beautiful visitor is on an errand to execute the judgment of Daniel and destroy the world! Implicit faith is due to the sacred prophets:—the difficulty lies in fallible constructions and calculations by imaginative laymen. However, nothing is too incredible not to have some believers. *Credo, quia impossibile.*

Lord Derby, though physically excruciated by the gout, continues politically in the groove of good luck. The public revenue has augmented beyond expectation. Some, to be sure, predict a deficit of £6,000,000 at the end of the year:—but the most sagacious are unable to perceive whence it can arise. The ministry are allowed six months longer life by their sanguine opponents:—the lapse of that period brings them to the second month of the parliamentary session, and what may then be the topics of eventful discussion it is impossible to foresee. Reform will not shake them.

Lord Canning has written a very able defence of his policy against the attack made in Lord Ellenborough's celebrated despatch, condemning his confiscating proclamation. His defence, to be sure, consists more in averments of intention than in denying facts: arguing it to be wise to declare the territorial forfeitures, but not to retain them:—to restore or re-distribute them.

The Czar says he will visit Paris and London, *if possible*, in the spring. He had better move slowly in the cause of serf-emancipation, or his boyars will make the visit *impossible.* He has been, as it were, "stumping" his empire: and his published addresses are underlaid by an apparent consciousness that the task which baffled his father may endanger him.

Always faithfully yrs.

## No. 221.—TO MR. MARKOE.

LONDON, October 8, 1858.

MY DEAR MARKOE,—You never write. The steamers bring me nothing. I hope you are taking your fall trip, for that will be your best apology by giving me the assurance that your health is invigorating.

I suppose an Ex-Premier may be likened to an "archangel ruined," and so, worthy even in his fall, of some respect. Well!—the ladies, by a rapid interchange of notes, so fixed it that we closed our vagabondish month of September by a visit of five days to Broadlands, Lord Palmerston's delightful residence in Hants. What a lovely region of country. That river Tesk! running at the foot of the lawn, in all sorts of curves, limpid, crystalline, sparkling, murmuring, with the quick-eyed trout stemming its current while seemingly motionless three feet below the surface! The huge elms, with trunks thirty feet in girth: the towering cypresses: the pinnacled cedars: the age-worn oaks: the magnolia grandifloras with their capacious (but not fragrant) white flowers: the glowing beds of roses, geraniums, rhododendrons, heliotropes, pinks, chrysanthemums—the sculptured vases, fountains, cascades: the interminable park, clusters of trees, gravel walks, and clouds of ever-cawing rooks:—and there, right in front, high in the heavens, yet glittering in the rippling Tesk, shines the magnificently tail-bearing Comet!

Don't ask me about paintings and rare objects of *vertu*. I am not now in their vein. Take them to be multitudinous and infinitely curious. I want to boast, that while Morphy was challenging and beating all Europe at chess in Paris, I was following his illustrious and patriotic example by conquering the conqueror of Derby at billiards, and by outshooting him marvellously during a five hours' tramp after partridges:—he in the finished jaunty costume of a thoroughbred English sportsman, I under my heavy beaver, in common frock coat, and light thin boots. Our coveys were shy, and required more than usual activity of pursuit, and it was glorious to see how this veteran managed to keep up his animation and brisk step to the very last: dressing and coming to dinner too in an hour afterwards as if he had been upon a satin sofa all day.

Don't abuse me for this harum-scarum style of epistle. If I stopped long enough to arrange ideas and words, I should be worse fagged than I was in shooting, and you would lose this precious piece of fanfaronade by the flight of my Bag.

Ever faithfully yrs.

---

## No. 222.—TO MR. CASS.

LONDON, October 15, 1858.

MY DEAR SIR,—The Emperor and his resolute minister Walewski shew no yielding on their device of black emigrants from Africa to the West Indies. You have doubtless noticed the new case of the ship "*Charles et Georges*" seized off Mozambique by the Portuguese, first for being in prohibited waters, and second for carrying on the prohibited trade. She was crammed with negroes, and crowded with fetters: both of which "our great and good ally" vindicates by the presence of a public "*Commissaire de France*" on board. Sent for condemnation to Lisbon, two Imperial line-of-battle-ships have repaired thither, anchored in the stream, and demand that either she shall be forthwith surrendered, with indemnity, or that Louis Napoleon's diplomatic representative shall repair to Paris. Of course, poor Portugal will have to succumb, violate her own laws, annul the judgments of her courts, and sacrifice the vested rights of her subjects. There is a talk of saving honor, etc., by a mediation. What will England say? *Vive la sainte alliance?*—maugre the capture of a slave-ship *flagrante delicto.*

His Prussian Majesty has finally withdrawn before a Regent, and may be regarded as a "dissolving view." Like several other supernumerary royalties, he ceases to be talked of, and must soon either die or be forgotten.

The condition of the Venezuelan controversy is just now somewhat inaccessible. Lord M. sticks tenaciously to his "shooting box" in Scotland, and nobody in London cares a pinch of snuff for all the parties concerned. Monagas is reported to be in Paris. But your ex-minister, Eames, must by this time have repaired to Washington and put you *au fait*. A loose rumor represents the difficulty as settled by mutual concession.

The Duke and Duchess of Malakoff, married two days ago, ought to be in London this afternoon. Thus far the Crimean conqueror has been a model of loyal acquiescence to a command which secured for him a combination of Venus and Juno. His predecessor, as I suspected in one of my former letters to you, is longing to return to Albert Gate:—and his pretty countess haunts, like a desponding spirit, the courtly scenes of her past enjoyment.

The Association of Social Science, met and still sitting at Liverpool, is really exhibiting great ability and vigor. Still it is noticeable what an infinity of talent and trouble they expend in proving positions long since accepted by us as almost axiomatic truths. Lords John Russell, Brougham, and Shaftesbury are the leading figures.

Though no chance of acting efficiently for some time is apparent, I hope our Coast Survey is on the alert to seize the first opportunity offered by the Cable for fixing the longitude by means of clocks at each end. Men of science are referring to this here.

Always faithfully yrs.

---

## No. 223.—TO MR. CASS.

LONDON, October 22, 1858.

MY DEAR SIR,—The first duty and pleasure of the moment is to thank you for your private letter of the 4th instant.

I wish I could answer your enquiry as to the personal deportment of the explosive *pétard* of the Foreign Office:—but I cannot:—he has been shooting grouse or stalking deer in Scotland, or perhaps, preparing like an irritated lion for another spring, he coolly for the present lies low and keeps dark. However, to speak seriously and sincerely, my impression is that his rage exhausted itself in his note from Potsdam, that he has not a drop left with which to treat my reply, and that we shall slowly (on my part very slowly) resume our previous relation. You will have seen that our diplomatic correspondence on other topics has not had the faintest smack of this particular acid.

Will you have the Bahamas? They are not as attractive as Cuba, and scarcely comparable to the bay of Samana:—but they lie in the great thoroughfare of our Gulf, and might yield a cluster of harbors for coaling or against storms. What will you bid for them? The "Baron E. Graves van der Smissen," a highly intelligent Dutchman of about 33, claims them or rather their sovereignty as vested in himself and co-heirs under an express grant of Charles I. The Baron is a grandson of Admiral Graves, whom I knew here in 1814, who had been naturalized in the United States and married there. The Baron can and will deploy a perfect title:—he has undertaken to put it on paper, to exhibit copies of deeds, and to set forth the chain of proofs. His price is reasonable. Will you offer?

I send you the copy of a letter addressed to me by a surgeon of the 2d West India Regiment. He thinks himself entitled to a share of the $3000 appropriated in June last to make suitable acknowledgments to the Jamaica authorities for the relief extended to the sick officers and crew of the Susquehanna. Not, as it would seem, that he actually partook in the kind offices rendered, but that he was on board of the vessel which carried the sufferers to New York, might have succored their bodies had his aid been invoked, and no doubt soothed their minds by the consciousness that he was at hand. The surgeon might quote precedents of high authority.

The Chinese Treaties are still favorite topics. Of course, John Bull claims all the merit. Even Baron Gros was on the point of yielding to the views of forbearance and national courtesy inculcated by Mr. Reed:—but Lord Elgin held on his course sternly.

The Queen returned from Edinburgh to Windsor Castle on Wednesday last:—of course with her usual "*entourage*." All the peripatetic royalties have gone back to their homes.

I am strongly inclined to convey to you my speculations on the drift of political affairs just now, this side of the Atlantic:—but this letter is already too long, and you are too busy for generalities. To me, let me say briefly, the indications of approaching change, convulsion, and war, are marked and multitudinous. "Watchman, what of the night?" Shadows, clouds, and darkness rest upon it. Keep our western star steadily shining, that the world may see it above the storm.

Always faithfully yrs.

---

## No. 224.—TO MR. CASS.

LONDON, October 26, 1858.

MY DEAR SIR,—What of Lord M.?—you will ask. Well! these collateral entanglements about words are by no means the easiest to unravel: and they who rush impetuously into them must sometimes be fain to creep backwards out as they may. His lordship would appear unable or unwilling to put in a replication to my answer, and so resolved, after six weeks' meditation and a visit to the Premier at Knowsley, to bury the hatchet with short blessing, and with as much grace as his nature would allow. He invited me to the F. O. and I went yesterday at 4 P.M. I entertain a high and sincere respect for the Earl:—none the less because as a British statesman he has done the United States justice on a point of momentous concern long in angry controversy. Let me then restrict myself to saying that after I had tranquilly looked at him for one or two minutes, waiting the communication he had invited me to receive, he went on to talk, discursively and incongruously upon all sorts of topics, without for one instant adverting to the one uppermost in my thoughts, and the one which it was impossible not to perceive was the bee in his own bonnet. A pointless and profitless course of commonplace was selected as the harmless means of bridging over the fissure in our relations. He began by awkwardly saying that though he had requested to see me, he really had nothing to communicate; and he proved his words by much talk on ordinary topics which he forbore to illuminate by the least novelty of idea. I saw very soon that the controlling sentiment was "the least said soonest mended;" and I abstained, during the fifteen minutes' visit, from interfering in the slightest degree with what was no doubt prescribed as the course fittest and fairest for all concerned. There then is an end of that tantamarara: *redeunt saturnia regna:*—and you may rest assured that your minister is henceforward safe from such storms.

Lord Malmesbury's department would seem to me to give him something better to attend to than deer-stalking. This abandonment of Portugal to the swoop of the Imperial eagle, on a point too of so much professed tenderness, puts a sharp arrow into the quiver, as well as a broad grin on the face, of the Palmerstonian opposition. One of two things:—either the government of Lord Derby did, or did not, intervene to shield at least the honor of their feeble friend:—if they did, why was their intervention repelled by their dear ally?—if they did not, why thus palpably sink from the position of a first rate power? The question grates closely on the very spirit which, suddenly evoked by Milner Gibson, deposed Lord Palmerston. The French editors, too, are taking now pretty much the contemptuous and defiant attitude taken by the French colonels then. Popular feeling is rousing: and by the time Parliament meets, it may become a small hurricane like that of February last, only taking the opposite direction.

Flags, as well as feathers, shew how the wind blows. On the very day that Portugal surrendered the "*Charles et Georges*" at the summons of Louis Napoleon, Marshal Pelissier, for the first time, hoisted over his embassy at Albert Gate, the tricolor, and there it has continued, flouting the air, and exciting curious enquiries as to its import. Just at the same time, as if to console by blandishment, the excellent Count and Countess Lavradio are commanded to Windsor Castle. Of course, the despatch of the Count soothed the Court of Lisbon with the idea that his flattering reception at such a juncture was an ample equivalent for the loss of the slaver.

The controversy about the Jewish boy, who was baptized into Christianity by a sort of nurse, then taken in charge by the Roman priests as a brand plucked and to be saved from the burning, and as to whose restoration to his parents the Pope says "*non possumus*," is in full blast all over Europe. It is egging on Louis Napoleon to a quarrel with the Holy Father; some say, nothing loth to find pleas for re-enacting his uncle's coronation courtship of Pius VII. If the case of this child, Mortara, were for judgment before King Solomon, he would be puzzled, as he was once before:—and I think that I perceive that his reference to the headsman is a hint for the disposition of such knotty points not altogether forgotten, though perhaps perverted. The lad, at a college of catechumens, is reported very, very ill.

Much power of oratory expended on her Majesty's subjects of late! as a general current, not unlike the dull, turbid, and repulsive Thames of the last summer solstice. Mr. John Bright, M.P. for Birmingham, has, however, in addressing his constituents the day before yesterday, made a stirring speech on Reform, almost sufficiently democratic for a 4th of July at Tammany Hall. This rich cream is more to one's taste than the bonny-clabber of the Liverpool meeting of the Social Science Association. One result of these agitations is striking, and is apparent more to veterans than to novices like myself:—they are said to foreshadow the early downfall of the present ministry. In his brief compliment to Lord John Russell, Mr. Bright is thought to have indicated the only Premier the Manchester party will accept as successor to Derby.

Always faithfully yrs.

---

## No. 225.—TO MR. GILPIN.

LONDON, October 31, 1858.

MY DEAR GILPIN,—Mr. Bright's picture of England's domestic politics must have its "pendant" on foreign policy:—so here it is, and perhaps you will say the better of the two.

I forget whether even a scrap of the eloquence of either of the Gracchi has come down to us: (how is that?) they were always favorites of mine:—now take the two speeches of Mr. Bright together, and do they not give him a claim to rank with these jewels of Cornelia, and as a diamond of the first water?

Always faithfully yrs.

## No. 226.—TO MR. CASS.

LONDON, November 5, 1858.

MY DEAR SIR,—One can't help being struck by the singular sensitiveness which seems to prevail here about a French invasion. All the stump speakers, all the daily papers, all the ponderous periodicals, do their best to argue it down, or laugh it off. This very effort keeps it on the *qui vive*. Two days ago, at Queenstown, in Ireland, a junior lieutenant, left by superiors in command of a war steamer, took it into his head, after a late dinner given to some shore companions, to signalize the occasion by a succession of salutes. He fired away, larboard and starboard, for some twenty minutes, and this far in the night. *Conticuere omnes, intentique:*—"the French are come!" the whole town shook with panic. Officers convened, movements were concerted, deputations arranged, and imaginative ladies fainted. Returning silence set guessing at work; and when day came it was soon ascertained that the eccentric and insubordinate son of a gallant old Admiral had kicked up all that there was of a "French invasion." In revenge for the terror he had inspired, he was arrested; and I suspect he will have a hard time of it for causing the universal apprehension to betray itself. All this is natural when you consider the peculiar locality, press, principles, pretensions, and antecedents of England. As her hand is ready against every other nation, she instinctively feels that the hand of any one sufficiently powerful must be against her.

The *Times* of this morning contains a merciless column against the present ambassador of France. It rakes up the savage exploit of burning 500 Arabs in their rocky den, and quotes the strong denunciations pronounced at the time in Paris against so barbarous an act. What is meant hereby? To make London, like the refuge of his victims, too hot to hold Pelissier? To prepare the reinstatement of Persigny? Or is it a mere catering to the existing and swelling discontent with the Imperial ally? Most likely, the last:—for the *Times* has gone far and deep in multiplying attacks on Louis Napoleon, especially since his treatment of the Portuguese for intermeddling with the black emigration scheme.

London is reviving. The members of the cabinet have returned to their official residences. The Queen has held a Privy Council at Windsor. Courts of Justice have begun business. Galleries of Art are opening. Science is marshalling her lectures. Soirées, theatres, and equipages are agog. "The noise of battle hurtles in the air." Be patient a little while, and I shall have more dainty food to dish up in these "*notæ variorum.*"

Always faithfully yrs.

---

## No. 227.—TO MR. CASS.

LONDON, November 12, 1858.

MY DEAR SIR,—Mr. Pickens has sent me by a private messenger such loads of despatches from St. Petersburg, which he describes to me in a note as specially confidential, that I shrink from putting anything in the Bag which can distract your attention, especially at the season when the Message is on the anvil.

Count Montalembert would seem to have a peculiar relish for martyrdom. His pamphlet of panegyric upon England in derogation of France introduces him to a criminal court in the manner most acceptable to the Emperor, for it brings the national feeling to co-operate with the Crown in its policy of silencing the Press. The gauntlet thus indiscreetly thrown is instantly picked up by one who, in so doing, loses the character of oppressor and becomes, as against a hated rival, the champion of his country. This result is being aided by the *Times*, which devotes countless columns of exultation to the republication of the essay. The Count's purpose was doubtless a generous and brave one:—but like many an imprudent advocate, he has, in his anglomaniac zeal, given to his cause the very worst stab it has yet received.

In general opinion here, the *Morning Herald* is the government paper. It has latterly sought to be interesting by commenting upon our uncontrollable tendency to expand and annex. The Monroe doctrine is stigmatized as a "*sop addressed to American vanity:*" and it is insisted that on the other, as on this side of the Atlantic, a "*balance of power must be upheld.*" Yesterday the Central American States were the pivot on which these remarks revolved; to-day it is Mexico, and the necessity of European intervention to preserve her demoralized weakness from sinking into our athletic embrace is distinctly stated. Now, this is all fanfaronade if it be not ministerial:—but if the latter, it mounts into importance, is inconsistent with protestations to which I have heretofore listened at the Foreign Office and have formally reported to you, and is entitled to grave attention. Spain may yet under the auspices of England be tempted to make a spasmodic effort for the restoration of her Mexican dominion. A word, a single word, importing American unanimity and inflexibility on the topic, would crush the egg-shell project forever.

You have doubtless observed the French Emperor's retreat from his free emigration scheme as to the negroes; his letter to Prince Jerome directing a thorough investigation, and hinting that white slavery is perhaps as good as black, and that Coolies may be made to work as well as Africans. Some persons are ill-natured enough to regard this as a mere ironical feint on the part of his Majesty. I do not. He is a sincere politic penitent. "*Les Amis des Noirs*" are at once numerous and fashionable in Paris:—while pig-tailed and scalp-tufted Chinese are rare and no go.

Always faithfully yrs.

---

## No. 228.—TO MR. FAIR.

LONDON, November 16, 1858.

MY DEAR SIR,—Your letter of the 13th instant is just received.

The positive provision of the act of 1856, that "no attaché shall be allowed in any case," has, I presume, been conformed to by our foreign legations since it became known. I am aware of but a single instance of what bore the appearance of its evasion:—that of a young gentleman whose card, brought in to me about a year ago, described him as "*secrétaire intime de S. E. le Ministre des*

*États-Unis.*" Perhaps as personal or private secretary he obtained all the circulation he desired.

The mischief against which the law is aimed had long been noticed at the department of State, and was often embarrassing to our diplomatic representatives. Under the old usage, unpaid attachés might be created without stint as to number: and a train so composed was thought, and justly thought, to give *éclat* to a mission. Now it frequently happened that the minister, always conscious of the invidious nature of *selecting* from his young countrymen, preferred giving his appointments without discrimination and to every one who asked. American attachés became as plentiful as blackberries, and sometimes deranged by their intermeddling the business of, or by their deportment, threw discredit upon, the legation. Congress, moved no doubt by the Secretary of State, Gov. Marcy, who was pitiless against shewy pretension, struck at the root of the evil by an express prohibition. I have occasionally wished to possess the discretion:—but on the whole perceive many inconveniences in which I should be involved by it, and have therefore no reluctance in strictly complying with the law.

Do me the favor to believe that it will always give me pleasure to be allowed to interchange with you views on public topics.

Faithfully and respectfully yrs.

---

## No. 229.—TO MR. CASS.

London, November 19, 1858.

My dear Sir,—You will find in the Bag of to-day a despatch addressed to Mr. Toucey which conveys an interesting document respecting the pay and allowances of British naval officers, and will enable him satisfactorily, as far as this country is concerned, to answer a resolution of the House of last session. Pray expedite his reception of it.

You will have noticed that England has rather tired of the Protectorate assigned to her over the Ionian Islands, and is planning to pick the plum out of the pudding, that is, to retain Corfu, as a military post, and let the rest go to Greece, or elsewhere. This course, hardly reconcilable with her public obligations, must be made at least plausibly proper:—and so Lord Derby has lately sent Mr. Gladstone to visit these Homeric regions and to report what is best to be done, not doubting that he will reach the conclusion already attained by the cabinet. The member for the Oxford University, the finished scholar and too musical rhetorician—the *Preston*, as I might describe him, of the House of Commons - scarcely crossed the Channel, in his progress up the Mediterranean, before out came a series of official documents in the newspapers shewing that the alleged enquiry for which he was appointed had been fully, effectually, and satisfactorily made by the British representative actually there. All the opposition at once open cry. It is termed a shabby and treacherous treatment of an eminent statesman, who committed himself by accepting office under this ministry merely because he wished to render a patriotic service. Mr. Gladstone is depicted as placed in a most awkward and ludicrous predicament:—to get out of which it is predicted that he will at once throw up his commission in disgust. What follows on the heel of this seemingly well-founded explosion? Why, another complication. The Colonial Department, under the signature of Sir Edw'd Bulwer Lytton's private secretary, alleges that the official documents have been surreptitiously taken from the files and published, without the assent or knowledge of her Majesty's government! This is the present almost absorbing topic. No doubt the desire is great to "fan the embers" of a quarrel which may induce the Peelites to merge into the ranks of opposition.

The appointment by Prince Jerome of Count Persigny, whose anglomania is even greater than that of Montalembert, to be president of the committee to examine and report upon the nature of the Black Emigrant scheme, removes all doubt, and is thought to denote a foregone conclusion in the Imperial mind to give it up.

Lords Palmerston and Clarendon have gone to Compiègne, and the political *réunion*, or rather the réunion of politicians at that place, is regarded as something significant. Of one thing its significance is strong, to wit, that her Majesty's late Premier and principal Secretary for

Foreign Affairs are being very careless of their popularity at home. This visit of theirs gives countenance to the subservient predilection of which they have been accused, and the belief in which produced their fall on the 19th of February last. Ordinary minds draw ordinary conclusions, and this sort of intimacy, wholly uncalled for in the existing state of feeling among the masses of both countries, gives rise to the most prejudicial inferences.

Parliament has undergone a second prorogation, to the 2d of January, when a similar formality will be enacted for the first week in February and—for *the despatch of business.*

Lord Elgin's two brothers, Bruces, mount the back of his Chinese Treaty, one as Ambassador to Pekin, the other as Governor to the Prince of Wales.

Since my last week's note, I observed in a newspaper's correspondent at Madrid that, after a long interview held with the Foreign Secretary by the English and French ministers, a squadron had been ordered to Vera Cruz.

Always faithfully yrs.

---

## No. 230.—TO MR. TOUCEY.

LONDON, November 29, 1858.

MY DEAR SIR,—After my letter to you, returning the credit on the Barings for $500, Colonel Guernsey obtained the written consent of the Queen to his engaging in our service, and shewed me a note from Mr. Hammond saying that the document was at the Foreign Office, to be had on the payment of about fifty dollars office fees. He exhibited also strong testimonials from the Duke of Cambridge, General Burgoyne, General Evans, General Hill, etc. etc., as to his military qualifications; and he impressed me with a conviction that his familiarity with the topographical features and garrison equipments of Paraguay, would make his presence on board our squadron quite useful. Military operations, dependent upon the depth of water in the river, could not begin before February:—so that there was ample time for him to reach Buenos Ayres.

I determined to send him: and arranged with Messrs.

Baring Brothers & Co., for an advance of $500 to pay his expenses out. During the whole of last week, I expected him daily at the legation to complete the transaction, bring me her Majesty's leave, take his money, letters and final instructions, and speed to the rendezvous. I agreed that his compensation should be at the rate of pay allowed in our army to a Lieutenant-Colonel of Engineers. He came not: and my two successive notes to you of the 23d and 26th instant were written in impatient expectation of his coming.

The mystery of his dilatory action has been suddenly solved. The evening newspaper of last Saturday, the *Globe*, contained a detailed examination at the Bow Street Police Court on that morning, shewing his arrest and commitment upon the criminal charge of having stolen the much-talked-of Ionian despatches from the Colonial Office! So, there is an end to this Free Knight:—he won't destroy Lopez; he won't disgrace the American service, and he won't pocket our cash! I send you a printed narrative.

Always faithfully yrs.

---

## No. 231.—TO MR. SPEAKER DENNISON.

LONDON, December 4, 1858.

MY DEAR SIR,—I beg you to excuse my apparent remissness in not before answering your note of the 22d ultimo:—attributable to a short absence from town and a press of official engagements.

The spirit of party, in America as in all free countries, is prone to goad in moments of excitement to acts of injustice. Majorities, each in turn, may abuse power by dealing with the minority impatiently and illiberally. But what has long stood its ground as a rule of legislative action, surviving changes in party ascendency and the criticism of tranquil times, must be presumed to possess substantive and independent merit. Such I regard to be the case with our Congressional "*Previous Question.*"

It is not practised in the Senate, whose numbers are comparatively few and graver in age. But in the House of Representatives it is resorted to, with a view to expedite measures known to be exigent, and to break through the entangling meshes of amendments, or to close a worn-out debate. The Rules of the House, carefully matured in advance, prescribe its modes of use and its effects. It has disadvantages no doubt:—but its conceded beneficial working on the whole has preserved it through shifting currents of political storms. Public opinion, which soon becomes all-powerful with us, has never yet condemned the "Previous Question" as exercised in the House. On the contrary, it has been generally esteemed, as well by the enlightened as the popular mind, a check upon factious dissipation of time and money, and a wholesome corrective to profuse or "bunkum" speaking.

Your "distinguished American who was in London last year" had perhaps personally suffered under the rule, and owed it a grudge. If he mentioned the instances of the Annexation of Texas and the Fugitive Slave Law as unaccompanied by discussion, he was sadly in error. Pardon a few particulars to shew this.

The former question not only occupied the whole country during the Presidential canvass of 1844, in which one party made it the principal and victorious issue, for the popular verdict, but, after being recommended to Congress by President Tyler in his Message on the 3d of December of that year, it was on the 19th, in the form of a Joint Resolution, referred to the "Committee of the whole House on the State of the Union;" and thenceforward, at fifteen full meetings of the House in Committee, during nearly half the session, it was debated with great ability (but "*usque ad nauseam*"), and it was only (a directory order for closing the discussion having passed the House on the 21st of January, '45, by 102 to 54), finally decided under the "Previous Question" on the 25th of January, '45, 120 to 98.

Being now transferred to the Senate, it underwent farther and more elaborate consideration. The same question had engaged that body upon movements of its own members. One Senator, McDuffie, had introduced a joint resolution for the annexation of Texas, on the 10th December, '44: another, Niles, on 7th January, '45: and a third, Foster, on the 13th January:—but the great debate, or pitched battle, was reserved for the coming House measure. That measure came in on the 28th January, '45, was sent to a committee, was reported upon *adversely* on the 4th of February, but was taken up in its order on the 13th February: and thenceforward, at every daily meeting of the Senate, and sometimes twice a day, it was the standing order and exclusive topic, until the 27th of February (within four days of the close of the session of Congress), when, debate being drained to the lees, no one capable or willing to add another word, it passed by a majority of two votes only.

I very much doubt whether any act of legislation has undergone a more thorough, full, fair, and satisfactory discussion than did the annexation of Texas by Congress.

As to the Fugitive Slave Law, the sphere of its discussion was, owing to exceedingly special circumstances, almost exclusively the Senate. It was introduced there by the Committee on the Judiciary, on the 16th of January, 1850, and was soon after made by Mr. Clay one of a set or cluster of measures which constituted his celebrated Compromise of that year. As a feature in his comprehensive plan, it underwent debate, as unrestricted as able, for *thirty-three days*. So much time, indeed, was taken up by these discussions, that the bill did not reach the House of Representatives until the 26th of August, nine months from the opening of the session. As a component and indispensable part of the adjusted compromise, its prompt adoption, in the approved shape, was required by the state and voice of the country. It passed upon a demand for the "Previous Question," on the 12th of September, 109 to 76:—and Congress closed one of its longest and most agitated sessions in about two weeks afterwards.

I have gone into these two cited instances of what is thought an abuse of the "Previous Question" by the House of Representatives, as pieces of legislative history which you will perhaps think interesting, and principally to shew you how little they justify the grumblers against its exercise.

I have said, it has not found its way into the Senate. But there is another expedient there for maintaining, on emergencies, the rightful power of the majority to control the business of the Body:—that is, a motion to lay whatever is under discussion *upon the table:* whence, indeed, it may be subsequently taken, but not without a successful motion to that effect.

Always very faithfully yrs.

---

## No. 232.—TO MR. CASS.

LONDON, December 10, 1858.

MY DEAR SIR,—The young *roués* of London, on crossing the Atlantic, would naturally be curious to see the wild life of the Western savages. No one, therefore, doubted the rumor, published two days ago, that the three English noblemen who have been travelling in the States, had penetrated far into the northwest of Canada, had had a fight with a tribe of natives, and were all murdered. The sensation produced was after their own hearts. Fortunately, Lord Shaftesbury, one of the fathers, had received an explanation of the story and was able yesterday, as he says "*providentially*" (for his lordship is of the class particularly pious) to contradict "the massacre" taken from "American journals" whose origin is only "the murder of two traders" by Indians last August. Poor traders!—still, we are all pleased to hear that the nobles are safe.

Louis Napoleon and Montalembert are still at their game of chess. It is the Emperor's move. The epigrammatic pardon (whose sting lay in reminding the Count that he was among the faithful actors of the 2d of December) is spurned, and the appeal perfected. Can his Majesty pardon what Mr. Berryer reasons and the court may adjudge to be no offence? Various are the opinions on this subtle point. The Count is pushing boldly before the Judges to checkmate his adversary:—let him take heed, lest by the sudden refusal of the Procureur Imperial to make another move, the game takes the unsatisfactory turn of a "*stale.*" That would subject him to the "*loi des suspects*" of last February for the rest of his life, or rather for the rest of the Emperor's reign, which promises to be the shorter of the two. Professors Morphy and Stanton, hide your diminished heads!

A bitter hatred to each other is vented daily by the masses on the two sides of the Channel. It is getting beyond the power of repression by the respective governments. As I ventured to foresee would be the case, the visit of Lords Palmerston and Clarendon to Compiègne has brought a cataract of reproaches upon their heads. Count Montalembert is prosecuted without a single popular murmur, because he praises England. Where is the wisdom that can tell which of these two nations is right in her hostility? Or are both wrong? One thing is clear to the rest of the world, to wit, that it is easier to like a volatile Frenchman than a bullying Briton. Here is a mangy M. P.—one Henry Drummond—an F. R. S. (which may sometimes mean a Fellow Rather Savage), who, because he chooses to pick a controversy with Mr. Bright, snarls at the whole world, and especially snaps at the United States in the following precious sentences:—"*Their pretended love of freedom is the most barefaced falsehood that ever existed. They are utterly without private or public honor, and the only people on earth who ever avowed that gain was their sole object in every relationship of life.*" *That* from an F. R. S. of 72! Out upon such fellowship. If English philosophy deal in calumny, in what may not English anger and arrogance deal? We can't honestly say "*ab uno disce omnes:*"—but, in reference to national attributes, it is impossible not to acquiesce in the "*ex pede Herculem.*" Drummond, it may be feared, is a specimen brick.

A careless phrase or two, let drop at a review by the King of Sardinia, combined with a general restlessness and discontent in the north of Italy, fanned by the anti-Austrian feeling in France, gives promise of an outbreak in the spring. Let it come. For really Europe, under the auspices of a Bonaparte too, is retrograding so fast into mediæval wretchedness, that nothing can save it but a grand smash. This is not mine, but the sentiment of the day. At present, Victor Emmanuel is busy in riveting the affections of Russia, conceding Villafranca, and entertaining most cordially H. I. H. the Grand Duke Constantine and his household.

I ought to hurry in retracting some of the conclusions expressed in my last, drawn from the premature publicity given to the despatches of the High Commissioner of the Ionian Islands. It now appears that these documents were purloined by a military engineer (upon whom, by-the-by, Mr. Toucey and I were very near conferring the immortality of sharing in our Paraguay demonstration) from the Colonial Office; that their contents never had received the approval of government: and that the duty of adhering to provisions of the Treaty of 1815 establishing the Protectorate is recognized and avowed. To be sure, this would seem to reduce the extraordinary and vaunted mission of Mr. Gladstone to a mere act of patronage.

Lord Derby steers more skilfully than was anticipated. A few things have recently deepened the groove in which he moves. The proclamation of the Queen on assuming the sovereignty of her 200,000,000 of Indian subjects, obtains unanimous praise. It is ascribed to Lord Stanley. So, the discountenance given to the efforts of ship owners to unsettle free-trade by insisting upon sharing in our coast trade as a right of reciprocity, is commended by the opposition. Then again the decided aversion to filibustering, manifested in the repulse of Rajah Brooke of Sarawak, is favorably contrasted with the foreign policy of Lord Palmerston, and what perhaps just now tells powerfully on popular sentiment is the cooler distance taken towards French rulers and men, set in contrast with the course of their rivals both before and since downfall. It is said that Lord Palmerston frankly declares that a change would not at present be an improvement. Mr. Lowe, whom you had in Washington two years ago, a man of great political acuteness, told a large dinner party of his constituents two days ago, that he was unflinchingly devoted to the late Premier, but that his restoration could not be thought of for a year or two to come. All things are uncertain:—but I am inclined to think that, sportsman as he is, more of the *stable* will be found in Lord Derby than in most prime ministers.

Always faithfully yrs.

---

## No. 233.—TO MR. CASS.

LONDON, December 17, 1858.

MY DEAR SIR,—Mr. Toucey, like all the London public, will be surprised to hear that my quondam recruit for Paraguay, Colonel William Guernsey, has been tried for larceny of the Ionian despatches and—acquitted! His dexterous counsel triumphed over the Attorney-General and the court;—making the jury believe that to purloin in order to publish an official paper, not to appropriate it to his own profit, was an offence which lacked the essential quality of a felony. Government prosecutions thrive only in France:—here, as with us, juries like to rescue hapless sufferers from the grasp of authority.

You will have noticed that while the Emperor's commissioners are actively engaged in ascertaining for him the real character of free emigration from Africa, and just at the moment when they are supposed to be ready to report in its favor, a case like that of the "*Charles et Georges*" occurs on the *western* coast of Africa. The zealous commander of H. M. S. "Alecto" (you remember that name, don't you, in connection with Cobb & Ellis's "Caroline"?), egged on by the President of Liberia, captured the French vessel "Phœnix," with an Imperial representative on board and negroes stowed in the hold. The culpable craft was taken to Monrovia. As this government lost, in the estimation of Europe, much of its dignity by failing to shield Portugal from the peremptory resentment of Louis Napoleon, it may be willing to lose a little more by disavowing Captain Hunt's act, and pointing to President Benson as the scape-goat.

The Reform leader, Mr. Bright, is steadily making headway. He successfully, if not victoriously, withstands the combined contumely of the *Times*, the *Morning Herald*, and *Punch*. His speeches are read by everybody: his photographs hang in all public nooks and corners: his audiences are multitudinous and enthusiastic. If he maintain his attitude in the House of Commons, and once enforce a principle by carrying a measure, it will be difficult to assign a limit to his progress.

All the world are on tiptoe for *the* Message. It cannot reach us until two days after this letter shall have left Liverpool. These democratic state papers have now for more than half a century been giving annually their ponderous blows upon the intelligence and integrity of Europe, until they seem to be accepted as the periodical strokes of some great spiritual bell marking the advances of humanity.

I am disposed to think, notwithstanding some equivocal indications, that you will not be harassed with fresh complications in Central America, arising out of the landing of troops. Mr. Seymour Fitzgerald, of the Foreign Office, has just proclaimed with emphasis that non-intervention is Lord Derby's cardinal principle:—and, to say the truth, I have more confidence in Mr. Fitzgerald than in the Earl of Malmesbury.

Always faithfully yrs.

---

## No. 234.—TO MR. CASS.

LONDON, December 24, 1858.

MY DEAR SIR,—During the last day or two a protracted spell of some six or eight weeks of wretchedly dark and damp weather has been broken in upon by glimpses of sunshine. Let us postpone the project of suicide, at least during the festivities of Christmas. So, many compliments of the season to you!

General Pierce is tracing the vestiges of his executive predecessor Tiberius at the delicious little island of Capri in the mouth of the Bay of Naples. I heard from him yesterday. The cold at Florence was disagreeable and unkind to Mrs P., who, though improved by travelling, is still exceedingly delicate. The picturesque islet promises much better, and will be adhered to until the close of next month. Thence, to Rome.

It is difficult to say whether the game of chess played by Napoleon and Montalembert has dwindled to a drawn one, or which of the champions comes off the better The Count exults in having by his appeal proved the absurdity of his pardon; in reversing that portion of his sentence which subjected him to the arbitrary provisions of the February law of "suspects;" and in reducing by one half the term of his imprisonment. The Emperor, on his part, makes a merit of mercy, fastens upon his victim the discredit of petty police offences, has him roundly lashed for anglomania by the eloquence of the Procureur-Général, Destange, and either puts him in jail for three months or forces him to swallow the pill of a pardon. No political result can follow: because there is nothing excessive in the penalties, and praise of England is treason to France, in the sense of the Blouses.

You must not be too credulous of the Earl of Eglintoun's Proclamation. There may be secret societies in Ireland as elsewhere: apprentices, clerks, and counterboys achieve importance and notoriety by mysterious affiliation:—but there are no revolutionists, and no filibusters. The arrests thus far have pompously secured some twenty lads of 14 or 15 years of age, accused of drilling at night in the open fields, and one girl charged with writing sedition! And these are the heroes said to be awaiting the arrival of Generals Walker and Henningsen! It is hard to discover a decent apology for all the police pother of the Viceregal government.

The signal failure of General Prim in the Spanish legislature to have a war with Mexico discountenanced, would seem enough to put you all upon your guard. The only question is whether the invasion which it means is to be a joint one by France, England, and Spain, or a separate one by Spain only.

No doubt your news from China is later than mine. But it may not be amiss to say that my last letter from Mr. Reed is dated Shanghai, 20th October. He had returned from Japan, and was engaged with a new tariff. He quits for home about the present time, and contemplated reaching London, via Bombay, Egypt, Malta, and Italy, in March next.

Always faithfully yrs.

---

## No. 235.—TO MR. CASS.

LONDON, December 31, 1858.

MY DEAR SIR,—Mr. H. F. Polydore, a much-respected English solicitor, desires to express his thanks all round, for the rescue of his young daughter from the sink of Mormonism. I enclose you a copy of his exceedingly well-worded letter to me. The facts are doubtless fresh in your remembrance. As the incidents which preceded the child's abduction, and captivity in Utah, have been extensively published, and as her restoration to her father is a pleasing episode of warlike operations, I suggest the propriety of letting Mr. Polydore's gratitude find vent through the *Intelligencer* and *Union*.

You are tired hearing of Montalembert, are you not? Well, this is "positively for the last time." He is pardoned *again*, nett and comprehensively, without a witticism, and even his companion in offence, the straw publisher of the *Correspondant* shares the Imperial quotation of Uncle Toby's address to the fly—"there, go: room enough in the world for both of us!"

As the result of the bold speeches made by Dufaure and Berryer on this trial, I think the press in Paris appears disposed to resume a little more liberty. It is plausibly argued that the prevailing silence fosters secret disaffection, and that the dynasty founded on universal suffrage and aiming at universal good, must be invigorated by a certain legally limited freedom of discussion. Fortunately for the world, despotism cannot be rational.

I suppose you have noticed the admirable example set by the Servians, how to effect a revolution promptly, quietly, and without shedding a drop of blood. Almost as smooth a process as our State-constitution-making. The people of Servia discovered their Prince Alexander to be no better than he should be:—they invited an extraordinary session of an old body called the Shupkina (something analogous to the French States-General), and when this assembly met, it composedly adopted a resolution deposing Alexander, who took sanctuary in a Turkish garrison, and recalling, as purified by adversity, their former Prince Milosch. The scale is small, but the fact as a movement of popular self-government is immense: and how it will be regarded by the adjacent neighbors, Austria, Russia, and Turkey, is an interesting question.

Annexation of contiguities is an impulse of governments at once instinctive and irresistible. All past nations have exhibited the disease in its natural form, and all existing ones are constantly breaking out with it. Here now is Greece, little, delicate, infantine Greece, eager to embrace and absorb Corfu, Kefalonia, Zante, and the others of the seven Ionian Islands! No child ever had the measles more virulently. Mr. Gladstone finds a sympathizing disorder impetuously proclaiming itself among the islanders wherever he goes. What's to be done? The Colonial minister, Bulwer Lytton, seems, by a very neat despatch, recently written to Lord High Commissioner Young, disposed to treat the case as the old physicians treated the small-pox, by fastening down the window sash, excluding the air, locking the door, throwing the key away, and preventing all spread of the malady by declaring intercourse impossible! This won't do, Sir Edward! You have, by sending the Homeric statesman on his mission, created the occasion for a full and frank interchange of sentiment, and must not now turn a deaf ear to unanimous utterances. Parliament will no doubt, as soon as it meets, be exercised upon this topic. The Manchester men are in favor of letting people whom they do not regard as fellow-subjects manage their own destinies as they like best.

Although I am before an 8 or 10 feet wide window, extending to the ceiling, I have not been able, from 11 o'clock in the day, to write this letter without the aid of two candles. Such has been the wretched, smoky, foggy, dirty, rainy atmosphere for the greater part of six or eight weeks! One comfort:—my daughter reports Paris to be quite as bad, if not worse.

Always faithfully yrs.

---

## No. 236.—TO MR. PIERCE.

LONDON, January 2, 1859.

MY DEAR SIR,—Your letter of the 15th ultimo reached me some days ago, and communicated so much pleasure that I have chafed a good deal under the pressure of engagements which prevented an immediate reply. It was warmly welcomed because in the first place it assured me of the well-being of Mrs. Pierce and yourself, and, in the second place, it flattered me with the intimation that my course of action in this arduous diplomatic post had not disappointed the expectations of the gentleman who sent me to it. Many, many thanks for the kindness.

What you have noticed in the newspapers about me has, as far as I myself know, no foundation whatever. I have not invited a recall, and do not believe one to be contemplated. At this particular moment, the step would be an unwise one, and would be so until the Central American complications are definitively unravelled and settled. The period for their adjustment is not far off. On purely public considerations, there should be no change in this mission *pendente lite*. As to private considerations, I confess myself agreeably disappointed by the hospitality and respect which have invariably been shewn me:—but my anglomania is not sufficiently intense and concentrated to survive three years' close observation of the mediæval barbarism of caste by which the social intercourse of this country is broadly and painfully marked. Democracy is less at ease in England than in Imperial France or Russia.

How I should have enjoyed being with you at Capri! In the course of my life I have made several desperate efforts to get to Italy:—one, forty-four years ago, at Ghent, trunk packed, and bills of exchange ready, when the veto of Mr. Gallatin interposed, and whisked me off to Mr. Madison. By-the-by, Miss Julia Kavanagh, in a course of volumes, has given us her "summer and winter in the two Sicilies" so agreeably that I commend it to Mrs. P. while she is yet in the scenes described.

The Persia, which arrived yesterday, brought nothing worth telling from home. A sharp letter of Mr. Slidell's published on Judge Douglas. A fight on the Avenue between two members of Congress, Messrs. English and Montgomery. Governor Wise nominated for 1860 by the *Richmond Enquirer*. A message from the Governor of South Carolina recommending the dissolution of the Union and the creation of a Southern Confederacy. Lord Napier's recall universally regretted. Public sentiment, recently much excited by British folly at San Juan, has swung to the opposite extreme and represents everything to be settled.

Mrs. D. sends her best regards to Mrs. P., as we all do *en masse*.

Always faithfully yrs.

## No. 237.—TO MR. MARKOE.

LONDON, January 9, 1859.

MY DEAR MARKOE,—Your last letter springs from too solicitous a friendship and shews me that you are greatly more anxious about this mission than I can bring myself to be.

It is about eighteen months since I wrote to General —— in reply to a kindly meant intervention on his part, and explained the principle of public action on which alone the President would probably act, and on which alone I could consent to accept or retain any foreign appointment whatever. That letter was, with more than my usual caution, enclosed to you unsealed, and, if it obtained the sanction of your friendship, it was to go to the General, and from him to Mr. Buchanan as I did not doubt. You approved, and it went on its way. I believe its contents gave no dissatisfaction to the President:—indeed, they were such as could not be a cause of difference between men of just and honorable sentiments. Well, that letter marked out my permanent attitude as respects this post, and I am without any new motive or reason for changing it in the slightest particular. I cannot perceive that what I have been doing for nearly three years has suddenly become wrong:—and unless that were to stare me in the face, why am I virtually to admit my error?

It is wished that I should write letters to the President himself and so avoid a threatened storm. Perhaps I write oftener than any minister ever did:—what I write goes to the President, but it is addressed to the Secretary of State, because it would really be intrusive in me, considered personally or officially, to be perpetually courting the eye of the Executive with matters which, though interesting or entertaining, are more private than public. I do not believe that Mr. Buchanan can view this in a different light. He is too much a man of the world not to see that my notes to General Cass, on the topics they contain, are really as open to him, and indeed his whole cabinet, as to the Secretary. Their shape only saves them from the wretched fate of public despatches. I wrote to General Pierce but once, as he was on the eve of quitting Washington.

As to the prospective storm, so like a tempest in a teapot, I cannot see whence, where, how, or why it is to blow:—but if it rage fiercely enough to tumble the Capitol into Goose Creek, I would not stir one inch to avert or allay it. Precedents are as plentiful as blackberries: and the minister has clearly the right to make what arrangements with the government he deems will best secure the character, dignity, and interests of the station he is about holding which that government approves. My notions upon the subject are the results of experience and observation. When I went to Russia in '37, Mr. Van Buren invited me to take as secretary a gentleman unknown to me except as unreliable, and I declined. Every one of our legations furnishes, almost annually, proofs how far ill-assorted public agents disturb their business, depreciate their character, and torture their incumbents. These things have to be encountered by many, but when it is possible to avoid them it is wise to do so.

Everybody knows that nothing is so easily found, when wanted, as a pretext. If one thing don't answer, another will. Now, if there be a disposition to assail—of which it is naked justice to say I have seen no proof whatever—how practically absurd it would be to expect to sweeten that disposition, or foil it, by disingenuous and altered action! Even in the light of personal policy, every man only lays himself more open to attack by abandoning the position he deliberately and openly took at the outset. Having taken a stand, unless convinced that it is wrong, he had better accept firmly all its consequences.

I should not write thus to anybody else. You have a right to my inmost thoughts. And though I cannot adopt the course of action you recommend, I am profoundly convinced that it has sprung out of a friendship I am proud to have kindled and to reciprocate.

Always faithfully yrs.

## No. 238.—TO MR. CASS.

LONDON, January 14, 1859.

MY DEAR SIR,—The signs of war accumulate. Since the oracular words to Baron Hübner on New-Year's day, every sort of soothing and explanatory construction has been attempted in the Paris newspapers to no purpose.* The Bulls and Bears are convinced, and funds are steadily going down. Austria has hurried into Lombardy thirty thousand additional men. The address of the Sardinian King to the legislature, just assembled, was clearly martial, and drew forth loud manifestations of popular adhesion. But it is in the arranged marriage that veteran politicians see conclusive proof. Victor Emmanuel, though ranking among young sovereigns, is in his thirty-ninth year of age and has a daughter, Clothilde, of attractive sixteen, whom he gives to Prince Napoleon. Their engagement is publicly announced. The Prince, only two years younger than his father-in-law, quits Paris to-morrow for Turin, to spend a week in courtship of his girl-bride. This is admirable preparation for a Bonapartean kingdom of Savoy.

Two or three other war-pointing straws are in the wind. Baron Hübner is reported, prematurely I suspect, to have suddenly left the French capital for Vienna. The French marshals and generals, absent from their respective posts, are ordered to return to them. And the Austrian vessels of war in the Adriatic are exhibiting more than customary uneasiness and activity. I have thus, I believe, like a faithful Pliny, given you the leading premonitory symptoms of the approaching eruption.

---

* DIARY: *January 3d*, 1859, *Monday.*—"The first flash of lightning precursive of the storm has startled everybody. The French Emperor at his Levee held on the 1st instant, Saturday, addressed the following words to Baron Hübner, the Austrian minister, with marked excitement and emphasis:—'*Je regrette que nos relations avec votre Gouvernement ne soient pas aussi bonnes que par le passé:—mais je vous prie de dire à l'Empereur que mes sentimens personnels pour lui ne sont pas changés.*' Marshal Vaillant, who was by, followed it up by adding to the minister: 'After that, I suppose I am not at liberty to shake hands with you.' This sudden revelation of the purpose as to Italy is a striking imitation of the conduct of Napoleon I. towards the British ambassador, Lord Whitworth, preparatory to the rupture of the Treaty of Amiens. To be sure, there is more graciousness, less downright insult in it."

It may be doubted whether our great and good friend the Czar will find it quite convenient to pay his promised visits in May next to Paris and thence through *Cherbourg*, to London. I ventured, from my remembrance of what his sterner father experienced, to predict, in the course of a letter to you a year ago, that his ardor for serf-enfranchisement would receive a check from his nobles and might disturb the Empire. Well! the committee to whom the matter has been entrusted, and who manifested great zeal, have suddenly insisted that the reform shall not stop half way, that it must be extended to other classes besides the serfs, and (tell it not in Gath!) that *the States General* should be convoked! Of course Imperial indignation will be roused:—but what can be done? His Majesty set the ball rolling, and these really revolutionary ideas emanate from the very Council charged to keep it rolling. There is something in reform like the electrical fluid:—generate it once and it will run to the end of the wire. In England, long training has taught how to effect it "bit by bit:"—but in Russia the spirit is a novelty—how to fetter or graduate it unknown.

The heir apparent to the Protestant British Crown is off to Rome. His visit, though the result of natural and laudable curiosity, is not the most prudent or wise thing that could be done. The press has already regarded it with jealousy. "No Popery" is a chord which is made to vibrate in England just now with the slightest touch. He may not be converted:—but, if he ever reign, he will be taunted, by one party or the other, with the taint of the Vatican. In France, an ultramontane journal has already interpreted this tour of the Prince of Wales to mean such an approach to Roman Catholicism as is involved in the alleged Puseyism of Queen Victoria! The age (17) and character of the lad invest his course of travel with other aspects of hazard.

Two days ago, the 3d of February, was fixed upon for the meeting of Parliament. Her Majesty's Proclamation appeared and the farther prorogation to that day, and then for the despatch of business took place. All the ministers are now at their posts in London. Their scheme of electoral representation, though avowedly on the anvil, has been kept profoundly secret. Although there are several other important topics on which, during the recess, they have laid themselves open to serious interpellations, this of Reform, notwithstanding the affected disdain of "John Bright," is the impracticable maelstrom which endangers their safety.

Always faithfully yrs.

---

## No. 239.—TO MR. KNOTT.

THE Minister of the United States has received the note of the 18th inst. addressed to him by Mr. S. Dyer Knott from "Alphington, Devon," requesting an autograph.

Now, "*Alphington, Devon,*" are words singularly persuasive with the minister, who yet hopes to secure before he recrosses the Atlantic, a daguerreotype sketch of the Church of that Parish.

Let there be, then, a Yankee bargain.

The minister will send his autograph with pleasure to Mr. Knott, if Mr. Knott will kindly procure and send to the minister a mem. from the proper functionary of the entry in the Register or Record of the Church at "*Alphington, Devon,*" of the declaration of Banns and the marriage of "*Alexander James Dallas and Arabella Mucia Smith,*" who became husband and wife in that Church about 1780 or 1781, and who, subsequently emigrating to America, in the course of ten years summoned the minister into being.

Such a mem. with a a note of whatever fee should be remitted the functionary, will, on being received, be instantly followed by the transmission to Mr. Knott of the minister's thanks and autograph.

Is it a bargain?

LEGATION OF THE UNITED STATES,<br>
LONDON, January 19, 1859.

---

## No. 240.—TO MR. CASS.

LONDON, January 21, 1859.

MY DEAR SIR,—I have tried, during the last week, for your benefit, to form a judgment on the probabilities of war. It is no easy thing to do so. Opposite views, hopes, and interests are in loud and indefatigable conflict. Facts are invented or exaggerated every day on one side or the other. Schemes to lift or lower the rates on the Parisian Bourse are hourly creating panics or composure, both alike treacherous. Immense efforts have clearly for their sole object to arrest or mitigate the effect, upon property and prices, of Napoleon's sudden revelation of "*the situation*" on New-Year's day. It is impossible to deduce anything satisfactory from this boisterous chaos of statements and denials. There is no safety for opinion in attempting to discriminate between them. What, then, is there no clue to the labyrinth? None, except to set aside all the contradictory clamors and pretences of the last three weeks, and coolly weigh the import of the admitted international incidents bearing on the question. 1. The foregone conclusion in the Imperial mind of France as uttered to Baron Hübner. 2. The rapid concentration of Austrian forces in Italy. 3. The explosive disaffection of all that part of Italy. 4. The vigorous speech of Victor Emmanuel and the enthusiastic echo it evoked from the Sardinian legislature. 5. The nuptials which unite the destinies of the two dynasties, Bonapartist and Piedmont. 6. The military *vis a tergo* to which Louis Napoleon is subject. 7. The ambitious *entrainement* of both sovereigns. 8. The vast armies and wounded pride of Austria. 9. The death of Ferdinand II. (Bomba) just announced. He was 49 years of age. His successor, Francis, Duke of Calabria, is 23, and married but recently a German princess, though it must be remembered that his mother was an aunt, and that he himself is therefore a cousin, of Victor Emmanuel.

War may be averted. The moneyed power of Europe may keep it off. But the advancing apparition is obvious to sight, like a comet "shaking its fiery tresses in the air."

The last number (January, '59) of the Edinburgh Review, just distributed, has come in aid of the Parliamentary Reformers, in a short but effective article. Its inculcation is an adherence to the principle of the Act of 1832, with such practical extensions "as the great innovator Time" calls for: and, asserting every free government to be founded on a system of compromises, it insists upon a plan which shall duly combine numbers, property, intelligence, and locality. Its language is moderate and persuasive:—and I think it may be regarded as foreshadowing what will be realized.

Always faithfully yrs.

---

## No. 241.—TO MR. KNOTT.

LONDON, January 26, 1859.

MY DEAR SIR,—You have executed your part of the proposed fanciful bargain so promptly and so kindly that I feel ashamed of the little to be done on my side. Something more than a humble autograph must prove how much pleasure you have given. I propose, as soon as I can command the time, to tell you briefly the brilliant career run, in the new world, by the *disobedient* couple who, at the ages of 21 and 16, fled from the house of an aunt named Barlow, at Devonport, and were married in Alphington Church on the 4th of September, 1780

I must beg you not to place me under any heavier obligation by taking the trouble to search for and send me a sketch of the Church. An engagement with an admirable artist was entered into some two years ago:—he undertook to accompany me, with his instruments, into Devon, at a moment's warning, and give me a perfect daguerreotype of a venerable building, which to me has a higher charm than architecture or picturesque position can possibly confer.

You are right as to the witness, Charles Stuart Dallas: —he was my father's elder brother: and adhering to the island of Jamaica, accumulated a large fortune as a lawyer. His son was recently Speaker of the House of Assembly.

I consider myself strictly bound, independent of this letter, to furnish for your curiosity album the accompanying detached and worthless signature of,

Dear Sir, very sincerely

Your obliged humble servant.

## No. 242.—TO COL. MURRAY.

LONDON, January 28, 1859.

MY DEAR SIR,—My present object is special and urgent. I know your energy and activity when once under way in a good cause, and I want to stir into immediate movement yourself and through you, your Mayor, Collector, District Attorney, etc. etc. The King of Naples has consigned to New York, as a sort of New-Year's gift, a collection of about 200 of his political victims, among whom are those noble specimens of the *genus homo*, Poerio and Settembrini. All good men here wish them health, honor, and happiness. Brown, Shipley & Co., of Liverpool, will address their branch in your city most generously about them. Bomba has sent them to Cadiz, whence they are to be shipped in merchant vessels.* They are probably now a third of their way across the Atlantic. Some persons dread the operation of a State or municipal law which would reject them as convicts and paupers palmed upon your poorhouses. Do, in the name of all that is just and generous, prevent anything of the sort. Rather give these inflexible foes of tyranny the ovation they merit on reaching our shores. I shall hide my diminished head if you act otherwise.

Always faithfully yrs.

---

## No. 243.—TO MR. SICKLES.

LONDON, January 28, 1859.

DEAR SIR,—You will have noticed that the King of Naples has recently liberated some two hundred of his political prisoners upon certain conditions, among others exile in America. He will suffer them no nearer than

---

* They left Cadiz on board the American ship "David Steward," Capt. Prentiss:—but, when at sea, combined to compel the officers of the vessel to shape her course for Ireland; and, going into Cork, were received with great enthusiasm and hospitality.

New York. They were sent to Cadiz, to be thence forwarded on board of one or more merchant vessels, and are probably now crossing the Atlantic. Among them are Poerio and Settembrini, who, the best known and appreciated, may be regarded as types of the entire company.

Now any man of liberal thought and generous feeling must wish that the sufferings and wants of these victims of tyranny should be cared for and lightened wherever they go. Fears are entertained that, as destitute convicts and paupers, they may be repelled at New York by some State or municipal law and thrust back into the cells of Bomba. For God's sake, move heaven and earth to prevent the possibility of an incident which, coming from our country, would require endless explanation, and would be the thrust of an icicle through the heart of every friend to constitutional liberty in Europe.

I am very truly and respectfully yrs.

---

## No. 244.—TO MR. CASS.

LONDON, January 28, 1859.

MY DEAR SIR,—His Majesty of Naples, though supposed a sufferer by partial paralysis (courteously ycleped rheumatism), did not die, as was somewhat victoriously announced by the *Morning Post.* He is recovering fast; and let us hope that his political victims, to whose pardon he has managed to give the torturing keenness of exile, may yet, *auspice Napoleoncino vel Muratto*, find means to confront him somewhere on the plains of Italy:—the nearer to one or the other crater of Vesuvius or Etna, eager to receive him, the better.

I returned a call of Lord Lyons two days ago. A war steamer takes him to Boston or New York on the 15th of February. I knew his father, the Admiral, and was therefore partially inclined towards him. Perhaps, he may succeed in pleasing as well as Lord Napier, though the latter has the immense advantage of being charmingly married. A legation without a lady is but half composed:—a column sans capital, piano sans pedal, coiffure sans curls. I suspect the ages of the two lords are much the same:—Lyons is 42. He lives at Norfolk House, whose Duke married his sister.

An official decree is out in Paris, prohibiting free negro emigration on board French vessels from the *eastern* coast of Africa. Whether this affects the existing contract of Regis & Co. may be doubted. As far as it goes, however, it is a homage to the British monomania.

The marriage at which, according to the French phrase, I *assisted* just one year ago (25th January, '58) in St. James's Palace, was yesterday signalized at 1 P.M. by the production of an heir to the Prussian throne. The annunciation shot from Berlin to Windsor in six minutes. Her Majesty has become a grandmother while yet some three or four months short of 40.

Always faithfully yrs.

---

## No. 245.—TO MR. CASS.

LONDON, February 4, 1859.

MY DEAR SIR,—Of course your British legation were in full force representing you in the House of Lords yesterday at the opening of Parliament by the Queen.

The Speech, though unusually long, was extremely cautious both in what it said and in what it left unsaid. In referring, in the fourth clause, to the desire "to maintain inviolate the faith of public treaties" and to contribute "to the preservation of the general peace," you find the key to the remarkably bold and anti-Napoleonic exposition of policy made by Lord Derby in the evening. I listened very attentively to the outspoken Premier, and was led to the conclusion, 1. that he was making rather a menacing effort to arrest a war which he feared was impending: 2. that he chose an attitude of neutrality, and 3. that if obliged by events to change that, he would embrace the Austrian cause.

A telegram reached the Brazilian minister yesterday, to the effect that his sovereign had been invited to act as mediator between the United States and Paraguay, and that his Imperial Majesty had consented to do so.

Since the 1st of January, and *a fortiori* since the marriage of Prince Napoleon and Princess Clothilde, I have not been able to doubt that hostilities would soon, upon some pretext or other, *be made* to break out on the banks of the Ticino between the confronting troops of Piedmont and Austria. That now is all that is wanting to produce a French rush into Lombardy. My opinion is confirmed by a letter which has just been received here from Mr. Guizot. Lord Brougham, immediately from Cannes, a sort of observatory for Mediterranean and Italian politics, told the Peers last night that the popular sentiment was altogether undeniable and universal. It is barely possible, nevertheless, that the unanimity of Parliament may check the impetuosity of Victor Emmanuel and Louis Napoleon.

Always faithfully yrs.

---

## No. 246.—TO MR. CASS.

LONDON, February 11, 1859.

MY DEAR SIR,—You will perceive by the map transmitted how easy a thing it is to settle to one's mind a reconstruction of European nations, *on paper*. Some thousands of this document crossed the Channel three days ago, copies of it have been multiplied on this side, and many a startled and staring diplomat has had his nightmare under the weight of so fantastic a sheet. Rumor preluded it as a Napoleonic study and cartoon direct from the Imperial press. Farther scrutiny seems to ascribe the invention to a Belgian priest. Then, again, it is thought to be a monster device which, by the argument of contrast, may make the mere expulsion of Austria from Italy seem a small affair.

Since my last week's note, two very strong shadows of the coming event have been thrown on the dial of time: a pamphlet* plainly if not avowedly Bonapartean, entitled

---

* DIARY: *February* 5, 1859, *Saturday.*—"A tremendous Pamphlet just out in Paris. It is obviously the offspring of Imperial 'inspiration.' Nothing could be more like '*Les Idées Napoléoniennes.*' Its title is 'Napoléon III. et l'Italie.' It inculcates with remarkable power and dis-

"Napoleon III. et l'Italie," and a speech from the throne to the French Chambers:—both, in my judgment, powerful yet guarded expressions of an unalterable purpose. The pamphlet is a manifesto and appeal really unanswerable, or answerable only by the charge of ambitious motives:—the speech is assailable and assailed, merely because it forbore to repeat from the Queen's address to Parliament the inviolable character of the Treaties of 1815—those monuments of the overthrow of "My Uncle"! Austria may be expected to circulate her reply through diplomatic channels:—*audi alteram partem!*—but the controversy advances and embitters.

To these indications must be added the return of bodies of troops from Algeria to Marseilles, the storing of fabulous amounts of ammunition, the gradual adoption of a warlike tone by the Parisian press, the fifty million loan voted by the legislative chamber of Sardinia in a paroxysm of anti-Austrian ardor, and, last not least, the very decided written and oral utterances of Count Cavour, whose position as a wise, virtuous, patriotic, and skilful statesman is overtopped by no one in Europe.

But what's the prevailing opinion? Some wish peace to continue, and that wish is father to their judgment. Others deem it a duty to humanity to clamor down war. Many of the best thinkers are mystified by conflicting representations, and incapable of forming a conclusion or even a firm guess. I have recently and most industriously attended the soirées, to deduce from their chatting coteries, for your enlightenment, the general impression. Well!—at the Marquess of Salisbury's, at Lord Palmerston's, at Lord Derby's, and particularly at the Prussian minister's last night, the current of opinion ran war, not immediate, but inevitable war. Her Majesty's cousin, the Commander-in-chief, personally intimate with the Imperial character, disclaims emphatically any doubt about it.

Do you notice how amusingly the Union-loving senti-

---

tinctness the necessity of preserving the peace of Europe by insisting diplomatically and if need be militarily upon the withdrawal of Austria from Lombardy, and the construction of an Italian Confederation of Nationalities. It opens by a distinct declaration of aversion to the Treaties of 1815:—no wonder, for they are the monuments of the degradation of France and the Bonapartes by the Holy Alliance. This splendid manifesto is clearly meant as a semi-official preface to a great drama."

ment of the Principalities has flouted the injunction of the Congress of Paris in 1856? It was formally decided by that august body that they should live separate and apart, and each have her independent Hospodar. The elections coming on, Moldavia chose for her chief Prince Couza, and Wallachia ran after and chose the very same man for herself, thus concentrating in one personage the executive authorities of both states! There's a complication for you! The Sultan is said to be enraged:—he can, however, like Austria in reference to the revolution in Servia, do nothing alone beyond a protest: he must await the reassembling of the Conference, an event whose non-concurrence is among the possibilities on the cards.

I will not release you from this note until I apprise you that my admirable and able friend Mr. Richard Cobden will go by the same steamer, Canada, to the United States. He has just called and bade me good-bye. He will strive to reach Washington before the dispersing day of the 4th of March. Bid him, All Hail!

Always faithfully yrs.

---

## No. 247.—TO MR. WINTHROP.

LONDON, February 17, 1859.

MY DEAR MR. WINTHROP,—Your letter in regard to the recall of Lord Napier and the shameless explanation of it attempted in the Boston paper by a penny-a-liner correspondent here, deserved a prompt acknowledgment. I think your appreciation of his lordship strictly just. We cannot hope to have a more acceptable British minister at Washington. A great mistake is involved in his removal; and though his successor be quite unexceptionable, the *rôle* he played in cementing the kindly feelings of the two countries can scarcely be acted with equal efficiency by any one else.

I am not quite sure that the ministry were insensible to the motive imputed for the treatment of this distinguished gentleman. Some of our travelling countrymen are inconsiderate enough to bring abroad the party asperities they cultivate at home; and though in the general they take nothing by doing so, or rather are positively disrelished for their lack of natural patriotism, still occasionally and on particular points they achieve more mischief to the country than it is easy to repair.

You do not, I perceive, shrink from the sarcasm of Carlyle, who, in his Life of Frederick the Great, calls all *antiquaries* by Scott's descriptive cognomen, Dryasdust. I forward you a diploma sent to me from Somerset House.

Always faithfully yrs.

---

## No. 248.—TO MR. CASS.

LONDON, February 18, 1859.

MY DEAR SIR,—The unanimity in Parliament on the still pending war question seems to have a composing effect as to party differences. Nothing as yet has ruffled the smooth current of legislation. Even the Right of Search, which gave Lord Clarendon an opportunity to awaken a titter at the expense of Lord Malmesbury, passed off without leaving a furrow behind it. By-the-by, her Majesty's principal Secretary of State for Foreign Affairs said that a series of naval instructions, as to the mode of verifying the flags of traders, had been prepared by France and England, and were now under consideration at Washington. He anticipates from their adoption an international millennium. Pray suffer me to see this, not quintuple, but tripartite proposal.

I have a letter from Mr. Reed, of the 10th ultimo, Colombo, Ceylon. He expects to leave Bombay behind him on the 25th, to be in Malta on the 14th February, in Rome on 1st March, and here before April. I am thus particular to enable you, if occasion occur, to let Mr. Ward know how he may run a fair chance of meeting his returning predecessor.

I have no modifications to make in the views heretofore expressed as to the likelihood of a struggle over a new map of Italy. Every well ascertained incident throws fresh light and reality on the prospect. The Bulls and Bears are fertile in rumors to help along their speculative objects:—but the steady, calm, and vigorous manner in which both the great parties are taking what Mr. Madison called their "attitude and armor" permits one conclusion only. It is barely possible that the Conference about to be held in Paris to deal with the contempt committed by Hospodar Couza—a sort of political bigamy—may wish *ampliare jurisdictionem*, and to throw oil upon the troubled waters:—but the matter has gone too far, and backing down, even to preserve the peace of Europe, is un-imperial and too shockingly distasteful.

The relations of the mutually dependent partners, Messrs. Demand and Supply, are oddly illustrated just now. There's a plethora of money everywhere, and down comes a cataract of projected public loans! Mr. Bates tells me the Austrian proposals have failed. Turkey, like a Phœnix, makes her own fire with her own fuel. Sardinia designs to try the same experiment for the fifty millions of "lire" she wants. Lord Stanley thinks nothing of asking from English capitalists, for his new empire of India, thirty-five millions of dollars.

The Court of the "Parvenu" has signalized itself by the introduction of a new feature of etiquette. At the grand ball at the Hotel de Ville, two days ago, in honor of the recent marriage, the girl-bride, like a "little Miss Creeper left in the lurch," instead of being handed into the crowded salon by Prince Napoleon her husband, was permitted to walk behind him! Magnificent, cry all the newspapers!

Always faithfully yrs.

---

## No. 249.—TO MR. CASS.

LONDON, March 1, 1859.

MY DEAR SIR,—The review which Lord Palmerston took in his speech last Friday evening of the causes and character of quarrel just now between France and Austria, was marked by more than his usual discretion and forbearance. Mr. Disraeli, in making answer to his enquiries, shewed equal sense of the dignity due to the occasion:—and his announcement as to the prospect of preserving peace was uncommonly effective. But I am disposed to think that those who heard him were a little misled by their hopes, and did not notice the extremely measured and cautious words (no doubt pre-arranged, for they were repeated later in the evening by Lord Malmesbury in the Lords) which he used. "Her Majesty's government had received communications from which they *had reason to infer* that the two powers would withdraw their respective armies from the Papal States simultaneously, and upon the invitation of the Pope."

A very extraordinary result is expected to be achieved over the cabinet of Vienna by the energy, skill, and suppleness of Lord Cowley:—no less than its acceding, notwithstanding all its recent acts and language to the contrary, to the original proposal of Louis Napoleon. One is accustomed to predicate of Austrian statesmanship nothing but pretension and obstinacy:—and the ministry will be singularly lucky if, in the full tide of these characteristic qualities, they get Francis Joseph to "eat his leek." They themselves entertain grave doubts:—for Lord Lyndhurst told me that when the Premier heard of what Mr. Disraeli had said in the Commons, he remarked "he has gone too far"! Such an expression lacks reliance on the diplomatic expedient. In Paris, it would seem to be very little relied upon:—indeed, there the evacuation of the Papal States is but a small part of the solution of the Italian question.

Pray let me ask you to give consideration to the accompanying copy of an advertisement which contains matter of great historical interest to our country. The two hundred letters and documents connected with the negotiation of what Mr. Adams called "Our Treaty of Independence," and the map of the United States traced by Franklin, ought certainly to be in your department. I can receive the expression of the President's wishes upon the subject before the 6th of April, the day appointed for the sale.

I was last evening seven continuous hours in the diplomatic gallery of the House of Commons, listening to the introduction of Lord Derby's Reform bill. It is as infinitesimal a dose as any homœopath could administer, and is essentially a mere sham of words. Lord John Russell denounced it at once; Mr. Bright termed it frivolous, trifling, absurd, and disgusting. Not a shadow of enfranchisement extended to the working classes. Lord Palmerston and his serried ranks of friends remained quiet, while the measure underwent violent castigation from the ultra Liberals and was falteringly sustained on the Treasury side. Mr. Walpole, Home Secretary, and Mr. Henley, President of the Board of Trade, have resigned: Lord John Manners is expected to follow suit: General Peel is said to be giving way for Lord Elgin, and Sir E. B. Lytton for Gladstone. On the whole, the cabinet seems spontaneously dissolving.

Mr. Ward and his family have been here for the past week. I have been able to keep him advised of Mr. Reed's course and progress homewards. He will meet that gentleman in Paris on the 15th instant, whither he proceeds to-morrow. You have probably already heard that there has been fresh fighting near Canton between the English troops and Chinese braves, as late as the 8th of January. It is said that the Imperial government secretly disclaim Lord Elgin's Treaty as the work of compulsion.

Always faithfully yrs.

---

## No. 250.—TO MR. CASS.

LONDON, March 4, 1859.

MY DEAR SIR,—Her Majesty's government have been caucusing. Lord Derby invited two hundred and eight of his partisans of the House of Commons to meet him at the Treasury Department in Downing Street on Tuesday last:—the gravamen, the Reform bill. He plumply informed the assembled gentlemen that every one of them must vote for every part and the entirety of the measure unflinchingly: and that, if it finally failed, he would dissolve Parliament. It is customary to regard our President, not in the light of the Sovereign here, but as a Prime Minister:—now, what would be thought of him all over the world, and what would the Representatives say and do, if our Chief Executive were to take a leaf out of Lord Derby's book, and, surrounded by his cabinet, were to indoctrinate, menace, and marshal the legislative phalanx?

I think we should all be long before we heard the last of it. This jumble of separate and co-ordinate powers is the natural, if not necessary consequence of permitting ministers to hold seats in Parliament:—a practice accompanied by certain administrative advantages, though subversive of fundamental principle. Be this as it may, Lord Derby had his caucus, and he and they have resolved to go it blind for the bill, the whole bill, and nothing but the bill. Now, I can't express a confident opinion as to how this will end, and I must tell you why. Lord Palmerston is at heart no reformer; he does not wish to reattain power upon that issue: and he would probably be averse to larger concessions of political franchise than are made by Mr. Disraeli. I have observed, upon this topic, unequivocal symptoms of *rapprochement* between his followers and those of Lord Derby; and, to defeat the ultra Liberals, Bright, Gibson, Roebuck, and Russell (!), they may find themselves on a test vote in the same lobby. Generally speaking, it is thought the bill cannot be saved, and that a dissolution is unavoidable. *Nous verrons* on next Monday fortnight, or shortly after.

Plon-Plon, having sacrificed himself to the Imperial policy by marrying a youthful princess, swells with self-importance, and takes airs:—snaps his fingers at the Treaties of 1815: and snubs Persigny, even in the great presence at the Tuileries, and to the well-affected amazement of the Court, by loudly telling him that, let England or all Europe say what they please, the honor and safety of France demand and will exact the independence and nationality of Italy.

Lord Cowley is on his return to Paris:—but the fruits of his mission remain undivulged:—while "*rentes*" are sinking and armies concentrating, the Kaiser at Vienna openly abusing the Kaiser on the Seine, the Holy Father and Cardinal Antonelli "ungratefully insulting" France, and the remains of the patriot Dandolo are being buried at Milan in a row!

Mr. Gladstone is said to be coming home to fill the Colonial Office now occupied by Sir E. B. Lytton. He is conveniently at present in Piedmont, interchanging views with Count Cavour.

I am afraid I have overwhelmed you lately with official despatches. The constant effort is to prevent accumulation and to be brief. I was told by Mr. P., at Cambridge House last night, that, in the Foreign Office, Lord Lyons and Lord Stratford de Redcliffe were esteemed their ablest writers.

Always faithfully yrs.

---

## No. 251.—TO MRS. BACHE.

LONDON, March 10, 1859.

MY DEAR SISTER,—Julia has made for you copies of a series of small notes which have passed between a gentleman living at *Alphington* and myself, the contents of which will I think interest and amuse you. The whole, except the photograph of the church, are enclosed.

I meet at the leading receptions and soirées no one more punctually than Mrs. Mansfield, your Baltimore friend of early life. Her son has been distinguished as a general in the Indian war:—and she is sedulously engaged in chaperoning her grand-daughter, about 18, through the mazes of a first season out.

All the inferior world of Europe is waiting impatiently to know what the two angry Emperors of France and Austria are going to do:—to make war or prolong peace. At this moment, after much vaporing and bluster, there is a lull—inspiring hope which enables the stock exchanges of Paris, Vienna, and London to take a little breath. It is attributed to the supposed success of Lord Cowley's mediatory mission, and it may be dispelled in twenty-four hours by some fresh blast. There is obvious dissension in the French cabinet on the point:—Prince Napoleon though just married upon the strength of his belligerent inclinations, resigning his ministry of Algiers and retreating before his adversaries, Messrs. Walewski and Fould. This is likely to tell.

Dallas has, I presume, recorded his annual victory over the enemies of the Coast Survey. You would be surprised if told how much anxious interest is expressed here in his labors.

I am told that your spirits are good, that you do not

suffer pain, and that you enjoy the presence of affectionate children and friends. Such news is comforting.

Always your devoted brother.

---

## No 252.—TO PROFESSOR ALEXANDER.

LONDON, March 11, 1859.

MY DEAR PROFESSOR,—Thank you very many times for your obliging and most agreeable notes. Nothing but positive lack of time has prevented my writing in reply:—and now, with the Bag yawning for its food by my side, I must be brief.

If there be such a volume as the Parliamentary Rules of Order and Debate, I will procure and send you a copy:—"else wherefore breathe I in a Christian land?" I'll catch the Speaker by the button, or Lord John by his keen circling look, at the next reception, and soon know the truth. If it exist, consider it yours.

We have reached a very brisk part of the rampant "season," and yet retain our health and senses. Pray remember us all most cordially to Mrs. A.

Always faithfully yrs.

---

## No. 253.—TO MR. CASS.

LONDON, March 11, 1859.

MY DEAR SIR,—Our friend her Majesty's principal Secretary of State for Foreign Affairs has been subjected to a heavy critical bombardment, in both parliamentary chambers, for what was represented as his dulness, indifference, and mismanagement of the "*Charles et Georges*" affair between France and Portugal. Lord John Russell was extremely and unusually tart. In defence, but one really good speech was made, that by Cairns, the clever Solicitor-General. Had not the prospect of expelling the ministry upon their Reform bill assumed an almost certain aspect, I think the Opposition would have rallied on this field. and carried a vote of censure.

Lord Cowley gets back to-day from Vienna. Nothing yet known as to what he has achieved: and that circumstance in itself leads me to suspect that in his main and indispensable point, the abandonment of the special treaties, he returns as he went. The government must have been apprised by the electric telegraph of any decidedly favorable concession, and would be eager to tell it. Their omission to do so, in the existing tremulous state of stocks, would be regarded as almost criminal.

Napoleoncino, alias Prince Napoleon, alias Prince Jérome, alias Plon-Plon, has retreated before his adversaries in council, Walewski and Fould, from the ministry of Algeria. He is perhaps too impatient and impetuous:—wanting at once to give the *quid pro quo* for his bride by devotion to the policy of Victor Emmanuel. To that complexion, postpone it as they may, it will come at last. A sweep in the Imperial cabinet is no improbable occurrence as soon as the failure of their agent Lord Cowley is ascertained. It will be the first step in a great European war.

Two days ago the harbor of Cork was invaded by the revolted Neapolitan prisoners whom the gracious Sovereign of the Sicilies had consigned to New York on board of an American vessel! They have been welcomed with loud hurras and open arms. These victims of royal perjury and cruelty, headed by Poerio and Settembrini, are irreproachable, talented, and upright men, whose presence in London will probably tap many a purse and spread many a table.

It is perhaps incumbent upon me, at least thus informally, to say that the Queen, at her dinner last evening, very graciously enquired about the President and Miss Lane, of whose health I was fortunately enabled by a recent private letter to give welcome assurances. Her Majesty has really been benefited by becoming a grandmother.

Always faithfully yrs.

## No. 254.—TO SIR E. B. LYTTON.

LONDON, March 17, 1859.

MY DEAR SIR EDWARD,—Your note of yesterday reached me late at night.

Our Senate is, in its several aspects, legislative, executive, and judicial When acting executively, it sits with closed doors, deliberates on treaties sent to it for ratification or rejection by the President, and on appointments to office. With these functions the House of Representatives has nothing to do. Foreign affairs necessarily engage the Senate largely:—not merely the Committee, but the body itself:—the Committee is only an agent to examine closely and report in detail.

But you are not strictly right in saying that the House of Representatives "does not discuss foreign affairs." There are many cases in which negotiations with foreign nations end in tariffs, or engagements to pay money:—these to be carried out, require legislation, and so become *legitimately* topics of discussion in the House. And there prevails a practice which rather irregularly and *illegitimately* constantly converts the representative chamber into an arena for discoursing "*de omnibus rebus et quibusdam aliis.*" This happens whenever on motion it resolves itself into a "Committee of the Whole on the State of the Union:"—the comprehensive character of which opens every field of debate, domestic and foreign:—practically, a great safety valve

Faithfully yrs.

---

## No. 255.—TO MR. CASS.

LONDON, March 18, 1859.

MY DEAR SIR,—Among the veteran and vigilant statesmen whom I meet in clusters at social gatherings there would seem to be an almost unanimous belief that war is inevitable. To be sure, the course taken by the inferior sovereignties of Germany has been calculated to check the impetuous progress of the French Emperor, for it threatens a revival of the Coalition of 1815: and we are still kept in the dark as to what has been effected by Lord Cowley, which may possibly transfer all difficulties to the domain of diplomacy:—but, the immense military preparations on both sides, and the mutually incriminating tone of their state papers and journals, daily diminish the probability of peace. I am told that in the commercial circles of the City the conviction is so strong that bets have been offered that the first gun has been fired! Austria is evidently greatly emboldened by the attitude of Prussia, the utterances of the German Confederates, and the intervention of this government. At Vienna, her inflation has chalked the walls with the vowels, A. E. I. O. U.—which do plainly signify that "*Austriæ Est Imperare Orbi Universo:*"—and smacks of the democratic arrogance which we may remember adorned the fences and bricks of Washington, "54.40 *or fight*"!

To welcome and relieve the Neapolitan prisoners landed at Queenstown is the order of the day. Very imposing committees are already formed and generous contributions made. You are entitled to know that, owing to some letters written home, I was wanted on the first committee organized, but declined, pleading the restraints and reserves attached to position. I think I perceive that this hospitable movement is very much, if not exclusively, in the hands of Liberals:—not unnaturally.

The first prosecution of the members of the "Phœnix Society" in Ireland has failed, although pressed with ability and energy by the Attorney-General, Whiteside. The jury disagreed. It is becoming a religious struggle: and apart from the big words used in the indictment, the acts of the conspirators appear very frivolous. A government should ignore the fantasies and follies of exuberant youth: —*nec Deus intersit nisi dignus vindice nodus.*

I am on tiptoe for the Cass-Yrissari and Ousely treaties: taking it for granted that Nicaragua will baptize them as twins at or about the same time.

Our winter has been remarkably mild, more so than fifty years have witnessed. Little or no ice formed; and fruit trees in full blossom three weeks ago. Lord Eversley (the late Speaker, Lefevre) told me that he has covered his trees, down in Hampshire, with *woollen netting* to protect them from any possible return of frost.

Always faithfully yrs.

## No. 256.—TO PROFESSOR OWEN.

LONDON, March 18, 1859.

MY DEAR DR. OWEN,—After thorough search, one volume only of Commodore Perry's visit to Japan has been found in the legation:—and that I now send you. Let me beg you to retain it *sine die*. At a future day I hope to be able to send you its mate.

Very faithfully yrs.

---

## No. 257.—TO MR. KNOTT.

LONDON, March 19, 1859.

DEAR SIR,—I am afraid that my tardiness in acknowledging the great kindness of your last letter, accompanied by a sketch of Alphington Church, may have lost me some of your good will. I must throw myself upon your indulgence, simply assuring you that my engagements have been constant and monopolizing.

The delay has relieved me of one perplexity:—how to fulfil, without too much intrusion upon a stranger, the promise respecting the career in America of those whose Banns were declared in Alphington in 1780. Since making the promise, I have received a very valuable work published in my native city of Philadelphia, called "A Dictionary of British and American Authors:"—and herein I find a short notice of my father which contains quite as much as you ought to be troubled with. So my daughter has been good enough to transcribe this article, and I enclose it.

Allow me to repeat to you the very grateful thanks with which I shall always remember the part you have taken in our correspondence.

You enquire whether either of my parents resided in Alphington when they were married. I believe not. My mother was at the time under the care of an aunt, a venerable single lady named Barlow, whose home was in Devonport.

Faithfully and respectfully yrs.

## No. 258.—TO MR. CASS.

LONDON, March 25, 1859.

MY DEAR SIR,—We may now safely conclude, as I formerly surmised, that Lord Cowley's mission to Vienna produced—nothing. So close, however, upon its heels came a proposal from the Russian Czar for a Congress, that an undiscriminating public has given his lordship the merit of that suggestion. This European Areopagus will be constituted of plenipotentiaries from France, Russia, Austria, England, and Prussia; Count Cavour goes to Paris to insist upon the presence of Piedmont, and it may be that considering the peculiarly Italian purpose of the consultation, the minor States of the peninsula may creep in. As all such assemblages are designed, not so much to confer and discuss, as to give impetus and weight to a decision already reached by one or more of the cabinets, I think we shan't be wide of the mark if we anticipate that the issue of a scheme of settlement devised at St. Petersburg, and instantly adopted at the Tuileries, will bear hard upon Austria. Thence springs the question, will it be frankly acquiesced in?—Assuredly not: and so nothing will have been gained by the expedient except those inestimable matters—time for preparation and a temporary rise in stocks. We are already told that Prince Napoleon is designed to be the "*alter Ego*" of his Imperial cousin at the Congress. The landing at Cannes suddenly dispersed a body of this sort in 1815; and, indeed, unless there be great haste in meeting at Geneva, or Aix-la-Chapelle, all accounts agree in predicting a revolutionary movement in or near Rome, or a conflict on the Ticino, which will supersede all deliberation:—the *decies repetita* story of Brennus.

An amusing and much-laughed-at instance of Lord M.'s propensity to indoctrinate with simple and wholesome truths, took place in the "*Charles et Georges*" case, when he pinioned the veteran Malakoff to his *fauteuil* at Windsor Castle, and inculcated "*the immortal truth*, that time undermined prejudices as well as unveiled facts."

You will notice that last night's debate in the House of Commons, brought out through Mr. Seymour Fitzgerald,

Under Secretary of State, the acknowledgment that "representations had been made by the French government respecting the conduct of her Majesty's commander of the steam sloop '*Alecto*' (Hunt!) in boarding the Phœnix while the latter was engaged in procuring laborers (under the system which had been so much discussed) on the west coast of Africa." When the particulars of this domiciliary visit are laid upon the table, they may help Cobb & Ellis to form an estimate of the real character of the self-justified agent of maritime police who so harmlessly seized, carried off, and kept in durance vile, for two days, their dirty little "Caroline."

The government's Reform bill has occupied the House of Commons every day of this week, except Wednesday, and many suppose the debate will not close before Tuesday night next, 29th March. Amid a mass of "intolerable rubbish," there are here and there speeches made of real power, as well on one side as on the other. Bulwer Lytton, the Colonial Secretary and charming novelist, defended the bill in a manner which would have done honor to Fox, Chatham, Sheridan, or Erskine, in his palmiest day. Cairns, the Solicitor-General, was equally successful. Lord John Russell, whose motion aims to strike down the bill and the ministry too, has been supported ably from every section of the Liberal party, and partially from the Tories. Sir Charles Wood, Sidney Herbert, Bernal Osborne, John Bright, and Milner Gibson have taken leading parts. Nobody doubts the result; except perhaps myself. I cannot, until he himself declares it, believe that Lord Palmerston and his personal tail will contribute to what cannot, with their assistance, fail to be the triumphant Premiership of Lord John Russell. Lord Palmerston was to have addressed the House last night, and, according to universal conviction, in maintenance of the motion:—he will speak to-night, and let us see whether he does not, in some way or other, repress the expanding glories of his rival. Perhaps, for this purpose, he may dexterously yield to Mr. Gladstone, or Sir James Graham.

Always faithfully yrs.

## No. 259.—TO MR. CASS.

LONDON, April 1, 1859.

MY DEAR SIR,—In the House of Commons, at 1 o'clock this morning, the resolution of Lord John Russell, immolating the ministerial Bill of Reform, was carried by a majority of 39 out of 621 votes. An adjournment took place to Monday the 4th instant, giving to the cabinet an opportunity to determine on their course, whether of a new bill, a resignation, or a dissolution of Parliament. Much could be said in favor of each of these courses: but my knowledge of Lord Derby and his colleagues induces me to believe that the last will be preferred. Certain formal and indispensable steps of supply must be first taken, and the maturing of these may consume a week or ten days. It is not impossible that, in the generous hour of triumph, the opposition may allow to be wasted as much time, I think about a fortnight, as is necessary to ripen the title of Mr. Disraeli to a pension of two thousand pounds annually for an aggregate service of two years. It is hard to see such luscious fruit turn to ashes on the eve of being clutched. The disinterested independence of Mr. Walpole in resigning when similarly tempted to hold on, has, however, been greatly eulogized.

If a new ministry, who are likely to compose it? There is no redundant ability, experience, and influence at command. As to the Premiership, the hostile attitude of Palmerston and Russell must embarrass:—for you will notice that, agreeably to the anticipation with which I closed my letter of this day last week, the former of these gentlemen, while sustaining the motion of the latter, took a course to damage any ambitious hopes its author might entertain very seriously. Some speak of Lord Granville as the chief who could enlist both in an administration and bridge the gulf which divides them. Others think a Russell Reform cabinet may be made stronger (through the Radicals) without than with Palmerston. Sir James Graham and Mr. Milner Gibson will doubtless be provided with seats. On the Department of Foreign Affairs, Lord Clarendon seems to have an almost undisputed lien:—and that is *our* principal concern.

No place yet definitively fixed for the proposed Congress. Berlin, Geneva, Baden-Baden, and Mannheim have been successively named. As to its result, meet where and when it may, the opinion I have heretofore expressed remains unchanged. Count Cavour has returned from a victorious sojourn at the Tuileries to Turin, radiant with smiles:—and Count Cavour's vista has no limit short of relieving Italy of every Austrian foot.

I am afraid that these two great topics have lost some of their interest:—but until they are on the track of human affairs in a settled shape, I don't know how to avoid them. So, be merciful.

Always faithfully yrs.

---

## No. 260.—TO MR. CASS.

LONDON, April 15, 1859.

MY DEAR SIR,—A thin and glimmering ray of possible peace has suddenly shone on the dark cloud of approaching war. My colleague and neighbor, the Belgian minister, regards it as a rainbow, precursive of a bright sky. He may possibly be right:—but I cannot say that the incident appears to me of much importance. It is the last proposal made by Austria:—that there shall be a general disarmament, and the Italian question referred for definitive adjudication to the Congress at Baden. Now, what is this but an affectation of fairness?—an offer originating in financial difficulty, and which cannot, without self-stultification, be accepted by the quarrelling powers. Accordingly France replies at once, she has not armed, and cannot therefore disarm:—a reply about as ingenuous as the proposal itself. Sardinia declares she cannot safely, and therefore will not, take a single step backward, while her enemy remains in Lombardo-Venetia. The truth is, it is essential to both parties to satisfy the opinion of Germany: and hence the game of constantly recurring efforts to put each other in the wrong. The instant these efforts are exhausted, artillery will be heard, whether preceded by a declaration or not. The acknowledged and extraordinary popularity of Louis Napoleon, notwithstanding all that he has been doing since the 1st of January last, amply disproves the change in the French character which it is the fashion here to insist has been effected by the last eight years of peace. They love glory, and will follow *this* Bonaparte in pursuit of it just as readily and heedlessly as they did the other.

On this absorbing subject we are promised by the cabinet a full development of the course they have taken, and of the actual "situation." It was designed for this evening, but was last night postponed to Monday next. My own impression is that we shall be told of the failure of every mediating effort, and perhaps of an impending declaration of war by Austria against Piedmont, which will be a "tocsin" to France.

Mr. Reed reached here the evening before the last. He must have crossed Senator Clingman on his way to Paris. He tells me Mr. Mason has no doubt of war.

I am quite sensible how much your time must be filled up with more peremptory claims, and therefore am really very grateful for your delightfully long note of the 18th ultimo.

The members of the Commons are very generally off to the hustings. It is not easy to form a House. The election will be a spirited one:—perhaps at some places it may be marked by violence. Mr. Cobden is up for Rochdale;—his armor borne in his absence by his Patroclus, Mr. Bright, who has no dread of his own defeat at Birmingham. The dissolution finds little favor with either party. When coolly considered by-and-by, it will be looked upon as a most unnecessary and dangerous departure from the settled principles and practices of this government:—a step, however, rather stimulating towards republicanization.

Always faithfully yrs.

---

## No. 261.—TO MR. CORYELL.

LONDON, April 21, 1859.

MY DEAR SIR,—Your letter of the 4th instant is before me, and I thank you for its contents. It is impossible for me to be more active in private correspondence than I am. There are so many subjects for official thought and attention constantly arising that I am obliged to rest satisfied with the modicum of personal writing within my power. I bombard General Cass by every steamer.

What a deplorable picture you draw of the condition of our good old party! It must be much worse, however, before I can persuade myself to think that there is real danger. As to my own action, I have grown old sticking inveterately to one groove of straight line motion, out of which I have neither the wish nor the ability to budge. My faith in pure democracy is now exactly what it was when I embraced or inhaled it fifty years ago. Perhaps this will be esteemed blind idolatry. Be it so. I steer by an old compass: and, sink or swim, amid shallows, rocks, flats, or icebergs, I'll keep on to the last. When I see men, like fretful painters, displeased with their own work and dashing their brushes in a rage at the canvas, I feel more pity than surprise at an intemperance which visits the imperfection of a slight part upon the great whole Because they can't make a nose as straight, or an eye as blue, as they conceive it ought to be, they indignantly spoil their still beautiful creation. None do more harm to fundamentals than they who are over-righteous and are "wise in their own conceit." You must make the application of these "saws:" for you perceive I have a latent reluctance to do so.

So, the delusive chirrup with which warm-hearted friends are wont periodically to be excited as with an intermittent, has again, for the fifth time, buzzed in the breeze! At this distance it is quite inaudible. The speaking-trumpets of the press communicate no sound of the sort. The cars are crammed with candidates steaming to Charleston. I'll accept cheerfully any one of them: preferring to be sure a Southerner, but never discontented with the best practicable result. When we can't do the best, let us at least do the best we can. Be the candidate whom he may, nail the flag, and never despair of the Republic!

We have not got war yet, though I expect it every day. France and Austria have had a protracted game of political chess, and I rather think the former will prove the Morphy of the occasion. The number of men under arms in Europe, fully equipped and ready to give battle, may be estimated at two millions five hundred thousand. These are the bulwarks of despotic thrones! Can we wonder that thrones still stand?

Remember, when you have a chance, to give my kindest regards to Mr. Ingham:—also Judge Joel Jones, etc.

Very faithfully yrs.

---

## No. 262.—TO MR. CASS.

LONDON, April 22, 1859.

MY DEAR SIR,—I see a good deal of Baron Poerio, the minister in '49, and ever since the imprisoned victim, of the now dying King of Naples. He is a short, slender gentleman, rather bald, of unaffected quiet-toned manners, and of clear mind. I should presume him to be about 55; he attracts much kind notice, and circulates actively. The deportment of all these escaped prisoners has been, since they reached England, most admirably becoming. They are not generally military men, but they seem to regard the Sardinian army as their natural resource.

Two brilliant intellects of the 19th century have just died out: De Tocqueville, at Cannes, on Saturday last, and Lady Morgan, at London, on the preceding Wednesday.

The heavy sword of Brennus has suddenly been pitched into the scales, though not exactly from the quarter I had anticipated. Yesterday morning, the funds rose, Lord Malmesbury's indefatigable and inexhaustible proposals for peace, disarmament, and a Congress seemed everywhere accepted, and even my obstinate convictions were giving way; when, crack! came the thunderclap of the afternoon's telegram from Turin, announcing that Giulai, the Austrian Commander-in-chief at Milan, had summoned Piedmont to disperse her soldiers and volunteers under penalty of war and invasion at the expiration of three days! I do not believe the fact to be so, but it *looks* very much as if England had busied herself in administering opiates and sedatives to Louis Napoleon, while the black double-headed eagle was stretching its wings for a spring and a swoop. For, what can Victor Emmanuel do now? He must fly before the immense forces he is wholly incapable of repelling; his capitals must fall in quick succession: and when he is irreparably ruined, and perhaps a suicide after the fashion of his father, then possibly France, delirious with shame, may rush to revenge him. If the French take up this notion, that their honor has been compromised by too blind a reliance upon their dear allies, whither will they not impetuously turn to strike? Scotch "second sight" is hardly necessary to make palpable the crowded harbor and bristling batteries of Cherbourg. And Queen Victoria is without her Parliament, her Channel without a fleet, her coasts without defences, and her militia without arms or practice! Here is a complication from which you may deduce the likelihood of a violent demand for the restoration of Lord Palmerston, the recognized War minister, to power.

I wish Congress could be persuaded to place at the disposition of the American minister here a reasonable credit with the house of Barings, to be applied, under Presidential sanction in each case, to the purchase of rare relics illustrative of our national history. Besides the catalogue of Franklinian and Revolutionary articles sold on the 6th instant, but which you plead poverty for not buying, here is a manuscript of extreme interest by Bradford, the narrator of the preparations, voyage, and settlement of the Pilgrims, *quorum pars fuit:* and here, telling a tale of our complete and minute custom-house subserviency, while colonies, to the London establishment, is the very copperplate whence were struck, and sent over, certificates of assessed valuations of imports!

Always faithfully yrs.

---

## No. 263.—TO MR. CASS.

LONDON, April 29, 1859.

MY DEAR SIR,—The Foreign Office and the Exchange are equally under a panic. Stocks are tumbling headlong, with curses louder and deeper than any heard since '48. As to Lord Malmesbury, he is fiercely assailed in the newspapers for absence and neglect of duty at an appalling crisis. It will turn out, as I believe, that the Secretary, over-zealous to avert war, has hurried to Paris to present in person England's final offer of mediation. The treaty of alliance offensive and defensive between Russia and France, executed three days after the date of the Austrian summons to Piedmont, and immediately announced, has created general surprise and consternation. The Czar's troops are in two armies of observation, composedly exercising surveillance, one on the eastern frontier of Prussia, the other not distant from the eastern frontier of Austria. They will cross the boundary at the signal of Louis Napoleon, who sped from Paris yesterday for a field of battle in the vicinity of that of Marengo. The Duke of Malakoff is still here, and possibly may linger for several days:—but he has left what I take to be his farewell cards. He has often said that the Emperor was no general and never could be one. His Majesty has nevertheless organized a magnificent campaign, and if he come out as well as he goes into it, the Marshal will be obliged to eat his words. In the course of the present week the soil of Piedmont will be trodden by little less than 350,000 armed men, marshalled by three sovereigns, and bent on a pitched battle whose importance far transcends that of Waterloo.

The perplexities and tribulations of Lord Malmesbury are, as we may readily imagine, *au comble.* But the real state of things is every instant thrown into doubt by fresh telegrams across the Channel. Since I began this letter, a distinction is taken between *a treaty* offensive and defensive, and *a perfect understanding*, in explanation of the Czar's attitude. Bonaparte's quitting Paris is said not to be definitive, and hence he don't empower the regency *to act:*—he will be back before he enters Italy. He is gaining time by forbearing to slam the door against mediation. All the while, however, it is certain that immense bodies of troops are pouring across the frontiers of Piedmont.

Should this European war proceed, of which I have hardly had a doubt since the 1st of January, would it not be well to suggest to General Floyd the expediency of allowing some of our most promising officers to witness its operations? Vast improvements in military weapons, it is said, will have their first practical trials; and the French Emperor has studied out, and meditates exhibiting, new strategical movements, the very hints of which have thrown all the young Gallic mousquetaires into ecstacies. For my own part, I should like to see, if the combatants would permit it, an American historiographer, Major Delafield for instance, at or near every battle.

The election is going on with less agitation than was expected. The coffers of the Carlton Club are crammed with means for "paying expenses."

Always faithfully yrs.

---

## No. 264.—TO MR. CASS.

LONDON, May 3, 1859.

MY DEAR SIR,—It may be important that you should promptly know the judgment passed by this government upon the proceedings of their negotiator in Nicaragua; and I therefore availed myself of the earliest opportunity by the Arago from Southampton. The tone of censure used by Lord Malmesbury is somewhat softened in my report. Such unexplained departures from prescribed duty could, he said, be only attributed "to the loss of his faculties"!

I introduced conversation by complimentary reference to the Secretary's great exertions for the preservation of peace in Europe. The truth is, I *felt* the extraordinary alteration his appearance had undergone. He looked *abattu*, exhausted, worn, grave: as if ten years of suffering had intervened since I last saw him. He said he had given fourteen hours of every day for two months to efforts to keep people from fighting, but fight they would, in spite of everything he had been able to say or do:—all mediation or intercession was at an end:—and (pausing to reflect) they fight this very day!

War then is opened. The white-coated legions, with their black double-headed eagles, have crossed the Ticino, and Austria is in Piedmont on the banks of the Sesia! Nothing as yet but a lively skirmish:—the Sardinians killing a colonel and fifteen privates, and then retreating.

The French are hastening to the theatre of action, through all the passes, in great corps and high spirits:—forty thousand of them at Genoa from Algeria and Toulon. Revolution has exploded at the approach of the tricolor in Tuscany (whose ducal family have fled), in Parma (whose duchess is among the missing), in Modena; and even in Rome, popular "manifestations," after taking a decided course, tending to the overthrow of the Pope's secular power, have only been suspended by the persuasive exhortation of the French General Guyon. The respective diplomatic vindications of the three belligerents are now addressed and circulated at the bar of European opinion. Napoleon, however, is still in Paris, and Malakoff in London.

At present the policy of maintaining a pacific neutrality is here ascendant. All the hustings proclaim it. The pipe of every section, Derby, Palmerston, Russell, or Bright, discourses the same eloquent music. Yet the Mediterranean squadrons and garrisons are reinforced, and the Channel fleet is in process of doubling. Volunteers, too, are drilling with rifles:—the militia embodying:—and the coast fortifications are anxiously brushed up. There is no knowing, indeed, in what direction the lava of a volcano may scoop its channel.

The complexion of the new House of Commons cannot yet be determined. The Conservatives will gain, say their adversaries, about ten members,—not enough to enable them to retain the government. Lord Palmerston anticipates another ministry, and another dissolution consequent upon the adoption of another Reform bill in less than a twelvemonth.

Always faithfully yrs.

---

## No. 265.—TO MR. T.

LONDON, May 7, 1859.

MY DEAR SIR,—I got yours of the 2d instant with its enclosure.

When Mr. —— asks "for such information, in regard to international law, as will define the rights, obligations, and responsibilities of neutral ships," he asks a *pamphlet*, not to be struck off (according to the newly coined phrase) as quick as 1 o'clock. I think it one of the most violently unreasonable requests ever made to a public officer who has current business exacting attention. If I can manage to get time enough to compress a few leading principles, rules, and cases, within something short of an octavo, you may have a chance to hear from me; otherwise, hint to Mr. —— that what he wants he can easiest and safest procure by administering a handsome fee to some eminent professional counsel.

Faithfully yrs.

---

## No. 266.—TO MR. PICKENS.

LONDON, May 8, 1859.

MY DEAR SIR,—Your highly interesting letter of the 19th ultimo would have been answered before, but that our Central American relations suddenly required rectification here and exacted exclusive zeal. It will be a source of great pleasure to me to exchange thoughts with you occasionally. I cherish many delightful remembrances of my short residence in St. Petersburg during the years '37, '38, and '39, and feel much interest in the movements of the present Czar, in their bearing on foreign politics, or domestic ameliorations. He became of age while I was at his father's Court.

The condition of things at home seems rapidly improving. All the elements of prosperity are vigorously pushing upwards. Coal, iron, cotton, corn, railways, are emerging from the fogs of panic. An excess of imports is apprehended:—a dangerous consequence, but sure proof, of renovated enterprise. The incumbent of the Treasury, after suffering the chilly horrors of emptiness, will have to watch and subdue the tendencies to repletion.

The Paraguay Armada returns; having accomplished very little, but that little quite enough. Peace and good will are pearls for which we must sometimes pay a high price. We probably saved in the future a good deal by the size and vigor of the demonstration.

The very equivocal—rather the unequivocally wrong—

course taken by the British negotiator in Nicaragua, threatened to necessitate a similar movement in that quarter. I think, however, it will be abstained from. The fault was clearly more in Sir William G. Ousely than in the local statesmen; and the remedy sent from the Foreign Office will doubtless be efficacious; we shall have the Cass-Yrissari Treaty *pure et simple:* the transit opened, permanently neutral to all the world; the Mosquito Protectorate at an end; and the Bay Islands restored to Honduras:—these arrangements leaving the Clayton-Bulwer Treaty free of contestable points.

If, in addition to the Right of Search question, the China question, the Paraguay question, and the Central American question, the President shall be able to adjust advantageously the wretched Mexican question, his foreign policy will stand a very good chance of being esteemed historically as fortunate, no matter how his personal popularity at home may stand.

The existing war is an exceedingly interesting event. Of the real, though distant, source whence it springs, one can scarcely doubt. When you hear of an unaccountable murder, you ask "who benefits by it?" It is possible that Italy may incidentally be relieved of Austrian tyranny: but the Emperor of Russia would appease his Sire's ghost by occupying the halls of Stamboul, and a large print of the foot of Napoleon I. is indelible at the base of the great Pyramid. At the expiration of this struggle, unless the maritime power of England energetically intervene, the Crescent will have disappeared from Europe, and Egypt be annexed to Algeria. That is the only logical end to the beginning.

Just now, the public men of Great Britain, high and low, in and out of office, on the hustings and in private, unanimously inculcate neutrality. The policy is wise,—for the time being: but it will not continue wise or safe, as soon as the vista shall open of a redistribution of empire in especial reference to the crowns at Paris and St. Petersburg. For one, or two, or three years, England may husband her vast resources and concentrate her scattered forces: and then, on seeing the danger patent, she will find herself able to compel a peace. You will probably have remarked that the instant her efforts at mediation failed, she pushed forward the doubling of her fleets, the restoration of her garrisons, the embodying of her militia, the recall of her troops, and the recruiting of seamen with a ten-pounds bounty. I am quite satisfied that she will try to avoid being drawn into the maelstrom of war, until she feels so strong and so secure that she can, by going one side or the other, bring it to a close. Up to the point of driving the Austrians into the Adriatic, my sympathies all run with the Italians, and even with Louis Napoleon: "*après cela, rien si non le déluge!*"

I agree with you in believing that our American interests are beyond the reach of injury by this war. Indeed, as neutral carriers, our merchant vessels may be much benefited; especially under the operation of the 2d, 3d, and 4th clauses of the "Declaration concerning Maritime Law" in the Treaty of Paris of April, '56, although Mr. Marcy refused his assent.

Always faithfully yrs.

---

## No. 267.—TO MR. CASS.

LONDON, May 13, 1859.

MY DEAR SIR,—There are but two topics, the war on the Po and the fight at the Polls. The latter is just closing:—shewing twenty Liberal members captured by the enemy, but still leaving a large superiority of force, say 55, with the opposition. Is it not quite shocking to perceive that, in this highly moral and religious country, so given to inculcate virtuous principles and practices upon "all the world and the rest of mankind," this change of twenty constituencies is authoritatively (Sir James Graham), scarce disputably, attributed to bribery, bribery with a Carlton Club fund!

Governments are very generally and distinctly announcing neutrality as the order of the day. In the actual war, Russia declares herself neutral: so does Prussia: so does Switzerland: so does Belgium: so does Holland: so does the Roman Pontiff: so does expiring Bomba: so does Denmark: and so shortly will England, either by orders in Council, or unequivocal declarations in Parliament. Thus the war in Italy assumes the aspect of a prize fight:

three bruisers without backers hemmed in by a complete *cordon* of neutrals. How long this *cordon* will last; whether it will not soon prove itself a rope of sand; whether the German States will not be frightened into fits of intermeddling; whether Russia may not on tiptoe creep to the bedside of the "sick man;" whether Hungary may not invite the Czar to liberate her on his way to enlarge Greece by territorial annexations; and whether splicing Egypt to Algeria may not fall like "a stunner" upon Britannia: are all speculative questions of easy starting but of slow solution.

The French Emperor reached Genoa yesterday. To-day he is doubtless in Turin. Whether he will execute his promise and get to Milan in three weeks, *nous verrons.* He left Paris on the surge of the highest swell of popular enthusiasm, and (a comforting fact) carrying in his portfolio the spontaneous pledges of the "Mariamne" and the Socialists that they would guaranty the safety of his dynasty and family during his absence. His command is already 180,000 men.

We are bound to celebrate her Majesty's birthday on the 19th instant at the Drawing Room in St. James's Palace, at the Foreign Office dinner, and at the Prime Ministers' ball: and all this by conventional arrangement, when the excellent Queen was really born on the 24th of May. Quite immaterial, when once settled.

Marshal Malakoff is succeeded at this court by corporation-scolding Count Persigny. The former went off in a huff, at being sent to Nancy to await the possibility of getting the command of a division at some future day. Perhaps it is intended that, in order to have a pretence for concentrating the army, he shall do something to provoke a German breach of neutrality. Since his marriage, I think he has become "the soldier tired of war's alarms."

Lord Napier and family arrived safely at Plymouth a few days ago.

Always faithfully yrs.

## No. 268.—TO MR. H.

LONDON, May 17, 1859.

DEAR SIR,—Your note of the 14th instant was handed to me yesterday. In it you request my opinion as to your contracts to ship provisions and coals to France, and as to your position in executing these contracts, per English vessels, under the recently issued Proclamation of the Queen.

You leave me in the dark as to the dates and terms of the contracts, the expressed purposes to which your supplies are destined, the nominal parties, and the places of delivery. All these are matters which, more or less, affect the character of your proceedings. One thing, however, is I believe indisputable:—your contracts are with the Imperial government, not with private persons, and it would be difficult, therefore, should obstacles interpose, to resist the presumption that your shipments were designed for military, not domestic use.

The penalties and forfeitures provided in the act of George III. recited in the Proclamation, are meant to enforce a high national policy, that of strict neutrality in an actual war between two foreign powers. Such shipments as you propose would certainly help the belligerent movements of one of these powers injuriously to the other: if that be undeniable, do they not necessarily violate the neutrality proclaimed? and so subject the shipper to prosecution for misdemeanor and his vessels to condemnation. If the Proclamation means less than this, it is mere pretence.

But perhaps you hope that the doctrine promulgated in the *Times* is sound, to wit, that the statute does not apply to American citizens or vessels. I am sorry to be obliged to think otherwise. The very words of the act refer to "any person" and "any vessels." Our citizens domiciled as merchants in England, and our ships in British ports, cannot claim immunity from the operation of the statute upon any principle of which I am aware.

These views are hastily submitted to you. I should much have preferred expressing them orally:—because I do not like to give a hurried opinion on so grave a topic. Please, regard them as confidential.

Let me conclude by saying that, notwithstanding the suggestions I have made, the shipment of *provisions only* seems to me so little likely to be noticed or complained of by Austrians, that, were I embarked in the business, I should not be deterred from going on.

Very respectfully yrs.

---

## No. 269.—TO LADY S.

LONDON, May 18, 1859.

MY DEAR LADY S.,—Your note of the 16th instant in reference to Mr. —— has had all the favorable consideration which any request from you is sure to command from me. I cannot doubt the excellent qualities of one whom you desire to serve:—and in promptly conforming to your wish, it would be a source of additional satisfaction to me to contribute, however slightly or indirectly, to an appointment which would please the several highly cherished friends whom you name.

If on any occasion Lord Malmesbury were to honor me by touching on the subject and asking my opinion, I might feel at liberty to express myself in harmony with your suggestions. But, to go farther than this, or to initiate the topic, is out of my power, as I am prohibited by positive law. What course of conduct heretofore pursued by the representatives of the United States at any foreign Court may have suggested the expediency of the legislative injunction is unknown to me:—but in 1856 Congress passed an act prescribing, among other matters, that "*no diplomatic officer shall recommend any person, at home or abroad, for any employment of trust or profit under the government of the country in which he is located:* nor ask or accept for himself or any other person any present, emolument, pecuniary favor, office or title of any kind from any such government."

This law, my dear Lady S., renders me powerless to aid your gracious object: and I have no mode of mitigating the regret felt at abstaining to execute your wish except by frankly shewing the obligation of duty.

The departure of his Grace, the Duke of Leeds, shocked

us all by its suddenness. Short as our acquaintance with him was, the kindly and generous features of his character had produced an impression not to be easily effaced.

With the sincerest respect I am, my dear Lady S.,

Always faithfully yrs.

---

## No. 270.—TO MR. CASS.

LONDON, May 20, 1859.

MY DEAR SIR,—Lord and Lady Napier had a prosperous and quick voyage home. They are full of grateful remembrances for kindnesses, and express themselves to everybody with warmth.

Your representative at the Court of Lisbon, the gallant General Morgan, is at present here. He escorts Mrs. Morgan to Liverpool, on her way to the United States by the steamer of to-morrow. They did us credit yesterday at the birthday Drawing Room of the Queen.

We were thirty-two plates at the diplomatic feast of the Foreign Office. Among us shone, in a perfect wilderness of diamonds, Prince Obrenovitch, son of the recently reinstated Miloch of Servia. This specimen of the race is exceedingly imposing, and dwarfs nearer and older royalties.

What of a battle?—coming, not yet come. Strategy, manœuvre, observation, inspection, distribution, but no fight. They say we are to hear of one to-night. Sympathizing with Italy, I almost fear the news:—the Austrians have been so cautious and concentrated, the allies so dashing, brisk, and loud. Then the military theories of Louis Napoleon, however brilliant, do not give the confidence imparted by the experience and practice of Hess and Gyulai. And again, even the Emperor himself apprehends mischief from the rash levity of his new troops. I would be content to ensure a drawn game or two for the next month.

Count Persigny has resumed his embassy. He said to me yesterday that he would not have come, had he not regarded his coming as an earnest of the Emperor's good will towards England. Something, then, makes it expedient to prop up the belief of that good will even by small matters! Words have lost their efficacy. No wonder, for the world is pretty generally convinced that the extraordinary armament of this country has its impulse in the knowledge of the secretly agreed designs between Russia and France. I think the leaning of sentiment and comment too here is towards Austria. The *Times* has managed, it is said through the agency of Lord Aberdeen, to plant a "special correspondent" at the head-quarters of the Tedeschi on the Po: and able letters have already appeared, eulogizing and vindicating the invaders. The Regent of Prussia, too, father-in-law of *our* Princess Royal, in his farewell address to the dissolving landtag, though still ambiguous, shews more anti-gallicanism than was expected.

The new Parliament convenes in ten days. The Liberal majority is fifty-one, nominally: in reality, it may sometimes be many more, and sometimes wholly disappear, according to the questions for decision. Great exertions are being made to keep the party united, until at least a change of government be effected. If Reform be early brought upon the *tapis*, the ministry will fall: but if, as I hear, a resort be had to any other expedient, such for instance as a vote of want of confidence, on account of failure to prevent the war, or on imputations of electioneering corruption, the "independent members" will bolt, and Lord Derby be firmer than ever. I am, as you know, not much of a political conjurer: but, were I to wager, it would be that the cabinet will last another year.

Always faithfully yrs.

---

## No. 271.—TO MR. T.

(*Unofficial.*) London, May 22, 1859.

My dear Sir,—If I do not misapply the present Sabbath, I am afraid that an answer to your letter of the 20th instant will run a chance of almost indefinite postponement. Perhaps, too, what may be said will reach all the practical objects aimed at by your friend.

The memorandum, now returned to you, of the legislative provisions by which our shipping, in its titles, transfers, and privileges, is governed, however correct in itself, does not seem to me applicable to the enquiry on foot. Our custom-house regulations are not what you want. You are seeking a solution of the illusory problem started in several newspapers since the Queen's Proclamation of neutrality, to wit, whether the penalties prescribed by the act of George III. can be avoided by shippers in England, if they employ American instead of British bottoms and flags. Now, on this question, our peculiar customs laws have no bearing whatever.

1. When a war is declared or explodes between two or more nations, the normal relation of other nations to that war is one of neutrality: signifying, engaged on neither side.

2. To preserve unquestioned this condition of neutrality, some governments deem it expedient to warn and deter the people by threatening with penalties and forfeitures; other governments simply go on their usual course, having nothing to say or do with quarrels which don't concern or involve them, and leaving intercourse and commerce to private enterprise and prudence. Great Britain, on the occurrence of the actual war, has chosen the former proceeding: the United States have mostly heretofore, and probably will now, take the latter. This difference in the manner of municipal action towards their respective peoples does not, in the slightest degree, vary the character of their international relation:—they are both neutral to the fullest extent.

3. The statute of George III., recited in her Majesty's Proclamation, makes amenable to domestic or municipal criminal procedure, certain acts tending to bring the national neutrality into suspicion, against which we in the United States have not thought it necessary to take such stringent steps. Both countries have what are called permanent neutrality laws (ours you will find dated the 20th April, 1818), but the offences made punishable are not the same in reality or in terms.

4. Observe that the language of the statute Geo. III. very properly makes the penalty and forfeiture attached to the commission of the described misdemeanor, applicable to all "*persons*" and "*ships*" within British jurisdiction. It would have been strange if "*foreigners*,"

domiciled Americans or any other class, had been allowed an immunity for offences alleged to endanger the national good faith, honor, and interests. We have not declared in our criminal code the acts thus denounced to be misdemeanors: but had we done so, certainly aliens or strangers would have been made equally liable with citizens.

5. Breaches of neutrality are of various kinds and followed by various consequences. It is impossible, for me at least, to state in advance every case that would be construed into a breach. Take it as a fundamental rule that fraudulent neutrality is no neutrality: and, then, that in general a violation is committed by supplying one of the belligerents, directly or indirectly, with contraband of war.

6. What articles are contraband of war must be too commonly known to require mention. They are, broadly and comprehensively, such things as contribute to, and are designed for, military use. Provisions may become contraband, if destined to feed a population intentionally condemned, by siege or other plan of operations, to starvation: and the necessities of steam navigation would seem, in these modern times, by parity of reason, to convert coals into contraband, if freighted for a belligerent navy.

7. I have been surprised, under the influence of these views, at finding some portion of the English press making the unusual concession that commerce can be more safely carried on from their ports in American ships and under the American flag than with their own. This compliment has too little foundation to be accepted. As I have said, both nations are neutrals, in reference to the war now waging. To be sure, an English merchant in Liverpool, who fits out an English vessel in the Mersey, with a cargo of coals or salt beef, and orders her to Toulon, may be, and his ship also, in more immediate peril than would be an American merchant in New York who fits out an American vessel in the Hudson with a like cargo for the same French port: but the greater peril does not spring out of the nationality of the citizen or ship: it is the consequence of a local criminal law, the statute of George III., which at Liverpool applies indiscriminately to every person and every vessel, but which at New York don't exist at all. On the high seas, in the view of the parties at war, and in reference to the

doctrine of contraband, as the two nations are equally neutral, it is quite immaterial whether the carrying craft be British or American. If the freight be internationally lawful, it is as secure against invasion in one as in the other:—if it be unlawful, it will in both be liable to seizure and condemnation.

8. War has its rights as well as neutrality. These rights, in regard to maritime captures, are enforced by courts of admiralty, whose decisions rest, or ought to rest, upon the established principles of international law. Whether a vessel seized for breach of neutrality be good prize or not, is often a complicated, nice, and difficult question, requiring the closest study of facts, documents, circumstances, and designs. In every civilized country, admiralty tribunals have been established to which either party to a war may resort with alleged prizes to obtain judicial decrees of condemnation, unless, indeed, for the stricter maintenance of neutrality, such resort has been prohibited.

But you will say enough, and more than enough! I believe so too. These suggestions have been made, to indicate what I conceive to be the right track of thought on the new phase of our commercial relations by which your mind is exercised. Each of them could be amplified into the pamphlet held over you *in terrorem*, by illustrations, exceptions, and book authorities;—but I forbear to do what would consume much precious time (both mine and yours) without yielding a corresponding profit. One reflection I *must* add: indeed "situated as I am" (as Sir Patrick Plenipo adroitly intimates), I do not feel at liberty to omit it: viz. that what I have written to you on this grave topic, if used at all, should be used with extreme discretion.

Faithfully yours.

---

## No. 272.—TO MR. DILLER.

(*Unofficial.*) LONDON, May 24, 1859.

MY DEAR SIR,—I have received your excellent letter of the 20th instant. It is one among many from our foreign consuls which the war has induced. All, I believe, are anxious to do right:—but all are not as inflexible to surrounding and misleading influences as I take great pleasure in finding you to be.

Your law on the mooted topic is incontestably sound, and your official morality, in refusing to be an agent to effectuate a fraudulent cover, not to be questioned. Never do what is tainted even with the suspicion of *mala fides.* In God's name, why should the seal or the flag of the United States be debased by bolstering or disguising what is false? We should recoil from such profanation instinctively.

There is a certain amount of discretion vested in you by the 637th paragraph of the Regulations. There should be *proof* that 1. the *purchaser* is a citizen of the United States, and 2. that the transaction is *bona fide:*—and *you* are to determine whether that *proof be satisfactory:* you are the officer to be *satisfied:* and though I would never embarrass a fair transaction of business by captious difficulties as to evidence, yet, if I doubted its integrity, I would probe it resolutely, and exact all-sufficient proof.

Of your power to administer an oath whenever you think it necessary or proper in fulfilling your duties, no doubt can possibly be entertained since the passage of the 24th section of the act of the 18th of August, 1856.

I will only add that the advantage to be derived by one neutral ship-owner in selling to another neutral, even as a cover, is imperceptible to me: for, in time of war, no flag can protect against the belligerent right of search.

Very respectfully and faithfully yrs.

---

## No. 273.—TO MR. DE LA HENRIÈRE.

London, May 25, 1859.

Sir,—I beg to thank you for your note received two days ago, and for the spirited little volume, the Handbook of Reform, which accompanied it.

As the dispassionate conclusion of an enlightened stranger, your estimate of the Constitution of my country is exceedingly welcome. Born under the beneficent operation of that instrument, I have yet to experience my first doubt of its great wisdom, or to shew my first reluctance to maintain it unaltered.

With sentiments of esteem and good will,

I have the honor to be, sir, yrs.

---

## No. 274.—TO MR. CASS.

London, May 27, 1859.

My dear Sir,—The French Ambassador fairly cornered me at a reception the day before yesterday, and with unmistakable *empressement* and perseverance went through an elaborate vindication of the Emperor's entire course respecting the war. It was necessary to give my whole attention:—for Count Persigny speaks poor English, and is too courteous to insist upon his own tongue, though I hinted he might. Well! he produced in my mind a conviction that Napoleon III. regards it as essential to his dynastic and national policy that he should end the war and leave Italy to her own population and self-government, as soon as he has driven the Austrians into the Adriatic. Nothing, said his Excellency, can be more unjust and preposterous than the English notion that he wishes to go beyond the independence of Lombardo-Venetia: that he wants crowns for his cousins: and is preparing to confront all Europe in battle. If anything of that sort result from the intermeddling of the German States, the fault will not be his. Securing the Peninsula against revolution, and France against its contagion, by giving the oppressed and misgoverned people the power to act for themselves, is the great guaranty he proposes to effect for his throne and fame. Victory, it is true, deals with the general as brandy deals with the toper:—but inebriation may possibly be escaped, and the Count has implicit faith in the strong head of his Majesty. So have I.

Once or twice heretofore you have had my deduction from various and numerous small matters, that the tendency of the Derby government is to *rapprochement* with Austria. That, I am convinced, is their gravitation.

Neutrality, vigorously arming neutrality, as long as Napoleon has his hands full in Lombardy, and while Prussia is settling the Germanic pre-eminence: but, when all's ready, the ministry, in harmony with the Court, will elude the popular vigilance and place England, before she is aware of it, at the head of a general coalition hostile to France. One event may defeat this,—a ministerial change: for all admit that no administration which could be formed by Lord Granville, Lord John Russell, or Lord Palmerston, would allow the pacific position, now unanimously chosen, to be disturbed, in order to reinstate or uphold the oppression of Italy.

Her Majesty's mother, the Duchess of Kent, about 73, has just undergone a severe and alarming attack. Should it prove fatal, the Queen's affliction will be ample ground for putting off any rough handling of her official servants. The Tories would rejoice, as brands from the burning, if they could tranquilly tide over the next two months. Poor old lady! she little thinks that such hopes have been kindled by the report of her illness!

Senator Seward has been here a week, and purposes to remain until November. Sir Henry Holland talks of visiting the President in September. He likes the sea, and has American investments.

The battle of Montibello, though unquestionably a French success, is not esteemed here as much more than a sanguinary skirmish with little result.

Always faithfully yrs.

---

## No. 275.—TO MR. MARKOE.

LONDON, June 1, 1859.

MY DEAR MARKOE,—The military movements in Italy are very engrossing. To-day brings us a second sanguinary fight at Palestro; in which the Piedmontese carry off the palm, and the Austrians are beaten. Their chief, Gyulai, is reported among the slain. The carnage, both here and at Montibello, is out of all proportion with the result as affecting the campaign.

In the north, at Como, Garibaldi has received a check;

a thing that will do him no permanent harm, for he was moving on, like mad Anthony, rather recklessly, too much despising his adversary. A little more caution and armament, and he may yet be the first in Milan. One can't help wishing this, for he is their best type of liberty and independence:—republican, *ab ovo usque ad mala.*

Odd enough, I am getting to believe in the sincerity of Louis Napoleon's professions about the only purpose of the present war. I have persuaded myself into the conviction that it is the interest of his dynasty and fame and future power to stop, at least for some years, as soon as he drowns the Austrians in the Adriatic:—and as he has sagacity enough to see his interest, so, setting aside the notion that a despot can be a liberator, he may see his own selfish and solid advantage in accomplishing what all Europe will praise him for, if he be content as soon as it is done. Of course, Englishmen and Germans can't reason in this way; they remember too keenly, and are nervous.

Prussia is fast taking the pre-eminence and lead among the German powers. If Austria yield her the *pas* in political arrangement, she may be flattered to a *rapprochement*, and then if the French Emperor forget the moderation inculcated by Eugénie, she, with England at her side, will create a coalition for the House of Hapsburg, which even Russia might not be averse to joining, and which Napoleon is not vigorous enough to withstand.

Always faithfully yrs.

---

## No. 276.—TO MR. CASS.

London, June 3, 1859.

My dear Sir,—I am told by a confidential and reliable Whig, that all efforts to bridge over the chasm between "Lord Pam and Lord John" have failed. Neither will enter a new government except as Prime Minister. If such be the irremediable fact, the great Liberal party, with its majority of fifty in the House of Commons, must fly to pieces on the first occasion next week, leaving Lord Derby "calm as a summer's morning." Mr. Roebuck, the fiercest of the Independents or Radicals, and Sir John

Ramsden, a sterling member of her Majesty's opposition, have recently made speeches which disclose a very unpromising prospect for those who covet seats on the Treasury bench.

The battle of Palestro was signalized by the exhibition of great daring on the part of Victor Emmanuel, and by *the first command given by Louis Napoleon*, which directed the Zouaves to an irresistible attack. It was reported, but without foundation, that Gyulai had been killed. As the allies contemplate a combined movement to cross the Po in face of the Austrians, a general and most destructive conflict is hourly expected.

Some of our distinguished army officers, Crittenden, Carr, Todd, Leroy, Clitz, have been attracted to this side of the Atlantic by the war. They would like to be observers at head-quarters:—but there are, I fear, insuperable obstacles in their way.

The legation was, the day before yesterday, specially honored by receiving her Majesty's commands inviting Bishop Delancey, of New York, and Mr. Senator Seward, to a concert at Buckingham Palace. The Queen graciously permitted the presentation of Mr. Seward between the acts of music:—I had, some weeks ago, introduced the Bishop at a regular Levee.

This morning I received official notice that her Majesty will in person open Parliament on the 7th instant. What has been doing since the 31st May is preliminary only: the election of Speaker, Mr. Denison again, and swearing in of members.

You will doubtless have seen in the public journals, or received from our consul there, Mr. Ferdinand Sarmiento, the official notification of the blockade of Venice by the French fleet. This is, I believe, the first maritime act of the kind in the present war. All the belligerents have referred to the Treaty of Paris of 1856 for their rule as to blockades:—we did not adopt the declaration contained in that treaty, but I suppose the rule would act upon all commerce without discrimination.

Always faithfully yrs.

## No. 277.—TO MR. CASS.

LONDON, June 17, 1859.

MY DEAR SIR,—The world's movements have latterly been brisk:—the Tories driven out, and the Austrians beyond the Adda! To signalize these events duly, I send you a list of the new government, and the huge blue-book of correspondence on "the affairs of Italy" from the Foreign Office. Of the first, it may be said that, like the pudding, its proof will be in the eating:—the flavor is not peculiarly palatable to us, but it may improve on tasting. Of the second, this is clearly true, that it does great credit to the industry and fairness of Lord Malmesbury as a European statesman: the Continent will read and digest it with avidity, and perhaps hasten to regret the downfall of Lord Derby. These gentlemen, after all, quit power with grace:—a grace that has emboldened the Queen, notwithstanding the condemnatory vote of the Commons, to confer the Garter on the retiring Premier, and the red ribbon of the Bath upon his principal Secretary of Foreign Affairs, as also upon his first Lord of the Admiralty, Sir John Pakington.

The virtues of a caucus were signally shewn by the opposition. They convened to the number of 274, the day preceding the opening of Parliament: were addressed by Palmerston, Russell, Bright: and although tempted into dissension by Roebuck, Lindsay, and Horsman, they steadily resolved to move an amendment to the Address, declaring a want of confidence in her Majesty's ministers. After nearly a week's debate, the amendment prevailed, in a House of 633, by a majority of 13. Had no preliminary and conciliatory meeting shewn the possibility of union on interchanges of mutual pledges, it is quite certain that the government would have stood.

The distinctive feature of the new cabinet, as a political agency on this side of the Atlantic, is an avowed sympathy with the Italian cause as espoused by Napoleon III. To be sure, neither Palmerston, Russell, Granville, nor Gladstone will dream of quitting neutrality in order to aid that cause:—but as soon as it triumphs by the expulsion of Austrian power from the Peninsula, they will firmly insist upon a peace by their mediation, and upon guaranties of independence and improved administration. If you can afford a few hours, I recommend to your perusal that cogently argumentative and wonderfully witty book, About's "*Question Romaine.*" You will there see, dissected and phosphorescent, the corruptions which make changes absolutely indispensable. I think the opportunity is at hand for their cure:—but it will be like drying the sores of Lazarus.

You will observe that the cabinet I send you requires the Queen's assent:—that will be announced in the two Houses of Parliament this afternoon, and probably without modification. On the score of ability, it will pass unchallenged. A greater infusion of "Independent Liberals" and less of "Peelites" might have improved the "pudding." Whether Mr. Cobden will accept the Board of Trade is questionable: he and Mr. Milner Gibson are the representative men of the extreme left "below the gangway," and they rather seem fobbed off with *pièces de résistance*, hard and homely places. Mr. Gladstone and Mr. Cardwell are assigned the posts for which they are respectively admirably fitted: but, as to the former,—just radiant under the patronage of Lord Derby, eulogistic of rotten boroughs as nurseries of statesmen, and voting unabated confidence in ministers—one "wonders how the devil he got there!" The three plain Misters, pray remark, are counterpoised by a cluster of Dukes:—Newcastle, Argyll, Somerset; the best tried and least exceptionable of their class. A happy hit brings in Lord Elgin, and makes the government overwhelmingly strong in the House of Peers:—even though the despotic Lord John preferred himself to Lord Clarendon, who *may* most justly question the wisdom of the preference. *Personally*, the Premier has limited himself to keeping his faithful "corporal's guard" the three Sirs, Wood, Lewis, and Grey. A "broad-bottomed" administration here was once short-lived:—perhaps one on a "broad basis" (for that was the improved phraseology of the present coalition) may last a little longer. Bottom and Basis! tweedledum and tweedledee! the *end* may be the same.

The Austrian Emperor has taken command of his army in Italy, as a preliminary to a last desperate battle. He stands at bay in what military men call "the famous quadrilateral position," or the area flanked and defended by four great fortresses. The allies will undoubtedly rush upon him: if their attack succeed, the work of the campaign may be regarded as accomplished, for they will then have nothing to do but to invest the garrisons, and await the inevitable capture of Venice by the French fleet. There is really no reason why the war should not be closed by November next:—for, observe, that the attitudes respectively taken by Russia and Prussia, per their recent diplomatic manifestoes, render it in the highest degree improbable that any testy or terrified member of the Germanic body will intermeddle with the struggle. Thus localized, like a malignant disease boarded up in an infected district, it must soon die out. I do not say that all difficulty will cease when war ceases and Francis Joseph renounces his provinces:—for it is quite obvious that as arms are laid down, up will spring a multitudinous crop of complications respecting the Pope, the Legations, the Duchies, and the Two Sicilies:—but these fall to the department of diplomacy.

Always faithfully yrs.

---

## No. 278.—TO MR. CASS.

LONDON, June 24, 1859.

MY DEAR SIR,—The new ministry are *in*, but not fairly under way. Until re-elected to their seats, vacated by accepting office, those of the House are busy with their constituents. With some it will probably be a hard road to travel:—among these Mr. Gladstone, the Chancellor of the Exchequer, and Mr. Sidney Herbert, Secretary of War. The former, but recently twice chosen by the University of Oxford, has exasperated toryism by joining Lord Palmerston, and I am assured by a gentleman just returned from that seat of learning and conservatism that he will be defeated by his competitor the Marquis of Chandos. It will be something odd if circumstances should make it appear that, in his panegyric about two months ago on nomination boroughs, he was under the influence of a prophetic spirit as to his own impending necessities. Herbert is hated for his Romanism (he built a church which for excess of ornamentation illustrates a bad taste run mad) and for being a Peelite.

The expenditures of the government of Lord Derby in military defences are beginning to be denounced, and it is said Mr. Gladstone intends their reduction. This design is connected with the sympathy felt in the Italian cause, more genuine and sincere than that of the preceding ministry, with the greater devotion to the French alliance, and with the perception that the extraordinary armament of England is represented at Paris as a menace to France, while it sets an example of which the continental states avail themselves. Prussia has put on her coat of mail and seems more than half inclined to forbid the allies crossing the Mincio. In taking this step she would undoubtedly place herself at the head of the German Confederation:—but she prudently looks right and left: on the right, for an intimation from Lord Palmerston, and on the left, to note the Muscovite *corps d'armée.* The step once taken, unless Victor Emmanuel and his all-powerful colleague are willing to eat dirt, a thing altogether incredible, the war, like a vast maelstrom, will very rapidly if not instantly suck into its vortex every European nation. I don't think anything can be done to restore peace until both Lombardy and Venetia are independent; aiming at that, the struggle has, in the course of six weeks, sacrificed some fifty thousand lives.

Do you observe that, animated by the republican spirit of our Congress of '89, the Hospodar of Wallachia and Moldavia, Couza, has actually abolished all titles except those descriptive of official duty and authorized by the new Constitution?

The Queen's concert on Wednesday was graced by the presence of the Belgian King and members of his family. The deaf, and loud-talking, Prince Esterhazy was there also. Movements in these elevated circles are just now supposed all to have their meaning. What is the import of his Majesty's? Is it to act as medium between Palmerston and Prussia? Is it to fan the flame of Germanism in this Court? Speculation is rife. Leopold could not withstand the reconstruction of the map of Europe, which a great and authentic literary discovery has proved that even

Charles X. sketched and encouraged, and which Louis Napoleon may be provoked into attempting.

Don't say, "rather dull!"—for my consciousness is so sensitive that, if you do, I shall hear it on this side of the water.

Always faithfully yrs.

---

### No. 279.—TO MR. CASS.

LONDON, July 1, 1859.

MY DEAR SIR,—With equal personal safety and *éclat*, Mr. Cobden has crossed the Atlantic, and Napoleon III. the Mincio:—the former welcomed by troops of eulogizing friends, the latter accompanied by a victorious army.

You will notice the very warm expressions of Mr. Cobden about the kindness he experienced in the United States. They are among his earliest outpourings on landing in Liverpool. *We* could not act otherwise: *he* might have imitated Basil Hall, or Morpeth, or Dickens, or Grattan.

At the Queen's ball the night before last, I met Milner Gibson, Lord Clarence Paget, Monckton Milnes, Charles Villiers, and others of that ilk, whom I was astonished to find ignorant of the advent of Mr. Cobden. Their anxiety was extreme to ascertain whether from what he had said and done, there was a likelihood of his accepting the Board of Trade. They wanted him to do it:—but obviously feared his Roman inflexibility. His decision is yet unknown; and the advice of Mr. Bright may disincline him to the post. The woman who deliberates is lost:—it may be so with the politician, and I rather infer from silence and suspense that Mr. Cobden consents. It is a matter of almost vital importance to the Palmerston-Russell ministry, both of whom met him, ere he landed, with letters of invitation and courtesy.

Mr. Gladstone will be re-elected member for the University. He has been violently shaken, almost toppled over; but he will retain his seat. The election closes this afternoon. Mr. Secretary Cobb, with fellow feeling, will felicitate his brother financier on his good luck in finding the national income better than it was a year ago. The customs, and indeed all the sources of revenue except the income tax, have been very productive.

There is a singular identity of character in the battles in Lombardy. The last, that of Solferino, like those of Palestro, Montibello, and Magenta, can scarcely be said to be a victory for either belligerent: almost a drawn, certainly an inconclusive, though a horribly bloody, fight. The Austrians, under the command of their Emperor, against respectful but urgent remonstrances of General Hess, advanced across the Mincio, 200,000 strong, to meet the coming French and Sardinians, 180,000, and struggling for fifteen hours on a field of fifteen miles in length, with alternations of success and failure, finally retreated unpursued and in order over the river, amid the natural obstacles and terrors of a dark tempestuous deluge. The French Emperor, it is undeniable, exhibited consummate strategetical ability, combined with omnipresent activity and reckless courage. Gossip, not credited, says that one of his epaulettes was shot off by a Tyrolese rifleman.

It is impossible to see one's way through the many complications incident to this war. I think the chances of a general European convulsion, revolutionary as well as merely belligerent, have been largely increased by recent events. At Vienna, I am told by Mr. Villiers, who referred to letters received by his brother, the popular rage and mortification are threatening to explode against the incapacity of the sovereign and his generals. All the French diplomatic and consular agents in Turkey have been mustered at Paris, have received fresh instructions, and have gone back to work up a rebellion against the "sick man" of which the Czar may avail himself. The covert but obvious encouragement given to Kossuth and Klapka, if it do not lead to insurrection in Hungary, can hardly fail to exasperate into action some of the German States, and as sure as any of them crosses the frontier to aid Austria, Bonaparte, now raising 450,000 new levies and thus lifting his forces in and out of France to a figure exceeding a million, will burst like a torrent over the Rhine. Prussia, with all her dignity and composure, secretly dreads this irruption, and is indefatigable to repress the angry spirits of the Confederation:—yet Saxony, through *her* Metternich, Beust, replies to Gortschakoff's warning in a tone plausible and taunting. Rumor, to be sure, brings upon the *tapis* armistices, mediations, concessions:—but clearly the moment for any of these is not yet:—and precipitancy in proposing them would make matters worse, by leading to their scornful and irreparable rejection. Louis Napoleon has deemed it inexpedient to rouse the enmity of the forty thousand Roman Catholic priests in France by countenancing any assault upon the secular dominions or power of the Holy Father:—yet it may be doubted whether the revolutionary patriots of the Peninsula will be satisfied with this forbearance. It must also be remembered, as a fact established historically if not argumentatively, that blood once tasted, the craving for it becomes, as Senator Seward would say, "irrepressible," and that Bonaparte's triumphant conscripts may insist upon no halt until they reach Vienna. Even Professor Espy, though claiming the ability to raise a storm, did not, I believe, pretend to the power of dispelling it.

Mr. Murphy, your representative at the Hague, has just visited me. He accompanies some members of his family to Liverpool to embark them for the United States.

Ex-Speaker Winthrop has reached England, intending to travel, first through the island and then on the Continent.

Always faithfully yrs.

---

## No. 280.—TO MR. CASS.

LONDON, July 8, 1859.

MY DEAR SIR,—I have been anxious to do something which would shew my attention to the joint resolution of Congress on the Tobacco Trade to which your printed circular of the 20th April last applies. The unsettled condition of the ministry suspended everything for a time:—but I had some conversations which led me to think that a change in the duties favorable to our purpose could not be looked for. Suddenly, I notice the newspaper paragraph which is enclosed: the foundation for which may possibly be found real when Mr. Gladstone opens on his budget.

An armistice between the two Imperial fighters seems agreed to, though its duration and terms remain to be fixed by commissioners. I have reason to believe this measure, altogether operating in favor of Italian independence and almost necessarily leading to peace, to be the result of prompt and energetic steps taken by Lord John Russell, backed by the Prussian Regent. If this be so, the new cabinet in Downing Street will have consolidated itself and resumed for England the prestige in Europe so much impaired of late. Yesterday I had the pleasure to dine with her Majesty's principal Secretary of State for Foreign Affairs, and late at night bustled to the *soirée* of the Secretary of the Admiralty, Lord Clarence Paget. I returned from these two excursions of fashionable gaiety with the conclusion mentioned.

It is remarkable how little confidence is expressed by the leading intellects here in the designs of the Emperor Napoleon, whom they nevertheless still call their "great ally." His total want of sincerity and truth, even in his most formal public documents, is regarded, in every theory as to his course, to be a conceded postulate. The dread that he may yet direct his now acknowledged military genius towards this country is almost universal. Lord Lyndhurst, you will have noticed, and Lord Brougham have sounded the alarm in the House of Peers:—and even Mr. Cobden, though he declares that he sees no danger of invasion, bends before the prevailing nervousness, and is willing to double the national debt rather than have a French army for a month in London!

The terrors of the Thames are taking rank with those of Bonaparte. Pestilence is thought to be brewing in its waters. The horrid odors which accompany its returning tide are worse now than during the heats of last summer. Members of Parliament, suffering seriously, are perplexed what to do, for they fear to excite among the wretched classes of this vast population an apprehension of cholera. They are careful what they say upon the subject, and will work hard in order to adjourn soon. The armistice may give a better grace to this purpose.

General Pierce reached London on Tuesday last, the 5th instant, from Brighton, where he had been for several days. He is in excellent health. For the benefit of Mrs. Pierce, who is still very delicate, he has taken lodgings at the village of Norwood, close to the Crystal Palace. He will perhaps remain in England until late in the autumn.

Always faithfully yrs.

---

## No. 281.—TO MR. EVERETT.

LONDON, July 13, 1859.

MY DEAR MR. EVERETT,—Your letter of the 28th ult. reached me the day before yesterday. Its enclosure and accompaniment came safely also. I obtained from Count Bernstorff the exact address, and have sent to Mr. Miller as you desired, the letter for "his Excellency Baron Bunsen, Heidelberg, Grand Duchy of Baden, Germany."

The power of your pen is strongly and delightfully shewn by the eulogy of Thomas Dowse. "Phœbus! what a name to fill the long resounding trump of Fame!" I am a little exercised with the doubt whether you had a conscientious right to set him thus in amber:—and would be greatly pleased to hear, through the medium of Judge Edmonds, whether the modest spirit of the leather-dresser don't shrink from your brilliant casing, and "wonder how the d—— he got there!" Certain humble merits, one likes to see drawn out, and given the fame they were prevented achieving by circumstances. But had Dowse those merits? Was he a practical philanthropist? Was he an ardent patriot? Did he devote a long life to useful public purposes? Is it enough for the immortality you have conferred, that he had selfish though correct tastes, and took delight in books and pictures which he held to, notwithstanding nephews and nieces, until he felt he could keep them no longer, and then passed them to your Historical Society? As an author, does he prove a title to the splendid niche you have worked, by twenty short lines on Franklin, or by paying for a monumental column? He was lame, and no doubt that lameness helped to make him solitary, selfish, and silent:—but how many thousands suffer in this form who nevertheless seek society, love their kind, and charm with sentiment and wit?—which are the worthier? Have you not in fact thrown a handful of pearls—to where they were not claimed and are ill suited? You see, I am jealous that such consummate power of rhetoric should expend itself indifferently upon a Washington or a Dowse.

I shall be happy to welcome you to London, and must beg you not to hesitate a moment to charge me with any commissions or wishes I am able to execute.

Always, my dear sir, sincerely yrs.

---

## No. 282.—TO MR. A. DICKENS.

LONDON, July 15, 1859.

MY DEAR MR. DICKENS,—I got your note of the 1st ultimo, and went straight to enquire the reputation of the auricular professors so full of promise in the advertisement you enclosed. Nothing good could be picked up:—but, finally, the parties in command of countless names, were charged with conspiracy to defraud, before the Recorder, and, after much evidence, were each sent to 18 months' imprisonment. I send you the report of the case.

There is, however, another invention of which I have heard, and to which I shall direct my attention. A lady, by whom I sat at a dinner, observing that my right ear was imperfect, invited me to look into hers; and there I noticed, tightly embedded and scarcely visible, a miniature trumpet. It effectually restored her power to hear, and she employed it whenever she went into society for a limited time. But she had a vague dread of its *modus operandi*. The compression of something like a delicate watch-spring, one end of which kept the tiny instrument in the ear, and the other passed through the hair to the top of the cranium, was sure to produce pain, occasionally violent. She recommended my trying it:—but really her look at the time made me think it better to be content with the good organ *left*. I will, however, search farther, and let you have the result. Nothing would give me more sincere pleasure than being able to send you some relief.

Always faithfully yrs.

## No. 283.—TO MR. CASS.

LONDON, July 15, 1859.

MY DEAR SIR,—The quick incidents of the day are generally thought full of approaching mischief. The peace of the two Emperors, signed at Villafranca on the 11th instant, is not yet clearly comprehended, but every one sees that something *not seen* has rehabilitated Austria in Italy at the very moment she was being extinguished:—every one sees that Sardinia has been coldly thrown her stipulated pound of flesh without a drop of blood in it:—every one sees that the despotic principle rejoices in an overshadowing triumvirate:—every one sees that the movements of Prussia and the press of England are already in the crucible to produce the amalgam of another war:—every one sees that the eagles which flew across the Alps can as rapidly perch upon the hills around Cherbourg:—every one sees that the abrupt abandonment of one programme necessitates the annunciation of a second still more exciting and acceptable:—in fine, every one sees, or thinks he sees, a huge finger, or an air-drawn dagger, over the "Invalides," pointing to the chalky cliffs of perfidious Albion. There are not wanting those who already give up the struggle, who deem successful resistance impossible, and who would rather propitiate than exasperate the invader. One public and forcible writer recommends an immediate appeal to the liberty-loving and arms-wielding citizens of the United States! All this springs from exaggerated alarm: an alarm to which the recent shifts of Imperial policy lend the character of patriotism.

Napoleon is looked for in Paris to-day. Some have fancifully thought that neither his own army, nor the revolutionists, nor the corps of Garibaldi would suffer him to quit Italy alive. He comes without his soldiers, and postpones an ovation until they arrive to participate in it.

I have written several rather lengthy notes to enquiring consular functionaries on the rights and duties of neutrality. The trouble might have been saved, for the present at least. As the newspapers report you to be engaged on a comprehensive manifesto of the kind, I hope you will have finished it before you hear of the peace.

Pray notice the denunciations passed by Lord Brougham and other anti-slavers upon the horrors and infamies of the Coolie trade. Poor Jamaica! she can't be allowed labor, black or white.

Always faithfully yrs.

---

## No. 284.—TO MONCKTON MILNES, M. P.

LONDON, July 28, 1859.

MY DEAR SIR,—The subject of your note of the 25th instant has, for many years, engaged the attention of my predecessors and myself. I have meditated sending you the dead fruits of our efforts:—hence my delay in answering:—but I find that doing so would involve too much copying either for the short time you have left me or for your patience.

If, as an M. P. you have access to the pigeon-holes of the Foreign Office, you can perhaps come across a long letter addressed by Mr. Buchanan to Lord Clarendon, on the 1st March, 1855. This letter was the epilogue of many conferences. It offers *three* articles for consideration, the *third* of which was intended to remedy the practices of which the Pamphlet "*Unpunished Cruelties*" so justly and persuasively complains, and the mode of cure was precisely the enlargement of consular jurisdiction you suggest.

The project failed, and my efforts to revive it have been fruitless:—much, I believe, against the personal leanings of Lord Clarendon, but under authoritative opinions from Law Officers of the Crown, who saw something in the arrangement incompatible with fundamentals. Certainly, a good deal of novelty and machinery may be seen, which, according to the constitutions and laws of both countries, can only be vindicated on the maxim, *consensus tollit errorem*.

Possibly a Parliamentary Resolution (if that be in order) recommending a Consular Convention with the United States, to arrest these mischiefs and others of a kindred character, might embolden the ministry to make the experiment even under the frowns of the lawyers. I believe it would work practically well.

Faithfully yrs.

---

## No. 285.—TO MR. CASS.

LONDON, July 29, 1859.

MY DEAR SIR,—One life is not much, and yet sometimes, though far from protracted, it witnesses, in its course, really wonderful progress. When I started, men of taste were not very laudatory in front of paintings by Copley, Trumbull, West, and Stewart. To be sure, we praised, because we had no idea of not being patriotic even more than critical, and, perhaps, because we knew no better. Well! God bless the aspiring genius of my countrymen, we are already at the head of sculpture, and here comes "*The Heart of the Andes*," to challenge competition from any century of old Europe. The chief dilettanti, Lord Lansdowne, considers it an unequalled *picture*, and Lord Stanley, who has travelled these Cordilleras, pronounces it a faithful *portrait*. No landscape was ever yet put on canvas more absorbing, more rich in varieties of beauty, or more true to nature. I wish it were of our Rocky Mountains! *N'importe*, it hails from the easel of "Church, of New York."

It seems possible to delineate the heart of the Andes, but who will undertake to map out that of Louis Napoleon? What is really in contemplation, at present, as to the future, no man ventures to assert. There are reticences which cannot be dragged forth, depths unfathomable, darkness impenetrable:—or it may be, that drifting on the current of events, and watchful only for the approved opportunity, the avenger of Waterloo calmly bides his time. At Zurich, the peace will be given definite shape. Will it be followed by a European Congress? What for? Simply to do what was left undone at Paris in 1856, to soothe the seething cauldron of revolution in Italy? Lord John Russell, in his speech last night on foreign affairs, threw but a faint light athwart the gloom. He was cautious almost to cowardice. Remark, however, that apparently without intending it, he developed the *ruse* to which, at Villafranca, Francis Joseph became dupe:—conclusively shewing that the draft of terms of mediation and peace, shewn as if agreed upon by Prussia, England, and Russia, and which he has characterized as worse on the part of his "natural allies" than those of his conqueror, was concocted in the bureau of Count Walewski, never assented to here or at Berlin, and was therefore most deceptively used by Napoleon in the interview with his brother Emperor. If there be a Congress—resisted only by Austria—England will hardly withhold her presence:—for though she has nothing to do with the points to be adjusted, and is choice in praise of non-intervention, yet Lord John (for such is the pith of his address in the Commons) has read and felt the "melancholy chaunts" of Petrarch and Leopardi! How capital this in a parliamentary leader!

Bonaparte has determined that his armaments, both on land and sea, shall be "*remises sur le pied de la paix*," and Great Britain breathes "freer and deeper." His *pied de la paix* is probably what it was when he told Austria the same thing just before he threw 150,000 men across the Alps. It is, however, extremely annoying to be in constant panic; and so a prodigious effort will be made here to restore the public equanimity, on the basis of this most oracular and illusory phrase in the *Moniteur*. The alarm has certainly been universal and excessive. Lord Lyndhurst exhibited its extent when he forcibly inculcated "distrust, distrust, distrust." How, indeed, is it possible for a manufacturing and trading people, who are not familiar with the use of arms and who cannot muster a force of 100,000 men, to banish "distrust" when they see but thirty miles off, under the absolute control of a victorious avenger, a standing and irresistible army, with numerous steam transports ready to annihilate the distance in three hours? Ay, but the Channel fleet!—unfortunately nobody knows where it is, and everybody knows that it is not ubiquitous.

I have had on hand lately many of my distinguished fellow-citizens. Mr. Seward, Mr. Sumner, Mr. Motley, General Pierce, Mr. Winthrop, and lots of others whom it has afforded equal pride and pleasure to welcome to my diplomatic domain. They scatter, however, rapidly:—some to the attractive mountains of Switzerland:—some to the capital or "vine-covered hills and gay regions of France:"—some to the Scotch and Irish lakes:—some nestle in the Isle of Wight:—and some take a long sight for the Pyramids, the Holy Sepulchre, or the Acropolis. Anywhere and quick, rather than remain breathing the unusually hot malaria of London, and the pestiferous effluvia of the Thames. Parliament will, I think, soon follow this rational example. Though the day of adjournment be not yet fixed, many members assure me that the session cannot be protracted beyond the 18th proximo.

The committees of the House have been laying bare the corruptions of the last election. Bribery in every shape, bold and unblushing. Employments secured, public offices promised, executions paid, and golden sovereigns openly laid upon tables to be picked up by voters! A more scandalous exhibition cannot be imagined. A contest costs, in this utterly shameless way, not less than thirty thousand dollars, to the victor. One of the unseated gentlemen is ———, who married an heiress, and who "bled" profusely to attain "position." The thing is so little regarded that when, on the evening his election was declared null, I met him at Mr. Sidney Herbert's, he was full of fun about it, and smiling sympathies passed current through the company. When matters come to this point, which are we to prefer, the universal suffrage under Napoleonic surveillance by Prefects, or English limited suffrage gorged with golden baits?

We are promised, in the newspapers, visits from the three Emperors in the course of the summer. I have no idea that the promises are more than "canards."

Always faithfully yrs.

---

## No. 286.—TO MR. CASS.

LONDON, August 5, 1859.

MY DEAR SIR,—It seems agreed, that at the last election, both political parties, Conservative and Liberal, thrust their arms to the elbows into the depths of bribery. The expositions made before scrutinizing committees of the direct and open use of money amount almost to the burlesque. In his fierce indignation, Mr. Roebuck drags the case of a member for Bodman before the House this afternoon. Now, this gentleman occupies a half-way house between Whigs and Tories, and fairly represents both:—is a scholar, author, and old legislator:—yet is he personally picked out and denounced for undeniable corruption! He is striving to escape the *éclat* by a compromise with his assailant and by accepting the Chiltern Hundreds:—but Mr. Gladstone claims this myth as the only sphere of patronage attached to the Chancellorship of the Exchequer, and denies him the sanctuary unless he first plausibly explains. Let us see whether the onslaught of Mr. Roebuck be not something of a feint, intended to subside into a fizzle.

Opportunities of personal intercourse with Lord John Russell occur just now less frequently, owing to the death of his father-in-law, the Earl of Minto, a few days ago, in his 78th year.

We are expecting an inundation of Russian Imperial visitors. The Czar himself was supposed coming, but that is given up. The Grand Duke Constantine is hourly looked for, and was thought to have reached Osborne last Sunday merely because a sudden convocation of ministers at that royal residence was noticed. The Grand Duchess Maria, whom I saw married to Maximilian the Prince of Leuchtenberg in July, 1839,* and who, having

* DIARY: *July* 14, 1839, *Sunday.*—"Went to the Winter Palace, agreeably to invitations, to witness the marriage of the Grand Duchess Maria and Prince Maximilian of Leuchtenberg. Julia, Elizabeth, and Sophia, having obtained tickets of admission through the kind activity of the French Ambassadress (Madame de Barante), were escorted by Madame Daschkoff to a window gallery in the Chapel which overlooked the ceremony. The foreign ministers and their ladies, after waiting with the general company for some time, were shewn by Count Woronzoff into the Chapel and arranged on the two sides nearest to the chancel, forming an alley for the Imperial cortége. Among us were interspersed Count Nesselrode, General Count Woronzoff, Governor of Odessa, Count Orloff, Count Platen (Russian Ambassador of Paris), the Marquess of Anglesea and his three sons, Count Levaschoff, Count Cancrine, Count Tschernyschew, etc., etc., etc. We noticed that two pairs of pigeons entered at the open windows, and alighted, after flying round the dome, over the altar:—an incident that may have been accidental, but which many conceived to have been prearranged. The Metropolitan and a concourse of twenty or thirty Priests, robed in rich vestments of crimson thickly crossed with

lost her husband some seven years ago, lost it is said also by a subsequent *mésalliance* her caste, has found her way to Torquay with a miniature Court or *entourage* of some six or seven. She is represented as rivalling, in the arts of diplomatic intrigue, the late Princess Lieven:—Is that a *rôle* to be played now and here? *Quien sabe?*

I hope you will specially authorize me to meet at once any proposition for a Consular Convention which this government may make in consequence of the motion of Mr. Milnes in the House of Commons, explained in my official despatch of to-day. There are other points of great practical interest beside the "unpunished cruelties" to be attended to. You will find these detailed in the admirable draft of a treaty submitted by Mr. Buchanan in 1855 and the correspondence connected with it. The obstacle encountered at that time may possibly be now kept out of view: especially if you should instruct me to say that a total suppression of that obstacle, and the full attainment of the arrest of merchant-seamen deserters, are *sine qua nons* to any arrangement whatever. The humani-

---

gold embroidery, and with mitres glittering with jewels and enamel pictures—some bearing the sacred images and others carrying wax lights—stationed themselves at the grand entrance to receive the Imperial party. Everybody wore their richest clothing:—all the ladies having long trains, and all, except the diplomatic ones, having the Kakoshinnick brilliantly studded with diamonds, or otherwise ornamented. The bride wore a superb diadem of diamonds and on the very top of her head a crown of the same description. Her train was an immense one of crimson velvet deeply bordered with ermine. Of the religious ceremonies I could understand nothing:—they were exceedingly tedious. There was an interchange of rings between the bride and groom effected through the agency of the Metropolitan: they sipped the consecrated wine from the same golden goblet: and during a part of the proceeding, for about twenty minutes while the Metropolitan was reading to them, golden crowns were held over the heads of the couple—over that of the Grand Duchess by her brother the Hereditary Grand Duke Alexander, and over that of the Prince by Count Pahlen. At one time the couple were led, with their hands united by the Metropolitan, three times round the altar. At the close of the ceremony, the groom handed his bride to the Emperor, who bade him embrace her, and then followed the family felicitations and kissing. The Court choir performed the great Te Deum most effectively, and the cannon of the Fortress, aided by peals from all the huge bells of the innumerable churches, sent forth a deafening yet exhilarating uproar. After kissing a number of the Priests in succession, the Imperial circle left the Greek Chapel and went to where a temporary Roman Catholic Chapel had been constructed in some interior apartment, and the marriage ceremony was repeated. We got home as expeditiously as we could at about 4 o'clock."

tarian zeal which in a case of black and white discriminates in favor of the former, may accept compensation founded on the prevention of "unpunished cruelties."

Parliament may drag its slow length along for another week.

Always faithfully yrs.

---

## No. 287.—TO COL. MURRAY.

LONDON, August 5, 1859.

MY DEAR COLONEL MURRAY,—Your letter of the 1st June, enclosing one from Mrs. —— and another addressed to the Queen, has reached me.

Instinct makes me always anxious to do what any lady seriously desires me to do. Independent, therefore, of some misplaced suggestions made by your fair friend, it would and will give me pleasure to accomplish her object, if I discover a mode of doing it compatible with fundamental rules. At this Court, it is much easier to manage an important national negotiation than to break through the gossamery fencework with which aristocratic exclusiveness has hedged in the sovereign. I would personally prefer entering upon a complicated question of peace or war, to manœuvring for the mere autograph of her Majesty. The request, no matter how meritorious its purpose, involves considerations of extreme delicacy:—its gratification would set a precedent of which millions would be eager to avail themselves:—the sale of the signature might be a mortifying one:—and the danger of its misapplication by an unknown purchaser is not slight.

Besides this, Mrs. —— has transmitted the letter to the Queen *sealed*, and has not sent me a copy of it. I cannot break the seal, have no certainty of its precise character, and am therefore without the means of giving to an intermediary officer of the government or of the Court the indispensable knowledge of what it is he is conveying to her Majesty.

You will do me a favor by explaining to Mr. S. and to Mrs. —— the embarrassments I feel:—assuring them at the same time that my disposition to meet their wish is sincere and will be watchful.

Always faithfully yrs.

---

## No. 288.—TO MR. CASS.

LONDON, August 19, 1859.

MY DEAR SIR,—The Queen goes to Scotland in the course of three or four days: and, as her Majesty must be accompanied by one or the other of the Secretaries of State, she takes with her on the present occasion our "*chef*," Lord John Russell. He has engaged a house in the vicinity of Balmoral, and may remain resident there for five or six weeks. I am almost the only member of the diplomatic corps who may possibly miss him, my colleagues having diverged from London to all quarters of the compass.

Louis Napoleon has certainly the art of concentrating upon himself the universal gaze. No one else in Europe is just now visible, and everybody intently watches each successive movement. He is another Blondin, whose figure is strongly delineated on the sky, advancing steadily upon a tight rope, over a boiling and unfathomable abyss. At this moment, he is doing the graceful. One decree amnesties all political prisoners under sentence or "*proscrits:*"—this opens France to about two thousand of her ejected sons, among them Changarnier, Louis Blanc, and Victor Hugo. Another fiat enjoins the promptest execution of the amnesty in all the colonies, to be hailed with rapture at Cayenne. And a third launches a ray of promise at the press, by nullifying all the warnings that have been given. At his recent fête the clap-traps were innumerable and irresistible. The speech to the banqueting generals was short, frank, and soothing. Victory seems to have given him confidence, and confidence brings into play the generosity of his nature. Or, is it purely the attitudinizing of a skilful acrobat?—So thinks Louis Blanc.

Mr. Cobden's two addresses to his constituents of Rochdale maintained in undiminished solidity his past reputation. I presume I was the only foreign minister invited by the Committee to his *soirée;* and it would have given me peculiar pleasure to attend. As, however, I am scrupulous of participating in party politics here, it was without regret that I found myself obliged to be elsewhere. Everybody praised these speeches, their force, originality and tone. His explanation of his refusal to enter the ministry is at once so manly and conciliatory that many regard it as a sort of pledge to take the place offered, some six months or a year hence. According to conventional ideas in England, he is too strong a man on the Liberal side to be allowed to remain out of the government.

The Great Eastern (she has resumed her original name, because positively destined to ply between this and Australia), after trying the suppleness of her joints by an experimental trip, will, on 15th of September next, bridge the ocean between the two Portlands, Portland in Dorsetshire and Portland in Maine. She is open to passengers, and Sir Henry Holland and I have calculated that she may accomplish the transit in five days. What if she do! an Atlantic voyage in 120 hours!

Always faithfully yrs.

---

## No. 289.—TO SENATOR G. W. JONES, BOGOTA.

LONDON, August 27, 1859.

MY DEAR SIR,—Immediately on the receipt of your letter, I took the necessary steps to enable you to have by return packet, the *Daily Times* and the *Illustrated News*. It is to be hoped therefore that you will get them at the time you get this. The subscription, as you directed, was made for one year: and finding payment in advance indispensable, rather than allow you to be disappointed I sent the money. Copies of the papers are enclosed.

The real state of things in Europe is never what it superficially appears to be. The press is wise to a certain extent, and is always striving to seem wiser:—but the select few who wield the powers of nations cover their designs in impenetrable mystery, which is only broken by sudden action. Hence it is dangerous to speculate as you wish me to. The Zurich Conference proceeds slowly:—it is scarcely across the threshold. A Congress is yet uncertain, though more likely than it was a month ago. The Peace of Villafranca adds nothing to the security of this country; far, very far otherwise. She steadily advances in armament and apprehension:—so much so, that she is hazarding her polity by training her yeomanry to the use of the rifle.

I am just now on a visit to Brighton, whose attractions are too great for much letter-writing.

Always faithfully yrs.

---

## No. 290.—TO MR. GILPIN.

BRIGHTON, August 29, 1859.

MY DEAR MR. GILPIN,—The manner in which I have had your silence accounted for worries me a good deal. I am told that you are not well, and have been ailing for some time. If this be mistaken rumor, pray let me hear so, as soon as you can and as shortly as you please.

London is a horrid hole in hot seasons. The Thames, the Serpentine, the sewers, the crowd, the dust, are all horrid. So, we have escaped, and taken a house here for a month:—close to the sea on the Marine Parade, with a balcony whence we look across the Atlantic up to the corner of Spruce and 11th Streets. I must have been made sensitive to atmospherical conditions by continued stay in the murky Babylon sixty miles off, for I never before noticed such purity and perfection of air as we are breathing. Merely to inhale it seems to satisfy us all:—and, although nearly a week since we came, we have felt no inclination to *do* the sights of the city, beyond the Cliff, the Pavilion, and the Pier. As to company, catch us at it!

I can't get a word from home about politics, although really feeling my habitual interest in the customary tangle. The democratic embroglio seems to be eschewed as a disagreeable topic, which one's friends erroneously suppose I can't want to hear about. Don't they know that distance blends and softens coloring? What seems to shock them, as for instance Wise's letter to Donnelly, creates with me only a smile at its *naïveté!* Mr. Everett sent me that little epistle, as if he regarded it as almost the crack of our doom: I read it, and, strange to say, laughed at so characteristic a specimen of eccentricity at full gallop.

But if people won't indite politics to me, how dare I venture on politics to them? Simply because what is exotic is relished in every locality. Well! Europe is lulling at this moment. Crowns are perplexed by efforts to rectify the blunders they have been committing. They can't bear to be sneered at for incompetency and rashness, and so they hugger-mugger at Zurich to put things to rights. Will they succeed? Yes, if Plon-Plon be planted in Tuscany:—yes, if the so-called Italian Washington, Garibaldi, be strong enough to inaugurate the Confederation and upset the Pope:—yes, if the Iron Crown, filched from Milan and locked up in Vienna, be sent in a satin reticule worked with golden bees, to the Charlemagne bathing at St. Sauveur:—yes, if Victor Emmanuel, dropping the victor and assuming the chafferer, will agree to pay more gold than his people have yet paid blood, for Lombardy:—and finally, which ought to be firstly, yes, if Lord Palmerston will consent, which he won't, to a Congress without his condition precedent. Otherwise no, no, no.

Something like a squadron of cavalry has just gone by, —here on the brink of the ocean!—with carbines under arm!! Take that as an indication of the "English Craze" at present raging about invasion and armament. They can't sleep quietly for Cherbourg, looking as if ready to vent itself in this direction, or Lille, looking as if ready to brush away our Uncle Leopold.

General respects and regards to Mrs. G.

Always faithfully yrs.

## No. 291.—TO MR. CASS.

BRIGHTON, September 1, 1859.

MY DEAR SIR,—You must not suppose me slow or dull as to the main topic of the despatch to-day. I think of nothing else, feel all the urgency of the case, and will omit nothing. If professions mean anything, an abundance of steam has been let on to accelerate the engine in reaching every one of the stations in quick succession—all, in the course of two or three months. But, while from this point a brisk readiness may shew itself, there can certainly be nothing expected from the Isthmus but delay, prevarication, and petulance. Without fancying to exist a profligate disregard of good faith and truth, the fault is not here, but there.

Her Majesty took with her to Balmoral, the day before yesterday, as the Secretary of State "in waiting," *not* Lord John Russell, but Sir George Grey. This change of programme was simultaneous with a sudden summons addressed to all the scattered cabinet for a meeting in Downing Street: — and they came rattling from every quarter of the compass. As Polonius would say, put that and that together and it may not be difficult to surmise that "something's in the wind." What that something may really be; whether the belligerent aspect of an increase of French force at Lille, designed to overawe and prevent the Belgic fortifications at Antwerp, or the emergency created by the determination of a large body of English soldiers not to re-enlist but to return home from India, or the new aspect of the Napoleonic policy as regards the banished dukes in Italy, or the still meditated Congress, nobody can tell. The Conference at Zurich engages little attention:—seeming to divide its time between apoplexy (Count Colloredo) and waiting for instructions.

Have you ever been at Brighton? I am here for several weeks, owing to the adoption of some new system of drainage in London which imposes the necessity of repulsive repairs in my quarters. The rapidity of travel on the railway here, the regular express train darting at the rate of sixty miles an hour, puts me as near to the Foreign

Office as Mr. Bodisco or Mr. Crampton was to the Department of State, when residing on the hills of Georgetown. Judged by difference of atmosphere, however, I am a thousand leagues away:—a boundless sea, a dazzling sky, a clear, pure, and bracing air, and endless lines of white palaces surmounting chalky cliffs; such are the features of Brighton.

Always faithfully yrs.

P.S.—By a memorandum just received, I find that the presence of Sir George Grey with the Queen during her journey to Scotland misled me, when I concluded that he had been substituted for Lord John Russell. The Foreign Secretary, with his family, left London two days ago for Abergeldie Castle, assigned by her Majesty as their residence while she remains at Balmoral. Before his lordship's return, ample time will elapse to enable me to hear again from you as to Wyke and Central America.

---

## No. 292.—TO PROFESSOR BACHE.

BRIGHTON, September 5, 1859.

MY DEAR PROFESSOR,—Your note, accompanied by the letter of Mr. G. W. Blunt respecting Lights on the Bahamas, reached me a day or two ago. I have been here ten days, and intend staying two weeks more, in order to enable my landlord to make some offensive repairs as to drainage and painting. I mention this to explain why, at a distance from records, I don't give, in what I am going to say, exact dates and results.

By enquiry at the Treasury Department you will be able to obtain full information as to the extent to which this government deems it expedient to go in constructing Light-houses on the Bahama Islands. And should additional ones be called for, you will find the course heretofore taken to have been this:—Mr. Guthrie during the summer of '56 wrote to me to see whether I could get more Lights put up by the government, and if not, whether I could induce them to authorize the United States to build them. I begged him to furnish me with the evidence upon which he thought the Lights necessary and at what points. He sent me a Report from the Light-house Board, and a very admirable and large manuscript chart: on the strength of these, I went to work. After transmitting all the ideas and explanations in my power in writing, I had several conversations with Lord Stanley of Alderley, and other members of the Board of Trade, on the subject. If I remember aright, they took a long time to deliberate, and finally they expressed to me, through the Foreign Office, the opinion that the Lights already up were sufficient, and that those suggested by our Board could really be of no aid to navigation. All this will, I take for granted, be on file in the Treasury Department:—certainly, my correspondence with Governor Marcy cannot but indicate every step taken.

If a renewed effort be thought expedient, let it begin by such measures in the Light-house Board as will develope the positive want; then a representation to Mr. Cobb; then an application by him to the Secretary of State requesting him to direct my exertions to the attainment of the desired objects.

Always faithfully yrs.

---

## No. 293.—TO MR. CASS.

LONDON, September 15, 1859.

MY DEAR SIR,—It would seem that on this side of the Atlantic we are about entering upon a fresh score of important public events.

1. The tangled condition of the Italian question is already regarded as incapable of solution except by the sword. Since the *Moniteur* avowed Napoleon's altered attitude as to the Duchies, nothing but hasty belligerent action by either the French or Austrian forces lingering in Lombardy, is looked for as a result of the Imperial conjunction at Arenenberg. A step not the less willingly made, perhaps, because it slightly promises to draw this government out of their entrenchment of neutrality and non-intervention.

2. The attempt of the allied fleet in China to *force* a

pathway to Pekin for their ambassadors has been unexpectedly baffled by an army of Mongols at the Taku forts. Four hundred and seventy-eight of the peremptory assailants were killed and wounded, among them sixteen officers, including the British Admiral (Hope) and two captains. Three vessels of war were sunk, and the squadron retreated to Shanghai! Of course this news, which reached here by telegram from the secretary of the British minister in China, via Constantinople and Alexandria, on the 12th instant, has caused great solicitude and excitement. The feeling is none the less sharp because the story goes that our envoy, Mr. Ward, politely characterized as the "*submissive republican*," has quietly found his way to the capital and been cordially welcomed. I think Mr. Reed foresaw the likelihood of these events, as consequences of too harsh and dictatorial a manner. The fiery cross is, of course, rapidly circulating, and the croaking ravens of the press all "bellow for revenge." Observe, that the Chinese objected, not to the ambassadors, but to their naval and military escort; a distinction *with* great difference.

3. The aspect of India too is inauspicious and sullen. Financial matters get worse and worse. The English soldiers in Bengal, to the number of eight or ten thousand, disregarding the remonstrances of Lord Clyde, insist upon discharge, and are returning home. Rebels are still on foot, fighting the Sikhs in Nepaul. It is curious as a political coincidence, that just at this moment an emissary, M. de Sercy (was he not once in Washington?), of the devoted ally, has come back from a thorough exploration of Hindostan, and has officially reported to his superior, Count Walewski, that everything there threatens confusion and ruin!

Our friends in Portland, remembering the "frantic follies" incident to the landing of the western end of the Atlantic Cable, must be cautious in preparing a glorification on the coming of the Great Eastern. Her progress down the Channel was partially interrupted, opposite the town of Hastings, by the tremendous and murderous explosion of one of her water-funnels, killing by scalding some seven or eight of her engineers, and, without seriously affecting the body of the huge vessel, knocking saloons and staterooms into such pi as must occasion a month or more's delay for repair. The stock of the company has gone up because the ship didn't go down:—a strong illustration of how to make the best of a bad bargain.

Lord John Russell continues in Scotland, and may not be in Downing Street for a month to come.

You have noticed that Hospodar Couza has been permitted by the Conference at Paris to retain his two political brides, Moldavia and Wallachia, provided he keeps them apart from one another. The federative principle is making its way.

In Russia, the generous Czar is countenancing the creation of elective municipalities, with powers of local government.

Always faithfully yrs.

---

## No. 294.—TO MR. CASS.

LONDON, September 23, 1859.

MY DEAR SIR,—The Sentinel aloft must have smiled at the superfluous philanthropy which wasted our blood and treasure in searching for Sir John Franklin. He and his associates were all dead before we resolved to share in the scientific honor of restoring them to their country. The officer sent out by Lady Franklin in the screw vessel the Fox, F. L. McClintock, has returned with manuscripts and relics, found in the undisturbed desolation of Arctic cold, which disclose the sad secret. The gallant explorer perished more than twelve years ago, on the 11th of June, 1847. The details of this successful discovery are exceedingly interesting, minute, and authentic.

Public sentiment is somewhat inflamed by the imperfect accounts we have received of General Harney's proceeding at the islet of San Juan, and the prospect of collision arising out of Governor Douglas', so-called, prompt and judicious course to substitute the Royal standard for the Stars and Stripes. The provincial chief in the far northwest seems to have taken a leaf out of the book of Admiral Hope in the extreme east, and, without asking explanations or purposes, resolves to cut the matter short by Sappers and Miners. It is possible that the General may have been precipitate, and, if so, the Governor should have abstained from following a bad example. Public agents, except in cases of necessity, should await their cue from their superiors, and not, defensively or offensively, assume to involve two nations in war. Patience is a great power, and never fails to strengthen the party that exercises it.

General Duff Green was kind enough, on reaching England, to run down to Brighton, and to place in my hands his several commendatory credentials. I detained him to dinner, and we were all much gratified with his flourishing accounts of the Washington Panorama. I am yet a little at fault in forming a practical conception of what he aims at by his visit, if it be more than to obtain the co-operation of capitalists in building his projected railway across Texas. His views as to the political relations of the United States, England, and Mexico, are broad, comprehensive, and sound: and as he naturally likes to inculcate them, he shall have all the opportunities among the public men here I can fairly give him. At the moment, however, in the slang phrase, nobody is in London, and that nobody will be in London for some weeks to come.

Two ninety-two gun steamers have been ordered by the Admiralty to prepare for sea: probably as members of the contemplated Anglo-Gallican expedition to revisit the Taku forts at the mouth of the Peiho:—possibly, to see how the Sappers and Miners get on in San Juan.

Zurich still fizzles slowly. Arenenberg postponed. A Congress getting put aside, the loadstone is at Biarritz, and thither diplomats of all sorts are thronging from every European Court. The Belgian monarch returns from the Imperial hug, with the conviction that he has bagged an Italian kingdom for his younger son. Æsop's Lion holding his levee is magnificently revived, with a new corps of performers and fresh decorations.

Always faithfully yrs.

## No. 295.—TO MR. CASS.

LONDON, September 30, 1859.

MY DEAR SIR,—Governor Douglas of Vancouver has sent to London an explanatory and accusatory messenger, Col. J. S. Hawkins. This "gallant" officer, who reached here on the 27th instant, went straight to the Foreign Office and "transacted business." A systematic effort to place General Harney in the category of "American filibusters" and to put our government in the wrong as to the channel or Canal de Haro, is of course just now the outburst of newspaper loyalty and patriotism. In deploying the argument there is manifest ignorance or misrepresentation:—take as illustration that they say.

1. We never made claim till gold was found on Frazer's River!—a naked untruth.

2. The island is of no use to us!—yet it lies south of 49° and fronts our coast its whole length.

3. It is in the track of British intercourse with Vancouver! not unless that intercourse pass through admitted American territory.

4. Starting from a point on the 49th degree, we can't reach the Canal de Haro by sailing "southerly" as the treaty directs!—most assuredly we can:—"southerly" is not equivalent to "due south," but on the contrary implies a partial admixture of easting or westing: and it is obvious to inspection that to proceed from the given point to Rosario Strait much more easting has to be taken than need be taken of westing to get to the Canal de Haro.

5. At the date of the treaty, no "Channel" navigated or known, but that of Rosario! Untrue again:—the name Haro is itself disproof given by one of its oldest and earliest, if not its very first, navigator.

I hope General Harney will disclose good cause for his proceeding:—for if he do, San Juan is too clearly ours to be allowed again to go adrift.

Lord John Russell, though a veteran and able statesman, has perhaps rarely if ever visited Scotland before the present season:—for he has just been admitted to the Freedom of the City of Aberdeen.

General Green is now, as always, sanguine of success in

his projects: what they are exactly I do not know. He has seen and indoctrinated Mr. Cobden and others of that ilk: and your letter emboldened me to give him personal notes of introduction to Lords Palmerston and John Russell. He talks of returning to you by the steamer of the 8th of October, but he will probably wait for the 15th.

Regimentals are your only wear for Europe. The tendency to enlarge military establishments, as *sine qua nons* of safety, is shewing itself almost everywhere among the minor States of Germany. The Continent, with unimportant exceptions, is covered with an agglomeration of camps. "Poor human nature!" sighed Jacob Faithful.

Nothing more burlesque than the laborious idleness and unproductiveness of the "three men of Gotham who went to sea in a bowl" at Zurich! They are about to make six bows to each other, and leave the future to a Congress which won't meet. Some gloomy quidnuncs anticipate an Austrian movement in Italy to restore the Dukes; Napoleon leaving the struggle to Victor Emmanuel and Garibaldi. The whole conduct of Central Italy has been so admirable that Lord John Russell openly avowed at Edinburgh that the ministry were with it. Perhaps a compromise upon King Plon-Plon, with indemnity to the excluded princes, may be the destination to which public opinion is agreed to be led.

The press looks at last in France fierce and nearly unanimous for law and legal trial against administrative caprice in warning and controlling its utterances. The minister, Duc de Padoue, or as he has been nicknamed, the Duke of Padlock, provoked great excitement by his measures; and now there are grave thinkers on this side of the Channel who predict that Bonaparte will soon follow in the footsteps of Charles the Tenth and Louis Philippe! Tell that to the marines. A devoted army of four hundred thousand men, with a great name at their head, just reburnished by Magenta and Solferino, are not readily put to flight by printer's blacking balls and types. There must be subsisting discontent to work upon.

The Turks say that Schamyl was bought not beaten, that gold corrupted all his followers, except the few with whom he took refuge in Gounib, a fortress which was esteemed to be impregnable. He bore himself sternly when captured:—was a bigoted Mohammedan fatalist: indulged in pretensions to supernatural colloquies with the Prophet:—he was brave, patriotic, and national, sometimes cruel:—how will he fare in St. Petersburg?—probably better than the prisoner of St. Helena.

Mr. Ward has found his way to Pekin, though after a fashion somewhat comical. It may be that what appears to us ludicrous and derogatory was esteemed by the Celestial masters of ceremonies as the *ne plus ultra* of civility and etiquette to which they could go compatibly with their usages. Even the western barbarians would regard it as an act of unusual courtesy if an arriving envoy were facilitated to the seat of government by an express train or a coach and four, with an escort of purveyors, cooks, and valets. The floating or oxen-dragged chamber of the Chinese looks like their substitute for all this. I very much doubt its being meant as rude insolence. Very possibly French and English editors will so represent it:—but they are naturally nettled at Mr. Ward's success, and would not be unwilling to provoke us into joining the new military enterprise for vengeance. I send a slip of what the Paris *Pays* reports upon the subject.

Your highly recommended friend the ship builder, Daniel McKay, has been warmly welcomed here. It gave me pleasure to obtain for him from the Admiralty (as I immediately did notwithstanding Lord John Russell's absence) the run of the dock-yards and naval establishments.

Always faithfully yrs.

---

## No. 296.—TO MR. CASS.

London, October 14, 1859.

My dear Sir,—The Sovereigns of the French returned to their capital from Biarritz and Bordeaux late in the evening of the day before yesterday. In adverting to Italy's future he still restricts his speech to dubious oracular utterances. It would seem as if these and the long-drawn-out futilities at Zurich owe their origin to a reactionary policy, which for its excuse wants and waits such outbreaks as butchered Colonel Aviti at Parma.

The Imperial reply to the Archbishop is double: devotion to the Pope, and his abandonment by the withdrawal of French forces from Rome:—two pills, one opiate and soothing, the other inflammatory and alterative. *On dit* that a huge bolus is compounding for Victor Emmanuel in the form of a summons to foot the bill of his kinsman and ally for the expenses of the recent war:—say 250,000,000 of francs: — and this, it is expected, will eventuate in a compulsory compromise ceding Savoy.

The Local Science Association—not socialists, remember, oh! by no means—are mimicking the Institute this year at Bradford, in the West Riding of York. Lord Shaftesbury presides, recapitulates, and preaches: Lord Brougham thunders in ferocious eloquence against Bribery and Bonaparte: and there is a perfect flood of philosophers, each holding in his hand a homœopathic dose of science which he complacently regards as a panacea for some one or other of life's evils. Onward, gentlemen! the Augean stable is large and crammed with filth, but each of your countless crowd is a self-esteemed Hercules! *Eurèka, Eurèka!* Victor Hugo's new poem, at present in two, but designed hereafter to be extended six octavos more, "*La Légende des Siècles,*" has prophesied the end of all this labor after perfection, and says that man *must* invade the skies through clouds and stars!—certainly, and the Association, during its short existence of three years, has already ballooned us into the former.

Some strange, discredited but adhesive, rumors are just now afloat, chilling the funds somewhat. Rome has risen into revolution:—how can that be while Guyon is still there? The French and English squadrons off Morocco have had a conflict:—all circumstances considered, *se non è vero, è ben trovato.* Baron de Bourqueney has gone off from Zurich in a laugh:—very natural, therefore likely to be true.

I am afraid that our lively countrymen at Portland will not have a chance this year to hail the Leviathan's advent. Little annoying accidents succeed each other almost as often as the monster moves; and there appears to be in the hold of the big ship, as in the Christian Church, an irreconcilable conflict between fate and free will, which disturbs her management. She has had her trial trip, was pushed to seventeen miles an hour, and resumed her tremendous anchorage, waiting for a visit from the Queen:—*but*, she pitched and rolled, while meeting or siding the waves, far more than exact mathematicians had calculated or foretold. *N'importe!*—she's a wonder.

Always faithfully yrs.

---

## No. 297.—TO LORD NAPIER.

London, October 19, 1859.

My dear Lord Napier,—Your kind note of the 30th ult. and the package for Mrs. E. were received after the lapse of several days:—the latter crossed the Atlantic in the Bag by the Europa of the 8th instant. Let me assure you that one of the most valued sources of permanent gratification which I have had the good fortune to meet with in my wanderings on the arid desert of diplomacy has been the acquaintance made with yourself and Lady Napier. This is so true, that I am wondering at the time which has elapsed without my answering your letter:—but perceive how exactingly General Cass has dealt with me.

There is no wisdom in the world:—it is a myth which seems possible but is never met with. Certainly it was unwise in the two governments to neglect their boundary:—certainly unwise in Harney to plant his *Picket* in a neutral enclosure: and nothing can transcend the *un*wisdom with which the newspapers, by taunts, sneers, and invective, fret and exasperate the wound inflicted upon the public sentiment of both countries. The President has rapped the general over the knuckles, has sent Scott to put an extinguisher upon him, and has openly declined to order any additional naval force to that distant "jumping-off place:" a course which you will agree with me in considering somewhat less unwise than the menacing one of hurrying off several screw 91's and a parade of more sappers and miners. This last is a sad error.

The Yankees are taking the matter coolly:—unanimous in disapproving Harney, and unanimous in believing the islet theirs. How the question may, at the coming session of Congress, be harangued into the Presidential canvass, you have seen enough to imagine. Your friends Seward and Douglas will think nothing said while aught remains to say, in carpentering a new plank for their respective platforms.

Mr. Everett cannot leave home. He has too many engagements as a writer and lecturer. His son came over and has gone to Cambridge.

Pray make my respectful regards acceptable to Lady Napier,

And believe me,
Always faithfully yrs.

---

## No. 298.—TO MR. CASS.

LONDON, October 28, 1859.

MY DEAR SIR, — Maps are statements, *oculis submissi fidelibus;* producing more permanent impression than mere words. Hence it is that, to affect the general mind, the London shops and their windows are being crowded with charts of the islands and channels between Vancouver and the Continent, purporting to delineate the boundary as provided in the Treaty of '46 by a deep "*red line,*" starting from a point in the Gulf of Georgia and running with pictorial emphasis down Rosario Strait. Mr. Webster in '42 allowed his technical tendencies to conjure up difficulties as regards a more ancient "*red line:*"—it was cunningly po-pohed by Lord Ashburton, when at the very moment there could be seen, in one of the governmental offices here, a carefully neglected map which had descended from the royal negotiators of '83, whose "*red line*" conclusively sustained the one rather punctiliously abandoned by our great lawyer. Mr. Webster erred on the right side, and nobly declined resting his case on what he had not proof to shew might not be a "*suggestio falsi:*"—but this highly moral monarchy then took, and has ever since kept, the fruits of an admitted "*suppressio veri.*" Ask them if the wrong ought not to be remedied, and what answer will you get? a shrug and a chuckle. By-and-by, we shall be appalled by the resurrection of some long buried map of Vancouver's, on which the "*red line*" will speak, as a voice from the grave, in corroboration of those now addressing the public eye. I see by an extract of a letter from some Washington correspondent, in the *Times* of this morning, that you have replied to the extraordinary instructions given on the subject of San Juan by Lord John to Lord Lyons before any intimation of General Harney's proceeding had crossed the Atlantic. My solicitude to see this reply is extreme, and I hope to receive it by the steamer due on Sunday or Monday next.

Mr. Lesseps, with his Suez scheme, lingers longer in the public gaze than M. Belly with his Nicaraguan. The latter gentleman seems to have fallen like the stick of a rocket:—but the Emperor Napoleon relieves the former from the averted gesture of the Sultan, pats him cheeringly on the back, and inculcates patience. When the Mediterranean becomes a French lake, which the alliance with Spain against the Moors brings into a shorter range of telescopic view than heretofore, it will be both more safe, and more economical in time and money to forward legions to India through a perforation in the Isthmus than round the Cape of Good Hope. This is perfectly understood and appreciated by all classes:—and hence you may have noticed that of three leading investing countries, contributing to the Lesseps project an aggregate of $22,669,900, Great Britain, the plethoric capitalist, offers only $408,500, Holland only $261,400, while France subscribes for the whole residue, $22,000,000!

It is rather a strange fact that the cousin of the "dear ally" should come ostentatiously to England, announced in advance as purposing to meet Queen Victoria on board the Great Eastern, should pay his visit to the big ship, should travel rapidly about, should stop in London several days, rest at Portsmouth, and finally go back to Paris without having had the honor of seeing or hearing from her Majesty at all! There may be something in Prince Napoleon, disagreeable and repulsive, though Mr. P. who chaperoned him through the Museum thinks otherwise; or there may have been dropped unguardedly a stitch in that mysterious woof of etiquette which surrounds royal intercourse:—whatever the cause, the truth is notorious and leads to all sorts of remark and surmise.

Lord Brougham is just now the order of the day. He

has been honored with a grand "Banquet" at Edinburgh, in the course of which, it is said, he pronounced an elaborate philippic against the Emperor of the French. Under the new act of Parliament authorizing the appointment (without salary) of a Chancellor of the Scotch University, he and the Duke of Buccleugh are competitors for the post. A good deal of critical analysis of their respective merits and demerits is circulating:—but I think the Lord Harry is far ahead.

Count Colloredo has succumbed, at Zurich, and the two incomplete treaties must be signed by a new and special minister from Austria.

The cabinet came to town yesterday from all points of the compass, and are now in session. On the 6th of November they will be here again and then remain to meet for five or six days in succession.

Yesterday Parliament was formally and further prorogued to the 15th of December, on the coming of which day it will be put over to the beginning of February.

One of this morning's journals prints a telegram from Hong-Kong, saying that Mr. Ward had not effected the ratification of the treaty *at Pekin*. Possibly:—but I doubt, on the foundation of a statement made to me by Major McDowell, recently an aid of and introduced by General Scott. He says that while at St. Petersburg, ten days ago, Mr. Pickens informed him that the Russian Minister of Foreign Affairs announced at an interview that Mr. Ward had been treated with the utmost respect and kindness, had exchanged ratifications, and was invited to drink tea with the Emperor! The truth is, that the contrast between peaceful and bullying diplomacy is becoming painfully clear, and must be obscured by *canards*.

The French Imperial Court go to Compiègne next month. Of course, dependent and fraternizing sovereigns are expected to rendezvous there. The Grand Duchess Maria, whose marriage I witnessed in 1839, and who has the unenviable reputation of being a consummate politician, will be first and most favored.

Always faithfully yrs.

## No. 299.—TO MR. REED.

LONDON, November 4, 1859.

MY DEAR SIR,—Yours of the 16th enclosed one addressed to Sir George Grey of Cape Colony. Until this morning, I was at a loss for his residence:—nobody as yet *being known* to be in London. He has your letter now.

The perversity about China is still surprising. Louis Napoleon will be held to his engagement for a joint expedition of vengeance, and that may shield the government from Parliamentary condemnation:—for, the high point of acting independently of their great ally is not yet reached, either on "the floor" or the hustings. Mr. Ward has on the whole acted well. I saw from the first, and so wrote home, that the box, on which our piqued friends here were so lavish of their wit and sneers, was in fact designed in kindness and courtesy. At Pekin they went very far in conceding their Court ceremonial in order to bring about an Imperial reception:—farther, in my opinion, than you would get the *Arbiter elegantiarum* of Queen Victoria, Sir Edward Cust, to go. *Crede experto.* But this is Europe, whose traditionary futilities of five hundred years must be respected; while those of Asia whose roots have been deepening for 3000 years are fit only to be bullied down! I thought Englishmen more right-minded and just than this Chinese experience shews them to be. All their newspapers except one, and their hustings orators without exception, take special pleasure in striving to make Mr. Ward ridiculous:—and yet they owe to the manly and generous impulses of this gentleman at the critical moment of fight before the Forts, the lives of their admiral and his officers, and the rescue of such of their gunboats as were capable of rescue! The inconsistencies of false pride know no end.

We have a war, a small war *in presenti* but a huge one *in futuro*, Spain *vs.* Morocco. This and the coming Congress are possibly the means wherewith to provoke a quarrel with England.

Truly yrs.

## No. 300.—TO MR. CASS.

LONDON, November 11, 1859.

MY DEAR SIR,—When you get this, the Message will probably be in print, possibly in Congress:—and I must express a confident assurance that upon considerations of a public and pressing nature it cannot reach here too soon.

The treaties of Zurich, after a succession of obstacles and delays approaching the burlesque, were on the point of signature, when the cabinet of Vienna, in the true virus of the age, suddenly felt the inspiration of money-making, stopped the pens as they touched the parchment, and asked 400,000 dollars more! "My representatives," said Napoleon, "do you attach your names and seals to those instruments, and leave them to remain incomplete if others so choose." This command bore a serious significance. So Francis Joseph made a virtue of necessity, withdrew his demand, and the treaties became *faits accomplis* late yesterday afternoon. "I tell the tale as it was told to me."

Count Montalembert does not feel himself martyred with sufficient emphasis. He was being forgotten:—a wretchedness quite intolerable to a Frenchman who has once tasted fame of any sort. So, now he has rushed into print with two strings to his bow, resolved to be sacrificed by Napoleon and sainted by the Pope. His *brochure* "*Pie IX. et La France en* 1849 *et en* 1859" has drawn upon the *Correspondant* an *avertissement;* and will probably make him once more the hero of a public prosecution. On the present occasion he does not, as he did on the last, enjoy the sustaining sympathies of John Bull: for that unselfish old gentleman has been thrown into a perfect splutter of vexation, by finding that this apostate from anglomania has branded his conduct as "*ignoble*"*!* the felicity of which epithet is not diminished by its belonging to both tongues.

Your late diplomatic representative at the Argentine Republic, Mr. B. C. Yancey, is here. Did he not hail from Georgia I should take him for the brother of the member I once knew from Alabama. He returns to the United

States in the *painful* predicament of Mr. P——, to settle and realize a fortune of a million left by a deceased father-in-law.

The foray of Ossowatomie Brown and his band has been commented upon here with a little less of the anti-slavery monomania than usual. The favorite cant ascribes it to "madness." To me there seems so much method in this madness that I cannot but regard the whole as meriting a thorough investigation by commission or committee. Our national future may depend upon the manner in which this plot is dissected and exhibited. To pass it over as a freak will ensure it many imitations. Besides, the conduct of those who were to be *forced* into liberty, willy-nilly, goes an immense way to shew the real character of their condition as laborers:—and at the same time may satisfy the most fanatic abolitionist how utterly nonsensical as well as desperate is the object at which he aims.

Always faithfully yrs.

---

## No. 301.—TO MRS. SCHOOLCRAFT.

LONDON, November 19, 1859.

MY DEAR MRS. SCHOOLCRAFT,—I received late in September last your letter of the 29th of August with its enclosed circular, and fear that I may have incurred your displeasure by submitting to the heavy pressure of official engagements before making this acknowledgment.

No one holds in higher estimation than I do the great success achieved by your husband in his history of the aboriginal race of our Continent;—and it will afford me sincere pleasure to avail myself of every opportunity to draw attention to the edition you contemplate publishing.

In June last I was the happy medium of conveying to the Queen the sixth volume of Mr. Schoolcraft's work, in the name of the President. I presume that the emphatic acknowledgment made by her Majesty, through Lord John Russell, the principal Secretary of State for Foreign Affairs, came to his knowledge. Her Majesty expressed her "very great pleasure in accepting this magnificent and interesting volume," and requested that I would have the goodness to convey to "the President her sincere thanks for the present of a work which reflects honor both upon its author, and upon the government under whose auspices it has been published." Such praise as this, from a Sovereign so universally beloved, and a Secretary so high in literary reputation, should give the work unlimited circulation.

I am, my dear Mrs. Schoolcraft, with profound respects to your husband,

Always faithfully yrs.

---

## No. 302.—TO MR. CASS.

LONDON, November 25, 1859.

MY DEAR SIR,—Since my despatch by the Europa of the 19th instant, nothing has occurred worthy of official communication.

I am told by Sir Henry Holland that Lord John Russell has, for the last four or five days, been so unwell as to be confined to his apartments. Even if this were not so, I have no reason to expect an early attention to the title or taking of San Juan. No doubt your thoughts have been turned to the expediency of having a limit assigned to all discussion upon the subject. It is not enough that we should be in possession, though it is a great deal.

Although I can imagine the multitudinous distractions to which, at the opening of the present Congress, you must be subjected, yet I doubt your being half as much puzzled how to act as Lord Palmerston and his colleagues now are or seem to be. On receiving, the other day, a deputation respecting an improvement in the Law of Bankruptcy, the Premier, thinking that the matter ought regularly to have been carried before Lord John Russell, amused his visitors by a comical excuse for that Secretary, in consequence of the deluge of difficulties pouring into his department from all quarters of the earth. To these cares may probably be soon added that of representing his country at the European Congress to convene in Paris, possibly as early as the 15th of December next.

Lord Cowley paid us a flying visit at the beginning of the present week, and is believed to have borne from Compiègne the cunning proposal of a simultaneous disarmament. No ministry could outlive for a week an attempt to arrest the actual movement for defence against possible invasion. Stop the Naval Reserve! Stop the Rifles! Stop the Armstrong guns on their way to the chalky cliffs! The astute Emperor probably understands this perfectly:—and only strengthens his own position and plans by offering what is sure to be refused.

A casual interchange of question, answer, and remark, at the Russian Embassy, with her Majesty's principal Secretary of State for Foreign Affairs. His lordship anticipates much good from the visit of General Scott to Bellevue:—he also has great confidence in the wisdom and forbearance of Admiral Baines:—his principal objection to Harney is the rough or rude style in which he replied to Governor Douglas' disproof of Hubb's story that the Hudson Bay's Company had threatened to carry off an American who had killed a pig! I expected him to tell me, but he did not, that Governor Douglas had been recalled. It is so rumored. Not a word yet from the new Envoy, Mr. Wyke, who *deflected* to Guatemala. I do not ascribe much importance to these chats *en salons*, but they are not wholly void of significance, and certainly in the one referred to I could perceive nothing inconsistent with the impressions heretofore conveyed to you.

I have just been told, by a perfectly established authority for penetrating and disseminating political secrets, that Garibaldi has been invited to Compiègne. The tyrant and the tribune in conclave! There is something Napoleonic in the conjunction: as it shews a consciousness that, of all the brood of monarchs, *he* alone, as the offspring of universal suffrage, can handle unharmed the hot irons of democracy.

Persons recently from Italy (English and American) say that no ejaculation is more frequently heard among the common people than "Oh! if we could only find a Washington!" Uttered in the sincerity of a trying crisis by the descendants of Brutus, Cato, Gracchus, etc., are we not excusable if proud of these words? Garibaldi is assuredly not an entire Washington: but he is as nearly so as perhaps any man can be not born on the Western Continent.

Prussia, stimulated by her traditions, is believed to intend, at the coming Congress, to press the adoption of Governor Marcy's proposal to substitute for the abolition of Privateering the entire immunity of private property from capture. It is perhaps to be regretted that we are not yet prepared for this beneficent measure. Our great instruments of war on the ocean are the swarms of volunteer clippers with which we can so harass the commerce of an enemy in all parts of the world as speedily to bring him to terms. We deprecate standing armies, huge navies, and our policy is not only peace but permanent disarmament. What's to become of us if this last and congenial resource be diplomatized out of our power?

Always faithfully yrs.

---

## No. 303.—TO MR. CASS.

LONDON, December 9, 1859.

MY DEAR SIR,—This note must be accommodated in size to the little patience you will have left after reading three dull despatches.

1. My confidence in the punctuality of steam inclines me, as you open this letter, to step out, mingle in your interchange of visits, and very heartily to wish you a merry Christmas!

2. The early meeting of Parliament, 24th January, is ascribed to a determination on the part of the cabinet to begin the session with a Reform bill, and to push it steadily through before the holidays. Mr. Bright has just announced at an assenting assemblage of reformers, that he will accept what is supposed to be the ministerial *projet*, namely the measure explained in the House by Lord John Russell, after the Derby administration had been fatally stricken: *i.e.* a ten-pound franchise in counties, a six-pound rental one for boroughs, with a large extinguishment of seats in small boroughs, and the transfer of those seats to more important constituencies.

3. This government were, through the Admiralty and admiral, so prompt, quiet, and effective in rescuing the property of Grinnell and Minturn, on board the Sea

Serpent, from the dangers of a violent mutiny, that though I may feel bound to say something, would it not be well that I should be authorized to convey *your* formal acknowledgments?

4. It is confidently believed, though not technically certain, that the Congress at Paris, which assembles on the 15th or 20th instant, will have Lord Cowley alone as the British representative.

5. For the first time in England, I was yesterday honored by a visit from Mr. Louis Kossuth. He looks much improved. He is somewhat subdued by long deferred hope making the heart sick. He does not, however, complain, even of Louis Napoleon. His eye brightens, and his arm makes an oratorical gesture, as he refers to the incidents transpiring in Hungary. He says he is growing old. I think not. He is but 57, and his beard only enriched with lines of silver scattered on light-brown.

6. Of course you have noticed the act of the four Liverpool merchants who undertook to eclipse the famous Sheffield Foreign Affairs Committee, by addressing a joint note of interrogation to the Emperor, demanding to know *what he meant.* The thing is too silly to be the burden of remark:—and yet H. I. Majesty has not let slip the opportunity of sending a few keen darts of mingled encouragement and scorn across the Channel. Nevertheless his reply don't silence the Laureate's invocation, "FORM, FORM, RIFLEMEN, FORM!" Drills are enacted everywhere. The Judges and Lawyers "play soldiering" every afternoon in Westminster Hall!

Always faithfully yrs.

---

## No. 304.—TO MR. CASS.

LONDON, December 16, 1859.

MY DEAR SIR,—Accept my best thanks for your full and kind letter of the 26th November last. I cannot think that the democratic statesmen of the United States will fail, under passionate excitement, to turn to the best account what appears to me the most auspicious period furnished by our political history for vindicating the social humanity, as well as the national wisdom, of the assailed clauses of the Constitution.

The diplomatic movement at the Porte, insisting upon the concession required by Mr. Lesseps, is very significant. The Sultan is beset by the combined representatives of France, Russia, Austria, Prussia (?), and Sardinia, who simultaneously demand that he shall recede from the engagement of his Prime Minister with Sir Henry Bulwer, and authorize the canal. Such a pressure is not to be resisted by the "sick man." It is, as I regard it, the suddenly revealed consummation of a profound Napoleonic policy, which has been characterized in a recently published and powerful pamphlet by Emile de Girardin, as the ultimately fatal thrust of the French rapier into the British cuirass.

Pius the Ninth commissions Cardinal Antonelli to the Congress at Paris. *That*, of course:—for he has no other competent man at his service; but then, feeling the majesty of the Pontificate, he formally claims for the representative of 160,000,000 of Roman Catholics the Presidency of the Assembly. The demand can scarcely be entertained by a Protestant power:—even France may be embarrassed by it:—nor is it altogether impossible, if it be seriously and firmly pressed, that the contemplated Congress may disperse in anger before organization. I wish this:—and would almost agree to be Mortara-ized, if the Holy Father would effect it:—for, in verity, as Europe is now composed, these general Congresses are mere trumps in the hands of a despotic copartnership.

All Ireland is getting to be deeply stirred. Meetings are numberless, crowded to excess, extremely violent, and openly proclaiming a higher loyalty than that to the Queen.

The Russian is beginning to perceive that he has a hard road to travel in effecting the emancipation or enfranchisement of the serfs. "The course of true love never did run smooth." Our wishes for his success are rather damped by the bold attitude and language of the dissenting nobles.

Senator Seward returned home the day before yesterday, I believe by the Arago. As I send you, from the Azores Consulate, a letter respecting the yacht "Wanderer," it may be agreeable to have the enclosed newspaper slips, reporting the subsequent career of her captain.

Always faithfully yrs.

---

## No. 305.—TO MR. CASS.

LONDON, December 23, 1859.

MY DEAR SIR,—A telegram from Galway brings news from the United States as late as the 13th instant, and announces that, at that date, there were still no Speaker and no Message! However provoking, pretty much as was expected. I cannot help thinking and hoping that the true cause will lose nothing by debate in the House:—but the consequent detention of the great annual exposition of national affairs is a grievance of no light weight.

The Congress at Paris being assured, either for the 5th or (to accommodate Gortschakoff) the 20th of January, and the Plenipotentiaries ascertained, the moment is seized for a Manifesto which discloses, if not dictates, the Napoleonic programme. This paper, entitled "*The Pope and the Congress*," passes from the Emperor to the public through the same funnel, Monsieur de la Guerronière, whence issued the celebrated pamphlet "*Napoleon III. et l'Italie*," which closely followed the sharp words to Hübner on the 1st January, '59, and in advance vindicated Palestro, Magenta, and Solferino. It is a most remarkable document:—leading through a series of lucid and forcible arguments to a conclusion with which all the world might be satisfied except perhaps the Pontiff and his Cardinals. It is here and there sprinkled with refreshing drops of sound democratic doctrine. The right of the Romagnese to choose their own government is not to be controverted, and that they have done so is a *fait accompli.* France can never coerce them back as subjects of the Pope. Let his Holiness remain an independent sovereign: his territory, Rome:—his police or protection, the troops of the Confederation:—his revenues, the guarantied contributions of the Catholic Powers, and of the 200,000,000 of his spiritual subjects:—his head and heart relieved from the distractions of administration; his pursuits those of contemplation, beneficence, prayer, concord, and peace!

All the high officers of government have gone to spend their Christmas holidays in their country homes. They will hardly rally here again before Twelfth-Night:—and then they will not have three weeks to prepare for Parliament.

The rumor was false that ascribed to the Pope a desire to have Antonelli preside over the Congress. A formal contradiction comes from Rome.

It is impossible to get at the truth as to the war in Morocco, or the tendency to outbreak in Hungary. Spain, however, has certainly met a more determined and numerous foe than she expected. If a few drenching storms, pregnant with cholera, dysentery, and ague, help the Moors, O'Donnell may be driven to his ships.

Always faithfully yrs.

---

## No. 306.—TO MR. P.

LONDON, December 25, 1859.

MY DEAR SIR,—The best thanks of Mr. Sanders and myself are due to you for the effort made to place the Petition before his Imperial Majesty. I received it back safely, and have transmitted it to Mr. Sanders, with the original note from the Department of Count Gortschakoff:—so that he can, if he wish, pursue his object by invoking the kindness of Mr. Stoeckl at Washington. More than twenty years ago, he was a gallant officer in the service of his country, Poland:—but the extinction of all hope there threw him upon the resources of his education and energy in the United States, and, as a fellow-citizen of ours, he has worked his way to general esteem and a competency.

The *brochure* just issued in Paris, nominally by M. de la Guerronière, discloses with eloquence and force the Napoleonic policy designed for adoption by the Congress. France will not permit the banished Dukes to be restored by arms: the position of the Romagnese is incontestably a *fait accompli*, and she cannot, consistently with her principles, compel them to resume an allegiance which they have unanimously and effectually thrown off: the temporal sovereignty of the Pontiff is essential to his spiritual independence, but it need not be territorially extensive, on the contrary it may best be restricted within the boundaries of Rome:—let his revenues be ample contributions from the Catholic Powers and Peoples; his sacred office freed from the distractions of administration; his subjects without liability to taxation; and his mind bent exclusively upon divine contemplation, magnificent ceremonials, prayers, and blessings! Such is substantially the *programme* for the proceedings at the Congress to assemble in Paris about the 20th January, 1860. It is a boldly delineated chart, whose lines are strongly marked, and to be misunderstood by nobody, least of all by the Holy Father or Francis Joseph. Will it be carried out? I would say, perhaps it will, if the Czar adhere to France, England, Prussia, and Sardinia.

Advices from home are to the 13th instant, when Congress was still without organization, no Speaker, no Message: nor is it very probable that any progress will be made until after the holidays. Naturally, so near the tentative foray at Harper's Ferry. and with a state of parties in the House which allows a fair hope to our friends, the excitement runs very high. I am waiting in momentary expectation of hearing of the arrival of the steamer Europa at Liverpool:—she will bring the news down to the 16th instant, and if that be important, an effort shall be made to send it to you.

Our relations with this government are once more serene. The effect of General Scott's visit is reassuring and tranquillizing. San Juan will be enlivened and protected by the presence of two small military companies, one from each country:—and then, the negotiation, as to the title to the island, renewed, will, I dare venture to say, be protracted pretty much as was the one about the Oregon boundary.

Pray present the best wishes of the season to Mrs. P. from all my family, and with my cordial salutations, believe me

Very faithfully yrs.

## No. 307.—TO MR. CASS.

LONDON, December 28, 1859.

MY DEAR SIR,—Sir H. H. calling to make sure that a prescription was effective, has just told me that Lord Macaulay died yesterday morning. His disease was in the heart, and probably attended by an effusion on the chest. Only 59:--made Peer about three years ago, but has never spoken in the House of Lords. During my time here, he has been residing two miles out of London, on Campden Hill. His high position in the world of literature will doubtless cause a deluge of obituary notices.

General Scott's adjustment at San Juan is esteemed satisfactory; although this good people, as is their wont, think they are entitled to more than enough, and growl askance at Picket's little anti-Indian company. The renewed assertion of their unquestionable title to the island, in the daily journals, may I think be regarded as an indication that something claiming to be an answer to your argument is on its way.

The Napoleonic pamphlet "*Le Pape et le Congrès*," which I mentioned in my last, is creating as much chuckle in England as tumult on the Continent. These mild and tolerant Episcopalians look upon it as a fatal stab inflicted upon the Scarlet Lady, by the favorite matricide. The Pontiff and the Cardinals are startled into activity:—Antonelli draws back the foot he had stretched towards France:—his intended colleague, already in Paris, Sacconi, demands official disclaimer by Walewski: even the Gallican Bishops seem shocked, and, with one or two exceptions, are "denying their master:"—and, behold! Count Kisseleff, the Czar's ambassador, though of the Greek Church, says the *brochure* won't do, that it is too democratic, and that the glorious example of Russia attests the wisdom of keeping united temporal and spiritual sovereignties! In the midst of this *fracas*, the unanimous "All Hail!" of Central Italy and Sardinia comes roaring over the Alps. It is almost a fair race between the two Congresses, the one at Paris and the other at Washington, which shall organize first and which first disperse. I rather incline to wager on the latter:—but we shall be better able to form an opinion how the heat will end, the day after to-morrow, the pregnant New-Year's Day, when the Papal Nuncio, heading the Diplomatic Body, may possibly evoke or provoke from the Oracle some illuminating remark like that darted upon Baron Hübner.

Do you notice that the old impracticable Boyars of Moscow have so worried and irritated the Emperor Alexander, on the question of serf-emancipation, that he declines spending his Christmas among them as has been the practice of the Court? A small fact, signifying much on that point.

The weather has become quite mild.

Always faithfully yrs.

---

## No. 308.—TO MR. EVERETT.

LONDON, January 5, 1860.

MY DEAR MR. EVERETT,—You must allow me to sight two birds (and beautiful birds they are!) with a single barrel. Mrs. S. B. some month or two ago had permitted me to retain the newspaper copy of your Webster Eulogy. I had indeed a *diplomatic purpose* to which to apply a part of it. Since then the pamphlet with your signature has been cordially welcomed. I can't tell you without seeming extravagant how much pleasure it has given me. During my first service in the Senate, my seat adjoined Mr. Webster's, and this accidental circumstance led to a constant interchange of remark on politics and persons. You can readily conceive how well I remember certain leading incidents of that his most brilliant and useful time.

Am I wrong in the impression that you and Mr. Webster were never in the Senate during the same session? It is to that I ascribe your not dropping a word, while enumerating his traits, upon his power as *an actor*. He was too grave a statesman to shew this except behind the curtain; but I have seen him, when the galleries were cleared and the doors closed, gesticulate against the "unmitigated tyrant," or repeat a whole scene from Cumberland, with an effectiveness equal to anything done by Demosthenes or Garrick.

In speaking of him as a diplomatist, the Eulogy supplies a most interesting narrative of what he did while negotiating the Treaty of '42, as to the Northeastern boundary, with "the red-lined map of '83." The view taken of this matter by the quondam British Consul of Boston, Grattan, may not have met your eye. I have it, cut from a recent *Times*, and send it enclosed.

All lovers of their country doing duty abroad must gratefully thank you for that grand invocation to Union delivered at Faneuil Hall. Nothing sounder, nothing truer, nothing finer. Such an appeal ought to be irresistible. And yet the infatuated and presumptuous men, authors really of all the mischief, know how to be deaf to everything but their own voices. Let them take heed:—for they who halloo on a robber and assassin may find Judge Lynch attracted by the sound. The poisoned chalice is often drained by those who mixed it.

Lord Macaulay takes his place in Poets' Corner on Monday next, the 9th of January.

Our friend Sir H. H. gives me most pleasant accounts of the happiness of your son at Cambridge, and of the high esteem niwhich he is held.

Always faithfully yrs.

---

## No. 309.—TO MR. CASS.

LONDON, January 6, 1860.

MY DEAR SIR,—We shall soon plunge *in medias res*, on this side of the water. The Premier's grand ministerial dinner is announced for the 21st instant: it precedes the opening of Parliament three days. The session promises to be interesting from the start, and may become eventful. Parties, however, are unusually tranquil. Certainly there are topics enough on which disagreement must arise:—the war with China, the Morocco policy, the future of Italy, and the Pope, Reform, Church Rates, Indian Finance, Rifle-corps, Ribbon-men:—but as yet the surface betrays no symptom of interior violence. The government can scarcely be said to have its majority in the House; and it is believed to be liable, from hour to hour, to explosive dissension: and yet, no one anticipates the advent of a new ministry from any checkmate in the Commons.

The earthy residuum of Macaulay will be deposited in the Poets' Corner of Westminster Abbey on Monday next:—and, as within three years he was "*created*" something better than other folks, the huge folding front door of the great Cathedral will be thrown open for his ashes, and he will not be required, as Stephenson was, to crawl his way through the little back door, occasionally rubbing and sticking against cold walls, to his immortality. But wherefore in the "Poets' Corner"? Assuredly he wrote verses, and good ones too:—but they were thrown into dark eclipse by his Essays and History. In this last department, wherein he chiselled hard at the column of his fame, his integrity has often been assailed:—and it may be that his dust is mingled with that of "Rare Ben Jonson," Shakspeare, Pope, to intimate that he excelled in fiction even when handling fact.

Count Walewski has ceased to be Napoleon's minister of Foreign Affairs. The acceptance of his resignation is in yesterday's *Moniteur*. He is succeeded, *ad interim*, by M. Baroche, permanently by Thouvenel, the ambassador at Constantinople. This change is, at once and everywhere, recognized as strongly if not conclusively significant of the Imperial determination to adhere to the scheme of the recent pamphlet "*Le Pape et le Congrès.*" In one aspect, it is anti-anglican:—for Thouvenel has signalized his mission at the Porte by routing Sir Henry Bulwer on the Suez Canal:—but in a more important bearing, that of the central independence of Italy and the limitation of the Supreme Pontiff's temporal sovereignty, it is all English. One consequence may, I think (though others don't), be safely predicated of this decided *coup d'état:*—there will be no Congress, or only such Congress as, in the absence of Czar, Kaiser, and Pope, will augment, instead of eradicate, the complications and uncertainties of the "situation." There is ample room on the astrologer's dial for a fresh coalition and another war.

I long, everybody longs, for the Message:—and yet after the lapse of a whole month from the beginning of the congressional session, here comes a newspaper saying that by this time it may just have reached the Capitol!

Always faithfully yrs.

---

## No. 310.—TO MR. CASS.

LONDON, January 13, 1860.

MY DEAR SIR,—I am much exercised by the misgovernment which appears to prevail on board of our merchant vessels. Acts of mutiny or murder are causing constant applications for rendition warrants. Four of these are at this moment pending. Can nothing legislative be devised to remedy a disease which must bring the service into disrepute, and ultimately injure our navigation and commerce? Would not Mr. Clay, Chairman of the Senate's Committee on Commerce, consider the subject? As akin to this topic, let me add that I shall to-morrow confer on the possibility of a Consular Convention;—a possibility regarded as very remote.

The Message came to us in full, two days ago. It is received with a deference and favor altogether unusual. The *Times* has dwelt upon it every morning in terms of compliment as to matter, tone, and style. The cheek-bursting Boreas of the *Advertiser*, full of abolition wind, is the only journal that has ventured a rabid roar in the other direction. Such official documents, however treated amid party heats at home, furnish to all lovers of American institutions abroad, as you very well know, inexhaustible sources of pride and gratification.

The Pope and the Emperor have crossed rapiers, and simultaneously lunged at each other. Napoleon's weapon is the more polished:—the Holy Father losing some of his discretion in extemporaneously addressing General Guyon under excitement caused by the really Imperial, though ostensibly anonymous pamphlet "*Le Pape et le Congrès.*" While Bonaparte soothingly and reverently couples with *his* "Happy New Year" the suggestion how wise it would be in the Pontiff to let the rebellious Romagnese go their way, his spiritual and infallible Chief anathematizes the *brochure* as "*un opuscule qu'on peut appeler un monument insigne d'hypocrisie et un tissu ignoble de contradictions"!* The width and depth of a breach thus created cannot be sounded:—and we look soon to see Rome evacuated by the French troops:—indeed both Guyon and Grammont are reported to have already left.

A writer of considerable talent, and a shrewd observer, has recently pressed upon public notice a sort of warning which it can do no harm to communicate to you. He shews, in the first place, a large increase made, and still making in the French Navy. Then he points to the quarrel about the Cod fisheries, purposely kept open. And he asks, what the armament is meant for?—ridicules the idea of an invasion of England, and announces the Napoleonic idea of a reconquest of Canada! A restoration of this great colony, half of whose population remain essentially French, would, he argues, give to Louis Napoleon a brilliant immortality, not otherwise within his reach.

Do you notice the dexterous manner in which the nobles of Russia have caused the Czar to halt in his plan of serf-emancipation? They address him through an imposing committee: profess to admire the generosity of his aims; and express a readiness to aid the movement, if it be accompanied by its indispensable and kindred props, freeholds, municipal representation, and liberty of the press! His Majesty has paused and still pauses.

A shadowy prospect only is thought to remain for a Congress at Paris. The common tendency is to back from it. Russia doubts, and Gortschakoff declines:—Austria thinks the programme proposed by France altogether irreconcilable with the agreements of Villafranca and Zurich, and too unpalatable to be swallowed. Pio Nono and Antonelli are completely staggered. Prussia is quite indifferent. England, after all, would seem to have brought about a condition of things which leaves to the alliance the command of the "situation," and unites her with Napoleon in securing the independence of Italy. The general opinion regards the alliance as closer and stronger than ever. Such I know are the ideas inculcated in the very highest circles of politics. It is not said "*we have joined Napoleon:*" that would involve an admission at which national pride recoils: but "*Napoleon has come over to our policy*" is a phrase heard in all quarters, amid flushes of exultation and rubbing of hands.

Always faithfully yrs.

---

## No. 311.—TO SIR G. LEWIS.

LONDON, January 18, 1860.

MY DEAR SIR GEORGE LEWIS,—I cannot too cordially thank you for the excellent pamphlet on Jurisdiction and Extradition which accompanied your note of the 16th instant. Having read it carefully, I do not find a single proposition in it to which I can decline adhering. It has given me a strong assurance that one who so perfectly understands his subject will devise modes of removing its practical embarrassments.

It is a high interest of all nations that great crimes should be punished. But they can be punished only by the jurisdiction within which they occur. The *Times* and the *Post* seem not to approve my interposition with the case at Cowes. One regards me as "protesting," the other as impeding the progress of justice. Not at all. The murders cannot be reached by English law. No English court would entertain a case of crime committed on the high seas on board of an American vessel. Not to intervene and not to offer the only competent jurisdiction, necessarily lead to the ultimate discharge and impunity of the malefactors. Their escape, owing to the imperfections of our extradition system, may be probable:—but without that proceeding it is certain. You and I may, I sincerely hope, contrive some mode of preventing the escape of culprits and witnesses, and remitting them promptly and effectively to the only jurisdiction, here or in the United States, where they can be dealt with. If we don't, each country becomes, more or less, a sanctuary for the other's worst criminals.

Many apologies and fresh thanks.

Always faithfully and most respectfully yrs.

## No. 312.—TO MR. CASS.

LONDON, January 20, 1860.

MY DEAR SIR,—There is great rejoicing that the French Emperor, in an official letter of instructions to Mr. Secretary Fould, of the 5th instant, has given his unqualified adhesion to the doctrine of Free Trade, and has directed the future to be fashioned accordingly. This grand *coup d'état* received its final impulsive blow from Mr. Cobden. That gentleman sought Paris ostensibly for a change of air about two months ago;—but those who watched his movements made public reports of frequent interviews with his Majesty: their conversation even was occasionally detailed: and now the *Moniteur* of last Sunday contains the economical dissertation and fiat which for ten days they elaborated upon the anvil between them! The French trading ports are naturally rejoiced: Bordeaux and Havre illuminated as soon as they appreciated the reach of the new policy: but, as with us, and as naturally, the manufacturing towns demand to be, and are promised to be, fully heard, before the system is practically put into operation in 1861. The paper is remarkable for the quarter whence it comes, and is the *third* in the series of Manifestoes by which its author has marked and continues to mark, in advance, every leap he takes: but to this public, and to us, "*qui ont passés par là*," it suggests nothing very forcible or new. Half an eye perceives how much this movement must strengthen the alliance.

We have dates to the 7th instant, and yet no Speaker! This is very bad in reference to the national business and interests:—but in its bearing upon political party, nothing better could be desired.

The Queen comes to London from Windsor on Monday next, the 23d, to open Parliament in person, at 2 o'clock on the following day. The Premier's summoning missive to the Liberal members has been out for a week. It promises immediate and important measures for legislation. Lord Derby, at a large dinner in Liverpool last night, seems to anticipate a quiet session.

Mr. Oliphant has made two volumes of considerable interest and attraction out of Lord Elgin's mission, particularly the visit to Japan. Though he credits the Earl, his patron, with qualities of sagacity, vigor, and tireless activity, I think one can detect, from a casual word dropped here and there, that the private Secretary's opinion leans towards the American style of pacifically opening China to commerce and intercourse. It is a part of the art of bookmaking, however, not to cloud the prospect of profit by offending any large class of readers.

After all, Macaulay did not get to his grave through the vast folding door of the Abbey:—the sublimation of his blood was too recent and imperfect:—

What *can* ennoble knaves or fools or cowards?
What?—a *single drop* from *any* of the Howards!

Always faithfully yrs.

---

## No. 313.—TO MR. CASS.

LONDON, January 27, 1860.

MY DEAR SIR,—Her Majesty's Speech on opening Parliament is of more length and interest than common. I send you herewith an official copy. In leaving the House of Lords, I met the Duke of Newcastle, Colonial Secretary, who said, "Well! you see we reciprocated the friendly remarks of the President!" I have no doubt that was the design:—but it would be highly un-English if, in carrying it out, they did not employ some word, or take a tone, making the civil intention questionable.

Earl Grey, though he argued with spirit and force, failed to get the support of Lord Derby to an amendment to the Address, and was obliged to withdraw it. He wished to condemn any regulations of tariff by commercial treaty:—this was a little too much in advance, for the one made with France through the active agency of Mr. Cobden had not been communicated to Parliament, and was not actually perfected by signature at the moment his lordship was assailing it.

There are many more than Mr. Cobden who claim the merit of having converted the French Emperor to Free Trade. Michel Chevallier had certainly much to do with it. So had Baroche. But I was enlightened by a long visit from Count Persigny, who coolly and volubly assumed the whole exploit. He declares that he has been at it these five years: that he developed, in successive elaborate papers sent to his Majesty, all the ramifications of the new policy: and that he returned from Paris only ten days ago, after a final and successful exertion of his personal influence. How will history decide among these rivals? Perhaps she may reach the conclusion that Prohibition and Protection yielded, after all, more to the Napoleonic fondness for change, for sudden and surprising *coups d'état*, than to the force of facts or logic.

I had the opportunity last evening of a free after-dinner chat with Lord John Russell respecting Mexico. He is much at a loss what to do: has little confidence in the public men of that country, except Juarez: is solicitous to avoid even the appearance of attacking the Monroe doctrine by intermeddling with their distracted condition:—the military strength of both contending parties is exhausted: and how enough energy was to be infused into either for executive government, without foreign aid, it was impossible to see.

The Great Eastern maintains her title of "The Unlucky:"—she has just lost Captain Harrison, drowned in going to the wharf, and her shareholders and directors are in a tempest of quarrel.

Always faithfully yrs.

---

## No. 314.—TO MR. CASS.

LONDON, February 3, 1860.

MY DEAR SIR,—I am strongly impelled, by a modest sense of demerit, *not* to send you the enclosed newspaper slip, reporting the interpellation of Lord John Russell by Mr. Monckton Milnes. It is, however, more important that you should see exactly where the proposed Consular Convention is, than that I should indulge *mauvaise honte*. May it not be necessary to clothe me with a Full Power for the special occasion? The negotiator does not manifest a very scrupulous regard for the technical obstacles interposed heretofore by the Crown Lawyers; and indeed has no reluctance to being esteemed equal, if not a little superior, in their own *spécialité*, to any of them.

It is not difficult to perceive that a good deal of the eagerness which prevails to back Bonaparte against the Pope springs rather from Protestant bigotry than love of Italian liberty. The Vatican is an old and preferred target for all the Locksleys of the press:—he who plants a shaft in that bull's-eye, has instantly the reward of a general shout. The new Encyclical letter exhibits more firmness than was predicated of Pio Nono. It has obliged the French Emperor summarily to suppress the leading organ of ultramontanism, *L'Univers*, and to throw himself upon the historical loyalty of the Gallican Church. He does so under the sanction of a special clause in the existing Constitution, and with graceful forbearance in regard to the Holy See. But Church and State are now squarely confronted, and the past, *decies repetita*, tells us what to look for as inevitable.

Your chargé in Paris will no doubt send you an early copy of the Anglo-franco Commercial treaty. Portions of it have got into the journals here:—but some details are still elaborating and incomplete. The manufacturing and mining opposition is active, impetuous, and outspoken:—it will put the reforming Emperor to a sharp trial.

The question of Savoy! aye, here it is at last. More than a year ago, I hazarded the "guess" that this Duchy was a stimulant to the anti-Austrian appetite. Well! it is sliding into France, under the operation of a quiet contract entered into at that very time with Victor Emmanuel. The secret has been well kept:—perhaps it would have been better to keep it so still, until this country had got more completely into the complicated meshes of the entangling alliance:—for John Bull is already out against his immovable nightmare, anybody's annexation but his own!

"*The Papal Question in a New Light*," by an American Diplomatist, is printing in Paris, and is from the pen of our recent Minister Resident at Lisbon, Mr. John L. O'Sullivan. The "new light" seems to consist in discovering the identity or strong analogy between the District of Columbia under our Constitution and Rome under the plan of the

Guerronière pamphlet. Only two-thirds of it, translated from French, have reached here.

The Chancellor of the Exchequer opens his budget on Monday next, the 6th inst. Royalty quits Windsor Castle for Buckingham Palace on the 12th:—and that infinitesimally simple measure, the Parliamentary Reform bill, comes up, for the first time since the world began, on the 21st instant.

Always faithfully yrs.

---

## No. 315.—TO MR. CASS.

London, February 10, 1860.

My dear Sir.—"What mighty contests rise from trivial things!" Every sort of mischief seems likely to flow from the ill-timed hoarseness of the Chancellor of the Exchequer. On Monday last, his throat refused its mellifluous tones to the eulogy of the budget:—he dared not venture, with a croaking voice, on a permanent income tax of nine-pence, a one-sided tariff-treaty with France, and an appropriation of thirteen millions sterling for the navy alone! It is announced as possible that he may undertake the task this evening. In the mean while discontent has so accumulated as to be dangerous, if not altogether impracticable. The delay has given opportunity to coalition; thence, a substantial condemnation of Cobden's arrangement; thence, a change in the government; thence, coldness or quarrel with France; and thence, finally, a general war! Extravagant as this may seem, I do assure you that the dismal foreboding is seen, felt, and expressed by every knot of politicians at the now numerous *soirées*:—and all the series of disasters unanimously attributed to the sore larynx of Mr. Gladstone.

There is some cause for suspecting, in the present House of Commons, a diminution in the zeal for Reform. On the night before last, the bill for abolishing Church Rates, sunk, from a majority six months ago of 74, down to one of 29: and last night, the ballot, after a hostile speech from Lord Palmerston, was rejected by a majority of 31.

These votes, united with the sensitive solicitude of Irish members about the Pope, tend to fresh party combinations fatal to the present ministry. Lord Derby and his friends are tranquilly watching the course of incidents, quite sure that the pear is rapidly ripening and must fall into their hands before two months elapse.

You will have noticed that the Peers were unanimous and firm against the annexation of Savoy to France. The address to the Queen moved by Lord Normanby was not pressed, on the ground that it gave a formality to the protest unnecessarily offensive to the Emperor. Victor Emmanuel and Count Cavour hold on tightly (as yet) to "the Cradle of the Royal House." The Parisian press is bent on forcing their grasp. The ministry here, after advising against the acquisition, are really indifferent, not seeing any danger in it, to the balance of power. Louis Napoleon seems in no hurry to proclaim his purpose, but all the world knows what it is, and are quite satisfied that sooner or later it must prevail.

I send, to occupy a cranny in your departmental library, a small volume on the present state of British shipping. It is written by a friend of mine, a member of the House, a large ship-owner, and a clear-headed man. His leading object, he tells me, is to arrest the movement towards the restoration of the Navigation Acts.

Always faithfully yrs.

---

## No. 316.—TO MR. CASS.

LONDON, February 17, 1860.

MY DEAR SIR,—I hurried through my letter this day last week in order to reach the House of Commons in time for Mr. Gladstone's grand performance on his two-stringed harmonium—the Budget and the Treaty. He spoke for four hours uninterruptedly, and with perfect mastery of his complicated subject; the very personification of self-convinced, eager, and unrelenting Free Trade! No mercy shewn to a solitary article taxed upon the principle of protection:—everything of the sort swept scornfully to the rubbish heap. In pushing his financial plane along the board, he has, here and there, say iron, coal, hops, and ribbons, cut more fiercely and deeply than is consistent with a prudent policy, and has roused a hornets' nest to sting his tariff in every quarter. But he has left his victims no means of escape. The commercial compact with Napoleon and the entire scheme of taxation are Siamese twins, the former dragging the latter over every obstacle. At a Conservative caucus, a resolution fatal to the ministry on this topic was rumored to have been adopted, and Mr. Disraeli was said to be sharpening his weapon for a home thrust on Monday next the 20th instant. I have, however, reason to disbelieve that this was the strategy finally agreed upon. Lord Derby does not wish to oust his rival at the present moment, and throw everything into sixes and sevens with France suddenly. The demonstration will cautiously avoid putting the enemy to flight. The debate in the Lords last evening was left in the hands of secondary men, Earls Airlie and Grey, and was signalized by the *absence* of Lords Derby and Malmesbury, although founded on a formal notice. The pear is not ripe.

You will notice the reply given last evening in the Commons to Mr. Liddell upon the subject of our Coasting Trade, by Lord John Russell. Perhaps, as you are referred to, I had better send you the enclosed slip.

His lordship, in answering Sir Robert Peel, conveyed to my mind the conviction that what I heretofore predicted about the annexation of Savoy to France cannot be prevented. Victor Emmanuel has been distinctly apprised by the Emperor that if his power and dominion were swollen by the accession of Central Italy, the Empire would not be safe with the Var as a boundary. Such a notice from the ally who is working out the aggrandizement of Piedmont involves a compact not to be disputed hereafter.

Lord Elgin goes back to China without delay, to relieve his brother Mr. Bruce, with whose course of action and despatch-writing public opinion is dissatisfied. Mr. Bruce indulged unfairly in catering to what he thought was the diseased appetite of the Foreign Office, by repeating false and frivolous stories of Mr. Ward's contemptuous treatment at Pekin. Lord Elgin is sanguine in the belief that he may preserve peace, and professes *that* to be his sole object. Remembering as we must that *he* extorted the Treaty of Tien-Tsin from Chinese fear, he would hardly seem the fittest agent for a friendly mission.

Always faithfully yrs.

---

## No. 317.—TO MR. CASS.

LONDON, February 24, 1860.

MY DEAR SIR,—There is no variation in the political tune. It is nothing but treaty and budget, and budget and treaty, at all times, and everywhere. I can perceive only a slight giving way on the part of the Chancellor of the Exchequer:—he sops the deep and dangerous baying of "the Trade," *i.e.* the licensed victuallers, by abandoning his proposed licensing for the sale of beer, confining it to wine. With this small exception, he pushes his entire scheme with perseverance and overshadowing ability. His firmness is bolstered by the collateral consciousness that the opposition hold in extreme dread another dissolution of Parliament. The technical assault of Mr. Disraeli on Monday last, was baffled with promptness. The debate may be extended far into the coming week.

There prevails something like a superstitious aversion on both sides to the proposed fight between Heenan and Sayers, for the Championship. The House of Commons will probably goad the government into preventive energy. The training of the Benicia Boy, in the Isle of Skye, is represented as admirable.

The Queen's Levee yesterday was amazingly tedious and uncomfortably cold:—relieved for a moment by the Royal sword descending upon the shoulders of the last explorer for Sir John Franklin. The knighthood of Captain McClintock, itself a mere name, closes with something like poetic justice this long protracted drama of sentiment.

There is a peculiar numbness (an allowable word?) at this moment about the Italian complications. No one can say how they stand. An occasional theorist anticipates the disclosure of a compromise between the Pope and the Emperor. Another will say that Napoleon lingers only until the Treaty, Budget, and Alliance are beyond a peradventure.

Always faithfully yrs.

---

## No. 318.—TO MR. CASS.

LONDON, March 6, 1860.

MY DEAR SIR,—On this side of the water, the mercury in the political barometer starts upward and sinks fast, very suddenly. The avowal of the Emperor in his address opening the legislative chamber on the 1st instant, certainly that he wanted and impliedly that he would have Savoy, has shocked the morality so unanimously and eloquently discoursed for a fortnight in the Palace of St. Stephens. That avowal takes firmness and form in the diplomatic notes addressed by Monsieur Thouvenel to the French ministers here and at Turin. Lords Palmerston and Russell are deeply committed against the annexation: and in the Commons last night they seemed perplexed in the extreme on discovering that the recently negotiated commercial treaty was in danger of defeat by the opposition as a primary protest against enlarging the limits of France. Still, I do not think Lord Derby and his wary associates prepared to take the helm, at the risk of encountering at once a Gallican tempest. The hour for that has not yet struck:—but they do much to consolidate the foundations of their party and to give it a European position, by seizing as theirs the popular dread of Napoleon's designs. Already there are symptoms of sensitive vigilance, if not of coalescing jealousy, in the intercourse and movements of Russia, Prussia, Austria, Germany, and Switzerland. This repeated "filling and backing" on the Italian points of policy bewilders interpretation and inculcates the expediency of a general "look-out."

I cannot say that when I read your last note on San Juan (to Lord John) there was the slightest indication of surprise or vexation on the part of her Majesty's minister. What you did was probably expected: or, at all events, Lord Lyons had written enough to take off the edge of astonishment. But, if Horace had not written *Nil admirari*, I should be inclined to ask, is it not wonderful how persistently and variously a bad cause is sometimes pressed? I went on Wednesday last to the reception of the Royal Geographical Society at the residence of their present President, Earl de Grey and Ripon, late Lord Goderich, and what do you think "stared me in the face with rapid strides"?—On the wall of the grand stairway, conspicuous to the eye of every comer, brilliant in coloring, was a gigantic map of the disputed Island, with its adjacent waters, and *a deeply red line, a quarter of an inch wide, running, as if unalterably convinced, down Rosario Strait!* Now, his lordship is not merely the præses among the manufacturers of charts, he is also an under Secretary of State for War! This sort of mural dogmatism can only deceive;—for, as you say, Rosario Strait is given up: the nailing, or plaistering, a concededly false pretension is unworthy a sage or statesman.

The French papers announce that your Plenipotentiary (Mr. Faulkner) presented his credentials to the Emperor, the day before yesterday (Sunday).

Always faithfully yrs.

---

## No. 319.—TO MR. CASS.

LONDON, March 9, 1860.

MY DEAR SIR,—I have too recently written to have any thing to say.

At the French Embassy on Tuesday evening last Count Persigny took the trouble to detail to me all the peculiar causes which justify his sovereign in annexing Savoy, or rather the "*slopes of the Alps*," and the extent to which he has been exasperated, not alone by the violent abuse in both Houses of Parliament, but also by the extraordinary diplomatic notes which Lord John Russell, ever since July last, has been scattering all over Europe, in deprecation of that resolutely adopted measure. The ambassador looks upon the state of things as threatening a war in the course of this spring.

The question of the treaty will be decided in the Commons to-night, on Mr. Byng's motion for an address to the Queen, conveying approbation. I do not doubt the success of the motion. Apart from the almost unanimous aversion to permitting France to have any of the Alpine passes, the ministry is overwhelmingly strong.

Always faithfully yrs.

---

## No. 320.—TO MR. MARKOE.

London, March 12, 1860.

My dear Markoe,—Your *billet* of the 21st February struck a spur into my intent, and caused me to drive in haste to one of the queerest and dirtiest little alleys I have yet seen in London. You marked (as everything delusive is now-a-days marked) with a "*red line*," on a certain page of catalogue, a group of *Facetiæ* as worthy of prompt pursuit. I rushed to 45 Booksellers' Row, Strand; and, would you believe it? the precious rarity had very recently been sold and no other copy was extant! I had to find consolation in shrugging my shoulders, and in gazing with wonder at the countless accumulations of old, weather-beaten, black, yellow, stained, greasy, big and diminutive volumes, encumbering both sides of the narrow and long streetlet into which I had picked my way on foot. Before vanishing from Mr. A.'s gloomy literary "Curiosity shop," I seized the accompanying list for the present *March* from off his ledge, and then gaspingly sought a gulp of fresh air.

What with China, French Treaty, San Juan, Savoy, Imperial Pamphlets, Counteractive Royal Coalitions, with the lively sessions of Parliament, the thoughts of diplomats are whipped, like spinning tops, into a stand-still of ceaseless activity. This mission is very different from that at St. Petersburg. There, I could yawn and doze, without end:—here, not an hour arrives without its budget, keeping me forever either in the deeply reflective or the excitedly *qui vive* mood. Which post is the better? I am not yet old and cold enough to hesitate in preferring this. I am not disposed to be dead before I die. After all, there is a charm in living fast, in being on the rack of vigilance, eagerness, hope, and hurrah, which goes at once not so much to the heart, as to the immortal spirit within. Of course I am referring to the enjoyments and bustle of the intellect, not to those of sense. London has an immense field for these, just below the Court and above the Counter: and, in that, range vast herds, titled and untitled, the philosophers, the littérateurs, the lawyers, the clergy, the editors, the politicians, the experimentalists on matter, mind, and morals, the painters, the sculptors, the musicians, the agriculturists, the florists, the photographers, etc., etc., etc. Any man who will anchor himself in this tide of incessant and roaring movement, and give himself to each wave of the flood as it passes, must, if he don't run mad, experience the highest degree of human enjoyment. All this is the better for not being exclusively English. Every country and every language contribute to the result. And all of it is essentially and absolutely apart from the pantomimic finery of royalty, or the grossness of mere money-changing. No doubt, the individuals have each and all their repulsive qualities:—but as a stirring whole, the thing is marvellous!

All well. Love to all.

Ever yrs.

---

## No. 321.—TO MR. CASS.

LONDON, March 16, 1860.

MY DEAR SIR,—The "Manchester School" have enabled Lord Palmerston to give two signal victories to the Treaty of Commerce with France, the majority in the Commons being 282 to 56, and in the Lords 68 to 38. The financial scheme of Mr. Gladstone, adapted to the treaty, proceeds almost *pari passu*, and we already read in the shop-windows French articles for sale "duty off."

If history *does* repeat itself, there are always some modifications, some slight shades of difference. That Bonaparte should bag Savoy, even with contemptuous disregard of the European Chart of 1815, is natural enough;—that he should do it, however, simultaneously with the closest embrace he has yet accorded to England, has a spice of novelty quite *piquante*. Such harmony in defiance of the "balance of power" and the annals of centuries, is wonderful.

Poor Switzerland points to the gash in her side for ruin's wasteful entrance and shrieks in vain for help! Victor Emmanuel, having attained the full proportions of manhood, parts with his "cradle" without a sigh. And the Savoyards, true to their wandering instincts, are rather eager than otherwise for the change of position.

The prevailing excess of the *entente cordiale* is worth watching. It may suggest the expediency of a less friendly tone with us. Our cotton surpasses General Scott as a great pacificator:—but the new Convention, opening vast markets for coal and iron, inspires exultation. In the *Times* of yesterday you will find the following lusty words: "San Juan American, and Vancouver's Island and Columbia British, are incompatible with peace." Heretofore there has been a chime of pens and presses, representing the *material* relations of the two countries as rendering war between them *impossible*. Let us see whether a variation is to be struck.

I have just had a visit from Mr ——. He has so absorbed me by descriptions of everything and everybody at home, as to oblige me to cut short this note. His conversational powers, always great, seem greater than ever. He goes to his consulate at Havre to-morrow, by way of Paris.

The season's circulation in what is termed high life will experience a damp check from the death, two days ago, of the Countess of Granville, wife of the President of the Privy Council. She was a general favorite.

Always faithfully yrs.

---

## No. 322.—TO MR. CASS.

LONDON, March 27, 1860.

MY DEAR SIR,—At the House of Commons last night, I listened to an outburst from Lord John Russell singularly at war with the Treaty of Commerce and pregnant with danger to the Alliance. It was, at the instant, provoked by a charge of "truckling" from Mr. Horsman;

and it announced, on the part of the ministry, as the consequences of recent negotiations with France respecting Savoy, the loss of all confidence in the assurances of the Emperor, and the duty of avoiding isolation in Europe by at once forming connections with other continental Powers interested in preserving the general balance. I have seen this movement preparing for a week past. Lord John has probably replied to the despatch of Mr. Thouvenel whose contents he refused to state, with the animation called for by a haughty tone. The *Times* has surprised its readers during four or five days with pungent articles on "fourberies de Scapin," "tricks of Figaro," and "insolence" of the new French Minister of Foreign Affairs. Considering the relations subsisting between the leading writers of this journal, and the chiefs of the cabinet, these pieces could only be regarded as preliminary to a foregone conclusion soon to be disclosed. The opposition loudly cheered: one of whom, while complimenting the perseverance of the mutinous Liberals, expressed a hope that, seeing the manly and patriotic course at last taken, government would now be unanimously sustained in upholding what were strongly asserted to be the interests, honor, safety, and sentiments of the British People. All this may, according to the genius of our epoch, blow over:—a few honeyed drops of soothing recantation from the lips of pre-eminent power may appease the rising storm: but I am inclined to think that the irrevocable bolt has been shot, and that while Lord John remains in his present post, Napoleon will consider this country as inimical and at work everywhere to thwart his views and restrict his influence.

It really would seem, according to the old couplet, that

> The pleasure is as great
> Of being cheated as to cheat,

for our acute countrymen almost hurry to be duped by the rogues on this side the Atlantic. They apparently like being, as lambs in hot weather, affectionately fleeced. Your letter on the newly contrived and extensive fraud reached me after I had received a number of eagerly enquiring notes, and after I had thoroughly ascertained the features, though not the authors of the conspiracy.* This is

* The contrivance was of the following fashion, and singularly successful. The conspirators in London ascertained the residences of individuals

about the tenth swindle which has invoked my detective faculties. Of course, artful and audacious rascals prearrange to mystify and baffle pursuit:—and I do not believe in the existence of police skill adequate to ferret out and bring to punishment the plotters of so wide ranged, and as it were international a scheme of pocket-picking as this. The knaves reckon much and naturally upon the indisposition to throw good money after bad: then, uncertainties of success give to distances an insurmountable aspect. But, *nous verrons.*

Admiral Van Dockum has ceased to represent Denmark at this Court; and Mr. Billé, the younger, whom we have known at Washington for many years, took the post of Plenipotentiary some five days ago.

I have just got the private note of which a copy is subjoined from Lord Clarence Paget, first Secretary of the Admiralty; and I must beg you to request Mr. Toucey to have the document therein referred to, if there be such a one, forwarded to me as promptly as possible. I have not been able to find anything of the sort among the books and papers sent to me.

Always faithfully yrs.

---

## No. 323.—TO MR. CASS.

LONDON, March 30, 1860.

MY DEAR SIR,—Pardon me for expressing a hope that you have not forgotten to obtain for me from Mr. Toucey the Report on our Naval Dock Yards requested by Lord Clarence Paget. Our countrymen are so constantly,

---

in most of the American States from local Directories. They sent by post numberless letters carefully addressed to all parts of the Union, especially to the interior. Each letter stated that the writer had accidentally discovered a Will or an Estate in which it appeared that his correspondent was largely interested:—that a claim if promptly asserted could be maintained upon accessible evidence: and that if it were wished that he should investigate records or collect proofs, he was ready to do so on receiving a trifling amount of money, say five or ten dollars, with which to meet preliminary fees or expenses. The bump of credulity and the smallness of the sum required made the suggestion irresistible to thousands, who could not too quickly transmit their cash to the appointed place.

through me, getting information of all kinds from the depths of the public offices here, that I feel it to be a duty to reciprocate whenever I can.

At the Queen's Levee on Wednesday the 28th instant, the Premier took occasion to converse about the Slave Trade. He expressed himself much gratified on noticing the promising plans you were preparing to pursue:—saying that the great difficulty arose from the facility yielded to the traffic by Cuba, and intimating that, as *we* objected to meddle with any vessel not carrying our Flag, and *they* had promised not to meddle with any that *did* carry it, perhaps the most effective plan, off that island, would be for the cruisers of the two nations, as he termed it, "to hunt in couples," the British cruiser overhauling and examining all vessels bearing colors not ours, and leaving the rest to us. I mention this because Lord Palmerston appeared to hold the idea as a favorite one, to be matured and formally proposed: and because it involves a striking recognition anew of the position you have enforced.

A Liberal Conservative Irish M. P. interpellates Lord John Russell this evening on the condition of the San Juan question. It will not be in my power to attend:—but I presume that his lordship will decline for the present any disclosure, unless indeed he regard your last as closing the negotiation, which is very unlikely. His troubles seem to crowd thick upon him just now. Nothing livelier than the agitation in the little diplomatic hive produced by his anti-Napoleonic explosion on Monday last. Persigny pale with passion, and the really stingless cluster of German Envoys buzzing unceasingly with a singular mixture of enjoyment and alarm!

I must not omit to state what it was pleasing to hear, when on Wednesday I dined at Buckingham Palace. During the conversation, which on such occasions, after the table is left, always takes place between the Queen and her guests, her Majesty enquired with the utmost kindness about the President and Miss Lane:—she was happy to hear of their continued health. I assured her that both would be delighted to know that they were thus remembered.

The Prince of Wales proceeds to Canada in July. His younger brother Alfred the midshipman, wishes to accompany him, but probably will not be allowed to do so.

The Duke of Newcastle, Secretary for the Colonies, and Lord St. Germans, Lord Steward, will go. The future King and his party will, I have reason to believe, visit Washington. Should there be an invitation?

The day assigned for Lord Elgin and Baron Gros to embark at Marseilles for China, is the 12th of April. He did not however appear surprised when I suggested the possibility that existing complications with France might stop him altogether.

I had the pleasure to introduce yesterday, at his request, your minister in Madrid to Lord John Russell. Mr. Preston's picture of his Spanish residence is not very flattering. He will cross the Atlantic in company with this note:—and, as he moves energetically and rapidly, may reach Washington as soon.

There is a rumor just from New York, that Cuba is at your disposal, though the price is not fixed. Bonaparte may have encouraged the substitution of a colony in Morocco for the precarious one in the Antilles. The rumor will require much confirmation before it gains belief.

Always faithfully yrs.

---

## No. 324.—TO LADY H.

London, April 5, 1860.

My dear Lady H.,—Allow me to express very cordial thanks for your note of last week, respecting the autographs placed in Leicester Square for sale at auction.

I could not find time until yesterday to visit these interesting relics. The signatures of Washington and Lord North are particularly attractive from historical association and relation. The bold broad hand of the former seems to contrast *rebelliously* with the delicate and tiny calligraphy of the latter.

Again, many thanks, very faithfully and most respectfully yrs.

## No. 325.—TO MR. CASS.

LONDON, April 6, 1860.

MY DEAR Sir,—Parliament, at the instance of Lord Palmerston, adjourned over on the night of the 3d to the 14th instant, that is, for the Easter Holidays. The members of both Houses are now distributed all over the kingdom and in the continental capitals. They left London at the moment when the relations of the Foreign Office were disturbed by despatches from Mons. Thouvenel to Mr. Persigny, and by an unexpectedly bold declaration from Lord John Russell that other allies than France must be sought for. Let us see in what mood they will reassemble. Those who stop in Paris, to assist at the grand *fête* of her Imperial Majesty, or to chat with Mr. Cobden, will probably have their "fretful porcupine" quills smoothed gently to their usual level. The Nephew is less irritably explosive than the Uncle, with equal tenacity of aim.

Spain is perhaps a reasonably good "quarter racer." She has shewn herself capable of a vigorous effort, of military skill, and of courage:—but she has tired soon. The Treaty of Peace with the Moors is not what O'Donnell was expected to dictate; and it will probably throw a shadow over his returning ovation. You of course notice that, almost simultaneously with the capture of the two steamers off Vera Cruz, the Governor of the Balearic Isles, Ortega, attempted a rebellious dash at the Crown of Queen Isabella and the inauguration of Don Carlos! This political pimple does not appear to have been thrown to the surface by any interior humors, and has exhaled of itself:—Ortega being chased by his own troops, no one can say whither.

A Papal Excommunication cannot be regarded as mere *brutum fulmen* as long as millions of devoted Roman Catholics are to be found in almost every country. Napoleon is alive to this:—and he hurries to exclude the lightning from his empire, by invoking an old, nearly obsolete law which prohibits the publication of foreign ecclesiastical acts without special license. To be sure, he is not "nominated in the bond:"—neither is Victor Emmanuel, nor in fact any one else:—but it is difficult to discriminate between their respective offences:—the alleged crime of despoiling the patrimony of St. Peter is flagrant,—don't the world know "*who have taken part*"? who "*perpetrated*," "*warranted*," "*supported*," "*helped*," "*counselled*," "*followed*," "*connived at*" it? Well, they are all comprehensively and indiscriminately anathematized and scourged out of the Church. Take an illustration of the immense influence of the Vatican:—the Duchess of ——, the granddaughter of Charles Carroll, ending her life in the quiet rural contentment of Protestant England, is said to have just sent the Holy Father a *cadeau* of a thousand guineas! Rest assured that we shall hear a great deal more than we have yet heard of the potency of this thunder.

An appeal to the Detective or ordinary Police respecting the frauds upon our citizens involves so large an expenditure, and so much official distraction and embarrassment, that I hesitate in believing that you intended both should be incurred. The falsehood and swindling character of the pretence have been completely ascertained, and I have written some dozen letters home upon the subject. Perhaps a short warning in the *Constitution* and *Intelligencer*, which proved effectual in a similar case about two years ago, might save many a man his four dollars. But can the government be reasonably expected to go farther? The mischief lies in the facility with which, in spite of all experience, our good countrymen allow themselves to act at once upon the faith of a boldly made promise. If they would only take the precaution, before parting with their money, to write to the legation, through your department, or directly, they would be shielded from the contrivances of rogues. If in your name I complain to Lord John Russell of the conspiracy, or in any other manner set the ball of criminal enquiry and punishment going, I commit the government to a responsibility for charges whose amount has no limit, and I also, I fear, subject myself and the secretaries and the archives, to the annoyance of judicial process. I can, and do, set a subpœna at defiance, as incompatible with my extra-territorial position:—but if I volunteer to begin the hunt, what then? Pray think for a moment on these practical suggestions.

Always faithfully yrs.

## No 326.—TO MR. CASS.

LONDON, April 13, 1860.

MY DEAR SIR,—Notwithstanding the undeviating and stern course adopted, the "*revendication*" of Savoy has its difficulties. I had the honor yesterday of a visit from Mr. de la Rive, the Swiss representative, and was much gratified by the candor and fulness of his conversation. He considers his country in great danger, and fears that, after what has been done, the Emperor will find himself unable to give her, in the direction of Geneva, the securities which, by the unanimous resolution of all parties, she is determined to exact. Mr. Persigny, to be sure, has encouraged him to hope that Napoleon will transfer an adequate circuit of territory to the Republic, the inviolability of which may be guarantied by a Congress. But he has the "mistrust" spoken of by Lord John Russell, and inclines to believe that Helvetian safety will ultimately have to be sought in an armed coalition with Germany, Prussia, Austria, and Russia. He is here to demonstrate the rights and perils of Swiss neutrality:—*perhaps* England may be persuaded to throw something in the balance weightier than mere remonstrance. An article of much force in the *Edinburgh Review* of the present month rather favors that "perhaps."

Our papers, I perceive, anticipate some pleasurable stir from the visit of the Prince of Wales. It is thought here that he will hasten back, and may probably only see Boston on his way to rejoin his ship. He is an ingenuous, good-looking lad; in expression taking after his mother, and in quiet polished tone of manner after his father. An article in a New York journal intimating the propriety and policy of his being invited, has been reprinted here; a symptom of the sensitive attachment universally felt for the Queen and her children.

Always faithfully yrs.

## No. 327.—TO MR. CASS.

LONDON, April 20, 1860.

MY DEAR SIR,—Had Doctor Franklin been in the House of Peers last night he would have found repeating the same favorite abuse of America to which he listened nearly a hundred years ago in the gallery of the Commons. Pray read the speech of Earl Grey; and observe with what oily unction he hands our present generation, from its highest to its humblest branch, to the mercies of the common hangman. Your people are venal, corrupt, and brutal: your State and Federal judiciary are demoralized and sunk: your legislatures, local and congressional, are mere spoilsmen, except when they are also ruffians: and your President himself and his cabinet are all floating in this ordure of crime! The excommunication is thorough. And on what bald pretence is this wholesale anathema of a nation founded?—simply on the fact that Lord John Russell's proposed measure of reform lowers the franchise from £10 to 6! It is difficult to trace the connection, but that matters not:—the opportunity was seized, if not made, to crucify transatlantic democracy. His lordship overshot his mark,—so the Earl of Granville told him—and he runs the risk of being permanently coupled in our affectionate remembrances with Attorney-General Wedderburne.

A vague uneasiness prevails as to the state of affairs on the Continent. Nor can this government with any certainty say whether their relations with the Emperor of France are amicable or repulsive. Events are hurrying on, especially in Italy, which must ripen to something definitive before a month is out. *On-dits* or *canards* are countless. Among these, a gentleman just from Paris (Mr. —— of the *Edinburgh Review*) reports that Lamoricière has Bonaparte's sanction for enlisting in the Papal service, that the French troops are not to be withdrawn from Rome, and that it is doubtful whether the mutual confidence between the Emperor and Victor Emmanuel can be prolonged.

I forgot, in my brief *critique* of Lord Grey's thunder, that he attributed to this mighty monarchy an amiable tendency to treat us as "spoilt children." The Treaty of '83 was a concession to "spoilt children;"—we were, like "spoilt children," permitted to flog our parent in 1813–'14:—the dismissal of Crampton was overlooked as the act of "spoilt children:" and our arrogant diplomacy was only tolerated because we are "spoilt children." Such phrases as these are alike unworthy of the scene, the subject, and the speaker:—rankling as venom in the hearts of individuals, yet puerile as regards the country.

Our disagreeable weather has continued until one does nothing but abuse the everlasting Nor'-Easter!

Always faithfully yrs.

---

## No. 328.—TO MR. CASS.

London, April 27, 1860.

My dear Sir,—I found great pleasure in reading, four times over, your despatch, to which the private letter of the 5th instant refers. There was nothing which hypercriticism could wish to alter. Pray take it for granted that I am not liable to be tired with reading any despatch of yours, however "lengthy:" on the contrary, it is both useful and agreeable, as in the effort to convey the contents justly to another, I become more thoroughly master of them myself, and moreover take a certain amusement in witnessing their legitimate effects upon the listener.

Until the last four months I doubted the existence of eloquence in England. Mr. Gladstone and Sir Bulwer Lytton have dispelled the doubt, by performances equal in force, beauty, and versatility to anything of Brinsley Sheridan's. The *Quarterly Review*, no friendly critic, pronounces the former's four hours' speech on the Budget, "the finest combination of reasoning and declamation that has ever been heard within the walls of the House of Commons:"—and again, "we find ourselves in the enchanted region of pure Gladstonism, that terrible combination of relentless logic and dauntless imagination." Bulwer, in assailing the Reform bill last night, rose to the same level. I cannot venture to predict the fate of that measure:—it is so moderate, that enthusiasm cannot be roused on its behalf:—if the vote were taken by ballot, it would be defeated, but the ayes and noes on a division are a formidable ordeal for those who love their seats.

Bad and unwholesome weather prolonged beyond all season. Everybody is victimized by rheumatism or uvula in some shape.

Always faithfully yrs.

---

## No. 329.—TO MR. CASS.

LONDON, May 4, 1860.

MY DEAR SIR,—On what is termed "the San Juan" difficulty, Lord John Russell was last night "interpellated" by Mr. Fitzgerald. If my knowledge of facts be correct, there is much indistinctness and confusion in his reply. I send it.

The Reform bill staggers along. The second reading is carried, but farther progress was suspended, amid loud jeering from the opposition, until the 4th of June next. The enemies of the measure have taken great pains, in both Houses of Parliament, to ventilate their hatred of American institutions, laws, and manners. Indeed, that course of atrabilious remark is rather cheered and encouraged by a large majority of both parties. We must manage to survive and smile:—especially as we are apt to give as hard as we receive.

On the Continent there would seem to be a momentary lull. Everybody, however, regards it as the stillness which precedes the storm. Each new day is expected to develope the coming *coup* A fresh map of Europe lies upon the table of every Parisian editor.

I am earnestly exhorted by a gentleman whom I do not know and never heard of, to inculcate upon my countrymen the duty and policy of intervening to stop the atrocious massacres committing in Sicily by Bomba Junior. He hopes nothing for the cause of humanity from England or France, but looks to us.

Our friend Mr. W. Beech Lawrence, of Rhode Island, has just issued a *brochure* in Paris, a light well-written essay, to vindicate the Southern form of labor, and to show its necessity if the new commercial policy of the Emperor is to be carried out. The "*Amis des Noirs*" are quite as numerous in France as here, and equally inaccessible to reason. Those of the *Débats* refused to publish any piece extenuating negro slavery:—and, under a sense of duty, he has flung out his pamphlet.

Always faithfully yrs.

---

## No. 330.—TO MR. CASS.

LONDON, May 11, 1860.

MY DEAR SIR,—The descent of Garibaldi upon Sicily, with a force not exceeding 2000, re-enacts the enterprise of distant centuries. He has managed with equal skill and boldness: allowing nothing to be suspected until he had pushed to sea, with all his companions, and securing a longer start ahead by cutting, on the instant of departure, all the loquacious electric wires in reach. The Island is rampant with insurrection, which his presence will organize and lead to success. Already the restricting epithet "North" is deemed misplaced in the title of the new Italian kingdom.

Mr. Gladstone's budget was uncomfortably near a fatal blow on the evening of Tuesday last. In a House of 428 he carried the repeal of the paper duty by a majority of nine only. Another such victory, and the opposition will be encouraged to a formidable assault.

Observe the affectionately polished terms in which Earl Grey and Lord John Russell cut each other up in a series of private though published notes. How worthy of imitation by our pugnacious members! "Dear Lord John," "Dear Lord Grey:"—can anything be more charming than this mode of pinning baseness and falsehood upon each other?

Although you would not tell me, I have known for some time, through Mr. Isturitz, that you decline taking any part in a Congress to deliberate on the means of effectually extinguishing the Slave Trade. I had been called upon by a diplomat some time ago on this subject. He said his government would follow in the footsteps of the United States: and after much conversation, he added—"Let me put a question: suppose my government to accept Lord John Russell's invitation, how would you regard her conduct?" I answered instantly, "As un-American and unfriendly." "Am I at liberty to write home to that effect?" "Certainly, as an expression of my individual sentiment and belief: the United States can never consent to be swamped in a European Congress:—in politics, we must be wary not to dovetail the two continents." From all I hear, this fresh effort to get a tribune whence to lecture the nations on religion and humanity will fail. Lord John will take nothing by his motion.

Always faithfully yrs.

---

## No. 331.—TO MR. C. J. INGERSOLL.

LONDON, May 21, 1860.

DEAR SIR,—Your letter of the 12th ultimo led me, in frequent conversations with eminent gentlemen, to seek a distinct answer to the question on British constitutional law which it proposed. Is there, in the making of leagues or treaties, a clearly defined line between the prerogative of the Crown and the power of Parliament? Without undertaking a dull and minute course of discrimination, let me give you my impressions.

What is called "the tendency of the age" shews itself strikingly on this subject. The great Commentator of last century may have been accurate:—he would require liberalization now. He told us that whatever international contracts the sovereign engaged in "no other power in the kingdom can legally delay, resist, or annul." That *dictum*, in its broad import, has ceased to be true. The impeachment of a bad minister is no longer the only recognized escape or remedy of an injurious treaty.

The Commercial Convention recently entered into with France, contains an *express* declaration that it shall not be valid unless "Her Britannic Majesty shall be authorized by the assent of her Parliament to execute the engagements contracted by her in its several articles." Such a clause is, I am assured, always introduced in modern treaties of this kind: and upon the present occasion its exigency was met by the adoption of a joint address to the Queen approving comprehensively the diplomatic programme.

I believe it safe to say, now-a-days, that a treaty which calls for a law in order to be executed, may be constitutionally nullified by the refusal of either House, the Commons or the Lords, to enact that law. If it be necessary to *assent*, it is competent to *dissent*. Treaties requiring appropriations of money: treaties establishing tariffs, or mutual terms of interchanging products: and treaties relinquishing territorial dominions, perhaps: sink into the power of Parliament. In the olden time, Blackstone would have been shocked if the Executive, bent upon fulfilling an international engagement, had thought it worth while to say more than "Pass the bill:—*stet pro ratione voluntas!*"

It may be doubted whether the check upon executive discretion be not, in this sphere of public agency, better ascertained here than with us. Chancellor Kent, I think, expressed astonishment and regret that a resolution, founded on the incidents of Jay's Treaty, was passed by the House of Representatives in 1796, declaring what is now understood to be settled English law and practice, that is, if a treaty depend for the execution of any of its stipulations upon a legislative act, the House could and should determine on the expediency of carrying it into effect or letting it abort. Whether the principle of that resolution was abandoned, or only pretermitted on the emergency of 1816, may be questioned. It disappoints expectation, but in reality is not illogical, that the treaty-making power when in the hands of a hereditary monarch should be more trammelled and restricted than when in the hands of an elective chief magistrate and Senate. I trust, however, that, should the controversy revive, our representatives may feel themselves, maugre Chancellor Kent, free to be at least as democratic as the British Commons. It is noticeable that the precedent of a parliamentary stand against a treaty was made during the ministry of Pitt, almost contemporaneously with Jay's: and that while on this side of the Atlantic the popular resistance triumphed, by leading to the withdrawal and abandonment of the measure, on our side, notwithstanding an agitation alike universal and violent, we were compelled to swallow, pure and undiluted, the strong concoction of the venerable Chief Justice.

Very sincerely and faithfully yrs.

---

## No. 332.—TO MR. CASS.

London, May 22, 1860.

My dear Sir,—Much tribulation was caused by a motion in the House of Lords to throw out, or reject, Mr. Gladstone's favorite measure for the repeal of the tax on paper. It was made by Lord Monteagle, backed hotly by Lord Derby, and after a violent debate of nine hours' duration, it was carried at 2 o'clock A. M. (this morning) by the overwhelming majority of 89 in a vote of 297. The friends of the bill stood upon the privilege of the Commons, to preserve untouched their control of the finances, and specially insisted that to reject a relief of taxation which had passed the House was equivalent to a fresh imposition. The blow is a harsh one on the Chancellor of the Exchequer: and, though it keeps him in deep water as far as national income is concerned, it deranges the system of his budget, and throws discredit upon his prudence. The garland of victory is proverbially fragile, and I shall not be surprised if Mr. Gladstone, nettled in the midst of elation, were suddenly to drop the seals of office.

Garibaldi's defeat of the Neapolitan forces arrived late last night pretty directly from Naples. I was told it in the House of Peers by Lord Wensleydale. The battle was fought in the vicinity of Palermo: and probably by this time young Bomba is on the road to Vienna.

Nobody questions the wonderful powers of Lord Brougham. His readiness at plagiarism upon himself is carried too far, and gives a stale look to some of his latter productions. At his inauguration as Chancellor of the University of Edinburgh, on Friday the 18th instant, he must have consumed a full half-hour in repeating his celebrated and superb parallel between the virtues of Washington and the vices of Napoleon I.

All the world will stream to Epsom to-morrow. The Prime Minister has formally given warning in the House of Commons that he regards the Derby Day as too sacred for legislative business:—he will move an adjournment over. By-the-by, his lordship is not a little addicted to fancies of the kind. The other day, he was obliged to expend heaps of solemn condemnation upon the approaching prize fight of Sayers and Heenan:—but he concluded by saying, with a bright twinkle in his eye, "Well! if it must come off—I hope Tom will beat."

Always faithfully yrs.

---

## No. 333.—TO MR. CASS.

London, June 1, 1860.

My dear Sir,—In the adjustment of the British Constitution, which you know is asserted to be the more perfect because imperfect, accommodating itself to the exigencies of progress, I think the popular principle about to make a fresh advance upon the oligarchical. The right of the Lords to intermeddle in any manner with money bills sent up by the Commons, as well repealing as imposing taxation, is for the first time broadly and vigorously denied. The precedents upon which Lords Monteagle, Lyndhurst, and Derby acted in throwing out the measure abolishing the paper duty, are discovered to lack in a slight degree exact applicability: and the Commons seize the occasion to push their privilege farther than it has hitherto gone, by absolutely excluding the Peers from the entire domain of the finances. New forms of bills may be devised for that purpose. Resolutions of a decided character will be introduced in the lower House. And though the actual offence of retaining the paper duty may glide into oblivion, it will become so only after its recurrence is rendered impossible. Such promises to be the issue of the present constitutional conflict between the legislative branches of Parliament.

My diplomatic colleagues very generally agree in considering the state of affairs on the Continent as unpromising and precarious. The "sick man" is once more an object of solicitude: and the unhappy Christians in Turkey are breaking the heart-strings of tender Prince Gortschakoff. Then, Prussia is carefully restoring the war-footing to her army, while Parisian pens are dropping persuasive pamphlets on the banks of the Rhine. Then, Spain, for some covert reason, instead of doffing, is actually riveting on, the helmets she donned in Morocco:—giving permanency to an army of 200,000, quartered in the Balearic Islands and on her northeastern coast. Then again, the intrigues and tentatives of the exiled Dukes of Tuscany and Modena get encouragement somewhere:—the despairing contortions of Helvetia in the tightening folds of the Gallic constrictor are extremely painful: Hungary is threatening Kaiser Francis with the treatment given to King John at Runnymede: the perturbations in Belgium are equally conspicuous in Leopold I. and Leopold's minister Van de Weyer: and finally, see the volcanic blaze of Garibaldi, whose head-quarters were established, with Sardinian flag in hand, by the brave chieftain himself in the centre of Palermo!

At last we hear from China. The Brother of the Sun and Moon has contumeliously flouted the terms arrogantly exacted by Mr. Bruce. Nothing seems left to the Allies but an advance on Pekin, and a race after the Emperor wheresoever he may fly. Whether a retreat like that of Thucydides and his ten thousand from Persia, may not be compelled by mere force of overpowering numbers, we must wait to see. Some straggling engineers and drill sergeants of Russia may possibly be backing the Celestials. The enclosed contains what Lord John Russell lately characterized as the "moderate" demands of this government!

*Le Box*, as the Parisians call the P. R., is renewing its hold upon the public taste. There are no heroes like those of the fist. Heenan and Sayers recall Hector and Achilles; and one of the panegyrists ranks them on the rolls of fame with Napoleon I. and Wellington! Each has stood, and still stands, in a pelting shower of gold:—each buckles on a belt sparkling with gems and ponderous with silver:—both are trumpeted from one end of the kingdom to the other: and even at the Derby, the high-mettled racers were forgotten in the universal eagerness to run after the Benicia Boy! The victory over law, civilization, order, and morality, is complete.

Always faithfully yrs.

---

## No. 334.—TO MR. CASS.

LONDON, June 15, 1860.

MY DEAR SIR,—Things are tranquillizing. Lord John Russell's Reform bill seemed to command too small a majority and has been withdrawn. The vacuum thus produced will enable Parliament to advance rapidly to a close. Agitation on the question of the exclusive financial privilege of the House, although kept alive, will mainly be reserved for the recess.

Indications make it quite clear that the second daughter of Queen Victoria, the Princess Alice, is about being merged into Dutch Royalty. John Bull has often counted the beads of his rosary, good-naturedly giving to each of them a blessing and a purse, and then growling at the budget.

A great conjunction takes place to-morrow or the next day at Baden-Baden. Napoleon III. has an interview with the Prince Regent of Prussia, and several sovereigns, Saxon, Bavarian, Hesse-Darmstadt, etc., propose to "assist" thereat. Europe has had recent experience of the consequences likely to flow from such consultative reunions. The Emperor, as his own Premier, is apt to state his "idea," to fix it impressively on those who listen, and to leave its complete execution as a thing, willy-nilly, to be done. No doubt, his fiat on the present occasion will point to the Rhine as the natural boundary of France: and one cannot perceive in any quarter the faintest readiness to resist. He will get it, *nunc vellunc:* possibly by diplomacy, for there is a deep dread of provoking him among the royalties, but, if not so, by an overpowering rush from Châlons.

The annals of Europe, though crowded with the names of great soldiers and seamen, do not furnish a parallel for Garibaldi:—so they call him the Washington of Italy. We

Americans may think the designation a little too flattering:—but in truth he has noble qualities, among which are most conspicuous the very firmness, sobriety, moderation, and devotion to duty, which characterized our national favorite. He has plucked Sicily from the Neapolitan crown by a series of rapid as well as prudent movements, and we may soon look for such insurrectionary collisions among the Lazzaroni as will induce him to cross the Strait of Messina and end the dynasty. All Europe is crying shame at Bomba junior for his barbarities—cannonading and shelling, firing and destroying his own city of Palermo and its population; and the dogma of divine right does not save him from universal condemnation.

Another trial trip by the Great Eastern preliminary to starting for New York on the 20th instant. They have been tinkering at her extensively for the last six months, and *perhaps* she is now a safe steamship:—but she don't promise to perform the voyage in less than ten or twelve days, she is still liable to many interruptions and accidents, and, on the whole, the report of the late excursion of twenty-four hours leaves me inclined to prefer a conveyance by the Adriatic, the Arago, or the Persia.

Our countrymen are crowding into London by hundreds. They are astonished at finding the cold wet weather which we have had all the spring.

Always faithfully yrs.

---

## No. 335.—TO MR. CASS.

LONDON, June 19, 1860.

MY DEAR SIR,—The cluster of kings and kinglets which met for two days at Baden, smiled unimaginable things at each other, and then dispersed as if enchanted with the wonders they had achieved, has opened a fresh and interesting field for speculation and prophecy. Simultaneous with the departure of Louis Napoleon from Paris was the appearance of a new pamphlet, "*France and Prussia*," by About. This performs the office assigned to the brochure "*Napoléon III. et l'Italie*," in February, 1859, which heralded the conquest of Lombardy, and the annexation of Savoy and Nice. The first moves in the game are alike:—Guerronière and About the summoning trumpets. "Reform the vices of your constitution: give up Divine Right: make your legislature what ours is, the offspring of universal suffrage: don't gasp at uttering democracy: expel your treacherous bureaucracy: and then, as soon as you concede to France her 'natural frontier,' she will expand you, as she has expanded Piedmont, into a United Germany." Such is the programme blandly unfolded to the Regent of Prussia, under Imperial inspiration! At Baden, Napoleon shook hands, drank tea, paid first visits, was the model of cordial good-fellowship, and when he left at night for the Tuileries, only dropped, as interpreting the drama, this little pamphlet of About. I send you as much of it as was in the *Herald* of yesterday morning.

The alarm here is somewhat on the increase. A commission has recently made report on the Public Defences, and its recommendations call for an expenditure of eleven or twelve millions of pounds sterling. French naval force is steadily augmenting. Lord Overstone appears in print, anxious about invasion. Colonel Jebb looks it coolly in the face, adverts to the three successive stages at one of which it may possibly be repelled, and finally, *supposing London to be captured*, looks to the probability of buying off the enemy!

The cold and wet continue without change. The Great Eastern anticipated her time, and left Southampton for New York on Sunday last the 17th instant. May she arrive safely!

Always faithfully yrs.

---

## No. 336.—TO MR. CASS.

LONDON, June 29, 1860.

MY DEAR SIR,—Strong and sincere gratification seems to have been given by the President's note to the Queen inviting the Prince of Wales to Washington. It is talked of in all circles; and the young gentleman himself is exuberant with delight. The Duke of Newcastle anticipates great enjoyment on the tour, and dwells much on its prospect. He expressed to me a solicitude to avoid, after quitting Canada, any proceeding, such as stopping for a short time at Cincinnati, which would be regarded as the slightest breach of the principle of etiquette that the first visit should be to the White House. Without being too strict in exaction, I have encouraged the expediency of travelling direct to the capital, and afterwards branching in any direction they please. This, I think it probable, will be the course. They calculate on reaching you about the close of September, and on re-embarking for home at New York about the middle of October:—allowing very little time to the United States. As we shall be involved in the universal and absorbing distractions of a Presidential election, perhaps it is well that it should be so. The programme for the voyage was officially published two days ago, making the start from Devonport on the 10th of July.

The legislative scene, like the fashionable season, is drawing to a close. Unless something unlooked for should break out, Parliament can hardly protract its session for another month.

England is laboring to convince herself that she is a military nation. Within the last week she has held two Reviews, one in Hyde Park of the Volunteer Rifles, and another at Aldershot of Regulars, counting an aggregate of about 45,000 men. Soon, she proposes to inaugurate a system of local games, making the skill in point-blank shooting the object of popular attainment:—like archery in olden times, only substituting the rifle for the crossbow. She went into ecstacies, as you may have noticed, at the tramp of her 20,000 volunteers, and almost trumpeted defiance to the 400,000 of France. Paris was highly amused. But, after all, there is something in this first taste of the voluntary principle which is really seductive, and may lead to important results. It is a bold and pregnant idea, that of putting rifles into English hands indiscriminately:—it may possibly end very differently from what is expected.

Our small screw steamer, of 6 guns, the Iroquois, Commander Palmer, is, under the requisition of Mr. Chandler, looking doggedly at the subordinates of young Bomba, and we may possibly witness something after the fashion of the Ingraham and Koszta incident. The King is getting so rapidly pushed off his throne, that he bows concessions in despair all round. A mere attitude will be quite enough for him.

Very sad rumors are afloat about the effects already produced, and the worse ones feared, from the continued cold and rain. The crops are in danger here, and indeed all through Europe. Prices of food are rising fearfully. The horrid weather is attributed by some to the great number and huge size of icebergs in the Atlantic.

Lord Elgin and Baron Gros seem to have lost everything but their lives by the wreck in the harbor of Galle.

Always faithfully yrs.

---

## No. 337.—TO MR. CASS.

LONDON, July 13, 1860.

MY DEAR SIR,—Mr. Longstreet, one of the delegates appointed by the President to the International Statistical Congress, has reached here in due time, but regrets to find that Mr. Lawrence, his colleague, left England in the Adriatic on the 20th ultimo. It is not impossible that this latter gentleman may be on his way hither. I have had sent to me by Mr. Faulkner from Paris, endorsed as from the Treasury Department, what I take to be his commission and therefore temporarily retain for him. Mr. Longstreet will, however, find other American associates in the Congress. Dr. Jarvis has been sent by the Massachusetts Association. This government, through Mr. Milner Gibson, invited my attendance at the initiation of the movement, but I declined for obvious reasons.

The Prince of Wales embarked in the "Hero" three days ago for Canada. His departure was signalized by naval demonstration and ceremony executed by the Channel fleet. He will go farther South than Washington only to visit Richmond.

The "sick man," as you have doubtless seen, is getting worse and worse. The Christians are being massacred by thousands in Syria, the Turkish forces too weak or unwilling to protect them. On both sides of the Channel, it is beginning to be seen that the Czar Nicholas had reason for his plans, and that Europe may soon be obliged to execute them. The two Emperors, Napoleon and Alexander, have a steady and longing eye upon the "New Map" I sent you two years ago, and are only impeded in their project of a coalesced triumvirate of military nations by the obstinate integrity of the Prussian Regent. How long that obstacle will last against the double pressure, right and left, depends much on the energies of Downing Street.

I listened attentively a few nights ago to a singular but striking speech by the Premier in the Commons. It was on the pending question of privilege, and elaborately excused, if it avoided defending, the rejection by the Lords of the bill remitting the paper duties. To me it savored strongly of a disposition to drop, or drive out, certain distasteful members of his cabinet—Lord John Russell, Mr. Gladstone, and Mr. Milner Gibson—for these gentlemen have resolutely and openly flung the gauntlet at the Peers, and are stirring up popular agitation in a manner rather disquieting. Yesterday there was convened at Liverpool what we should consider even in New York a roaring tumultuous meeting on this subject:—and here, three days ago, at the discussion of the topic by a numerous assemblage, a proposal to convene in Hyde Park was indiscreetly opposed by a threat of the newly raised Rifles!

The celebration on the 4th was enlivened by a capital speech from Layard (Nineveh Layard) and a very flat one by Dr. Mackay. Our own addresses and toasts were dishwater.

A fierce assault upon Sir Samuel Cunard and his line of steam ships is now in progress. The gravamen, an un-English concession to anti-negro tastes, by rules of government on board, which accommodated a sable Mrs. Putnam and her numerous family *separately* from other passengers. They demanded, and now the exclusively civilized press of England demands for them, that they shall eat, drink, sleep, and promenade, undiscriminated by color. What will Sir Samuel do? He has tried to avoid the onslaught, by justly regarding the matter as one to be determined by his own interest in controlling his own business:—but they threaten him with the withdrawal of all government aid and countenance, and the bolt of popular excommunication.

Always faithfully yrs.

---

## No. 338.—TO MR. CASS.

LONDON, August 3, 1860.

MY DEAR SIR,—The interest of Europe is just now concentrated on three novelties:—the filibustero Garibaldi, the Imperial letter-writer, and the religious massacres in Syria. Everything else is for the hour overshadowed.

The general is supposed to be slightly mutinous:—disregarding the advice of Victor Emmanuel, and fatally bent on seeing Naples. A telegram is daily looked for, announcing his landing on this side of the Strait: and it is said that there lies in the beautiful bay a fine steamship ready to receive the King and his household, as soon as the "Hero" touches the Continent. No reliance on the Royal forces: no trust in Lazzaroni: no safety but in quick flight: "the thief doth fear each bush an officer."

Napoleon's epistle to his "*cher Persigny*" is regarded as addressed to the British nation. Agreeably to the direction in it, the ambassador laid it before Lord John Russell, who told the House of Commons, and a bad translation appeared in the newspapers on the following morning. I send you a copy in the original French. No more remarkable State paper can well be imagined. He runs over the keys of Imperial policy with the rapid familiarity of a master hand, and seems to smile through his writing at the facility with which he gets over the hard passages of the last year's history. What does it mean? No one can say precisely. Perhaps more consideration must be given to it. But if, as some think, it was an inspiration of Mr. Cobden's (who continues in Paris) to help Mr. Bright's opposition to the immense expenditure on fortifications, it has failed, for that measure was carried in the House of Commons last night by a majority of 227.

The hair-trigger tendency to religious war is by no

means restricted to Syria. There, it has exploded into massacre fierce and undiscriminating:—but alarm prevails throughout the Turkish Empire, and the two great sects are everywhere watching each other with dangerous bitterness. Constantinople itself is in something like a state of siege. The Sultan has formally invited "the Great Powers," who signed the Treaty of Peace in 1856, to help his weakness. Bonaparte (exemplary Christian!) springs forward with alacrity, and was hastening his soldiers to Beyrout and Damascus, when Lord John Russell interposed the necessity of a previous programme of conditions and understandings. If the Zouaves are once bivouacked in the Lebanon, when will they leave it?

The Queen proceeds from London to Edinburgh during the night of the 6th and 7th instant, reviews the Scotch Riflemen on the afternoon of the 7th, and speeds to Balmoral. Her Majesty will probably visit her new granddaughter in Berlin early in September. Parliament gives no promise of immediate prorogation, yet London is being rapidly deserted.

Always faithfully yrs.

---

## No. 339.—TO MR. CASS.

LONDON, September 14, 1860.

MY DEAR SIR,—All eyes are fixed upon the movement of General Fanti, at the head of fifty thousand of Victor Emmanuel's forces, into the States of the Church. Guyon is ordered back to his post at Rome, taking with him ten thousand French, as a sort of body-guard for the Holy Father. Very little reliance is felt in Lamoricière, whose scum of foreign mercenaries only exasperate Italian feeling. The critical moment has arrived; and the Piedmontese cabinet seem suddenly to have taken against the Pope a new attitude of menace and violence. In his extremity, the hand of Bonaparte will be stretched out for his relief.

Garibaldi entered Naples on the 7th instant, and straightway, as if touched by a magic blight, the throne of Francis II. crumbled into dust. It is said that the King, while penning his farewell to his subjects, actually issued an order for the bombardment and sack of the city! What army he may be able to retain will pass to the ranks of Lamoricière. His own destination is yet doubtful:—perhaps Spain, may-be the interior of Germany, possibly Vienna.

On the 3d of next month, and at Warsaw, there will be an ominous conjunction of sovereignties, Russian, Austrian, Prussian, etc., and why? only to declare a negative, that they do not propose to coalesce against France. "Methinks they do protest too much."

The Queen returns from Balmoral to Osborne on Tuesday next, and forthwith prepares for a visit to the Continent. Lord John Russell will accompany her.

Nothing of much moment as yet from China:—the latest accounts intimate the probability of a battle about the middle of July, which, if it have taken place, should reach us now. In New Zealand the success of the natives against the British authorities has created an anxious feeling.

Quite a stir has been made about the character in which Mr. Wm. S. Lindsay, M. P., is visiting the United States. Lord John has certainly given it a slight infusion of the diplomatic decoction. So much so that I presume that gentleman will hasten his arrival at Washington, and may seek interviews with the President and yourself on various topics which one would think exclusively manageable by Lord Lyons. Mr. Lindsay called on me before quitting: and I inferred from his conversation that he hoped to do something *à la Cobden in Paris.*

London is lifeless:—all the world abroad: rain unabating: and cold annoying. It seems conceded that the harvests have been impaired to the extent of at least one-third. The great astronomer Herschel tells us in a published letter that he did not *predict* this season, but that many observations led him to *foresee* it.

Always faithfully yrs.

## No. 340.—TO MR. MARKOE.

LONDON, November 23, 1860.

MY DEAR M.,—It is much to be feared that all the patriotism and valor of Garibaldi have been wasted. He is essentially a republican; and so his rash levied troops who nevertheless conquered Sicily and Naples have been disbanded and dispersed, and himself bowed into the rocky islet of Caprera!

Of all interesting monuments of antiquity and power, commend me to Windsor Castle. Mrs. D. and I have just returned from a three days' visit there. We were lodged in the Tower of King Edward III.: and I mounted to the top of the "Round Tower," about three hundred feet above a base constructed by the soldiers of Julius Cæsar!! Then see the interminable and inexhaustible Corridor:—the Rubens Chamber: the Tapestry: the Royal Plate: the Hall of St. George: the Armory: the State apartments. It is far the most imposing and suitable Palace to be found in England or perhaps in Europe. Innumerable objects of art, paintings, sculptures, and highly ornamented cabinet works and vases are spread through the Corridor having reference to the incidents of the present reign. The first time the Queen, only seventeen years of age, presided at the Privy Council, forms an interesting picture, Lord Melbourne, her guardian and Prime Minister, in the attitude of addressing her from the farther side of the table, and looking as if struck by the dignity and ease of her carriage. Then the Duke of Wellington, in the presence of her Majesty and Prince Albert, assuming the office of godfather to one of her infants and presenting a richly jewelled casket, forms another. The glowing and gorgeous representation of the Coronation makes a third. Portraits and busts of Popes and Cardinals are excellent and numerous.

You may get this on the day of an opening row in Congress, and I hasten to close it, to avoid keeping you away. I have an infinite deal of nothing to say, but not a minute to say it in.

Always affectionately yrs.

## No. 341.—TO MR. D.

LONDON, November 16, 1860.

MY DEAR F.,—Your recent visitor the Prince of Wales, though he left Portland on the 20th October, only got to Plymouth yesterday. He had a disagreeable voyage and caused considerable anxiety and alarm. Several vessels had hurried out to scour the seas for him.

Empresses, you perceive, are becoming flighty. My old Dowager of Russia has taken final leave. The young Austrian, little cared for by her husband, has borrowed a steamer from Queen Victoria to carry her to the health-restoring climate of Madeira. And the lovely parvenu Eugénie, crossing the Channel in a common packet, and content with ordinary cabs, has actually reached Claridge's Hotel in Brook Street, *incog.*, and on her way to a ball at the Duchess of Hamilton's in Scotland! Is it possible there can be a transient miff with Louis Napoleon? These Imperial freaks set the world full of conjecture and gossip.

Garibaldi has gone to his rock between Sardinia and Corsica, Caprera: they say, to milk his cows, but one may suspect to cry over spilt cream. Though he still harps on a movement in the spring with a million of men, he probably feels that his great republican idea finds an insurmountable obstacle in the crown of Victor Emmanuel.

Always affectionately yrs.

---

## No. 342.—TO MR. MARKOE.

LONDON, March 1, 1861.

MY DEAR MARKOE,—Our latest news from the West plays like a thread of lightning on the horizon and rekindles hope. It is to the effect that the Convention assembled under the counsels of Virginia has under consideration a scheme of adjustment, including the best parts of those of Crittenden, Guthrie, and the Border States. Amen! Anything to save a great constitutional country from the self-immolating stroke of panic.

Storms have been unceasing during the last month, and the wrecks reported are numberless.

The Bishop of Poictiers, in an address to his clergy, has made a deadly lunge at the Emperor. Like the rest of the world, he regards the signature of "Laguerronière" to the recent pamphlet of "*Rome, France, and Italy*" as simply that of Louis Napoleon. He has the boldness to run openly a parallel which, in a Roman Catholic sense, stamps indelibly the Tuileries pamphleteer, in his treatment of the Pope, as *the modern "Pontius Pilate, washing his hands as he surrenders the Saviour to execution!"* The image is forcible, is colored into strong relief, and is destined to produce a powerful impression on Gallican consciences.

We have been treated at the Royal Geographical Society with a charming lecture on the scenery and course of the White Nile, the Mountains of the Moon, and the Gorillas in Africa, by our young American traveller Du Chaillu. He brought me an introductory, and has made a capital hit. The audience at Burlington House was immense, partly ladies. He was complimented at the close by fervent speeches from Professor Owen, Mr. Gladstone, and Captain Galton:—naturally, his gratification is unbounded. He began falteringly, seemingly intimidated by being in the presence of so great a crowd of strangers, and "as he knew only his minister Mr. Dallas, he was sure to receive his protection"!

The lease of the house I have occupied uninterruptedly for five years comes to an annual close on the 24th instant. By that time I may look to have a successor. I propose, therefore, quietly to forego farther housekeeping in London on that day, and to hold myself in readiness for homeward flight at any moment. Whoever may be sent to this post will be cordially welcomed by me, and facilitated in his first movements as far as may be in my power. I would advise him, as a measure for his own comfort, to rent the establishment I quit, provided it be repaired and refurnished, and to enlist the eight servants who have been with me from the beginning.

Always faithfully yrs.

## No. 343.—TO MR. SEWARD.

LONDON, March 26, 1861.

MY DEAR MR. SEWARD,—You must allow me to make my sincere acknowledgments for the personally kind messages received from you through Mr. Mason.

I shall take pleasure in giving to your representative, my successor, whoever he may be, a cordial welcome, and to place at his service any little aids or facilities with which my stay here may have made me familiar. I do not yet know who is likely to be your choice: and possibly he may not be within that range of acquaintances to whom I should feel at liberty to write. But I shall be happy to know that he has been apprised of my readiness to receive him. My own trial in '56 prepares me to believe that he cannot get himself and family ready to emigrate to London, without great inconvenience, short of two months hence, say by the 1st of June.* I hope for him about that time, and shall be happy to make arrangements with Lord John Russell for his comfortable landing at Liverpool or elsewhere.

Reiterating my thanks, I am truly your obliged and obedient servant.

---

* Mr. C. F. Adams reached London on the 11th May, 1861.

THE END.

PUBLICATIONS OF J. B. LIPPINCOTT & CO., Phila.

*Will be sent by Mail, post-paid, on receipt of price.*

---

## THE PEOPLE THE SOVEREIGNS.

Being a Comparison of the Government of the United States with those of the Republics which have existed before, with the Causes of their Decadence and Fall. By JAMES MONROE, Ex-President of the United States. Edited by SAMUEL L. GOUVERNEUR, his grandson and administrator. One vol. 12mo. Tinted paper. Extra Cloth. Price $1.75.

## A HISTORY OF SACERDOTAL CELIBACY.

An Historical Sketch of Sacerdotal Celibacy in the Christian Church. By HENRY C. LEA. In one octavo volume of nearly 600 pages. Extra Cloth. Price $3.75.

. . . The work has been laboriously and carefully prepared, and contains a complete history of ecclesiastical celibacy, traced through the different centuries and followed through all the changes of temporal government and religious authority. A very full index makes the book valuable and serviceable for reference upon the matters of which it treats.—*Boston Journal.*

## THE SEVEN WEEKS' WAR.

Its Antecedents and its Incidents. By H. M. HOZIER, F.C.S., F.G.S., Military Correspondent of the London Times with the Prussian Army during the German Campaign of 1866. Two vols. 8vo. With numerous Maps and Plans. Superfine paper. Extra Cloth. Price $10.00.

. . . All that Mr. Hozier saw of the great events of the war—and he saw a large share of them—he describes in clear and vivid language.—*London Saturday Review.*

## LIVES OF BOULTON AND WATT.

Principally from the original Soho MSS. Comprising also a History of the Invention and Introduction of the Steam Engine. By SAMUEL SMILES, author of "Lives of the Engineers," "Self-Help," "Industrial Biography," etc. With a Portrait of Watt and Boulton and numerous other Illustrations. Printed on fine toned paper. One vol. Royal 8vo. Strong Cloth. Price $10.00.

## HISTORY OF THE KNIGHTS TEMPLAR OF THE STATE OF PENNSYLVANIA.

Prepared and arranged from Original Papers, together with the Constitution, Decisions, Resolutions, and Forms of the R. E. Grand Commandery of Pennsylvania. By ALFRED CREIGH, LL.D., K. T. 33°. One vol. 12mo. Extra Cloth. Price $2.50.

. . . This work is an invaluable one to the fraternity, giving as it does a complete history of the Knights Templar from 1794 to November, 1866.—*Pittsburg Ev. Chronicle.*

---

## NEW AMERICA.

By WILLIAM HEPWORTH DIXON, Editor of "The Athenæum," and author of "The Holy Land," "William Penn," etc. With Illustrations from Original Photographs. Third Edition. Complete in one volume, Crown Octavo. Printed on tinted paper. Extra Cloth. Price $2.75.

In these graphic volumes Mr. Dixon sketches American men and women, sharply, vigorously, and truthfully, under every aspect. The smart Yankee, the grave politician, the senate and the stage, the pulpit and the prairie, loafers and philanthropists, crowded streets and the howling wilderness, the saloon and the boudoir, with women everywhere at full length—all passes on before us in some of the most vivid and brilliant pages ever written.—*Dublin University Magazine.*

## ELEMENTS OF ART CRITICISM.

A Text-book for Schools and Colleges, and a Hand-book for Amateurs and Artists. By G. W. SAMSON, D.D., President of Columbian College, Washington, D. C. Second Edition. Crown 8vo. Cloth. Price $3.50. Abridged Edition $1.75.

This work comprises a Treatise on the Principles of Man's Nature as addressed by Art, together with a Historic survey of the Methods of Art Execution in the departments of Drawing, Sculpture, Architecture, Painting, Landscape Gardening, and the Decorative Arts. The *Round Table* says: "The work is incontestably one of great as well as unique value."

## THE HISTORY OF ART.

By PROFESSOR WILHELM LUBKE. Translated by F. E. BUNNETT, translator of Grimm's "Life of Michael Angelo," etc. With 415 illustrations. Two vols. imperial 8vo. Beautifully printed from Old Faced type on toned paper, and handsomely bound in cloth.

## TERRA MARIÆ; or, Threads of Maryland Colonial History.

By EDWARD D. NEILL, one of the Secretaries of the President of the United States. 12mo. Extra Cloth. Price $2.00.

## COMING WONDERS, expected between 1867 and 1875.

By the Rev. M. BAXTER, author of "The Coming Battle." One vol. 12mo. Cloth. Price $1.00.

PUBLICATIONS OF J. B. LIPPINCOTT & CO.
**Will be sent by Mail on receipt of price.**

# INNER ROME:

## POLITICAL, RELIGIOUS, AND SOCIAL.

BY THE

REV. C. M. BUTLER, D.D.,

Professor of Ecclesiastical History in the Divinity School, Philadelphia; author of "The Book of Common Prayer interpreted by its History;" "Lectures on the Apocalypse;" "St. Paul in Rome," etc. etc. etc. 1 vol. 12mo. $1.75.

*From the Philadelphia Inquirer.*

. . . No modern volume within our knowledge has so thoroughly entered into an exposition of the government and the social condition of Rome.

*From the Cincinnati Gazette.*

The book is the result of personal observation as well as the careful study of documents only made public since the surrender of the Venitian capital to Victor Emmanuel. Hence we find disclosures of long permitted wrong, oppression, and cruelty, that startle us even in this day when rebellion has given so bloody a record of crime. It is the duty of every man to read a volume so opportune, and which so clearly indicates that the Old World is about to pass through an ordeal more severe, if possible, than that in which our own land and people have been tried, and, we trust, purified. We commend the volume to the student, the politician, and the practical man.

*From the Rev. Dr. S. I. Prime.*

. . . No book on Rome or Popery has met my eye so well fitted to show the world what Romanism is at Rome, as this book of yours.

*From Judge Advocate General Holt.*

My dear sir: I write to thank you sincerely for the volume "Inner Rome." . . . I have read it carefully and with much interest and instruction, and think you have done your friends and the country a good service in thus presenting to them the results of your diligent study of the principles and policy and habits of those who have now the guardianship of this "lone mother of dead empires." Be assured that I shall prize the offering alike for its own worth and as a token of that friendship with which you have so constantly honored me, and which I gladly and gratefully reciprocate.

*From the Rev. Horatius Bonar, D.D.*

My dear Dr. Butler; . . . I am busy with your work, and find it exceedingly interesting and instructive. One likes to get a view of the interior from one who knows it so well as you do; as for a traveler, like myself, he is not qualified for the task at all, and his pen can only sketch exteriors. You have seen a great deal both of Rome Inner and Rome Outer, and it is pleasant to be introduced by you into one chamber, and another, and another.